APA Handbook of
Intercultural
Communication

APA Handbook of
Intercultural
Communication

Edited by
David Matsumoto

American Psychological Association • Washington, DC
Walter de Gruyter, Inc. • New York, NY

Published by
American Psychological Association
750 First Street, NE
Washington, DC 20002
www.apa.org

APA Handbook of Intercultural Communication; David Matsumoto, Editor
Derived from original work edited by Helga Kotthoff and Helen Spencer-Oatey, Eds.; Peter Auer and Li Wei, Eds.; and Gerd Antos and Eija Ventola, Eds., in cooperation with Tilo Weber; and published by Mouton de Gruyter, an imprint of Walter de Gruyter GmbH & Co. KG.

Chapters 1–7 and 11–16 were originally published in *Handbook of Intercultural Communication*, Helga Kotthoff and Helen Spencer-Oatey, Eds., 2007, Berlin, copyright © 2007 by Walter de Gruyter GmbH & Co. KG. Chapters 8–9 were originally published in *Handbook of Multilingualism and Multilingual Communication*, Peter Auer and Li Wei, Eds., 2007, Berlin, copyright © 2007 by Walter de Gruyter GmbH & Co. KG. Chapter 10 was originally published in *Handbook of Interpersonal Communication*, Gerd Antos and Eija Ventola, Eds., in cooperation with Tilo Weber, 2008, Berlin, copyright © 2008 by Walter de Gruyter GmbH & Co. KG. All rights reserved.

To order
APA Order Department
P.O. Box 92984
Washington, DC 20090-2984
Tel: (800) 374-2721; Direct: (202) 336-5510
Fax: (202) 336-5502; TDD/TTY: (202) 336-6123
Online: www.apa.org/books/
E-mail: order@apa.org

Typeset in ITC New Century Schoolbook by IBT Global, Troy, NY

Printer: IBT Global, Troy, NY
Cover Designer: Naylor Design, Washington, DC

The opinions and statements published are the responsibility of the authors, and such opinions and statements do not necessarily represent the policies of the American Psychological Association.

Library of Congress Cataloging-in-Publication Data

APA handbook of intercultural communication / edited by David Matsumoto. — 1st ed.
   p. cm.
  Includes bibliographical references and index.
  ISBN-13: 978-1-4338-0778-7
  ISBN-10: 1-4338-0778-5
  ISBN-13: 978-1-4338-0779-4 (e-book)
  ISBN-10: 1-4338-0779-3 (e-book)
 1. Intercultural communication. I. Matsumoto, David Ricky. II. American Psychological Association.
  HM1211.A65 2010
  303.48'2—dc22   2009052506

British Library Cataloguing-in-Publication Data

A CIP record is available from the British Library.

Printed in the United States of America
First Edition

Contents

Contributors

Benjamin Bailey, PhD, University of Massachusetts Amherst

Madeleine Brabant, PhD, University of Queensland, Brisbane, Australia

Cindy Gallois, PhD, University of Queensland, Brisbane, Australia

Perry Hinton, DPhil, Oxford Brookes University, Oxford, England

J. Normann Jørgensen, University of Copenhagen, Denmark

Helga Kotthoff, German Department, Freiburg University of Education, Freiburg, Germany

Sabine Krajewski, DPhil, Macquarie University, Sydney, Australia

Jeffrey A. LeRoux, PhD, Center for Psychological Studies, Berkeley, CA

Jonathan Newton, PhD, Victoria University of Wellington, New Zealand

David Matsumoto, PhD, San Francisco State University, San Franciso, CA

Ingrid Piller, PhD, Macquarie University, Australia, Sydney, Australia

Pia Quist, PhD, University of Copenhagen, Denmark

Martin Reisigl, PhD, University of Vienna, Austria

Celia Roberts, King's College London, England

Martina Rost-Roth, PhD, The Free University of Berlin, Germany

Winfried Thielmann, DPhil, Ludwig-Maximilians-University Munich, Germany

Albert Scherr, Freiburg University of Education, Freiburg, Germany

Hartmut Schröder, PhD, European University Viadrina Frankfurt (Oder), Germany

Helen Spencer-Oatey, PhD, University of Warwick, Coventry, England

Janet Spreckels, PhD, Freiburg University of Education, Freiburg, Germany

Nathalie van Meurs, PhD, Open University, UK

Bernadette Watson, PhD, University of Queensland, Brisbane, Australia

Seung Hee Yoo, PhD, Yale University, New Haven, CT

Vladimir Žegarac, PhD, University of Bedfordshire, Luton, England

Introduction

What can be more important in today's world than communication? Communication is the fundamental process by which humans live as social animals. Because of communication we can come together to build families, social networks, and professional associations. Because of communication we can work with very different others toward a common goal. Because of communication we can organize sports, leisure, and recreational activities. And unfortunately, because of (mis)communication we can argue, fight, and wage war.

Thus, it is fitting that the study of communication is a field of active scientific and scholarly endeavor, and equally fitting that much of the state-of-the-art knowledge in this area be brought together in handbooks such as this one and its companion handbook, the *APA Handbook of Interpersonal Communication*. Communication has been studied from many different perspectives (e.g., basic and applied sciences) and disciplines (e.g., sociology, linguistics, psychology), and indeed today these efforts have amassed a wealth of information about communication. The purpose of these two handbooks is to compile, organize, and synthesize much of this knowledge.

It's important to have a working definition of *communication*, and as the reader will readily see, each of the chapters presents a common yet unique perspective on what such a definition may entail, either explicitly or implicitly. It may be impossible to arrive at a definition of communication with which all will agree. At the same time, I strongly believe that it is important for authors to make explicit their working definitions and for readers to be able to know what those working definitions are (and, of course, to have their own working definitions).

For me, a common thread among all definitions of communication involves some degree of message or information exchange between two or more interactants. Indeed, the encoding and decoding of such messages forms the foundation of any communication episode. And because this information exchange occurs through multiple channels and multiple signals, and through both verbal and nonverbal behaviors, communication is a rich, complex process.

I believe that one very important function of communication is the conveyance of intent (and, indeed, this is a perspective that is echoed by most of the authors in these volumes). One of the reasons why humans can produce and live very successfully in highly complex, layered social networks is because we can communicate intent and share intentions with others. Some scholars believe, in fact, that shared intentionality is an ability unique to humans (Tomasello, Carpenter, Call, Behne, and Moll 2005).

In my view, shared intentionality is one of the major reasons why human cultures have survived and thrived. While there are many definitions of *culture* (as there are of communication), I define culture as a meaning and information system that is transmitted across generations (Matsumoto and Juang 2007). Shared intentionality allows for human cultures to evolve and have three characteristics that nonhuman cultures do not: social complexity, differentiation, and institutionalization. And because communication is at the heart of the conveyance of intent and the production of shared intentionality, it is therefore at the heart of human cultural life. Without communication as we know it today, we would not have human cultures as we know them today. And the survival success story of humans, which has occurred because of the evolution of human cultures, would not have been possible without communication. For this reason alone, communication is an incredibly important topic not only for people today and tomorrow but also for humankind throughout the millennia.

An Evolving Understanding of Interpersonal and Intercultural Communication

Of the many potential ways of divvying up the field, one major method is the distinction between *interpersonal* and *intercultural* communication, the former referring to communication among individuals of the same cultural background using the same cultural framework, and the latter referring to communication among individuals who are agents of different cultures and who use different cultural frameworks. This distinction is important because of the implicit association of the communication process to cultural frames. Different cultures promote different procedures and meaning systems in the encoding and decoding of messages, and even when the same language is used, underlying cultural differences in frameworks can produce differences in meaning of the language (e.g., American vs. British vs. Australian English, or different meanings of the same terminology among branches of the military).

Sometimes, however, the distinction between interpersonal and intercultural communication can be blurred. After all, intercultural communication has traditionally been considered essentially interpersonal communication among people from different cultures. And given that no two people are exactly alike, even when from the same linguistic culture, almost any interpersonal communication can be considered (to some degree) intercultural (just ask any married couple whose members come from two different familial cultures).

I believe that, interestingly, much of the blurring of the distinction between interpersonal and intercultural communication has come about because of our increased understanding of *person* and *culture* and the intricate relationship between the two. Indeed, it is clear today that it is almost impossible to consider one without the other, and they both coevolved to have the capacities, abilities, competences, and dispositions that allow for communication to occur. Much of what you will read in the remaining chapters in both handbooks, therefore, reflects this fuzziness, which is inevitable given the nature of the topic area and the rather artificial distinction we scientists have placed in use.

Thus, although the distinction between interpersonal and intercultural communication has proven to be a very useful one in the field, it is not without pitfalls and limitations. Regardless, this distinction has been the major way in which research and theorizing has been organized in the field, and for that reason these handbooks maintain that distinction.

The Influence of Changing Technologies on Communication

Transportation and communication technologies have transformed our world in ways previously unimaginable, and they promise to continue to do so in the future. Communication no longer occurs just within the domain of face-to-face encounters. E-mail, Facebook, Twitter, Skype, and video teleconferencing have all changed the ways in which communication occurs. Moreover, transportation technologies bring people from disparate cultures together more easily today than ever, and it is not uncommon to communicate with people with very different cultural frameworks in our everyday lives, where it would have been unthinkable even 50 years ago. Fifty years from now we will likely be communicating with technologies we cannot even imagine today.

The dynamic nature of our ever-changing world brought about by technologies has produced new challenges in our ability to communicate effectively and efficiently. Understanding intent correctly is a major concern for businesses, governments, and individuals. Fittingly, a great deal of contemporary research has been directed toward understanding the ways in which communication has changed (or not) as a function of these evolving technologies, and this is reflected in many of the chapters in both handbooks. As technologies continue to evolve, so will the challenges they bring to bear on effective communication; future research efforts will undoubtedly keep up with these changes, resulting in a very dynamically fluid field of scientific endeavor.

The chapters in this handbook are the state of the art at this slice of time given the evolving nature of communication and our understanding of both communication and culture. This handbook is divided into two major sections, reflecting two broad ways in which work in each area has evolved. The first section deals with theoretical perspectives; chapters in this section provide different conceptual frameworks with which to understand the state-of-the-art knowledge in both fields. The second section deals with applications, describing how research findings have been instrumental to the development of intervention programs to improve communication, to the identification of key factors (competencies) that appear to be the key ingredients of effective communication, and to the examination of the efficacy of such programs.

Overview of the *APA Handbook of Intercultural Communication*

Theoretical Perspectives

This handbook begins with Chapter 1 by Žegarac, who provides a cognitive psychological account of communicative interaction within the context of culture. He views culture as a stable system of relations between visible things in the environment of people and their significances, shared by a group. He also views communication as the intent to convey information within a context (recall our discussion of intent above). Žegarac argues that communication intention is important, and intercultural communication can be understood as a cultural phenomenon from the perspective of the communicative intent. In particular, Žegarac's arguments for the concept of a mutual cognitive environment are particularly useful in understanding the role of culture in communication.

In Chapter 2, Brabant, Watson, and Gallois describe the social psychological perspectives concerning intercultural communication. Noting that the study of intercultural communication has a long history in social psychology, these authors describe the two main approaches to understanding and studying it from a psychological perspective: intercultural communication competence models and intergroup communication models. Brabant et al. correctly point out the limitations in both these traditions, and they suggest that theories that combine the two may be more powerful for predicting and explaining communication success and failure. In particular, they propose the communication accommodation theory as one such potential model, and they highlight future integrative research in the area.

In Chapter 3, Matsumoto, Yoo, and LeRoux focus on the role of emotion in intercultural communication and adaptation. As Brabant and colleagues point out in Chapter 2, there is much previous research in the area of intercultural competence and the knowledge, skills, and abilities associated with that area. Notably lacking, however, are approaches that incorporate emotion. Matsumoto and colleagues suggest that emotion, and especially emotion regulation, is a key ingredient of successful intercultural adaptation and communication. They describe research using their Intercultural Adjustment Potential Scale, which demonstrates the importance of emotion regulation and other factors in predicting intercultural competence and adaptation.

In Chapter 4, van Meurs and Spencer-Oatey focus on intercultural conflict. Many of us spend much of our time resolving conflicts, and these authors note that such conflicts are likely to increase in today's multicultural, highly technological world. The chapter provides an overview of key theoretical concepts related to conflict, explores the relationship between conflict and culture, and examines how intercultural conflicts may be exacerbated in intercultural encounters. Van Meurs and Spencer-Oatey note the limitations of current theoretical and empirical perspectives in terms of the study of intercultural conflict and suggest that multidisciplinary perspectives may provide more lucrative frameworks for theorizing and study.

In Chapter 5, Reisigl discusses the interesting and very relevant topic of discrimination, focusing on two types of discrimination: verbal and visual. He presents a discourse analytical framework that aids readers in understanding how verbal discourses can be used to promulgate social discrimination and that can be used to understand and study discrimination in methodical ways. In particular, Reisigl argues that the problem of social discrimination in discourses is far too complex to be understood and studied well with an exclusive focus on intercultural communication in a strict sense; therefore, he calls for interdisciplinary analyses that combine the analysis of intercultural communication with critical discourse analysis, as well as political, social psychological, economic, and legal analyses.

In Chapter 6, Thielmann suggests that extralinguistic phenomena play a crucial role in societal interaction. Because the latter consists of routines involving institutions and interactional patterns, such interactions are inherently cultural. Issues of power and dominance within intercultural communication are due to asymmetrical constellations within three constructs: societal structure, interactants' knowledge, and interactants' language. Thus, an understanding of power and dominance issues in intercultural communication requires an understanding of these three factors. Thielmann suggests that if students of intercultural communication take these factors into consideration, analyses of authentic intercultural discourse may be able to dissolve issues of power and dominance into the question of how people deal with asymmetric situation.

In Chapter 7, Spreckels and Kotthoff argue that intercultural encounters make it clear that interactants' identities constitute themselves in the interpersonal relationship and encounter, rather than being merely characteristics of individuals. They review traditional descriptions and frameworks of social identity, and they highlight the key concept of patchwork identities, suggesting that modern identities are often patchwork constructions that are based on the fluid and dynamic nature of relationships constructed during interactions. At the same time, identities need stability and confluence within cultures; thus, part of the associated politics of identity consists of the search for environments and relationships in which identities can assert themselves. Identities are driving forces that can bring people together or drive them apart, and the authors suggest that more social knowledge is required to understand this phenomenon, especially in our globalized world.

In Chapter 8, Bailey also discusses the issue of identity, suggesting that language is our primary semiotic tool for representing and negotiating social reality, including social identities. He argues that while some identity negotiations are conscious, most are not, and that a turn-by-run analysis of naturally occurring language and interaction is a means to understand how individuals, as social actors, position themselves and others. Bailey further argues that multilingual individuals have expanded sets of linguistic resources for the task of socially positioning self and other, and a broader range of social categories that can be activated during talk. He argues that what is distinctive about identity negotiations in multilingual contexts is not so much linguistic as it is social and political, and to analyze identity work in such contexts is to analyze the larger social and political systems in which identity operates.

In Chapter 9, Quist and Jørgensen discuss the interesting phenomenon known as *crossing*, which refers to the spontaneous acquisition and use of languages that are thought not to belong to the speaker. Crossing is related to code switching, stylization, and double voicing, and the authors approach the phenomenon in relation to processes of ethnic and social identity, and solidarity construction. Crossings are transgressions in the use of language that are open and observable acts performed with a purpose, which makes them an important and interesting source of knowledge about social meaning construction and negotiation.

In Chapter 10, Krajewski and Schröder deal with the interesting and relevant topics of silence and taboos. Noting that there is no such thing as antibehavior, they argue that any behavior—even silence—is communicative. As such, the interpretation of silence and its function differs from culture to culture, and cultural differences shape the meanings of silence across different contexts and individuals. Culture-related silence is related to the construct of taboos; they are characteristics of all forms of community, are prerequisites for organized coexistence, and prevent unnecessary disputes and conflicts. Taboos ensure the stability of a society, are the basis of the identity of individuals and groups, and thus are an important, albeit often unrecognized, part of understanding culture and communication.

Applied Perspectives

This section of the book begins with Chapter 11 by Roberts, who tackles the important question of intercultural communication in health care settings. Roberts notes that the applied linguistic literature on this topic is still sparse but growing; thus, Roberts argues that for this area to evolve, it is important for researchers to make connections with the larger literatures contributed by anthropology, sociology, linguistics, and psychology. Intercultural communication difficulties produce a lack of assumptions about role relations, differences in communicative style, and a lack of resources on both the health care provider and client/patient sides for negotiating understanding. Given the growing multicultural populations in the U.S. and elsewhere today, these issues are quickly coming to the forefront in both applied and empirical work.

In Chapter 12, Scherr discusses the role of schools as the institution that is important for not only language acquisition but also for the development of an individual's construction of his or her cultural membership, and the author argues that both aspects are thus intertwined in development. Scherr contends that schools, as national, state-managed institutions, bring forth collective identities and distinctions, and that how social and cultural heterogeneity is treated in schools is closely related to sociopolitical programs. That is, the various ways of dealing with cultural differences in education can be understood against the background of each country and culture's social and political situations, and the goals of their national policies.

In Chapter 13, Hinton examines the role of culture in the interpretation of the media. Although it is common to conceptualize the homogenization of cultural interpretations of media as indicative of a type of universality, Hinton argues instead that an examination of the cultural context of both the academic research and its audience reception is important to gain a full interpretation of what is happening in media interpretation. Utilizing a cultural analysis, Hinton suggests that globalization does not necessarily result in the promulgation of a dominant ideology (e.g., Western), but one that is contested and negotiated within the social practices of different cultures. That is, globalization is a process of complex connectivity, in which media products interact with home cultures to structure discourse around social concerns.

In Chapter 14, Piller provides an overview of recent research in cross-cultural intimate relationships, that is, those that are romantic and sexual. Focusing on the early parts of the formation of such relationships, Piller argues that cross-cultural communication cannot be defined by the identities of the interactants, but rather by what it is that the interactants orient to. Within this framework, communicative events are cross-cultural only if couples orient to cultural differences, and culture is a category that is actively constructed. Indeed, many couples, regardless of backgrounds, create their own minicultures, within which culture may or may not play an active role. Piller suggests that the more established a cross-cultural intimate relationship becomes, the rarer cross-cultural communication will be.

Intercultural communication is an important issue in many multinational and multicultural workplaces today, and businesses spend much time, effort, and resources in helping bridge gaps in communication among their workers. In Chapter 15, Newton describes work using authentic interactions taken from a large corpus of recordings made in a range of white and blue collar workplaces. Newton demonstrates that authentic materials are valuable resources for assisting migrants to become more informed, sensitive, flexible, and strategically equipped communicators in their second language. This work provides evidence that the expensive and complex business of collecting and analyzing authentic workplace interactions has worthwhile practical outcomes for those engaged in preparing people for communicative demands in the workplace.

Finally, in Chapter 16, Rost-Roth reviews the area of intercultural training. This area of research has blossomed in the past 30 years, and it has provided evidence that intercultural competence is a complex phenomenon and that intercultural training can be conceptualized in a multitude of dimensions. Rost-Roth discusses the need for training, typical target groups of training, and the types of training that are often available. In particular, the chapter describes in depth the use of simulations and role plays, critical incidents and culture assimilators, linguistic awareness of cultures, discourse analysis, and coaching. In particular, advantages and disadvantages of these multiple techniques are discussed, and readers are offered a broad menu of alternatives to understand intercultural training.

Conclusion

The chapters bring together much of the state-of-the-art literature on intercultural communication. They represent well the emerging and evolving nature of communication and its highly interconnected relationship with culture. They leverage research on new technologies and culture, and they highlight the pitfalls and challenges in understanding and studying communication today. Regardless of the approach, technology, and time period, human communication will continue to be one of the most important aspects of our lives and behaviors, and will form a bedrock for our families, communities, and society at large. The chapters in this volume will form the foundation for much theorizing and empirical work today and for the next generation of work in this area.

References

Matsumoto, David and Linda Juang. 2007. *Culture and Psychology* (4th ed.). Belmont, CA: Wadsworth.

Tomasello, Michael, Malinda Carpenter, Josep Call, Tanya Behne, and Henrike Moll. 2005. Understanding and sharing intentions: The origins of cultural cognition. *Behavioral & Brain Sciences* 28: 675–735.

Part I

Theoretical Perspectives

1 ——————————————————————————

A Cognitive Pragmatic Perspective
on Communication and Culture[1]

Vladimir Žegarac

1. Introduction

> I would define a social situation as an environment of mutual monitoring
> possibilities, anywhere within which an individual will find himself acces-
> sible to the naked senses of all others who are 'present', and similarly find
> them accessible to him.
>
> Goffman ([1964] 1972: 63)

The impact of Erving Goffman's work on the development of social approaches
to human interaction has been immense, but the fundamentally cognitive
character of his definition of "social situation"—clearly reflected in the notion
of "mutual monitoring"—has been largely ignored. This is apparent in the way
the term *situation* is characterized within Fishman's (1972: 48) sociolinguistics (as "the co-occurrence of two (or more) interlocutors related to each other
in a particular way, communicating about a particular topic, in a particular
setting"), in Halliday's (see Halliday and Hasan 1976: 22) functionalist view of
language (where *field*, *mode* and *tenor* are the key determinants of situations),
in Hymes' (1972) ethnographic approach to communication (in which the categories of *setting, participant, end, act sequence, key, instrumentalities, norms
of interaction and interpretation*, and *genre* provide a template for analysing
communicative events) and in much other work in the loosely defined field of
(social) pragmatics. To be sure, these authors are aware of the psychological
nature of *situation*. Thus, Halliday and Hasan (1976) observe:

> The term SITUATION, meaning the 'context of situation' in which a text
> is embedded, refers to all those extra-linguistic factors which have some
> bearing on the text itself. A word of caution is needed about this concept. At
> the moment, as the text of this Introduction is being composed, it is a typi-
> cal English October day in Palo Alto, California; a green hillside is visible

[1] In writing and rewriting this article I have benefited greatly from the help of many people. Special thanks to Robyn Carston and Helen Spencer-Oatey who always had time for my frequent que-
ries, and also to Kate Berardo, Joy Caley and Anna Mantzouka who have in various ways directly
contributed to the content of this text. The responsibility for all the remaining flaws is mine.

> outside the window, the sky is grey, and it is pouring with rain. This might seem to be part of the 'situation' of this text; but it is not, because it has **no relevance** to the meanings expressed, or to the words or grammatical patterns that are used to express them [emphasis VŽ].
>
> Halliday and Hasan (1976: 21)

Despite the general awareness that the concept of (*communication*) *situation* calls for a psychological explanation, existing definitions of this term tend to have a distinctly externalist-descriptive, rather than an internalist-explanatory flavour. The main aim of this article is to provide an introductory internalist, cognitive-psychological, account of communicative interaction in the context of culture. The lack of anything approximating a universally accepted theory of communication or a universally accepted theory of culture inevitably makes this endeavour possible only with some radical corner-cutting.

Although several natural points of contact between communication and culture have been identified in commonsense terms, the indissoluble link between the two has defied explanation. The following passage provides some intuitive support for the cognitive, Relevance-theoretic approach (Sperber and Wilson 1986/95) on which this article is based:

> Over time, the habitual interactions within communities take on familiar forms and structures, which we will call *the organization of meaning*. These structures are imposed upon the situations which people confront and are not determined by the situation itself. For example, the wink of an eye. Is it a physical reflex from dust in the eye? Or an invitation to a prospective date? Or could it be someone making fun of you to others? Perhaps a nervous tick? The wink itself is real, but its meaning is attributed to it by observers. The **attributed** meaning may or may not coincide with the **intended** meaning of the wink. Effective social interaction, though, depends on the **attributed** meaning and **intended** meaning coinciding [emphasis VŽ].
>
> Trompenaars and Hampden-Turner (1997: 24)

This passage suggests the following view: culture is a stable system of relations between (visible) things in the environment of people ("forms and structures") and their (invisible) significances, shared by a social group. (Note that the terms *cultural* and *social* are nearly synonymous. Following the common practice in social psychology and anthropology, I will call *cultural* those social things which are relatively stable and widespread.) This view of culture as a phenomenon suggests that particular cultures should be thought of as having fuzzy boundaries and that they can be identified in terms of indefinitely many various characteristics of social groups (such as: ethnicity, nation, profession, age group, sexual orientation).

Communication is different from other forms of social interaction in that it involves making evident the intention to convey information by integrating the evidence of this intention with the context. (It should be noted that the term *context* is used more broadly in social than in cognitive approaches to pragmatics. In social approaches *context* is the total linguistic and non-linguistic background to an act of communication. In Sperber and Wilson's (1986/95) cognitive account of communication, this term refers to a set of mentally represented assumptions which interacts with new information from various sources, including communication.) It is this communicative intention (i.e. the intention to make evident the intention to inform) that crucially distinguishes a (deliberate) wink from an involuntary twitch, which is also informative because it may provide evidence for various conclusions, such as: *the twitch was caused by dust in the eye.* The concept of *communicative intention* is important, because people generally pay attention to those phenomena which are evidently produced with the intention to convey information. For example, we tend to pay attention and attribute meanings to blinks, which we recognize as deliberate, rather than to twitches, which are likely to remain unnoticed, because they are not perceived as produced with the intention to convey information. Whilst culture is characterized by meanings shared within a social group, communication is a mode of social interaction through which new meanings can come to be shared. However, communication is generally at risk of failure, because the attribution of meaning depends on the interlocutors' ability to reason in the way intended by the communicator and to select the right context for the interpretation of the communicative act. As there is no guarantee that the addressee will interpret the communicative act in the way intended by the communicator, there can be no guarantee that the attributed and the intended meanings will coincide. Since a person's cultural knowledge crucially determines the contexts which are available to them, the risk of miscommunication is generally higher in interactions between people from different cultural backgrounds. Therefore, a plausible account of *inter*-cultural communication should provide answers to the following questions:

> What is cultural knowledge?
> How does cultural knowledge contribute to context?

I try to show that the theoretical backbone of Sperber's (1996) epidemiological approach to culture and Sperber and Wilson's (1986/95) Relevance-theoretic approach to communication provide explicit and well-motivated answers to these questions. The article is structured as follows: first, some of the main tenets of Relevance Theory are illustrated with a few examples of (inter-cultural) communication. Second, the epidemiological approach to culture is introduced, and a way of characterizing the distinction between *intra-* and *inter*-cultural communication is suggested. Finally, the framework of Relevance Theory is outlined in order to show how the contribution of cultural background to the context can be integrated with this approach to communication in a principled way.

2. Examples of a Relevance-Theoretic Account of (Inter-Cultural) Communication

In Relevance Theory terms, human cognition is geared towards improving the belief system of individuals and the most important type of social interaction through which this goal is pursued is called ostensive-inferential communication. On this view, an act of ostensive behaviour (such as a pointing gesture, a [deliberate] wink, or an utterance) makes evident the communicator's intention to inform the addressee/audience of something. Comprehension is an inference (i.e. reasoning) process which takes the evidence presented by the communicative act (i.e. an ostensive stimulus) and the context as inputs, and yields interpretations as outputs. These tenets of Relevance Theory are illustrated by the following examples of (*inter*-cultural) communication:

> (1) A British family had lived in an African country for several years. They had become familiar with the local language and culture. After the breakout of civil war in the region, they were forced to leave the country. Before leaving, they accepted the local peoples' offer of help and asked them to try and "rescue" some of their "special things". Quite some time later, they were somewhat surprised to find that their TV set and video recorder were the main rescued items.

In this case, the British participants did not take account of the context (i.e. the set of assumptions) in which their interlocutors would interpret the phrase "special things", despite their knowledge of the local culture (most likely, because they had to divide their attention between several pressing concerns, which made them revert to their more intuitive cultural mindset).[2]

In other instances of miscommunication, the intended interpretation is recognized, but it is not accepted. Consider Example (2):

> (2) [The following is an extract from an interview with Haldun Aydingün, the author of the book *The Divorced Man*, described in the Cyprus Turkish Airlines' in-flight magazine *Caretta* (September 2005) as "an entertaining look at the institution of marriage, how the institution and, more importantly, a break with this institution, affects men and their behaviour".]
>
> *Interviewer:* You make allusions to the male make-up and even say, "I wish the male body had a control button that would suppress sexual impulses". On the other hand, it is clear that you value faithfulness and the institution of marriage. Aren't these two somewhat contradictory?
>
> *Interviewee:* No, not in the manner you have just described. What I was trying to communicate here was the fact that the male sexual impulse was very basic, a need that had to be met. If sexuality is expressed in a healthy way in marriage then there is a chance that marriage and faithfulness can be non-contradictory.

The interviewee's intention to communicate that he holds modern views on gender relations is very salient in the interview from which this excerpt is taken. However, rather than accepting this message, many (Western European)

---

[2] Of course, whether the denotation of a particular expression, in this case "special things", is determined culturally or by individual people's values, attitudes etc. needs to be established on the basis of appropriate (ethnographic) evidence. In the situation described in (1), the evidence, which for space reasons cannot be presented here, strongly supports the view that electrical goods were considered particularly precious in the local culture.

readers will be more convinced by the inadvertently produced evidence of the interviewee's old-fashioned views which may easily appear sexist, or, at least, not politically correct, in the modern Western world (e.g. *A man's sexual needs are naturally stronger—more basic—than a woman's; Men are not able, or they are less able than women, to control their sexual impulses*, etc.). So, in this instance, communication will be less than successful in case the communicator has inadvertently conveyed some belief-assumptions which contradict those that he evidently intends to convey.

Miscommunication may also arise because some evidence of the communicative intention has not been recognized by the addressee:

> (3) At a meeting recently held in Japan, an American was discussing two alternative proposals with his colleagues, all of whom were native speakers of Japanese. The American was well schooled in the Japanese language and was, indeed, often called "fluent" by those around him. At this meeting, proposal A was contrasted to proposal B, and a consensus was reached about future action, and the meeting then dismissed. Upon leaving the room the American commented, "I think the group made a wise choice in accepting proposal A". A Japanese colleague, however, noted, "But proposal B was the group's choice". The American continued: "But I heard people say that proposal A was better". The Japanese colleague concluded, "Ah, you listened to the words but not to the pauses between the words".
>
> Brislin (1978: 205), quoted in Gutt (2000: 78)

In this situation, pauses were intended to be recognized as produced with the intention to convey something important for the interpretation of the words used (i.e. that the speaker merely acknowledges the hearer's view, whilst rejecting it politely). The hearer misunderstood the utterance because he had overlooked the communicative intent behind the pauses due to his lack of appropriate contextual cultural knowledge about the way pauses are used as ostensive stimuli.

The success of genuine communicative acts, such as (1) to (3), depends on the informative intention being recognized. However, in many situations the fulfilment of the informative intention depends on the informative intention not being recognized. Consider:

> (4) Situation: Zoë, a final year undergraduate, was waiting to see one of her lecturers to discuss her dissertation topic with him. After the lecturer had asked her a couple of times to wait a little bit longer, Zoë came up with an alternative action plan, and said, roughly:

"That's alright. I'll come to see you later this week. I'll first go and talk about it with Chloë. She's already started working on her dissertation, so she can help me with the topic".

What did Zoë intend to communicate to her lecturer? She overtly communicated that she did not mind coming another time and that she would come to see him much better prepared as a result of talking first to a fellow student. That was the informative intention that Zoë made evident (i.e. her communicative intention). But the lecturer drew a further conclusion on the basis of what Zoë had said. In his opinion, Zoë's friend Chloë had been going about her dissertation project in a way which did not provide the best example to follow, so he insisted that Zoë should stay and discuss her topic with him. As Zoë had not said (or otherwise made evident) anything that would indicate a negative attitude towards the lecturer, she did not communicate that she disapproved of waiting, that she did not think much of the help the lecturer would give her, that she would like to know what the lecturer thought about Chloë's work, and so on. A couple of years after she had graduated, the lecturer saw Zoë. He asked her if she remembered this incident and he told her how she had inadvertently made him change his mind, so he decided to talk to her without further delay. But Zoë corrected him: "No! That worked!" She explained that she had had the intention to inform the lecturer that it was desirable that he should see her promptly, but rather than making this intention evident, she had concealed it, hoping that he might reason in the way he actually did.

This example illustrates an important general point: in instances of overt communication, the communicator makes the informative intention evident and, in doing so, takes responsibility for what is communicated. There are various reasons for not wanting to convey information overtly, but people generally resort to covert social interaction when they do not wish to take responsibility for what they are trying to convey or when making the informative intention evident would jeopardize its fulfilment. In the situation described in (4), Zoë's informative intention (that the lecturer should change his mind and see her promptly, possibly also that he should reveal his opinion of Chloë's work) was fulfilled because it was concealed successfully.

Covert forms of information transmission are particularly important in intercultural social settings. For example, what might be a successful way to conceal the evidence of a particular informative intention in one culture, may seem transparent in the context of another. The following excerpt, taken from an open letter by the Cyprus Turkish Airlines' Acting Manager, published in the airline's in-flight magazine *Caretta* (September 2005), clearly illustrates this point:

(5) Welcome Aboard
   The hot summer season will soon be a thing of the past. Unfortunately, the aviation sector has experienced some uncomfortably hot moments this summer as well. The accident involving a plane from Southern Cyprus saddened all of us deeply. We would like to take this opportunity to convey our condolences to the people of Southern Cyprus and the aviation community.
   This accident, which grieved all of us so deeply, has shown once again just how seriously the aviation sector must take its responsibilities.
   [...]
   The Helios crash has been yet another reminder to the entire sector that there must not be negligence in even the smallest details.
   Our company has always operated with this mindset, constantly increasing and strengthening its precautions and efforts regarding flight safety and will continue to host its passengers with confidence.

The text from which this excerpt is taken makes evident the informative intention to express solidarity with another airline and the people affected by the accident, but many readers will reject this informative intention, because of what they take to be compelling evidence for the conclusion that the writer has a covert aim, a hidden agenda, as it were: to put down a rival company in order to promote his own. What must have seemed a clever and legitimate marketing move to the writer of the letter, is seen as a transparent, hypocritical and insensitive marketing ploy in the cultural context of many people in the intended readership.

These examples point to the importance of culture in context selection. Therefore, an explanatory approach to *inter*-cultural communication should provide an account of the way cultural knowledge is represented and used in communication.

3. The Epidemiological Approach to Culture

Like some other animals, humans represent mentally various aspects of the world they live in. Unlike any other animals, humans have the ability to form *metarepresentations*, i.e. belief-representations (*beliefs* hereafter) about the mental representations of their physical and psychological environments. Their ability to do this is evidenced by all things which are part of culture: a given thing is a hammer, not in virtue of the representation we form of its shape, form and other visible features, but because we make such representations the objects of various beliefs (e.g. that the thing in question is used for a particular purpose). To give another example, consider the mental representation of a particular thing (let's call it *A*) as a small stone. It is easy to think of circumstances which may lead one to make the mental representation: *A is a small stone* the object of beliefs, such as: *A is a small stone which can be used to keep the door open*, or *A is a small stone which can be used to prevent paper from flying off the desk when the window is open*. When such beliefs about the representation of *A as a small stone* become accepted by the members of a social group, A becomes an artefact: a doorstop or a paperweight. Of course, a typical artefact is a thing which has been designed and produced with a specific purpose in mind. However, what makes it a cultural thing is the existence of widespread and stable beliefs about (mental representations of) it, rather than the fact that it has been consciously designed and produced. It should also be noted that, when a mental representation of a psychological phenomenon, say, the emotional experience of anger, is metarepresented—in other words, when the representation of the direct experience of this emotion is made the object of some beliefs (such as: [this] *is the way one feels when something unpleasant one does not want to happen happens, although its occurrence could/should have been avoided*)—the direct emotional experience of anger becomes "visible" to the mind, and, therefore, available for symbolic representation and communication. In sum: the metarepresentational capacity is the human mind's capacity to think about itself and it is the biological prerequisite for the emergence of cultural categories.

Some important differences between the communicative behaviour of people and animals suggest that the metarepresentational capacity is unique to humans. For example, it is often observed that animals engage in complex forms of social behaviour: bees pass on to other bees information about the location of pollen-rich fields and lions hunt in groups by ambushing their prey. But a bee which "reads" another bee's dance gets the information content directly, as it were, without making the dance or its information content the object of beliefs (see von Frisch 1967). To give another example, we can realistically imagine a group of lions preparing for the hunt by taking positions through monitoring each other's movements and coordinating their actions in remarkably complex ways. However, the idea of lions planning the hunt by drawing lines in the sand and indicating with pebbles their respective positions relative to their prey is rather far-fetched. The ability to do this would involve the lions making representations such as: *A is a pebble*, the object of beliefs, such as: *A is a pebble which represents that antelope over there that we could hunt down*. But lions, bees and other animals do not have the metarepresentational capacity (i.e. the capacity to form beliefs about mental representations). That is why they are not capable of reasoning feats which even young children find easy and intuitive, or of the type of symbolic communication that comes naturally to humans. (This account of the role of *metarepresentations* in explaining culture simplifies greatly. For a more detailed discussion, see articles in Sperber 1996, 2000.)

While the metarepresentational capacity provides the basis for explaining our ability to think about our own and other people's minds and for the possibility of symbolic action, the theory of culture needs to explain how particular cultural representations emerge and spread. For example, we ought to be able to give an account of the way small wedge-shaped objects come to be thought of as doorstops, or how a given symbol, such as the expression "special things" in (1), comes to denote different sets of objects in different societies. In a series of publications Dan Sperber (see Sperber 1985, 1996) has developed the idea that explanations in the domain of culture should focus on a particular relation between psychological and ecological influences. On his view, a defining feature of social-cultural things is the relation between forms and structures, which are by and large in the environment of people, and mental representations, which are in individual people's minds/brains. Therefore, cultural categories should be seen as resulting from interactions between *intra*-individual, cognitive-psychological, mechanisms responsible for our ability to interpret the world, and *inter*-individual, social-cultural, mechanisms, such as communication, which enable us to disseminate these representations within and across human populations (see Sperber 1996: 49). On this view, cultures are not natural kinds. Rather, they consist of relatively stable patterns of a particular type of metarepresentation, which I will call *cultural representation*:

> Cultural representation: a metarepresentation which involves a stable three place relation between:
>
> - a mental representation (of a physical entity, event, direct emotional experience, etc.);
> - a belief about this mental representation (e.g. hammer, doorstop, love, anger); and
> - a sizable population made up of individuals (a nation, an ethnic group, an age group, a professional group, etc.) who share the same, or very similar, beliefs about particular types of mental representations over significant time spans.

Cultural representations emerge and spread through causal chains which involve mental representations and public productions (utterances, texts, pictures, artefacts in the environment of individuals) which are reproduced repeatedly and reasonably faithfully, thus achieving stability and wide distribution, through a process (very sketchily) illustrated in figure 1.

This approach is articulated in the context of an analogy between the study of culture and the study of epidemics. Just as there is no epidemic without individual organisms being infected by particular viruses or bacteria, there is no culture without representations being distributed in the brains/minds of individuals. This analogy is very suggestive in several ways. For instance, it is often observed that culture is both an individual and a social construct (see Matsumoto 1996: 18). There is no epidemic without diseased individuals, but the study of epidemics cannot be reduced to the study of individual pathology. By the same token, a culture cannot exist without some cultural representations being in the brains/minds of individuals, but it does not follow that the study of culture can be reduced to the study of individual psychology. Just as infections are in individual people's bodies, mental representations are in their minds/brains. And, just as the spreading of diseases is explained by investigating the interaction between strains of micro-organisms with the environment that they live in, the distribution of cultural representations is explained in terms of communicative, as well as other types of, interaction between people and their environment. From this perspective, the boundaries of a given culture are not any sharper than those of a given epidemic. An epidemic involves a population with many individuals being afflicted to varying degrees by a particular strain of micro-organisms over a continuous time span on a territory with fuzzy and unstable boundaries. And a culture involves a social group (such as a nation, ethnic group, profession, generation, etc.) defined in terms of similar cultural representations held by a significant proportion of the group's members. In other words, people are said to belong in the same culture to the extent that the set of their shared cultural representations is large. This characterization of a culture naturally accommodates the existence of multicultural nations, professions, etc. It also suggests a straightforward characterization of sub-culture, as a set of cultural representations within a given culture which are shared (mainly) by a subset of its members (e.g. teenagers, members of particular professions, different social classes within a national or ethnic cultural group, and so on).

On this view, individual cultures are epiphenomenal, rather than natural, things which owe their identities to the joint influences of a range of historical, political, economic, and various other factors. Therefore, *intra*-cultural communication could be characterized as communication between participants

Figure 1. Schema of the causal chain involved in the spreading of cultural representations.

who share most cultural representations, and *inter*-cultural communication, as communication between participants who share few cultural representations. This raises the following questions: how similar does the shared set of cultural representations of two individuals need to be, for communication between them to be considered *intra*-cultural? And conversely, how small should their shared set of cultural representations be, for communication between them to be considered *inter*-cultural? Plausible answers to these questions can be given in the context of two observations. First, some cultural representations are intuitively more important, or central, than others. This intuition seems to be based on two facts: (a) some cultural representations are more causally efficacious than others in terms of the extent to which they inform the beliefs and guide the actions of those who hold them, and (b) some of the beliefs and actions which are informed by cultural representations pertain to a greater number of spheres of social life than others. Therefore, the *centrality* of a cultural representation could be characterized as follows:

> Centrality of a cultural representation A cultural representation is central to the extent that it is causally efficacious across many spheres of social life.

For example, a system of religious beliefs may influence virtually all aspects of social life, whilst fashions tend to be, not only relatively short-lived, but they may also be confined to relatively isolated social-cultural domains (e.g. how to dress when going to a party). Therefore, cultural proximity/distance is a joint function of the number and the centrality of cultural representations:

> Cultural proximity/distance Two or more individuals/groups are culturally close to the extent that their shared set of cultural representations is large and to the extent that the centrality of these cultural representations is high.
>
> OR:
>
> Two or more individuals/groups are culturally distant to the extent that their shared set of cultural representations is small and to the extent that the centrality of these cultural representations is low.

Clearly, the greater the cultural closeness between people, the more able they will be to make accurate estimates of each other's cognitive resources (e.g. about the contextual assumptions available to other members of the same cultural group), and the better the chances of communicative success between them will be. Thus, in examples (1), (2), (3) and (5) cultural distance played a major role in the communicators' failure to achieve their goals.

Second, the shared cultural knowledge of two or more people may be adequate for communication in some situations, whilst being inadequate for communication in other situations. Therefore, the distinction between *intra*and *inter*-cultural communication should be related to situations of communication:

> Situation of intra-cultural communication A situation of communication in which the cultural distance between the participants is not significant

enough to have an adverse effect on communicative success, so it need not
be specially accommodated by the participants.

Situation of inter-cultural communication A situation in which the cultural distance between the participants is significant enough to have an
adverse effect on communicative success, unless it is appropriately accommodated by the participants.

This approach has a clear implication for the way in which research in the field
of inter-cultural communication might proceed:

1. establish the extent to which the intended and the attributed meanings
   of a given communicative act coincide;
2. find out the similarity between the context in which the communicative act was actually interpreted, and the context intended by the
   communicator;
3. find out the extent to which cultural representations have contributed
   to the gap between the actual and the intended context, and
4. assess the impact of those cultural representations on communicative
   success (taking account of their centrality).

An important methodological aspect of research along these lines is that
it is informed by robust intuitions about interpretations of communicative
acts and by empirical findings based on evidence from a range of different
sources. Note that these findings are independent of, and more reliable than,
any of the theoretical concepts which guide the research, so they can provide
a reasonably solid basis for testing hypotheses about the impact of culture
on communication between participants from particular cultural groups in
particular situations.

The importance of this methodological observation is further highlighted
by a major difference between cultures and epidemics. Epidemics result from
the replication of micro-organisms designed to multiply by producing virtually
identical copies of themselves. What needs to be explained are the circumstances in the environment which favour the emergence and the success of
strains of micro-organisms which are different from, rather than being identical copies of, their ancestors. In contrast to bacteria and viruses, human
brains/ minds are designed to transform, rather than to replicate, representations in the normal mode of operation. We generally synthesize information
forming new representations on the basis of perceptual inputs from the environment and already held representations. The outputs of such processes are
new representations which are more or less similar, rather than identical, to
the input ones. For example, reports of what a person has said only excep-
tionally preserve the exact form of the speaker's original utterance, and back-
translation seldom results in a text identical to the source-language original.
Only in exceptional circumstances do representations with highly similar
forms and contents replicate without significant changes over long time spans,
thus becoming part of culture.

This observation has two important consequences for the study of culture.
On the one hand, it suggests that cross-cultural similarity is more surprising

than cultural diversity. Since people live in vastly different physical environments, we might expect that cultures should differ rather more widely than they actually do. So, the main task for a theory of culture is to explain systematic cross-cultural similarities. On the other hand, cultural variation is the result of the diverse ecological circumstances in which human populations live. Therefore, it is extremely unlikely that these cultural variations fall in the scope of a general theory. Instead, descriptions and explanations in the social-cultural domain ought to be concerned with the study of the distribution of various cultural categories (e.g. artefacts, genres, art forms, "codes" of behaviour, etc.) in the context of a handful of fairly simple universal cognitive mechanisms and of myriad ecological factors. To give but one example, we are used to thinking of carrots as being of an orangey colour. In fact, the orange carrot is largely a cultural innovation which originated in Holland only several centuries ago, when the Dutch made their national colour the colour of the carrot. Before that time carrots, apparently, used to be of a dark-purplish hue. But this is not sufficient to explain the lasting (cross)-cultural success of this designer vegetable. It seems plausible to assume that our biological disposition to associate some colours, such as orange, with edible things, more readily than others, such as dark-purple, is a universal psychological factor which most likely played an important role in the appeal of orangey carrots to people. Of course, the cross-cultural success of the orange carrot also owes a great deal to other ecological factors, including cultural achievements, such as the advent of fairly effective means of transportation, international travel, and so on. In other words, orangey carrots were successful because they were persistently intuitively perceived as more desirable than their purplish ancestors, and because their production and transportation were relatively economical. This is a general point: successful cultural things are those which preserve an appreciable degree of perceived *relevance* in relatively large human populations over relatively significant time spans. Clearly, the term *relevance* can be used as a measure of (likely) cultural success only provided it is given explicit theoretical content.

4. Relevance in Cognition

The stability of representations over time and their geographical distribution owe much to a general functional feature of human cognition: its orientation towards improving the belief system of individuals. If this is indeed a major function of human cognition, then it should be characterized in terms of an efficiency measure, a cost benefit relation of some sort. This is true of any thing that has a function, as the following analogy with purposeful artefacts illustrates:

> Efficiency is some measure of benefit divided by cost. The benefit of a pot could be measured as the quantity of water that it holds. Cost can conveniently be measured in equivalent units: the quantity of material of the pot itself. Efficiency might be defined as the volume of water that a pot can hold divided by the volume of material that goes to make the pot itself.
>
> Dawkins (1996: 7)

Since the function of both communication and cognition is to bring about improvements in individuals' belief systems, cognitive gain constitutes the benefit side of the equation. As humans have finite cognitive resources and limited time for reasoning, planning and decision making, it seems plausible to assume that processing effort is the cost parameter in this cognitive efficiency measure. Sperber and Wilson (1986/95) call this measure relevance and define it as follows:

> Relevance
>
> A phenomenon is relevant to an individual:
> (a) to the extent that the cognitive effects achieved when it is processed in context are large, and
> (b) to the extent that the processing effort required for achieving the effects is small.
>
> Adapted from Sperber and Wilson (1986/95: 153)

On this view, the effect–effort ratio is not measured by mapping values on a numerical scale. People's estimates of effect and effort are based on the monitoring of symptomatic physico-chemical changes, and, when they are represented mentally, they take the form of judgements which are intuitive and comparative, rather than consciously calculated and absolute. These intuitive judgments are not merely retrospective but prospective: people have intuitions about how relevant the processing of a phenomenon is likely to be, not merely about how relevant a phenomenon which has been processed has turned out to be (cf. Sperber and Wilson 1986/95: 130–131). This characterization of relevance provides the basis for the following law-like generalization about human cognition:

> The Cognitive Principle of Relevance:
>
> Human cognition tends to be geared to the maximization of relevance.
>
> Sperber and Wilson (1995: 260)

The human cognitive system's orientation towards relevance provides one part of the explanation for the emergence and the success of cultural categories, including artefacts. On this approach, a plausible account of the success of the orange carrot might go, roughly, as follows: orangey carrots seemed more edible than purplish ones. Clearly, the assumption that a particular plant is edible generally interacts with other assumptions in more productive ways than the assumption that it is not likely to be edible (e.g. how to include it in various recipes). So, representations of orangey carrots seemed more relevant than those of purplish ones on the cognitive effects side. Moreover, if we assume that the two types of carrot are known to be equally beneficial foods, then representations of orangey carrots, which are more readily (that is, more intuitively) thought of as edible, will seem more relevant on the mental effort side as well: other things being equal, the more desirable a thing looks, the more cognitively salient it will be. And, the more cognitively salient something is, the less processing effort will be required for its mental representation and processing. It is interesting to note that the supremacy of orangey carrots is currently being challenged by research which shows that various types of non-orangey carrots (still grown in some parts of the world) are rich in natural substances which reduce the threat of cancer.[3] In light of general knowledge about the link between cancer and food, as well as the growing awareness of the increasing incidence of cancer, non-orangey carrots are likely to begin to seem more and more relevant to more and more people, largely as a result of the dissemination of representations of their beneficial properties by means of communication.

5. Relevance in Communication

Most of the time a vast range of stimuli impinge on our senses at a fairly high rate. Some of these stimuli pre-empt our attention (e.g. loud noises, flashes of light, etc.), thus creating an expectation that processing them will yield significant cognitive effects. Finally, some attention pre-empting stimuli are designed to create—and to be recognized as designed to create—the expectation that they are worth paying attention to (e.g. a [deliberate] wink, the sound of a door bell, a pointing gesture, an utterance, an unexpected silence or pause in speech, etc.). This last type of stimuli are called *ostensive stimuli*, and as mentioned in section 2, their use in conveying information is called ostensive-inferential communication. To recognize a stimulus as ostensive entitles the addressee to presume that whoever produced it did so because they thought this stimulus was worth paying attention to. Consider the following exchange from Chekhov's play *Three Sisters*:

> 6) Vershinin: . . . It's nice living here. But there's one rather strange thing, the station is fifteen miles from the town. And no one knows why.
>
> Soliony: I know why it is. [*Everyone looks at him*] Because if the station were nearer, it wouldn't be so far away, and as it is so far away, it can't be nearer [*An awkward silence*].
>
> Chekhov, *Three Sisters,* Act One

Soliony's conversational contribution is likely to meet with his interlocutors' disapproval because they have been made to expend gratuitous processing effort. By engaging in communication, Soliony creates the expectation that what he has to say deserves the attention of the others. In other words, he issues a promissory note to the effect that his interlocutors' expectation of cognitive reward will be fulfilled. As his remark is clearly irrelevant, he fails, not merely to fulfil an expectation that his interlocutors happen to have formed, but to honour a promise that he has made.

To sum up: human communication involves the production and interpretation of ostensive stimuli, which make evident the communicator's intention to convey some belief-assumptions. The communicator, by making evident her intention to inform the addressee, effectively issues a kind of promissory note to the effect that the utterance (or other ostensive stimulus) is worth paying

---

[3] See http://www.cals.wisc.edu/media/news/02_00/carrot_pigment.html for more information.

attention to. The Cognitive Principle of Relevance makes it possible to spell out the conditions under which this promise has been honoured: an act of communication is worth paying attention to, provided that doing so will lead to the derivation of enough cognitive effects to warrant at least some attention, without gratuitous expenditure of processing effort.

These observations on the role of the Cognitive Principle of Relevance in ostensive-inferential communication are more formally captured by the following generalization, known as the Communicative Principle of Relevance:

> Communicative Principle of Relevance:
>
> Every act of ostensive communication communicates a presumption of its own optimal relevance.
>
> Sperber and Wilson (1995: 260)

> Presumption of Optimal Relevance:
>
> (a) The ostensive stimulus is relevant enough for it to be worth the addressee's while to process it.
> (b) The ostensive stimulus is the most relevant one compatible with the communicator's abilities and preferences/goals.
>
> Adapted from Sperber and Wilson (1995: 270)

The principle of relevance provides the basis for a production strategy (followed by the communicator) and a comprehension strategy (followed by the addressee):

> Relevance-Theoretic Production Strategy
>
> Given your preferences/goals, choose the least effort-demanding option for the hearer.
>
> Žegarac (2004: 203)

> Relevance-Theoretic Comprehension Strategy
>
> (a) construct interpretations in order of accessibility (i.e. follow a path of least effort)
> (b) stop when your expectation of relevance is satisfied. Adapted from Carston (2002: 380)

The communicator's choice of signal is guided by two factors: their assumptions about the addressee (the addressee's knowledge and reasoning abilities) and the communicator's own preferences or goals. Thus, in examples (1) to (3), the communicator's poor assessment of the addressee's/audience's cognitive resources (more specifically, the availability and salience of particular contextual assumptions to the addressee/audience) is the cause of miscommunication. In (4) and (5), communicators try to manipulate the addressee/audience by concealing their informative intentions. Overt (i.e. ostensive) communication is a particularly efficient means for spreading representations, precisely because ostensive stimuli are presumed to come from a helpful source: if the addressee can assume that the ostensive stimulus is the best one that the communicator could have chosen in order to convey a particular set of belief-assumptions, they are in a position to narrow their search for cognitive effects.

The interpretation (i.e. the set of cognitive effects) which is most salient in the addressee's immediate context, is also the most likely to be optimally relevant. If it is not, the context is suitably adjusted (by discarding some assumptions and introducing others) until enough effects are derived for the communicative act to be found consistent with the Principle of Relevance (or until processing is abandoned and communication fails). Such adjustments to the context draw freely on the addressee's world knowledge, more technically, their cognitive environment:

> Cognitive environment (of an individual)
>
> The set of assumptions that are manifest to an individual at a given time.
>
> Carston (2002: 376)

Informally, the term "manifest" means "salient". In Relevance Theory, manifestness is defined as follows:

> Manifestness (of an assumption to an individual)
>
> The degree to which an individual is capable of mentally representing an assumption and holding it as true or probably true at a given moment.
>
> Carston (2002: 378)

The concept of cognitive environment is crucial in explaining ostensive-inferential communication, because a person's cognitive environment sets a limit on the contexts which are available to them. The concept of manifestness points to the fact that the cognitive environments of two (or more) people may differ, not only with respect to which assumptions are available to them at a given time, but also in terms of the extent to which they are able to represent them mentally and to use them in mental processing. Therefore, in deciding which ostensive stimulus to use, the communicator needs to assess which contextual assumptions are available to the addressee and how manifest they are to them. These judgements are based on the communicator's presumptions about the participants' shared cognitive environment. More technically, they are based on their mutual cognitive environment:

> Mutual cognitive environment
>
> A cognitive environment which is shared by a group of individuals and in which it is manifest to those individuals that they share it.
>
> Carston (2002: 378)

The notion of mutual cognitive environment is important because it sets a limit on the possibilities of communication, as illustrated in (7):

> (7) Situation: Kiki, a mutual acquaintance/friend of Maria's and Peter's, had told Peter in April that Maria would be coming to England in May, and that she was planning to see a few people, including him. She also asked him not to tell Maria that she had informed him of her planned visit. Peter was surprised, but he kept the "secret". He did not meet up with Maria in England as he was away on business at the time of her visit. However, unknown to Peter, Kiki disclosed to Maria what she had told him. So, for the next few

months, he remained under the impression that Maria was unaware of his knowledge of her visit to England. The following is an excerpt from their chat on the internet in which the assumption that Maria visited England in May, which was already in Peter's and Maria's shared cognitive environment, became mutually manifest to them:

[1] *Peter:* Are you going on holiday for the New Year and Christmas?
[2] *Maria:* Haven't quite made up my mind yet, but I'm probably going to Barbados to see Sharon and visit some other friends as well.
[3] *Peter:* Sounds good. Are you planning to visit England again?
[4] *Maria:* No, I did last June.
[5] *Peter:* Yeah, when I was in Beijing!
[6] *Maria:* Yes, when Kiki told you. I almost killed her!

People have clear intuitions about the distinction between assumptions which are mutually manifest (i.e. presumed shared) and those which are merely shared. For example, prior to the exchange in (7), the assumption *Maria visited England in June* was in Peter's and Maria's shared cognitive environment, but it was not in their mutual cognitive environment. Peter's affirmative response, [5], indicates that a previously shared assumption has now become mutually manifest to Maria and to him, and this opened up the possibility of communication on the topic of her visit to England earlier in the year.

It is important to note that the term (mutual) "manifestness" refers to the psychological disposition for mental representation. In (7), the assumption that Peter and Maria had known all along that Maria had visited England in June, became highly (mutually) manifest to them. Therefore, they represented it mentally, becoming fully conscious of it. However, the mutual cognitive environment that people draw upon in communication largely consists of background assumptions which are presumed shared by all people, or, at least, by all members of a particular community or group. Following Searle (1980), Carston (2002) refers to this set of assumptions as Background (with a capital *B*) and characterizes it as follows:

> We might usefully think of Background as a set of assumptions and practices that maintains a fairly steady degree of not very high manifestness, across time, in an individual's cognitive environment. A subset of the Background consists in assumptions/practices which make up the mutual cognitive environment of all (non-pathological) human beings—the deep Background; other subsets are the mutual cognitive environments of what can loosely be termed culturally defined groups of human beings—local Backgrounds.
>
> Carston (2002: 68)

Background is a useful technical term in that it identifies a subset of the interlocutors' presumed shared beliefs which play an important role in communication. For example, if any of the Background assumptions do not hold, the speaker should indicate this clearly. Failure to do so inevitably goes against the Principle of Relevance. Consider Example (8):

(8) *Mary:* I saw Peter yesterday.

Given our Background knowledge about people, it would not be rational for Mary to say: *I saw Peter yesterday* in order to convey the idea that she saw parts of Peter scattered round the room. According to the Principle of Relevance, the hearer is entitled to treat certain assumptions about the physical properties of people as taken for granted. These Background assumptions are not communicated, because they are already (presumed) held at maximal strength. Therefore, they do not need to be represented consciously in a given situation of communication.

Many cultural representations are an important part of the local (i.e. cultural) Background. They too are generally mutually manifest to the members of particular groups. They can be, and often are, taken for granted in communication between people who presume that they belong in the same culture. These cultural representations tend to be so intuitive to those who hold them that they often appear natural, rather than conventional, so they too are seldom consciously represented. That is why they are typically the loci of miscommunication in situations of inter-cultural communication, which suggests that cross-cultural training should focus primarily on the differences between the trainee's and the host group's local Backgrounds.

In light of these observations, the notions of cognitive environment and mutual cognitive environment can be related to cultural knowledge as follows:

> Cultural environment (of an individual)
>
> The set of cultural representations which are manifest to an individual at a given time.
>
> (In other words, the proper subset of an individual's cognitive environment which consists only of cultural representations.)
>
> Mutual cultural environment
>
> A cultural environment which is shared by two or more individuals and in which it is manifest to those individuals that they share it. (In other words, the proper subset of the mutual cognitive environment of two or more people, which consists only of cultural representations.)

On this view, the cultural environment of an individual is a subset of that individual's cognitive environment, and the mutual cultural environment of two or more people, is a subset of their mutual cognitive environment. The terms *cultural environment* and *mutual cultural environment* are useful because they provide a principled basis for distinguishing between issues relating to context selection in *inter-* and *intra-*cultural communication. Thus, in examples (1), (2), (3) and (5) miscommunication is largely due to the communicators' incorrect estimates of their and the addressee's/audience's mutual cultural environments. Of course, which assumptions will be in the mutual cultural environment of individuals from particular cultures is an empirical matter of the sort that social approaches to pragmatics are concerned with.

In Relevance Theory terms, communication involves the production and the interpretation of evidence of the communicative and the informative intentions. This evidence may be more or less conclusive. The more conclusive the evidence for some belief-assumptions presented by a communicative act, the more strongly those assumptions are communicated by that act. The Relevance-theoretic notion of communicative *strength* provides the basis for explaining the commonsense notions of *direct* and *indirect* communication. A particular assumption, or set of assumptions, has been communicated directly to the extent that the communicative act presents the addressee with conclusive evidence of the communicator's intention to make that assumption, or set of assumptions, more manifest. And conversely, the less conclusive the evidence of the communicator's intention to communicate a particular assumption, or set of assumptions, is, the more indirectly, i.e. *weakly*, that assumption, or set of assumptions, is communicated. It should be clear that what counts as sufficiently conclusive evidence of a particular communicative (or informative) intention in one culture, may be hopelessly poor evidence of this intention in the context of another. For example, in the situation described in (3), the Japanese participants presumed that pauses in their speech presented sufficiently strong evidence of their communicative intentions to be noticed by the American participant, whilst presenting suitably weak evidence of their informative intention to convey a rejection of the American participant's chosen plan. In Relevance-theory terms, the comprehension of a communicative act which presents less conclusive evidence for a particular informative intention requires more processing effort than one which presents more conclusive evidence for that informative intention. Therefore, a communicator aiming at optimal relevance should always choose the ostensive stimulus which provides the most conclusive evidence of their informative intention. It follows from this, that a communicative act which communicates a particular set of assumptions more weakly than is necessary for communicating that set of assumptions, will prompt the addressee to derive further contextual (i.e. cognitive) effects in order to offset the extra processing effort required for the interpretation. In other words, the addressee will assume that the informative intention is also somewhat different from that which would have been communicated by a more direct communicative act. Thus, the pauses in (3) communicate, not merely the rejection of the American colleague's chosen plan, but also some degree of concern on the part of the communicators for his positive face (see Brown and Levinson 1987). This suggests that cultural differences in the appropriate degree of (in)directness in communication, such as the one illustrated in (3), receive a natural explanation within the epidemiological approach to culture and the framework of Relevance Theory. The pervasive use of subtle ostensive stimuli within a society depends on the extent to which the mutual cultural environment of its members includes representations about their appropriate use. As Kate Berardo has impressed upon me, such a mutual cultural environment is more likely to be established in a relatively close-knit isolated society, such as Japan, which went through a period of two hundred and fifty years of cultural isolation. In contrast to the Japanese culture, the US culture emerged in a melting pot of diverse cultural influences in which the mutual cultural environment of its members was rather restricted, and this explains why the use of subtle ostensive stimuli, and various forms of communicative indirectness which depend on such stimuli, could not have developed and stabilized in US culture to the same extent as they did in Japan.

6. Conclusion

In this article I have tried to show how Sperber's (1996) epidemiological approach to culture and Sperber and Wilson's (1986/95) Relevance-theoretic account of human communication and cognition jointly provide an intuitive, simple and effective framework for analysing situations of *inter*-cultural communication. In particular, I have argued that the concept of *mutual cognitive environment*—in effect, a theoretically motivated equivalent of what Goffman ([1964] 1972: 63) termed "an environment of mutual monitoring possibilities"— can be related to culture in a way which brings us closer to an understanding of culture's role in communication.

References

Brislin, Richard W. 1978. Contributions of cross-cultural orientation programmes and power analysis to translation/interpretation. In: David Gerver and Wallace H.W. Sinaiko (eds.)/ *Language, Interpretation and Communication*. Proceedings of the NATO Symposium on Language and Communication, Venice, 26 Sept–1 Oct 1977. New York: Plenum Press.

Brown, Penelope and Steven Levinson. 1987. *Politeness*. Cambridge: Cambridge University Press.

Carston, Robyn. 2002. *Thoughts and Utterances: The Pragmatics of Explicit Communication*. Oxford: Blackwell Publishing.

Dawkins, Richard. 1996. *Climbing Mount Improbable*. London: Penguin Press.

Fishman, Joshua. 1972. The sociology of language. In: Pier P. Giglioli (ed.), *Language and Social Context*, 45–58. London: Penguin Books.

Goffman, Erving. 1964. The neglected situation. *American Anthropologist* 66 (6–2): 133–136. Reprinted in: Pier P. Giglioli 1972 (ed.), *Language and Social Context*, 61–66. London: Penguin Books.

Gutt, Ernst-August. 2000. *Translation and Relevance*. Manchester: St Jerome Publishers.

Halliday, Michael Alexander Kirkwood and Ruqaiya Hasan 1976 *Cohesion in English*. London: Longman.

Hymes, Dell. 1972. Models of the interaction of language and social life. In: John Gumperz and Dell Hymes (eds.), *Directions in Sociolinguistics: the Ethnography of Communication*, 35–71. New York: Holt, Reinhart and Winston.

Matsumoto, David. 1996. *Culture and Psychology*. Pacific Grove, CA: Brooks/Cole.

Searle, John. 1980. The background of meaning. In: John Searle, Ferenc Keifer and Manfred Bierwisch (eds.), *Speech Act Theory and Pragmatics*, 221–32. Dordrecht: Reidel.

Sperber, Dan. 1985. *On Anthropological Knowledge*. Cambridge: Cambridge University Press.

Sperber, Dan. 1996. *Explaining Culture*. Oxford: Blackwell.

Sperber, Dan (ed.). 2000. *Metarepresentations: A Multidisciplinary Perspective*. Oxford: Oxford University Press.

Sperber, Dan and Deirdre Wilson. 1986/95. *Relevance: Communication and Cognition*. Oxford: Blackwell. 2nd edition (with postface) 1995.

Sperber, Dan and Deirdre Wilson. 1995. Postface. In: Dan Sperber and Deirdre Wilson 1995 *Relevance: Communication and Cognition*, 2nd edn, 255–279. Oxford: Blackwell.

Trompenaars, Fons and Charles Hampden-Turner. 1997. *Riding the Waves of Culture: Understanding Cultural Diversity in Business*. London: Nicholas Brealey Publishing.

von Frisch, Karl. 1967. *The Dance Language and Orientation of Bees*. Cambridge, MA: Belknap Press of Harvard University Press.

Žegarac, Vladimir. 2004. Relevance theory and "the" in second language acquisition. *Second Language Research* 20(3): 193–211.

2

Psychological Perspectives: Social Psychology, Language, and Intercultural Communication

Madeleine Brabant, Bernadette Watson,
and Cindy Gallois

1. Introduction

Intercultural communication has a long history in social psychology and in many other fields. Indeed, the tradition of language and social psychology (LASP: e.g. Giles and Coupland 1991) emerged from studies of intercultural communication, as social psychologists in the 1960s and 70s aimed to add their own insights to research in linguistics and anthropology. Today, most scholars in language and social psychology consider intercultural encounters to be at the heart of their field (see Gallois, McKay and Pittam 2004).

Because the literature from psychology is so large, we can barely scratch its surface in a single chapter, and we have been very selective. Readers wanting more detail might wish to explore the series of volumes on intercultural communication published since the early 1980s by Sage, in particular the volumes on theories in intercultural communication (Gudykunst 2005; Kim and Gudykunst 1988; Wiseman 1995), as well as other chapters in this volume. In addition, there are many books (particularly Robinson and Giles 2001) and two major journals (*Journal of Cross-Cultural Psychology* and *International Journal of Intercultural Relations*) that have a largely psychological approach to intercultural communication. In this chapter, we attempt to describe the major features of the social-psychological perspective which distinguish it from other approaches, along with a critique of this perspective and some suggestions for the future.

We examine two major traditions in the study of intercultural communication in social psychology. The first of these traditions, the larger in terms of numbers of scholars and studies, is generally known as 'intercultural communication competence' (ICC). Key assumptions underpinning this research are, first, that intercultural communication is essentially interpersonal communication where interactants may not be using the same set of social and communication rules, and secondly, that if interactants acquire the relevant skills and knowledge, competent and effective communication will follow. The second tradition takes as its point of departure that intercultural communication is primarily 'intergroup' communication. Researchers in this tradition emphasize the socio-historical context and the intergroup relations between cultures. They argue that these factors are the main determinants of the motivations and behaviours in an intercultural encounter.

By critiquing these two social-psychological traditions, we highlight the following issues: (1) they address different aspects of intercultural interactions; (2) by themselves they are too limited; (3) theories that combine the two (e.g. Communication Accommodation Theory: see Gallois, Ogay and Giles 2005) provide powerful models for predicting and explaining communication success and failure, and (4) the perspective of psychology in understanding intercultural communication complements those of related disciplines.

1.1. Distinctive Features of the Psychological Perspective

From its earliest days, psychology emphasized individual behaviour. Even social psychology, which took as its core territory the study of group and larger processes, still starts with the individual as its unit of analysis and moves thence to explore the impact of other people and larger social variables on individuals. Not surprisingly, then, the interest of social psychologists in intercultural communication has tended to focus on individuals' attitudes and behaviour, with larger forces being encapsulated in terms of their impact on individual speakers and listeners. For intercultural communication, this has had consequences both for theory and methodology.

1.1.1. THEORY

1.1.1.1. Focus on motivation. Giles (1973) argued for the inclusion of motivation as a driving factor in all intergroup communication, rather than constructing speakers as (he argued) sociolinguistic automata. Since then, social psychologists have emphasized the motivational drivers in intercultural encounters. For example, Giles noted the capacity of speakers to change sociolinguistic style depending upon whether they liked and admired their interlocutor (or disliked the other person); this was the initial basis for Speech Accommodation Theory. Likewise, Lambert et al. (1960) noted the impact of language spoken (French or English) on listeners' evaluations of speakers, and argued that this process was anchored in the attitudes triggered by language. Psychological work in intercultural communication has always been based on the assumption that the attitudes, interactional goals, and motives of interlocutors determine their choice of language and nonverbal behaviour (with an emphasis on variables that are partly or fully under voluntary control), as well as their evaluation of it.

1.1.1.2. Focus on reception and evaluation. If motivation drives the way interactants approach an intercultural encounter, it also drives the way they perceive such an encounter. Thus, social psychologists have been interested largely in the impact of communication, rather than in the characteristics of communication *per se*. Thus, theory has highlighted the role of the attribution process in interpreting communication from members of another culture. Most psychological theory in this area, for example, has posited the value of an ethno-relative or intercultural perspective (e.g. Kim 1995, 2001; Triandis 1996) to more effective intercultural encounters. Whereas scholars in other fields may study in great detail the specific features of language and nonverbal communication, with little regard for the subtleties of their impact, social psychologists have tended to do the opposite.

1.1.1.3. Focus on identity. Perhaps the most distinctive feature of the social-psychological approach to intercultural communication is the central role given to identity, especially social identity. As the discussion below indicates, intercultural communication can be conceptualized almost entirely in terms of identity management (cf. Ting-Toomey 1993). The underlying assumption is that interactants bring their identity into an encounter, and may (or may not) negotiate a change in personal or social identity depending upon their evaluation of the encounter. In recent years, social psychologists have begun to explore the extent to which identity may emerge as a result of the communication process itself (e.g. Hecht 1993; Hecht et al. 2001), but there is still a tendency to construct identity as primary and communication as flowing from it.

1.1.2. METHODOLOGY

1.1.2.1. Questionnaires. The favourite measure of social psychologists is undoubtedly the questionnaire, and this method is probably the most common in the social-psychological study of intercultural communication. The advantage is that questionnaires are easy to administer and analyse, and a wide variety of attitude questions, norms, and knowledge of social variables can be tapped efficiently. The disadvantage is that they may not have much to do with situated behaviour in intercultural encounters. In a classic example of this, Bourhis (1983) asked French Canadians in Montreal whether they would change to English if a stranger asked them for help or directions. In his questionnaire study, the majority said they would not accommodate. When he observed actual behaviour in shops in Montreal, however, he noted that the vast majority of French speakers did accommodate to an English-speaking stranger. Work like this has highlighted the importance of tailoring the method to the research question. Questionnaires are excellent devices for studying overt attitudes, norms, and social rules, but they may be poor predictors of communication in context.

1.1.2.2. Simulated intercultural communication: Matched guise technique. Lambert and colleagues (1960) pioneered a uniquely social-psychological technique for the study of intercultural communication. The Matched Guise Technique (MGT) in its earliest form involved a single bilingual or multi-lingual speaker who recorded two or more monologues of relatively neutral content (e.g. giving directions in a city) in each of his languages (speakers were always male). The passages were exact translations of each other, so that speaker characteristics and content were controlled as much as possible. Later work

(see Giles and Powesland 1975) used the same technique to measure different accents within a language (e.g. RP, London, Scottish, Welsh accents in
English). The idea was that differences in evaluations of the speaker could be
attributed to the impact of the language or accent.

The MGT had the great advantage of being a fairly unobtrusive measure
of reception, and thus arguably less susceptible to social desirability and other
biases than direct techniques like questionnaires. On the other hand, it came
under fairly stringent critiques from within and outside psychology. First,
there had been an almost exclusive reliance on male speakers. Gallois and
Callan (1981) replicated some of the early work in Australia for male speakers,
but results were nearly reversed when the speakers were female. As it turns
out, other social group memberships (gender, age, professional role) and other
features of the context are extremely important influences on evaluations of
speakers, so that the decontextualized aspect of the MGT was called into question. On another front, Nolan (1983) pointed to the danger in assuming that
the same speaker across guises had the same characteristics. He noted that
speaker stereotypes about language (and even more, about accent) have a significant impact on vocal style. In addition, the diglossic nature of many bilingual environments means that speakers are unlikely to be equally at home in
both or all their languages for any particular content; once again, the impact
of contextual features cannot be ignored. In recent years, researchers have
tended to return to more direct measures of evaluation, but the MGT is still
seen regularly in the literature.

1.2. Interpersonal and Intergroup Approaches
to Intercultural Communication

After World War II, the interest of researchers in intercultural communication and miscommunication grew rapidly because of the negative reactions
received by Western sojourners and diplomats. In addition, large-scale immigration and human rights movements in many countries made communication
effectiveness and prejudice more salient than previously. During this period,
researchers concentrated on topics like social and display rules and communication effectiveness between cultures.

Hall (1959, 1966, 1981) proposed that most miscommunication across
cultures results from the operation of different rules or norms (e.g. interpersonal distance, where social norms are tied to values about aggressiveness
and sexuality). Interactants miscommunicate by interpreting the behaviour of
others using different rules as if the others were using their own rules. Hall
argued that if social rules could be brought to the surface and made explicit,
much of the heat would disappear from intercultural encounters, and communication would be more effective and positive. In a similar vein, Argyle,
Furnham and Graham (1981) defined social rules as socially shared expectations about appropriate and inappropriate behaviour in situations. They
argued that, while there are many cultural similarities in communication,
especially nonverbal communication, the differences still cause a great deal of
misunderstanding. Argyle and colleagues proposed training people to use the

social rules of another culture, to reduce the chance of miscommunication in an intercultural encounter. Triandis and Schwartz also argue for understanding intercultural dynamics from an interpersonal perspective (e.g. Schwartz 1999; Triandis 1996; Triandis and Suh 2002).

It is hard to overestimate the impact of this approach, particularly for communication skills training (see Matsumoto in this volume for a detailed discussion of the role of these variables in psychological adjustment in intercultural contexts). Almost all intercultural communication training conducted by psychologists takes Hall's and Argyle's work as its starting point. Only in very recent times has a serious critique of this approach appeared, arguing among other things that both interpersonal and intergroup factors are significant influences in many or all intercultural encounters (e.g. Gallois and Pittam 1996).

2. Intercultural Communication Competence (ICC)

The most direct descendant of Hall's and Argyle's work in social psychology is the tradition of intercultural communication competence. Researchers have posited a measurable level of effectiveness in an intercultural encounter but have not necessarily followed through with measurement. This approach focuses on the training of immigrants and sojourners who are motivated to attain a satisfactory level of communication competence in their host country (cf. Newton in this volume). We discuss three ICC models here, but there are many others (e.g. Singelis and Brown 1995; Matsumoto in this volume).

2.1. Anxiety and Uncertainty Management

Gudykunst's (1988, 1995) theory of anxiety and uncertainty management (AUM) gives priority to cultural traditions, values and norms over socio-political factors. He posits that individuals must experience optimal levels of anxiety and uncertainty to communicate effectively in intercultural encounters. The extent to which they experience uncomfortable or optimal levels of anxiety and uncertainty depends on their level of communication skills, motivation, and knowledge of general and specific cultural factors. The process of anxiety and uncertainty reduction through acquiring intercultural communication competence is performed by individuals qua individuals. To adapt to the ambiguity of a new situation, individuals perform tension-reducing and information seeking behaviours (Ball-Rokeach 1973). Gudykunst (1988) notes that much behaviour is habitual, and individuals are often not conscious of their behaviour (see Triandis 1996). Thus, when interacting with people from a different culture who do not share the same implicit theory of behaviour, sojourners become more conscious of their own behaviour.

Gudykunst (1988) posits individualism–collectivism (Hofstede 1983) as the major dimension of cultural variability influencing intergroup processes. People in individualistic cultures tend to apply the same value standards to

all, while those in collectivistic cultures tend to apply different value standards to members of their ingroups and outgroups. Triandis (1996) suggests
that collectivistic cultures emphasize the goals, needs and views of the ingroup
rather than individual pleasure, shared ingroup beliefs rather than unique
individual beliefs, and value cooperation with ingroup members rather than
individual outcomes. Gudykunst, thus, suggests that an increase in collectivism results in an increase in the differences in uncertainty reduction processes
(attributional confidence) between ingroup and outgroup communication.
Gudykunst (1995) proposes that the anxiety and uncertainty management
processes underlying both interpersonal and intergroup communication are
the same, highlighting the conceptualization of intercultural communication
as interpersonal communication across different social rules and values. Hubbert, Gudykunst and Guerrero's (1999) results, in a study of international students in the US, supported AUM theory.

2.2. Cross-Cultural Adaptation Theory

Kim's (1995, 2001) cross-cultural adaptation theory is based on the systems
concept that change is the consequence of stress and adaptation in a new cultural environment. The linkages in her model indicate mutual causations,
reflecting the open-systems principle of reciprocal functional relationships
among a system, its parts, and its environment. Kim proposes that a predis-
position by sojourners to communicate, in terms of personality and cultural
factors, is linked to more competent acquisition of the host communication
system, through interaction with the mass media and host individuals, along
with a loss or refocusing of interactions in the old culture. Thus, she assumes
that sojourners are differently motivated to become part of the new culture or
to adopt an intercultural identity. This process of adaptation is moderated by
the host environment, in that some environments are more tolerant of strangers and new behaviours and value systems.

Kim places a strong emphasis on sojourners acquiring what she refers to
as an intercultural identity; that is, an identity that is based in neither culture
but that sits between them. She describes this as an emerging identity that
develops out of the challenging and painful experiences of self-reorganization
under the demands of the new milieu. This intercultural identity is achieved
through prolonged experiences of trial and error; it is a new expanded identity
that is more than either the original identity or the identity of the host culture
(cf. Shibutani and Kwan 1965). The pressure on newcomers to conform comes
from the dominant group. As new learning occurs, deculturation from the old
culture also occurs. Kim describes a transformative process of stress–adaptation, where disequilibrium brought about by stress, uncertainty, and anxiety
allows self-reorganization and self-renewal.

Kim's (1995, 2001) theory identifies six dimensions that facilitate or impede
the process of cross-cultural adaptation. These dimensions reflect the experiences that individuals face in a new environment, through which they change
toward greater functional fitness and psychological health in the host environment and toward an intercultural identity. In Kim's view, adaptation by an

individual to a cultural environment occurs almost entirely in and through communication. Kim (2001) also highlights the practical issues that sojourners encounter, and her model provides a framework for the development of training programs.

2.3. Identity Negotiation Process Model

Ting-Toomey's (1993) identity negotiation process model proposes that identification is mediated by a dialectic of security–vulnerability and inclusion–differentiation, as well as by identity coherence and individual and collective self-esteem. The result of this dialectic determines cognitive, affective, and behavioural resourcefulness, and thus the extent to which the identity negotiation process in intercultural encounters is effective. The model posits that individuals in all cultures desire to be competent communicators in a diverse range of interactive situations, becoming competent through repeated practice. They also learn to deal with others appropriately and effectively through habitual routines. Ting-Toomey assumes that people desire positive group- and person-based identities in all types of communicative situations. According to the identity negotiation model, satisfactory outcomes include feelings of being understood, respected, and supported. As in most other models, outcome is contingent on the perceptions of the communicators in the interaction. Outcome also depends crucially on the willingness of interactants to practice mindfulness (i.e. thoughtful rather than automatic communication) with dissimilar others. To the extent that this happens, interactants should experience a high sense of identity satisfaction.

Identity understanding begins with gathering accurate identity information and being culturally sensitive in probing identity based-details. In addition, it involves the willingness to share facets of one's own self-conception with others in a culturally sensitive manner. A feeling of being respected and supported requires the mindful monitoring of one's verbal and nonverbal behaviour and norms in interacting with dissimilar others, and treating other salient social and personal identities with consideration and dignity. The consequences of the identity negotiation process affect the quality of relationships. Ting-Toomey's model provides the principles for training individuals to manage intercultural conflict.

2.4. Summary

Across all the ICC models described above, there are several common factors. The first is ethno-relativism (i.e. the ability of a stranger to take on the perspective of the unknown or new culture). The second is the need for the sojourner to obtain some education and knowledge about the new culture. The third is mindfulness, or the need for sojourners to engage with the new culture and to be constantly aware of their own as well as the new culture's values, norms, and behaviours. The final factor involves the belief that appropriate communication skills and knowledge will result in more effective communication.

This approach to intercultural communication and competence training has had a successful record in a number of contexts. Business travellers
in particular have experienced increased self-confidence and better results
in encounters with new cultures. Many students and immigrants have also
benefited, and immigrants often speak positively of training in this tradition.
Underlying the whole approach, however, are several key assumptions: that
people are unproblematically motivated to communicate well; that hosts are at
least tolerant of the efforts of sojourners; and that most intercultural interactions have mainly interpersonal salience. In brief, that there is no reason why
communication should not proceed smoothly if people are mindful and communicate skilfully. The ICC tradition does not try to explain contexts in which
miscommunication between two cultural groups may be inevitable despite the
best intentions of well-trained communicators. The intergroup approach we
describe below is aimed to explain and predict when intercultural communication is likely to fail.

3. Intercultural Interactions as Intergroup Encounters

The second main socio-psychological approach to intercultural communication
comes mainly from scholars in language and social psychology (LASP). These
researchers have been especially interested in contexts where two or more cultures co-exist, often in a state of social or power inequality, for many years (or
permanently). These include diglossic and other bilingual communities, long-
term immigrants, and intercultural contexts where interactants come from
different groups but use a common language (e.g. the countries of the UK).
Because of this, whereas the goal of ICC theories is communication competence, for this approach it is to understand prejudice, discrimination, conflict
between cultures, and how rivalry and antagonism can be reduced.

3.1. Second-Language Acquisition and Use

One of the earliest models in this tradition comes from Gardner and his colleagues (see Gardner 1985), and explores the intrinsic and extrinsic motivations for learning a second language. Extrinsically motivated learners attempt
to learn a second language for instrumental reasons (e.g. economic advantage,
job prospects), while those with intrinsic motivation have a genuine desire to
learn about and if possible become part of the new linguistic community. A key
assumption of this model is that the quality of interactions and the motivation
for language learning are based primarily on intergroup history, and driven as
much by motivation as by communication skill. In most contexts, one or more
communicative communities are advantaged and dominant, with prejudice
marked by negative, hostile or patronizing communication. The assumption
is that this is the norm in most intergroup encounters, so that less account is
taken of interpersonal relations between participants.

Clément and Gardner (2001) characterize second-language acquisition
as making the second language part of the individual's very being (i.e. they

posit intrinsic motivation as essential to effective L2 learning). This process involves at least some degree of identification with the other language community. Gardner and Clément (1990) distinguish three individual-difference variables in second-language acquisition that influence how well or quickly individuals learn another language: cognitive characteristics (language aptitude and language learning strategies), attitudes and motivation, and personality characteristics.

Contact with the second-language speaking group in naturalistic contexts is a key part of L2 acquisition (as it is for Kim 1995, 2001, albeit for different reasons). Positive benefits from language acquisition can only be achieved if the first language and culture are well established within the individual (Carey 1991; Clément 1984; Cummins and Swain 1986, Hamers and Blanc 1988; Landry and Allard 1992). The familial, educational, and social context should allow the development and transmission of the first language and culture. Ethnolinguistic vitality (Giles, Bourhis and Taylor 1977; Prujiner et al. 1984) is a closely related concept that is also relevant to second-language acquisition and use, as well as to the maintenance of the original ethnic identity. Ethnolinguistic vitality refers to the power and viability of an ethnic group in a specific context, as measured by the demographic representation of the community, its institutional representation and socio-economic status, and its position in the media and cultural landscape of the larger society. Vitality is important in second-language acquisition and use, as well as in maintenance of the original ethnic identity.

Research has also shown a consistent relationship between demographic, political, economic, and cultural capital factors and first-language retention and competence (Landry and Allard 1992; Landry, Allard and Henry 1996). The gap between structural or objective vitality and psychological vitality is bridged by recasting structural factors as subjective perceptions by individuals, so that vitality is now commonly measured through self-report questionnaire indices of perceptions (Bourhis, Giles and Rosenthal 1981). Researchers have found a relationship between objective and subjective ethnolinguistic vitality (Bourhis and Sachdev 1984; Landry and Allard 1992). Self-confidence in using the second language has been shown to be positively related to the degree of identification with the second-language group, and in the case of minority group members it is negatively correlated with identification to the first-language group (Noels and Clément 1996; Noels, Pon and Clément 1996). Competence in and preference for using the second language may entail, or may be perceived to entail, the loss of first language and culture (Cameron and Lalonde 1994; Clément, Gauthier and Noels 1993). Better adjustment and well-being are often correlated with greater self-confidence in using the second language and greater social support from the second language network (Clément, Michaud and Noels 1998; Noels and Clément 1996; Noels, Pon and Clément 1996), so that learning a second language may be a vector of individual psychological adjustment and collective language and culture loss (see Clément and Gardner 2001). Clearly, the socio-psychological understanding of second-language acquisition in this model is driven not by skills training (although ability and training are important), but by individual motivation and attitudes.

3.2. Social Identity Theory

Social identity theory was developed in part to explain the ways in which socio-cultural factors affect interaction (and thus communication) between different social groups and cultures (cf. Spreckels and Kotthoff in this volume). The theory rests on the assumption that the socio-historical context is the first factor influencing social behaviour, and thus the primary influence on interpersonal communication (Tajfel 1979; Tajfel and Turner 1979; Turner et al. 1987). The history of relations between two groups alone is sometimes enough to produce stereotypes about people in those groups, even though people who hold the stereotypes may be reluctant to admit this. The process of categorizing ourselves and others into groups or categories is ubiquitous and may be arbitrary (see Tajfel 1979). The process of stereotyping begins in the physical world, and stereotypes help to simplify and control judgments about strange situations. Individuals belong to a wide range of group memberships, ethnic and cultural groups, large-scale social categories (sex, race, age, social class, religion, etc.), occupational and other groups (Turner et al. 1987). When there is a history of conflict or social inequality between two groups, people tend to rationalize discriminatory behaviour through stereotypes.

In general, the theory posits that people describe their own group (ingroup) using dimensions on which it appears positive and salient, and describe the other groups (outgroups) in negative terms. Where there is social inequality, the dominant group may nevertheless be perceived as more intelligent, beautiful, and so forth, while the disadvantaged group is seen as submissive, uneducated, poor, but friendly by people in both groups (Lambert et al.'s work in 1960 was one of the first studies to show this clearly in an existing community, Montreal). Many structural features, including the differential use of dominant and non-dominant languages, reinforce such inequalities. For example, members of dominated groups are rarely given credit for their language abilities by members of the dominant group, but are stereotyped as stupid or criticized for their lack of perfect fluency by monolinguals. Much of social identity theory concerns the ways that structural inequalities influence the ways in which people construct and communicate their social identities, and how they use stereotypes and identity management to change or maintain the status quo (Taylor and McKirnan 1984).

3.3. A Typology of Intercultural Adaptation

Another approach that focuses on motivation is Berry's (1997) typology of intercultural adaptation. Berry (1980) was the first to propose that immigrant and host cultural identity could be portrayed as independent dimensions, rather than as extreme points of a single bipolar continuum. According to Berry's acculturation model, there are two dimensions yielding four acculturation strategies: 'integration', 'assimilation', 'separation' and 'marginalization' (Berry 1980). Integration reflects a desire to maintain key features of the immigrant cultural identity while adopting aspects of the majority culture (i.e. a high value placed on the original culture and the new culture). Assimilation reflects a desire by immigrants to relinquish their own cultural identity for the sake of adopting the cultural identity of the host majority (high value on the new culture but not the old one). Separation is characterized by the immigrant's desire to maintain all features of the original cultural identity while rejecting relationships with members of the majority host culture (high value on the old but not the new culture). Marginalization (more recently called *individualism*) characterizes individuals who reject both their own and the host community culture and emphasize another social identity (e.g. occupation), thereby losing contact with both their heritage culture and that of the host majority (low value placed on both the old and the new culture).

Acculturation orientations such as maintenance of the immigrant culture can be mediated by the extent to which immigrants feel accepted or discriminated against by host community (Bourhis and Gagnon 1994; Moghaddam, Taylor and Wright 1993). Bourhis et al. (1997) extended Berry's model to the societal level (see also Moïse and Bourhis 1994), positing that the match between individual and societal orientations determines the effectiveness of intercultural communication. Their model aims to present a more dynamic account of immigrant and host community acculturation in multicultural settings.

3.4. Summary

The second theory discussed here takes an intergroup approach to intercultural communication. From this perspective, researchers address the concept of ethnocentrism (a preference for all aspects of one's own culture relative to other cultures) as opposed to ethno-relativism. Good communicative outcomes may come out of the reduction in discriminatory language or harmful speech, more effective learning of the other culture's language, dialect, or style by members of both (all) cultures, better accommodation to the communication needs and behaviours of others, and better language and cultural maintenance by minority groups. Communication is viewed not so much as a skill but rather as the result of a motivation (identity maintenance or negotiation, reduction of prejudice, etc.), based on intergroup history. Miscommunication is construed not as a deficiency of the individual but rather as based on the motivations that underlie one or both interactants in an intercultural encounter.

This approach to intercultural communication acknowledges that because of the socio-historical context and intergroup relations, people may not be motivated to communicate well. Members of the dominant group may not be tolerant of the efforts made by members of a less dominant group, and in any case intergroup relations are salient in most interactions. In addition, in this approach there is an understanding that some encounters will not proceed smoothly and these encounters may be better avoided. One weakness of this perspective lies in the inherent complexities in these theoretical approaches that attempt a comprehensive explanation of intercultural encounters. By including so many variables, it is difficult to tease out when particular elements are salient in the model and when they are not.

3.5. Communication Accommodation Theory

Communication Accommodation Theory (CAT: e.g. Gallois et al. 1995; Giles, Coupland and Coupland 1991) is a theory of both intergroup and interpersonal communication, invoking the dual importance of both factors in predicting and understanding intergroup interactions. In our introduction, we noted that CAT proposes that communication has both interpersonal and intergroup elements. It is this combination that makes CAT such a powerful model. For example, Jones et al. (1999) used CAT to explain differences in the communication dynamics between Australian and Chinese students studying at an Australian university. Specifically, the cultural differences between these two cultural groups led to differing communication strategies and behaviours, as well as different perceptions of others' behaviour. In a different context, Watson and Gallois (1998) were able to explain why independent observers who watched a number of videotaped interactions between health professionals and their patients rated some as more satisfying and positive than others.

CAT developed from speech accommodation theory (Giles 1973) and provides communication scholars with an intergroup theory of intercultural communication. It has been influenced by both social identity theory and ethnolinguistic identity theory (see Gallois, Ogay and Giles 2005). CAT recognizes the importance of power and of macro-level societal factors. The theory posits that speakers orient towards interlocutors at varying levels of intergroup and interpersonal salience. Socio-historical factors and the goals of each interactant play a critical role in the levels of intergroup and interpersonal salience. In an intercultural context, therefore, intergroup rivalry may be a major but not the only influence on a speaker's choice of communication behaviours.

The primary thesis of CAT is that individuals interacting with others use communication strategies to achieve a desired social distance between themselves and interacting partners (Giles 1973; Giles et al. 1987). The goals of interactants drive the communication strategies that they exhibit. These strategies include approximation (convergence, divergence, and maintenance of language, accent, or other behaviours), discourse management (sharing or not of topics, register, etc.), interpretability (making communication clearer or more obscure), interpersonal control (more or less equal role relations), and emotional expression (more or less reassurance, etc.). As noted above, an interactant may perceive at certain times during the encounter that salience is simultaneously high intergroup and high interpersonal. In recent years (e.g. Gallois and Giles 1998; Gallois, Ogay and Giles 2005), the focus has been on summarizing the sociolinguistic strategies and goals into an overall accommodative stance (accommodation or reducing social distance, or non-accommodation or increasing it).

Approximation focuses on a speech partner's productive management of an interaction and refers to changes in speech patterns. Convergence is driven by a motivation to identify with or gain approval from an interlocutor (Bourhis and Giles 1977; Street and Giles 1982). Convergence may also arise out of the concern of ensuring the interaction flows more smoothly, which improves the effectiveness of communication (Gallois, Ogay and Giles 1995). Divergent behaviours are motivated at two levels to display distinctiveness from one's interlocutor. At the individual level, divergence may serve to accentuate differences or display disdain for the other. At the group level, divergence may emphasize a valued group identity (Cargile, Giles and Clément 1996; Tajfel 1979; Yaeger-Dror 1991). When there is a history of rivalry and inequality or the intergroup relationship is in flux, interactants tend to emphasize intergroup salience.

The other, non-approximation, strategies are also driven by each speech partner's goals. Interpretability refers to the extent to which conversational competence is focal and whether there exists understanding between interactants. Discourse management focuses on the conversational needs of each interactant and is concerned with the communication process rather than content. Interpersonal control concerns with issues of role and power relations between interactants and the extent to which one or other of the speech partners is constrained to a particular role. Where interactants' emotional and emotional needs are salient, emotional expression serves to reassure.

By situating intergroup encounters in a socio-historical context, CAT takes account of intergroup and interpersonal history, along with societal norms and values. CAT tracks an interaction between individuals, starting with the intergroup and interpersonal history and orientation they bring to the interaction, communication behaviours during the interaction, and perceptions and subsequent evaluations of the interaction. These evaluations then become part of the larger context that is taken to the next similar interaction. Gallois, Ogay and Giles (2005) suggest that intercultural encounters take place in the context of intergroup as well as interpersonal history, and in the context of different and sometimes contradictory social norms. Effective communication depends crucially on these factors. For this reason, ICC training models are likely to fail in certain contexts, because interactants are not motivated to communicate well or because intergroup norms restrict or prohibit the possibility of serious interpersonal communication (see Gallois 2003). It is essential for both theory development and applications that researchers take full account of the intergroup aspect of intercultural communication. CAT provides a comprehensive way to do this, without neglecting the interpersonal and idiosyncratic aspects of conversation.

4. Future Directions for the Socio-Psychological Approach to Intercultural Communication

As can be seen, these two major traditions in psychology about the study of intercultural communication have separate and complementary strengths and areas of application. The first one has fared well in contexts where speakers are motivated to communicate well and where intergroup history is either not salient (as in the case of individual travellers without strong views about the new culture) or not negative. Contrary to earlier predictions from Hall's (1959) work, cultural distance has proved less of a factor in communication and miscommunication than has intergroup history (see Gallois and Pittam 1996). The second tradition has aimed to explain interactions in settings of social inequality or intergroup rivalry. In general, researchers in this tradition are pessimistic about the possibility of effective communication and the potential of intercultural communication competence training. Instead, they concentrate on the description and explanation of settings of long-term and problematic intergroup contact.

Clearly it is important to theorize and address all these contexts, and no one theory of intercultural communication or training program presently does that (see Gallois 2003; Hajek and Giles 2003). A first step involves the careful analysis of a context in terms of intergroup relations, interpersonal relations, cultural values and norms, and skills and knowledge, in that order. A theory like CAT is well placed to do this. Gallois (2003) notes that in some situations, intergroup relations are so negative as to undermine any attempt to interact, no matter how skilled the interactants are. In such situations it may be better to attempt to alter social identity to embrace a larger, shared identity. In other contexts, individual orientation, the behaviours that occur in an interaction and the way they are perceived are the most important determinants of communication effectiveness. The very concept of effective communication is challenged by CAT and similar theories, because communication outcomes are posited as being as much in the eye of the beholder as in the actual behaviour of interactants (see Gallois and Giles 1998; Hajek and Giles 2003).

To conclude, there is much potential for more and deeper interactions between psychologists, emphasizing perceptions and motivations, and applied linguists, attending more to production. There are good examples of this kind of collaboration. One striking example is the collaboration between Coupland, Giles and their colleagues. This resulted among other things in their model (Coupland, Wiemann and Giles 1991) of miscommunication and problematic talk, which theorizes six causes of miscommunication ranging from inherent and unrecognized flaws in discourse through to socio-structural power imbalances (also likely to be unrecognized, albeit for different reasons). Models like this one, and theories like CAT, can provide a basis for understanding intercultural communication in context and as influenced by larger social and psychological factors. We hope that in another decade the research literature will reflect this amalgam.

References

Argyle, Michael, Adrian Furnham and Jean Ann Graham. 1981. *Social Situations*. Cambridge: Cambridge University Press.

Ball-Rokeach, Sandra. 1973. From persuasive ambiguity to definition of the situation. *Sociometry* 36: 378–389.

Berry, John W. 1980. Acculturation as varieties of adaptation. In: Amado Padilla (ed.), *Acculturation Theory, Models and Some New Findings*, 9–25. Boulder, CO: Westview.

Berry, John W. 1997. Immigration, acculturation, and adaptation. *Applied Psychology: An International Journal* 46: 5–68.

Bourhis, Richard. 1983. Language attitudes and self-reports of French-English usage in Quebec. *Journal of Multilingual and Multicultural Development* 4: 163–179.

Bourhis, Richard Y. and André Gagnon. 1994. Préjugés, discrimination et relations intergroupes. In: Robert J. Vallerand (ed.), *Les Fondements de la Psychologie Sociale*, 707–773. Boucherville, Québec: Gaëtan Morin.

Bourhis, Richard Y. and Howard Giles. 1977. The language of intergroup distinctiveness. In: Howard Giles (ed.), *Language, Ethnicity and Intergroup Relations*, 119–135. London: Academic Press.

Bourhis, Richard and Itesh Sachdev. 1984. Vitality perceptions of language "attitudes": some Canadian data. *Journal of Language and Social Psychology* 3: 97–126.

Bourhis, Richard, Howard Giles and Doreen Rosenthal 1981 Notes on the construction of a "Subjective Vitality Questionnaire" for ethnolinguistic groups. *Journal of Multilingual and Multicultural Development* 2: 144–155.

Bourhis, Richard Y., Léna C. Moïse, Stéphane Perreault and Sascha Sénécal. 1997. Towards an interactive acculturation model: a social psychological approach. *International Journal of Psychology* 32: 369–386.

Cameron, James E. and Richard N. Lalonde. 1994. Self-ethnicity and social group memberships in two generations of Italian Canadians. *Journal of Personality and Social Psychology* 20: 514–520.

Carey, Stephen T. 1991. The culture of literacy in majority and minority language schools. *Canadian Modern Language Review* 47: 950–976.

Cargile, Aaron, Howard Giles and Richard Clément. 1996. The role of language in ethnic conflict. In: Joseph B. Gittler (ed.), *Research in Human Social Conflict, Vol.1*, 189–208. Greenwich, CT: JAI Press.

Clément, Richard. 1984. Aspects socio-psycologiques de la communication inter-ethnique et de l'identité culturelle. *Recherches sociologiques* 15: 293–312.

Clément, Richard and Robert C. Gardner. 2001. Second language mastery. In: Howard Giles and W. Peter Robinson (eds.), *The New Handbook of Language and Social Psychology*, 489–504. London: Wiley.

Clément, Richard, Renée Gauthier and Kimberley Noels. 1993. Choix langagiers en milieu minoritaire: attitudes et identité concomitantes. *Revue Canadienne des Sciences du Comportement* 25: 149–164.

Clément, Richard, C. Michaud and Kimberley A. Noels. 1998. Effets acculturatifs du support social en situation de contact intergroupe. *Revue Québecoise de Psycologie* 19: 189–210.

Coupland, Nikolas, John M. Wiemann and Howard Giles. 1991. Talk as "problem" and communication as "miscommunication". An integrative analysis. In: Nikolas Coupland, Howard Giles and John M. Wiemann (eds.), *"Miscommunication" and Problematic Talk*, 1–17. Newbury Park, CA: Sage.

Cummins, Jim and Merrill Swain. 1986. *Bilingualism in Education*. New York: Longman.

Gallois, Cindy. 2003. Reconciliation through communication in intercultural encounters: potential or peril? *Journal of Communication* 53: 5–15.

Gallois, Cindy and Victor J. Callan. 1981. Personality impressions elicited by accented English speech. *Journal of Cross-Cultural Psychology* 12: 347–359.

Gallois, Cindy and Howard Giles. 1998. Accommodating mutual influence in intergroup encounters. In: Mark T. Palmer and George A. Barnett (eds.), *Mutual Influence in Interpersonal Communication: Theory and Research in Cognition, Affect and Behavior* (Vol. Progress in Communication Sciences, 135–162). Stamford, UK: Ablex Publishing Corporation.

Gallois, Cindy and Jeffery Pittam. 1996. Communication attitudes and accommodation in Australia: a culturally diverse English-dominant context. *International Journal of Psycholinguistics* 12: 193–212.

Gallois, Cindy, Howard Giles, Elizabeth Jones, Aaron C. Cargile and Hiroshi Ota. 1995. Accommodating intercultural encounters: elaborations and extensions. In: Richard L. Wiseman (ed.), *Intercultural Communication Theory*, 115–147. Thousand Oaks, CA: Sage.

Gallois, Cindy, Susan McKay and Jeffery Pittam. 2004. Intergroup communication and identity: intercultural, health, and organisational communication. In: Kristine Fitch and Robert Sanders (eds.), *Handbook of Language and Social Interaction*, 231–250. Mahwah, NJ: Erlbaum.

Gallois, Cindy, Tania Ogay and Howard Giles. 2005. Communication accommodation theory: a look back and a look ahead. In: William Gudykunst (ed.), *Theorizing about Intercultural Communication*, 121–148. Thousand Oaks, CA: Sage.

Gardner, Robert C. 1985. *Social Psychology and Second Language Learning: The Role of Attitudes and Motivation*. London: Edward Arnold.

Gardner, Robert C. and Richard Clément. 1990. Social psychological perspectives on second language acquisition. In: Howard Giles and W. Peter Robinson (eds.), *Handbook of Language and Social Psychology*, 495–518. Chichester: John Wiley and Sons.

Giles, Howard. 1973. Accent mobility: a model and some data. *Anthropological Linguistics* 15(2): 87–109.

Giles, Howard and Nikolas Coupland. 1991. *Language: Contexts and Consequences*. Milton Keynes: Open University Press.

Giles, Howard and Peter F. Powesland. 1975. *Speech Style and Social Evaluation*. London: Academic Press.

Giles, Howard, Richard Y. Bourhis and Donald M. Taylor. 1977. Towards a theory of language in ethnic group relations. In: Howard Giles (ed.), *Language, Ethnicity and Intergroup Relations*. London: Academic Press.

Giles, Howard, Justine Coupland and Nikolas Coupland (eds.). 1991. *Contexts of Accommodation: Developments in Applied Sociolinguistics* (Studies in Emotion and Social Interaction.) Cambridge: Cambridge University Press.

Giles, Howard, Anthony Mulac, James J. Bradac and Patricia Johnson. 1987. Speech accommodation theory: the first decade and beyond. In: Margaret McLaughlin (ed.), *Communication Yearbook*, Vol. 10, 13–48. Beverly Hills, CA: Sage.

Gudykunst, William B. 1988. Uncertainty and anxiety. In: Young Yun Kim and William B. Gudykunst (eds.), *Theories in Intercultural Communication*, 123–156. Newbury Park, CA: Sage.

Gudykunst, William B. 1995. Anxiety/uncertainty management theory: current status. In: Richard Wise-man (ed.), *Intercultural Communication Theory*, 8–58. Thousand Oaks, CA: Sage.

Gudykunst, William B. 2005. *Theorizing about Intercultural Communication*. Thousand Oaks, CA: Sage.

Hajek, Chris and Howard Giles. 200.3 Intercultural communication competence. A critique and alternative model. In: Brant Burleson and John Greene (eds), *Handbook of Communicative and Social Skills*, 935–957. Mahwah, NJ: LEA.

Hall, Edward T. 1959. *The Silent Language*. New York: Doubleday and Co.

Hall, Edward T. 1966. *The Hidden Dimension*. Garden City, NJ: Doubleday.

Hall, Edward T. 1981. *Beyond Culture*. Garden City, NJ: Doubleday.

Hamers, Josiane F. and Michel Blanc. 1988. *Bilinguality and Bilingualism*. Cambridge: Cambridge University Press.

Hecht, Michael L. 1993. 2002: a research odyssey toward the development of a communication theory of identity. *Communication Monographs* 60: 76–82.

Hecht, Michael L., Ronald L. Jackson II, Sheryl Lindsley, Susan Strauss and Karen E. Johnson. 2001. A layered approach to ethnicity: language and communication. In: W. Peter Robinson and Howard Giles (eds.), *The New Handbook of Language and Social Psychology*, 429–449. Chichester: Wiley.

Hofstede, Geert. 1983. Dimensions of national cultures in fifty countries and three regions. In: Jan B. Deregowski, Suzanne Dziurawiec and Robert C. Annis (eds.), *Expectations in Cross-cultural Psychology*, 335–355. Lisse: Swets and Zeitlinger.

Hubbert, Kimberley N., William B. Gudykunst and Sherrie L. Guerrero. 1999. Intergroup communication over time. *International Journal of Intercultural Relations* 23: 13–46.

Jones, Elizabeth, Cindy Gallois, Victor J. Callan and Michelle Barker. 1999. Strategies of accommodation: development of a coding system for conversational interaction. *Journal of Language and Social Psychology* 18: 125–152

Kim, Young Yun. 1995. Cross-cultural adaptation: an integrative theory. In: Richard L. Wiseman (ed.), *Intercultural Communication Theory*, 170–193. Thousand Oaks, CA: Sage.

Kim, Young Yun. 2001. *Becoming Intercultural: An Integrative Theory of Communication and Cross-cultural Adaptation*. Thousand Oaks, CA: Sage.

Kim, Young Yun and William B. Gudykunst. 1988. *Theories in Intercultural Communication* (International and Intercultural Communication Annual, Vol. 12). Newbury Park, CA: Sage.

Lambert, Wallace E., Richard Hodgson, Robert C. Gardner and Samuel Fillenbaum. 1960. Evaluational reactions to spoken languages. *Journal of Abnormal and Social Psychology* 60: 44–51.

Landry, Réal and Rodrigue Allard. 1992. Ethnolinguistic vitality and the bilingual development of minority and majority group students. In: William Fase, Koen Jaspaert and Sjaak Kroon (eds.), *Maintenance and Loss of Minority Languages*, 223–251. Amsterdam: John Benjamins.

Landry, Rodrigue, Réal Allard and Jacques Henry. 1996. French in south Louisiana: towards language loss. *Journal of Multilingual and Multicultural Development* 17: 442–468.

Matsumoto, David, Seung Hee Yoo and Jeffrey A. LeRoux. This volume. Emotion and intercultural adjustment, Chapter 3.

Moghaddam, Fathali M., Donald M. Taylor and C. Stephen Wright. 1993. *Social Psychology in Cross-cultural Perspective*. New York: Freeman.

Moïse, Léna C. and Richard Y. Bourhis. 1994. Langage et ethnicité: communication interculturelle à Montréal. *Canadian Ethnic Studies* 26: 86–107.

Newton, Jonathan. This volume. Adapting authentic workplace talk for workplace communication training, Chapter 15.

Noels, Kimberley and Richard Clément. 1996. Communicating across cultures: social determinants and acculturative consequences. *Canadian Journal of Behavioural Science* 28: 214–228.

Noels, Kimberley, Gordon Pon and Richard Clément. 1996. Language, identity, and adjustment: the role of linguistic self-confidence in the adjustment process. *Journal of Language and Social Psychology* 15: 246–264.

Nolan, Francis. 1983. *The Phonetic Basis of Speaker Recognition*. Cambridge: Cambridge University Press.

Prechtl, Elisabeth and Anne Davidson Lund. 2007. Intercultural competence and assessment: perspectives from the INCA project. In Helga Kotthoff and Helen Spencer-Oatey (eds.), *Handbook of Intercultural Communication*, 467–490. Berlin: Mouton de Gruyter.

Prujiner, Alain, Denise Deshaies, Josiane Hamers, Michel Blanc, Richard Clément and Réal Landry. 1984. *Variation du Comportement Langagier lorsque deux Langues sont en Contact*. Québec: International Centre for Research on Language Planning.

Robinson, W. Peter and Howard Giles (eds.). 2001. *The New Handbook of Language and Social Psychology*. Chichester: Wiley and Sons.

Schwartz, Shalom H. 1999. A theory of cultural values and some implications for work. *Applied Psychology: An international Review* 48: 23–47.

Shibutani, Tamotsu and Kian M. Kwan. 1965. *Ethnic Stratification: A Comparative Approach*. New York: Macmillan. Singelis,

Street, Richard L. and Howard Giles. 1982. Speech accommodation theory: a social cognitive approach to language and speech behavior. In: Michael E. Roloff and Charles R. Berger (eds.), *Social Cognition and Communication*, 193–226. Beverly Hills, CA: Sage.

Tajfel, Henri. 1979. Individuals and groups in social psychology. *British Journal of Social Psychology* 18: 183–190.

Tajfel, Henri and John C. Turner. 1979. An integrative theory of intergroup conflict. In: W.G. Austin and S. Worchel (eds.), *The Social Psychology of Intergroup Relations*, 33–53. Belmont, CA: Wadsworth.

Taylor, Donald and David J. McKirnan. 1984. A five-stage theory of intergroup behaviour. *British Journal of Social Psychology* 23: 291–300.

Theodore M. and William J. Brown. 1995. Culture, self, and collectivist communication: linking culture to individual behavior. *Human Communication Research* 21: 354–389.

Ting-Toomey, Stella. 1993. Communicative resourcefulness: an identity negotiation perspective. In: Richard L. Wiseman and Jolene Koester (eds.), *Intercultural Communication Competence* (International and Intercultural Communication Annual, Vol. 17, 72–111). Newbury Park, CA: Sage.

Triandis, Harry C. 1996. The psychological measurement of cultural syndromes. *American Psychologist* 51: 407–415

Triandis, Harry C. and Eunkook M. Suh. 2002. Cultural influences on personality. *Annual Review of Psychology* 53: 133–160.

Turner, John C., Michael Hogg, Penelope Oakes, Stephen Reicher and Margaret S. Wetherell. 1987. *Rediscovering the Social Group: A Self-categorisation Theory*. Oxford: Blackwell.

Watson, Bernadette and Cindy Gallois. 1998. Nurturing communication by health professionals toward patients: a communication accommodation theory approach. *Health Communication* 10: 343–355.

Wiseman, Richard 1995 *Intercultural Communication Theory*. Thousand Oaks, CA: Sage. Yaeger-Dror, Malcah 1991 Linguistic evidence for social psychological attitudes: Hypercorrection or [r] l by singers from a Mizrahi background. *Language and Communication* 11: 309–331.

3

Emotion and Intercultural Adjustment

David Matsumoto, Seung Hee Yoo, and Jeffrey A. LeRoux

Previous work on intercultural communication effectiveness has generally focused on its cognitive components, including cultural knowledge, language proficiency, and ethnocentrism. In this chapter, we examine the role of emotions in intercultural adjustment, and suggest that the ability to regulate emotion is one of the keys to effective intercultural communication. Our model focuses on the role of emotion in intercultural communication episodes, and particularly on the skills necessary for the resolution of intercultural conflict, arguing that emotion regulation is a gatekeeper ability that allows people to engage in successful conflict resolution that leads to effective, long-term intercultural communication.

Culture plays a large role in the communication process (see Žegarac in this volume). Building on that material, we first describe the concepts of intercultural adaptation and adjustment, then the factors that previous research has identified related to adjustment. We then discuss the role of emotions, but also highlight the importance of critical thinking and openness/flexibility, in a growth model of intercultural adjustment potential that has at its core the ability to regulate emotions. We review empirical support for this model, and then review literature examining cultural differences in emotion regulation. Throughout, we blend literature from both communication and psychology in producing a unique perspective on this topic.

1. Intercultural Adaptation and Adjustment

1.1. Definitions

One of the most important consequences of and processes associated with intercultural communication is intercultural adaptation and adjustment. We have found that it is important to make a distinction between adaptation and adjustment. On one hand we believe that adaptation is based in the sociocultural domain (Ward 2001); that is, it refers to the process of altering one's behaviour to fit in with a changed environment or circumstances, or as a response to social pressure. One of the most well known models of adaptation, for instance, is Berry's (Berry, Kim and Boski 1988) analysis of the interaction styles for sojourners, immigrants, and refugees. In this model, four categories of interaction style are identified: integrators, marginalizers, separators, and assimilators. These refer to behavioural changes made in response to different environments.

On the other hand we define adjustment as the subjective experiences that are associated with and result from attempts at adaptation, and that also motivate further adaptation. Previous researchers have incorporated a wide range of outcome measures as adjustment, including self-awareness and self-esteem (Kamal and Maruyama 1990), mood states (Stone Feinstein and Ward 1990), and health status (Babiker, Cox and Miller 1980; all cited in Ward 2001). Some have developed synthesizing strategies to integrate specific approaches in order to highlight a smaller number of features. For example, Brislin (1993) identified three factors of adjustment, including (1) having successful relationships with people from other cultures; (2) feeling that interactions are warm, cordial, respectful, and cooperative; and (3) accomplishing tasks in an effective and efficient manner. Gudykunst, Hammer and Wiseman (1977) included the ability to manage psychological stress effectively. Black and Stephens (1989) identified general adjustment involving daily activities, interaction adjustment involving interpersonal relations, and work adjustment related to work and tasks.

Adapting to a new culture can have both positive and negative adjustment outcomes. The positive consequences include gains in language competence; self-esteem, awareness, and health (Babiker, Cox and Miller 1980; Kamal and Maruyama 1990); self-confidence, positive mood, interpersonal relationships, and stress reduction (Matsumoto et al. 2001). Clearly when intercultural experiences go well, individuals report evolving in many qualitative, positive ways so that they are different, and better, individuals. These include the development of multicultural identities and multiple perspectives with which to engage the world.

Negative adjustment outcomes include psychological and psychosomatic concerns (Shin and Abell 1999); early return to one's home country (Montagliani and Giacalone 1998); emotional distress (Furukawa and Shibayama 1995); dysfunctional communication (Gao and Gudykunst 1991; Okazaki-Luff 1991); culture shock (Pederson 1995); depression, anxiety, diminished school and work performance, and difficulties in interpersonal relationships (Matsumoto et al. 2001). In extreme cases negative adjustment results in antisocial behaviour (gangs, substance abuse, crime) and even suicide. Fortunately all sojourners do not experience this wide range of psychological and physical health problems, but most have probably experienced *some* of these problems at some point in their sojourn.

Intercultural experience is comprised of continuous adaptation and adjustment to the differences with which we engage every day. This engagement is not easy because of the occurrence of misunderstandings due to cultural differences. Our ethnocentric and stereotypic ways of thinking, which are themselves normal psychological functions, make it easy for us to create negative value judgments about those differences and misunderstandings. Negative emotions are also associated with these judgments. These negative reactions make it difficult for us to engage in more constructive methods of interacting, and keep us from truly appreciating those differences and integrating with people who are different.

One of the goals, therefore, of intercultural adaptation is to adopt an adaptation pattern that minimizes these stresses and negative adjustment outcomes, and maximizes positive ones. Negative adjustment outcomes often serve as important motivators for continued or refined adaptations to the new environment, a concept that is rooted in the notion that emotions are motivational (Tomkins 1962, 1963) and that affect fuels the development of cognitive schemas (Piaget 1952). The development of strategies that deal with potential conflict and misunderstanding is imperative in order to produce successful and effective long-term intercultural communication and relationships.

1.2. Factors That Predict Adjustment

Studies have identified a wide range of variables such as knowledge, language proficiency, attitudes, previous experiences, levels of ethnocentrism, social support, cultural similarity, adventure, and self-construals as factors that influence intercultural adjustment (reviewed in Matsumoto et al. 2001; see also Brabant, Watson and Gallois in this volume) Among these, three factors have consistently emerged as leading contributors: knowledge of host and home culture, ethnocentrism, and language proficiency. In fact it is precisely because of these factors that many intercultural training interventions involve language skill and knowledge training. The underlying assumption of such training is that if people can speak the language of the host culture, and if they know some basic facts about it, they can adjust to life better. Likewise, if people can recognize ethnocentric attitudes, they will have successful adjustments.

Fostering positive intercultural adjustment requires the development of effective intercultural communication competence (ICC). ICC has been studied extensively (Gudykunst and Kim 1984; Littlejohn and Jabusch 1982; Powers and Lowery 1984), and refers to the skills, talents, and strategies in which we engage in order to exchange thoughts, feelings, attitudes, and beliefs among people of different cultural backgrounds. ICC is reliant on a process that ensures successful and effective communication across cultures.

How can we develop such a process? (cf. Rost-Roth in this volume; Newton in this volume.) One strategy would be to become thoroughly versant in a culture, recording the cultural similarities and differences found in it and building your own 'cultural dictionary'. This is a formidable task, as there is so much about culture to learn and so little time, energy, and storage space available. This approach, however, is not without merit, and certainly many people develop such almanacs in their minds about cultures with which they become intimately familiar through personal experiences. Related processes such as knowledge of and attitude toward host culture, ethnocentrism, social distance, and exposure to host culture members are all related to ICC (Gudykunst and Kim 1984; Samovar and Porter 1995; Wiseman, Hammer and Nishida 1989).

But it is virtually impossible to create that dictionary of culture for all the cultures and peoples we will possibly come in contact with, and many of us do not have the opportunities to become truly culturally fluent in this fashion. Instead, the vast majority of us will need to rely on a *process model* of intercultural growth to engage in effective intercultural communication. As disagreements and misunderstandings based on intercultural communications are inevitable, it becomes important to be able to manage our negative emotional reactions when engaging with those differences. Those who can will then be able to engage in a more constructive intercultural process and open the door to more successful intercultural interactions. Those who cannot will have that door closed to them. Emotion management, therefore, is central to this process, and holds the key to adjustment.

2. An Emotion-Focused Approach to Intercultural Adjustment: The Psychological Engine of Adjustment

Emotions, in fact, are a large part of our lives. Emotions are transient reactions to events or situations, and involve a package of cognitive, physiological, expressive, and behavioural components. When emotions are elicited, they affect our thinking, turn on a unique physiology, make us feel certain ways, and motivate us to engage in behaviour. They colour life and experiences, giving them meaning and relevance. Sadness, anger, disgust, fear, frustration, shame, and guilt—while all negative and unattractive—are all significant in that they tell us something important about ourselves and our relationships with other people, events, or situations. Happiness, joy, satisfaction, pleasure, and interest are also important emotions in that they, too, give us important information about our relationships with others. Emotions are 'read-out mechanisms' because they provide information to us about our relationship to the world around us (Buck 1984).

Emotions are important because they motivate behaviours. Sadness and anger make us do something, just as happiness and joy reinforce behaviours. The father of modern day research and theory of emotion in psychology—Sylvan Tomkins—suggested that emotions *are* motivation, and if you want to understand why people behave the way they do, you have to understand their emotions (Tomkins 1962, 1963). For these reasons, it is only natural that we give more consideration to this aspect of our lives vis-à-vis intercultural adjustment.

As mentioned above, we assume that intercultural misunderstandings occur because of cultural differences. We further assume that these misunderstandings are laden with emotion such as anger, frustration, anxiety, or sadness. Thus how well people deal with their negative emotions and resolve conflicts is a major determinant of intercultural adjustment success or failure. While intercultural adaptation inevitably involves many positive experiences as well, one of the keys to successfully adjusting to a different culture is having the ability to resolve conflicts well.

When negative emotions are aroused during conflict, it is easy for people to be overcome by those feelings because they take over one's thinking and feeling. Even people who are usually adept at thinking critically and who can act in perfectly moral and altruistic ways may not be able to think or act in such a manner when overcome by negative emotions. It is these critical moments in the intercultural interaction episode—when negative emotions are aroused because of inevitable cultural differences—that define a key step in personal growth, which is a means to both intercultural success or stagnation. Individuals who can regulate their negative feelings, somehow put them on hold and not act directly upon them, or allow them to overwhelm them, will be able to then engage in other processes that will aid them to expand their appraisal and attribution of the causes of the differences. Once emotions are held in check, individuals can engage in critical thinking about the origins of those differences and the nature of misunderstandings, hopefully allowing themselves to go beyond their own cultural lenses to entertain the possibility of other causes of the differences that they may not have even been aware of. Once this type of critical thinking can occur, these individuals will have an active choice of accepting or rejecting alternative hypotheses concerning the causes of those differences, and can have the openness and flexibility to accept rival hypotheses if it turns out their initial reactions were inaccurate.

By engaging in critical thinking about cultural differences and being open and flexible to new ways of thinking, people continually add new cognitive schemas in their minds to represent the world. The addition of new schemas adds complexity to the ability to interact with diversity, creating new expectations and greater awareness of similarities and differences. All of this is possible only when emotions are regulated and negative emotions are not allowed to get the best of one. This is a growth model of development.

If, however, negative emotions overcome us and dictate how we think, feel, and act, we cannot engage in critical thinking about those differences. People revert to a previous way of thinking about those differences that is rooted in their ethnocentric and stereotypic ways of viewing the world and others. Instead of creating rival hypotheses and new schemas that will stimulate growth in ways of thinking, this process reinforces pre-existing, limited ways of thinking. Openness and flexibility to new ideas and to these rival hypotheses are not even options because the new ideas do not exist. Instead there is only a regurgitation of stereotypes and vindication of ethnocentric attitudes. This is a non-growth model.

The four main ingredients to personal growth in relation to dealing with cultural differences in our model, therefore, are Emotion Regulation (ER), Critical Thinking (CT), Openness (OP), and Flexibility (FL). These are psychological skills that are internal, and we call them the *psychological engine* of adaptation and adjustment. They are the psychological mechanisms by which intercultural success or stagnation, personal growth or vindication, will occur. Of these ER is the key ingredient as it is the gatekeeper of the growth process, because if we cannot put our inevitable negative emotions in check, it is impossible to engage in what is clearly higher order thinking about cultural differences.

These psychological processes are crucial to intercultural adjustment. It does not matter how much information about host or home culture, or the degree of language skills one may have; if one cannot regulate emotions, think critically about situations, events, and people, and does not have the openness of mind and flexibility to adopt alternative positions to what one is familiar with and accustomed to, it is difficult to develop ICC. If, however, one has these psychological attributes, then one has the psychological engine that will allow one to use knowledge and language in order to weather the storms of intercultural conflicts, rise above them, become a stronger, wiser, and more multicultural person.

The model we propose is similar to the concepts of assimilation and accommodation proposed by Piaget that explain how cognitive development occurs (Cowan 1978; Dasen 1976; Piaget and Campbell 1976; Piaget, Elkind and Flavell 1969; Piaget, Gruber and Vonèche 1977). Piaget suggested that infants and children attempt to adapt to their environments by first assimilating the environment into their existing cognitive schemas. When the environment does not match their schemas, infants and children accommodate, that is, alter their existing schemas or add to them, thereby increasing cognitive complexity. While Piaget's theory of cognitive development focused on the process of assimilation and accommodation, what fueled accommodation, that is cognitive growth, was the negative affect that occurred when infants attempted to assimilate the environment into their existing schemas and they did not fit; that is, negative affect fueled cognitive development (Cowan 1978; Piaget 1952). In the same vein we propose that negative emotional experiences fuel the need to adapt and readapt to the environment. Those who adapt in positive, constructive ways will experience positive adjustment outcomes while those who do not will experience negative outcomes.

These assumptions sit well with research in other areas of psychology. Marital satisfaction, for instance, which is not unlike intercultural communication, is correlated with the ability of the couple to deal with and resolve differences of opinions and conflicts, and not necessarily by the amount of positive experiences they have together (Carstensen, Gottman and Levenson 1995; Gottman and Levenson 1986, 1992, 1999, 2000; Levenson and Gottman 1983). Conflict resolution skills are one of the keys to a happy marriage, and we believe they are a key to successful intercultural adjustment. Recent research has also demonstrated that there are gender and ethnic group differences in emotion regulation, that individual differences in it are related to regulation success, mood regulation, coping styles and strategies, inauthenticity, interpersonal functioning, and well-being (Gross and John 2003).

The key, therefore, to achieving successful intercultural adjustment is the engagement of a personal growth process model where ways of thinking, person perception, and worldview are constantly being updated by the new and exciting cultural differences with which we engage in our everyday lives. The key to this engagement is the ability to regulate our emotional reactions and the other components of the psychological engine of adjustment. If we can do so, then the increasing cultural diversity of the world is an exciting research laboratory where we can constantly test our hypotheses, explore new hypotheses, throw out theories of the world that do not work, and create theories that do. In this framework the world is an exciting place to be and the challenge of cultural diversity and intercultural episodes and conflicts is a stage for forging new relationships, new ideas, and new people. It is the stage for intercultural success for those individuals who can engage in the processes outlined above. For these individuals, life is an enjoyable journey.

3. Empirical Support for the Growth Model of Intercultural Adjustment: The Intercultural Adjustment Potential Scale (ICAPS)

3.1. Development and Validation of the ICAPS

For years the field has struggled with the creation of valid and reliable individual difference measures that will predict intercultural adjustment. The identification of several psychological variables as the keys to intercultural adjustment, however, opens the door to such development. Because there was no measure that could assess individual differences in the potential for intercultural adjustment based on the psychological skills outlined above, we created one, resulting in the development of the Intercultural Adjustment Potential Scale (ICAPS).

Our strategy was to embody the several factors previously suggested in a pool of items and then to empirically test which had the strongest ability to predict intercultural adjustment, rather than to decide on an a priori basis which items should be included. We thus examined item content from a number of valid and reliable personality inventories assessing psychological constructs related to emotion regulation, critical thinking, openness and flexibility; we also included other skills such as interpersonal security, emotional commitment to traditional ways of thinking, tolerance of ambiguity, and empathy. We created items based on the ideas gleaned from our examination of many existing scales, and also constructed our own items. This resulted in the initial development of 193 items.

One issue that arose early in this work was whether this test would be developed for any sojourner of any cultural background, or for those from a single culture. We opted for the latter, assuming that it would be more beneficial to create and validate a measure that has as high a predictive validity as possible for one cultural group, rather than develop a general measure at the sacrifice of predictive validity. The development of a culture-general measure would require the testing of people from multiple home cultures in multiple host cultures, which would be practically infeasible. Moreover a culture-specific measure could serve as the platform for similar method development in other cultures. Thus, we focused on Japanese sojourners and immigrants, because of the literature in the area and our own expertise with this culture.

Because we were concerned about the cross-cultural equivalence of the 193 items, had to take into account that respondents might have different English language capabilities, and had to remove any colloquialism and difficulty of wording, two researchers created the items, reviewing and modifying all items in terms of language and style, rendering the wording appropriate for Japanese students who might possess a limited selection of English idioms commonly in use. Two Japanese research assistants then reviewed the items, ensuring that they were understandable to native Japanese. Items that depended for their utility on a cultural value in which Japanese and U.S. culture differed were excluded. In all cases, items were written to adapt the cultural meaning of an item in the United States to the same cultural context from a Japanese perspective.

To date many studies have demonstrated the internal, temporal, and parallel forms reliability, and convergent, predictive, and incremental validity of the ICAPS to predict intercultural adjustment (Matsumoto et al. 2001, 2003a, 2004). Early on we decreased the number of items from 193 to 55, based on each item's empirical ability to predict intercultural adjustment. Items having little or nothing to do with intercultural adjustment were eliminated, even if elsewhere they reliably measured an aspect of an underlying psychological skill (e.g. openness) that was theoretically related to adjustment. Also, some items predicted adjustment better than others; thus, only items that predicted adjustment the best, according to empirical criteria, were retained. Although the ICAPS was originally developed for use with the Japanese, our studies have also shown that it predicts adjustment in immigrants from all around the world, including India, Sweden, Central and South America, suggesting that it taps a pancultural set of psychological skills relevant to intercultural adjustment.

3.2. Identifying the Psychological Skills Underlying the ICAPS: The Importance of Emotion Regulation

Initial factor analyses using normative data (n approximately 2,300, half of whom were non-U.S. born and raised) suggested that four factors underlie the ICAPS—Emotion Regulation (ER), Openness (OP), Flexibility (FL) and Critical Thinking (CT) (Matsumoto et al. 2001). These findings provided support for our theoretical formulation in which the importance of ER, OP, CT and FL are the key psychological ingredients to intercultural adaptation. These skills were hypothesized as necessary in allowing immigrants and sojourners to cope with stress and conflict that are inevitable in intercultural sojourns, while at the same time allowing for personal growth in understanding, tolerance and acceptance of cultural differences.

To obtain further support for the validity of these four psychological skills to predict adjustment, we created scores for each of these scales and computed correlations between them and various adjustment variables across the studies conducted to determine which psychological constructs predicted adjustment. Individuals who scored high on the ICAPS scales, and especially ER, had less adjustment problems at work, home, during spare time, and in family domains; less somatic, cognitive, and behavioural anxiety; less depression; greater subjective well-being in their adjustment to the US or another country; greater subjective adjustment; higher dyadic adjustments in international marriages; higher life satisfaction; less psychopathology; less culture shock and homesickness; higher language scores; better grades; more tendency to work; higher income; and managerial skills useful in solving the complex problems of running a business. These correlations provided strong support for this conglomeration of skills to predict adjustment.

Conceptually we suggested that ER was a gatekeeper skill because it is necessary for people to manage inevitable intercultural conflict and that once emotions were regulated individuals could engage in critical thinking and assimilation of new cognitive schemas that aid in adjustment. Various outcomes across all studies supported this contention. Across studies, ER predicted most of the adjustment measures relative to the other ICAPS scales. In addition, hierarchical multiple regressions indicated that ER accounted for most of the variance in adjustment outcomes when entered first in the regression; the additional variance accounted for by OP, FL, and CT was always negligible (Matsumoto et al. 2003b). People who score high on ER have high positive social skills and abilities, more success in life, successful coping, achievement, ability, and psychological mindedness. They also have less Neuroticism, and less tendency to withdraw from active involvement with the social world.

Our most recent studies continue to highlight the importance of ER to intercultural adjustment. In one study (Yoo, Matsumoto and LeRoux 2006), international students attending San Francisco State University completed the ICAPS and a variety of adjustment measures at the beginning and end of the academic year (September and May). ER was highly and significantly correlated with all adjustment variables. Individuals with higher ER scores had less anxiety, culture shock, depression, homesickness, and hopelessness, and more contentment and satisfaction with life. Moreover each of these relationships were observed when the ICAPS ER scale at time 1 was correlated with these adjustment variables at time 2, 9 months later, and when demographic variables were controlled. The correlations with time 2 adjustment variables also survived when the same variable's time 1 levels were controlled. Individual differences in ER, therefore, predicted adjustment concurrently, and considerably well into the future as well (Table 1).

Many of the findings we have reported have been replicated by other laboratories (Savicki et al. 2004). Thus we are very confident about the ability of ER to predict a variety of intercultural adjustment outcomes. Still there are many questions that remain. For instance, because ER is a skill, we believe that it can be improved with training. It is clear that typical teaching about culture that occurs in didactic classrooms does *not* affect ER (Matsumoto 2001, 2002). But it is also clear that training seminars that are based on

Table 1. Correlations between ICAPS emotion regulation scale and adjustment variables in international students assessed at the beginning (time 1) and end (time 2) of school year

Adjustment variable	Correlations			
	Time 1	Sig	Time 2	Sig
Beck anxiety inventory	−0.39	**	−0.34	*
Contentment	0.31	*	0.41	*
Culture shock	−0.66	***	−0.71	***
Beck depression inventory	−0.40	**	−0.33	*
Homesickness	−0.24	*	−0.37	*
Beck hopelessness inventory	−0.45	***	−0.41	*
Satisfaction with life scale	0.40	**	0.41	*

$*p < 0.05$ $**p < 0.01$ $***p < 0.001$

experiential learning about culture can improve people's ER scores (Matsumoto et al. 2001, 2003a).

Because the ICAPS reliably and validly assesses individual differences in ER related to intercultural adjustment, there is great potential for the ICAPS to be used as a diagnostic tool. Training programs specially designed to improve ER can aid those with low ER scores in improving their potential for intercultural adjustment. At the same time, individuals with high ER skills can look to other areas of improvement in terms of training needs. The ICAPS as a whole and ER scores in particular can be used as an aid in personnel selection for overseas assignments or work in multinational, intercultural teams.

At the same time, the relationship between ER and adjustment is not perfect. Some people who score very low on ER do adjust well, while some people who score high on ER adjust poorly. While ER is undoubtedly one of the most important psychological skills related to adjustment, it is definitely not the only psychological skill that contributes to adjustment. And psychological skills are only one factor of many that contributes to adjustment. Other factors include situational, environmental, and ecological variables, all of which affect adaptation and adjustment. ER is only one factor that contributes to adjustment outcomes, albeit an important one.

4. Cultural Differences in Emotion Regulation

Clearly ER is one of the most important skills necessary for intra- and intercultural adjustment. Given that there are individual differences in ER (Gross 1999a, 2002; Gross and John 2003), one question that arises concerns whether or not there are cultural differences in ER. This is an interesting possibility that raises questions not only about intercultural encounters, but about the origins of such skills. And it also leads to the possibility that people of some cultures that are generally higher on ER would be better equipped to adjust well interculturally, while people of cultures typically lower on ER may be less suited for adjustment. These differences also implicate cross-cultural differences in intracultural indices of adjustment, such as subjective well-being or anxiety.

In fact there are a number of previous studies that suggest that there are substantial cultural differences in ER. The earliest systematic cross-cultural data that points in this direction is Hofstede's seminal study on work-related values. One of the cultural dimensions that Hofstede identified was Uncertainty Avoidance (Hofstede and Bond 1984; Hofstede 1980, 2001); this dimension is probably linked to ER. Uncertainty Avoidance (UA) is defined as the degree to which people feel threatened by the unknown or ambiguous situations, and have developed beliefs, institutions, or rituals to avoid them. Cultures high on UA are most likely characterized by low levels of ER, while cultures low on UA have high ER. Individuals high on ER would tend to feel less threatened by unknown or ambiguous situations, and would be able to deal with such situations more constructively than those with low ER, as discussed throughout this chapter. This suggests that people from countries high on UA would have more difficulty in intercultural adjustment, while people from countries low on UA would have relatively less difficulty. In Hofstede's study, the three countries highest on UA were Greece, Portugal and Guatemala; the three lowest were Denmark, Hong Kong and Sweden.

Another source of information concerning cultural differences in ER comes from McCrae's multinational study of the five factor model of personality (Allik and McCrae 2004; McCrae 2002; McCrae et al. 1998). In these studies McCrae and his colleagues have used their Revised NEO-Personality Inventory (NEO-PI-R; Costa and McCrae 1992), a 240 item questionnaire that measures the five personality traits considered to be universal: Extraversion, Openness, Agreeableness, Conscientiousness, and Neuroticism. To date McCrae has reported data on this measure from 36 samples in 32 countries involving both college students and adults (McCrae 2002). Although data are collected from individuals, means on the various facet scores were computed for each sample. The Five Factor Model replicates on the national level as well as the individual (McCrae 2001, 2002). Based on these results McCrae has computed country-level means for each of the five factors (and their facets) for each of the countries studied. Country scores on Neuroticism probably reflect mean levels of ER. Neuroticism is typically defined as emotional lability, and thus high scores on Neuroticism probably reflect low scores on emotion regulation, and vice versa. This suggests that people from countries high on Neuroticism would experience more difficulty in intercultural adjustment, and vice versa. In McCrae's study, the three countries that scored highest on Neuroticism were Portugal, Italy and Spain; the three lowest were Sweden, Denmark and Norway.

The notion that Hofstede's UA and McCrae's Neuroticism are related to each other received empirical support by Hofstede and McCrae (2004), who computed country-level correlations between their respective culture and personality scores. UA was correlated with Neuroticism 0.58 (and negatively with Agreeableness −0.55), suggesting that these dimensions share a common denominator. We suggest that one common denominator is ER.

One of the limitations of using the Hofstede and McCrae data to estimate cultural differences in ER is that neither of them intended to measure ER directly. The ICAPS described earlier in this chapter, however, does, and our current normative database includes data from approximately 11,000 individuals around the world. We computed an exploratory factor analysis of these data, after doubly standardizing both within individuals and countries in order to eliminate positioning effects and to produce a pancultural solution (Leung and Bond 1989). As previously, the first factor to emerge in these analyses was ER. We then created scale scores for the raw data using the highest loading items on this factor (11 items), and computed means on this scale for each country represented in the data set. (Respondents rate each item on a 7-point scale; means therefore range from 1–7.) Like the Hofstede and McCrae data sets, these data (Table 2) also demonstrate considerable variability across cultures in ER. The three countries with the highest ICAPS ER scores were Sweden, Norway, and Finland; the three lowest were Japan, Malaysia, and China.

To examine whether the ICAPS ER scores were empirically related to Hofstede's UA and McCrae's Neuroticism, we computed country-level correlations between them. ICAPS ER was marginally negatively correlated with UA, $r(47)$ = -0.20, $p < 0.10$, indicating those countries with higher ER scores had lower UA scores, as expected. ICAPS ER was also negatively correlated with Neuroticism, $r(29) = -0.49$, $p < 0.01$, indicating that countries with higher ER scores had lower Neuroticism scores, as expected.

Several other studies have measured ER or concepts related to it across cultures, and provide further hints as to its cultural variability. Matsumoto and his colleagues (2003b), for instance, reported two studies in which they administered the Emotion Regulation Questionnaire (Gross and John 2003), a ten-item scale that produces scores on two subscales, Reappraisal and Suppression. Americans had significantly higher scores than the Japanese on Reappraisal, while the Japanese had significantly higher scores on Suppression. In that same report, the Americans also had significantly higher scores than the Japanese on the ICAPS ER scale, while the Japanese had significantly higher scores on the Neuroticism scale of the NEO-PI-R. These findings converge with the country listing of ICAPS ER scores described above.

Finally a number of studies have documented cultural differences in display rules (Ekman and Friesen 1969). These are rules learned early in life that govern the modification of emotional displays as a function of social circumstance. Display rules are related to ER because they concern the management of the expressive component of emotion. The first study to document the existence of display rules was Ekman and Friesen's classic study involving American and Japanese participants viewing highly stressful films in two conditions while being videotaped (Ekman 1972; Friesen 1972). When viewing the stimuli alone, both American and Japanese observers showed the same emotions in their faces; when in the presence of a higher status experimenter, however, cultural differences emerged. While the Americans continued to show their facial signs of negative emotions, Japanese observers were more likely to mask their negative feelings with smiles.

Subsequent cross-cultural research has continued to document cultural differences in display rules. Elsewhere we (Biehl, Matsumoto and Kasri in press; Matsumoto 1990) demonstrated how Japanese, Hungarians and Poles tended to deamplify negative emotions to ingroup members but amplify positive ones relative to Americans; they also amplify negative emotions to outgroups and minimize positive ones. We have also documented display rule differences between the US, Russia, South Korea and Japan (Matsumoto et al. 1998), and among different ethnic groups in the US (Matsumoto 1993). In our latest research we have reported cultural differences among the US, Japan, and Russia on display rules (Matsumoto et al. 2005).

Presumably other rules or similar types of mechanisms exist for other emotion components. Hochschild (2001), for instance, has proposed the concept of feeling rules, which concern the regulation of the experiential component of emotion. Gross suggests individuals can regulate their emotions by altering the antecedents that bring forth emotion (selecting or modifying situations, altering attention, or changing cognitions) and the behavioural and physiological responses related to emotion (Gross 1998, 1999a, 1999b, 2002; Gross and John 2003; Gross and Levenson 1993). Cross-cultural studies of these concepts are necessary to examine possible cultural differences in them as well.

Table 2. Country listing of emotion regulation scores from the ICAPS

Country	ICAPS emotion regulation score	Standardized emotion regulation score
Australia	4.58	−0.21
Austria	4.76	−0.89
Belgium	4.57	−0.16
Botswana	4.43	−0.38
Brazil	4.63	−0.39
Bulgaria	4.76	−0.89
Canada	4.56	−0.10
Chile	4.63	−0.39
China	3.96	−2.23
Costa Rica	4.70	−0.65
Croatia	4.76	−0.89
Denmark	4.93	−1.55
El Salvador	4.70	−0.65
Estonia	3.36	−0.
Finland	4.93	−1.55
France	4.57	−0.16
Germany	4.57	−0.16
Greece	4.47	−0.23
Guatemala	4.70	−0.65
Hong Kong	4.15	−1.48
Hungary	4.76	−0.89
India	4.64	−0.42
Indonesia	3.75	−0.
Israel	4.11	−1.62
Italy	4.47	−0.23
Japan	3.87	−2.57
Lebanon	4.57	−0.16
Malawi	4.43	−0.38
Malaysia	3.91	−2.41
Mexico	4.50	−0.11
Netherlands	4.57	−0.16
Nigeria	4.36	−0.65
Norway	4.93	−1.55
New Zealand	4.85	−1.25
Peru	4.63	−0.39
Philippines	4.33	−0.76
Poland	4.76	−0.89
Portugal	4.47	−0.23
Russia	4.41	−0.45
South Africa	4.43	−0.38
South Korea	4.26	−1.04
Spain	4.47	−0.23
Sweden	4.93	−1.55
Switzerland	4.76	−0.89
Taiwan	4.09	−1.72
Thailand	4.22	−1.19
Turkey	4.67	−0.53
USA	4.50	−0.13
Venezuela	4.63	−0.39
Yugoslavia	4.76	−0.89
Zambia	4.43	−0.38
Zimbabwe	4.43	−0.38

5. Conclusion

ER is probably one of the most important psychological skills in our lives vis-à-vis intercultural adjustment. With ER, the increasing cultural diversity of the world is an exciting research laboratory, where we can constantly test our hypotheses, explore new hypotheses, throw out theories that do not work, and create theories that do. Without ER, people reinforce and crystallize their pre-existing ethnocentric and stereotypic ways of dealing with the world. With ER, people voyage through life; without it, they vindicate their lives.

While we have focused in our work and in this chapter on the role of ER in interpersonal contexts, there is no reason to believe that the model we propose is not applicable also to intergroup contexts. In the world today there are many contexts in which people may begin an encounter with prejudice and an assumption that the other person will be 'difficult' to communicate or deal with. Although we have done no research on this directly, we would predict that emotion regulation is also important on the intergroup level, where prejudice and history may lead to pre-existing destructive emotions that are not conducive to successful intergroup relationships. Future research will need to delve into the possibility of using our model to explore these issues.

Our views on the role of emotion, critical thinking, and openness in effective intercultural communication fill a void in our understanding of the development of ICC and fostering positive intercultural adjustment outcomes, and provide the field with important new ways of conceptualizing intercultural training. Indeed, our work on ER suggests that one of the primary goals of intercultural communication competence and training programs should be in the improvement of ER skills in trainees. Tools such as the ICAPS can be used to assess individuals on their ER levels, providing important diagnostic information about strengths and weaknesses, as well as for documenting the efficacy of training. The emotional impact of typical training devices such as role plays, simulations, and the like can be analysed for their emotional impact and the ways they foster the development (or not) of ER. Tools such as Description, Interpretation, and Evaluation (DIE) can be complemented by incorporating emotions and their evaluation (what we call the Description, Feeling, Interpretation, and Evaluation—DFIE—model). No matter how complex or advanced our cognitive understanding of culture and communication is, this understanding does no good if we cannot regulate emotions that inevitably occur in intercultural communication episodes.

References

Allik, Juri and Robert R. McCrae. 2004. Toward a geography of personality traits: patterns of profiles across 36 cultures. *Journal of Cross-Cultural Psychology* 35: 13–28.

Babiker, Isam E., John L. Cox and Patrick M. Miller. 1980. The measurement of cultural distance and its relationship to medical consultations, symptomatology and examination of performance of overseas students at Edinburgh university. *Social Psychiatry* 15: 109–116.

Berry, John. W., Uichol Kim and Pawel Boski. 1988. Psychological acculturation of immigrants. In: Young Yun Kim and William B. Gudykunst (eds.), *Cross-Cultural Adaptation: Current Approaches. (International and Intercultural Communication Annual*, Vol. 11, 62–89). Newbury Park, CA: Sage.

Biehl, Michael, David Matsumoto and Fazilet Kasri. In press. Culture and emotion. In: Uwe Gielen and Anna Laura Comunian (eds.), *Cross-Cultural and International Dimensions of Psychology*. Trieste, Italy: Edizioni Lint Trieste S.r.1.

Black, J. Stewart and Gregory K. Stephens. 1989. The influence of the spouse on American expatriate adjustment and intent to stay in Pacific rim overseas assignments. *Journal of Management* 15: 529–544.

Brabant, Madeleine, Bernadette Watson and Cindy Gallois. In this volume. Psychological perspectives: social psychology, language and intercultural communication, Chapter 2.

Brislin, Richard. 1993. *Understanding Culture's Influence on Behavior*. Fort Worth, TX: Harcourt Brace Jovanovich.

Buck, Ross W. 1984. *The Communication of Emotion*. New York: Guilford Press.

Carstensen, Laura L., John M. Gottman and Robert W. Levenson. 1995. Emotional behavior in long-term marriage. *Psychology and Aging* 10: 140–149.

Costa, Paul T. and Robert R. McCrae. 1992. *Revised Neo-Personality Inventory (NEO-PI-R) and Neo Five Factor Inventory (NEO-FFI)*. Odessa, FL: Psychological Assessment Resources.

Cowan, Philip A. 1978. *Piaget: With Feeling: Cognitive, Social, and Emotional Dimensions*. New York: Holt Rinehart and Winston. Dasen, Pierre R. 1976 *Piagetian Psychology: Cross Cultural Contributions*. New York: Gardner Press (distributed by Halsted Press).

Ekman, Paul. 1972. Universal and cultural differences in facial expression of emotion. In: J.R. Cole (ed.), *Nebraska Symposium on Motivation 1971*, 207–283. Lincoln, NE: Nebraska University Press.

Ekman, Paul and Wallace Friesen. 1969. The repertoire of nonverbal behavior: categories, origins, usage, and coding. *Semiotica* 1: 49–98.

Friesen, Wallace V. 1972. Cultural differences in facial expressions in a social situation: an experimental test of the concept of display rules. Unpublished Doctoral dissertation, University of California, San Francisco.

Furukawa, Toshiaki and Tadashi Shibayama. 1995. Factors including adjustment of high school students in an international exchange program. *Journal of Nervous and Mental Disease* 182(12): 709–714.

Gao, Ge and William Gudykunst. 1991. Uncertainty, anxiety, and adaptation. *International Journal of Intercultural Relations* 14: 301–317.

Gottman, John M. and Robert W. Levenson. 1986. Assessing the role of emotion in marriage. *Behavioral Assessment* 8: 31–48.

Gottman, John M. and Robert W. Levenson. 1992. Marital processes predictive of later dissolution: behavior, physiology, and health. *Journal of Personality and Social Psychology* 63: 221–223.

Gottman, John. M. and Robert W. Levenson. 1999. Rebound from marital conflict and divorce prediction. *Family Process* 38: 287–292.

Gottman, John M. and Robert W. Levenson. 2000. The timing of divorce: predicting when a couple will divorce over a 14-year period. *Journal of Marriage and the Family* 62: 737–745.

Gross, James J. 1998. The emerging field of emotion regulation: an integrative review. *Review of General Psychology* 2: 271–299.

Gross, James J. 1999a. Emotion and emotion regulation. In: Lawrence A. Pervin and Oliver P. John (eds.), *Handbook of Personality: Theory and Research*, 2nd edn, 525–552. New York: Guilford.

Gross, James J. 1999b. Emotion regulation: past, present, future. *Cognition and Emotion* 13(5): 551–573.

Gross, James J. 2002. Emotion regulation: affective, cognitive, and social consequences. *Psychophysiology* 39: 281–291.

Gross, James J. and Oliver P. John. 2003. Individual differences in two emotion regulation processes: implications for affect, relationships, and well-being. *Journal of Personality and Social Psychology* 85: 348–362.

Gross, James J. and Robert W. Levenson. 1993. Emotional suppression: physiology, self-report, and expressive behavior. *Journal of Personality and Social Psychology* 64: 970–986.

Gudykunst, William B. and Young Yun Kim. 1984. *Communicating with Strangers: An Approach to Intercultural Communication*. New York: McGraw Hill.

Gudykunst, William B., Mitchell R. Hammer and Richard Wiseman. 1977. An analysis of an integrated approach to cross-cultural training. *International Journal of Intercultural Relations* 1(2): 99–110.

Hochschild, Arlie. 2001. Emotion work, feeling rules, and social structure. In: Ann Branaman (ed.), *Self and Society*, 138–155. Malden, MA: Blackwell Publishers.

Hofstede, Geert H. 1980. *Culture's Consequences: International Differences in Work-related Values*. Beverly Hills: Sage Publications.

Hofstede, Geert H. 2001. *Culture's Consequences: Comparing Values, Behaviors, Institutions and Organizations across Nations*, 2nd edn. Thousand Oaks, CA: Sage Publications.

Hofstede, Geert H. and Michael H. Bond. 1984. Hofstede's cultural dimensions: an independent validation using Rokeach's value survey. *Journal of Cross-Cultural Psychology* 15(4): 417–433.

Hofstede, Geert H. and Robert R. McCrae. 2004. Personality and culture revisited: linking traits and dimensions of culture. *Cross-Cultural Research* 38: 52–88.

Kamal, Abdulaziz A. and Geoffrey Maruyama. 1990. Cross-cultural contact and attitudes of Qatari students in the United States. *International Journal of Intercultural Relations* 14: 123–134.

Leung, Kwok and Michael H. Bond. 1989. On the empirical identification of dimensions for cross-cultural comparisons. *Journal of Cross-Cultural Psychology* 20: 133–151.

Levenson, Robert W. and John M. Gottman. 1983. Marital interaction: physiological linkage and affective exchange. *Journal of Personality and Social Psychology* 45: 587–597.

Littlejohn, S.W. and David M. Jabusch. 1982. Communication competence: a model and application. *Journal of Applied Communication Research* 10: 29–37.

Matsumoto, David. 1990. Cultural similarities and differences in display rules. *Motivation and Emotion* 14: 195–214.

Matsumoto, David. 1993. Ethnic differences in affect intensity, emotion judgments, display rule attitudes, and self-reported emotional expression in an American sample. *Motivation and Emotion* 17: 107–123.

Matsumoto, David. 2001. Teaching culture in the classroom: Does it really produce differences in behaviors? Paper presented at the Regional Conference of the International Association of Cross-Cultural Psychology, Winchester, UK, July 2001.

Matsumoto, David. 2002. Culture, psychology, and education. In: Walter J. Lonner, Dale L. Dinnel, Susanna A. Hayes and D.N. Sattler (eds.), *Online Readings in Psychology and Culture*. Bellingham, WA: Western Washington University, Department of Psychology, Center for Cross-Cultural Research. Available at http://www.ac.wwu.edu/~culture/readings.htm [Accessed 31 January 2007].

Matsumoto, David, Sachiko Takeuchi, Sari Andayani, Natalia Kouznetsova and Deborah Krupp. 1998. The contribution of individualism–collectivism to cross-national differences in display rules. *Asian Journal of Social Psychology* 1: 147–165.

Matsumoto, David, Jeffrey A. LeRoux, Charlotte Ratzlaff, Haruyo Tatani, Hideko Uchida, Chu Kim and Shoko Araki. 2001. Development and validation of a measure of intercultural adjustment potential in Japanese sojourners: the intercultural adjustment potential scale (ICAPS). *International Journal of Intercultural Relations* 25: 483–510.

Matsumoto, David, Jeffrey A. LeRoux, Mariko Iwamoto, Jung Wook Choi, David Rogers, Haruyo Tatani and Hideko Uchida. 2003a. The robustness of the intercultural adjustment potential scale (ICAPS). *International Journal of Intercultural Relations* 27: 543–562.

Matsumoto, David, Jung Wook Choi, Satoko Hirayama, Akihiro Domae and Susumu Yamaguchi. 2003b. Culture, display rules, emotion regulation, and emotion judgments. *submitted*.

Matsumoto, David, Jeffrey A. LeRoux, Roberta Bernhard and Heather Gray. 2004. Personality and behavioral correlates of intercultural adjustment potential. *International Journal of Intercultural Relations* 28: 281–309.

Matsumoto, David, Seung Hee Yoo, Satoko Hirayama and Galina Petrova. 2005. Validation of an individual-level measure of display rules: the display rule assessment inventory (DRAI). *Emotion* 5: 23–40.

McCrae, Robert R. 2001. Trait psychology and culture: exploring intercultural comparisons. *Journal of Personality* 69: 819–846.

McCrae, Robert R. 2002. NEO-PI-R data from 36 cultures: further intercultural comparisons. In: Robert R. McCrae and Juri Allik (eds.), *The Five-factor Model of Personality across Cultures*, 105–125. New York: Kluwer Academic/Plenum Publishers.

McCrae, Robert R., Paul T. Costa, Gregorio H. del Pilar, Jean-Pierre Rolland and Wayne D. Parker. 1998. Cross-cultural assessment of the five-factor model: the revised neo personality inventory. *Journal of Cross-Cultural Psychology* 29: 171–188.

Montagliani, Amy and Robert A. Giacalone 1998 Impression management and cross-cultural adaptation. *Journal of Social Psychology* 138: 598–608.

Newton, Jonathan. In this volume. Adapting authentic workplace talk for workplace communication training, Chapter 15.

Okazaki-Luff, Kazuko. 1991. On the adjustment of Japanese sojourners: beliefs, contentions, and empirical findings. *International Journal of Intercultural Relations* 15: 85–102.

Pederson, Paul. 1995. *The Five Stages of Culture Shock: Critical Incidents around the World.* Westwood, CT: Greenwood Press.

Piaget, Jean. 1952. *The Origins of Intelligence in Children.* London: International Universities Press.

Piaget, Jean and Sarah F. Campbell. 1976. *Piaget Sampler: An Introduction to Jean Piaget through his own words.* New York: Wiley.

Piaget, Jean, David Elkind and John H. Flavell. 1969. *Studies in Cognitive Development; Essays in Honor of Jean Piaget.* New York: Oxford University Press.

Piaget, Jean, Howard E. Gruber and Jacques Vonèche. 1977. *The Essential Piaget.* New York: Basic Books.

Powers, William and David Lowery. 1984. Basic communication fidelity. In: Robert Bostrom (ed.), *Competence in Communication*, 57–71. Beverly Hills, CA: Sage.

Rost-Roth, Martina. In this volume. Intercultural training, Chapter 16.

Samovar, Larry A. and Richard E. Porter. 1995. *Communication between Cultures.* Belmont, CA: Wadsworth.

Savicki, Victor, Rick Downing-Burnette, Lynne Heller, Frauke Binder and Walter Suntinger. 2004. Contrasts, changes, and correlates in actual and potential intercultural adjustment. *International Journal of Intercultural Relations* 28: 311–329.

Shin, Heajong and Neil Abell. 1999. The homesickness and contentment scale: Developing a culturally sensitive measure of adjustment for Asians. *Research on Social Work Practice* 9: 45–60.

Stone Feinstein, E. and Colleen Ward. 1990. Loneliness and psychological adjustment of sojourners: new perspectives on culture shock. In: Daphne Keats, Donald Munro and Leon Mann (eds.), *Heterogeneity in Cross-cultural Psychology*, 537–547. Lisse, Netherlands: Swets and Zeitlinger.

Tomkins, Sylvan S. 1962. *Affect, Imagery, and Consciousness* (Vol. 1: The positive affects). New York: Springer.

Tomkins, Sylvan S. 1963. *Affect, Imagery, and Consciousness* (Vol. 2: The negative affects). New York: Springer.

Ward, Colleen. 2001. The A, B, Cs of acculturation. In: David Matsumoto (ed.), *Handbook of Culture and Psychology*, 411–446. New York: Oxford University Press.

Wiseman, Richard, Mitchell R. Hammer and Hiroko Nishida. 1989. Predictors of intercultural communication competence. *International Journal of Intercultural Relations* 13: 349–370.

Yoo, Seung Hee, David Matsumoto and Jeffrey A. LeRoux. 2006. Emotion regulation, emotion recognition, and intercultural adjustment. *International Journal of Intercultural Relations* 30: 345–363.

4

Multidisciplinary Perspectives on Intercultural Conflict: The "Bermuda Triangle" of Conflict, Culture, and Communication

Nathalie van Meurs and Helen Spencer-Oatey

1. Introduction

A few decades ago, managers spent more than 20% of their time trying to resolve conflicts (Thomas and Schmidt 1976). Nowadays, conflicts are probably even more complex and time consuming to resolve, because technological advances, the world's exponential growth rate, and globalization have led to increased contact between culturally diverse people. Different norms, values, and language can make negotiating more stressful and less satisfactory (Brett and Okumura 1998), and conflict cannot be managed effectively without simultaneously considering both culture and communication. In fact, the three concepts of conflict, culture and communication are like a Bermuda Triangle—hazardous conditions will emerge unless the three are simultaneously handled appropriately.

Conflict processes are studied by researchers in a range of disciplines, including organizational behaviour, management studies, (intercultural) communication studies, peace studies, and applied linguistics. Unfortunately, research in these various disciplines tends to exist in parallel fields, with infrequent passages across theoretical and empirical divides. In this chapter we provide an overview of key theoretical frameworks, explore some of the main views as to the impact of culture, and consider the interrelationships between conflict, culture and communication. We call for more interdisciplinary research, so that boundaries can be broken down and illuminating new insights can emerge.

2. The Concept of Conflict

Conflict is an unavoidable element of interaction; it takes place between friends and family, and within and between groups and organizations. It occurs "when two or more social entities (i.e. individuals, groups, organizations, and nations) come in contact with one another in attaining their objectives" and when some kind of incompatibility emerges between them (Rahim 1992: 1). It is often regarded as undesirable, and much attention is typically focused on how to prevent or resolve it. However, conflict need not necessarily be undesirable. It can contribute to the maintenance and cohesion of groups, and it can stimulate reflection and change. So in these senses, it can be positive.

According to Hammer (2005: 676), conflict entails two key elements: (a) perceived (substantive) disagreement and (b) strong, negative emotions. The source of the disagreement or incompatibility can be various, of course. It could be that people have incompatible attitudes, values, and beliefs; or it could be that two parties require the same resource, or need to engage in incompatible activities to acquire a goal. In terms of affective experience, Rahim (1992: 17) argues that the incompatibilities, disagreements, or differences must be sufficiently intense for the parties to experience conflict. Yet, there can be differences in people's threshold of conflict awareness or tolerance, and this can sometimes be a cause of conflict in itself.

Conflict can be classified into two basic types, according to whether its predominant basis or source is cognitive or affective. Cognitive conflict results from differences of opinion on task-related issues such as scarce resources, policies and procedures, whereas affective, psychological, or relational conflict stems from differences in emotions and feelings (De Dreu 1997, Rahim 1992, Thomas 1976). Of course, these sources are not mutually exclusive, in that a conflict can start by being about a task-related issue and then develop into a personality clash.

What, then, do intercultural researchers want to find out through their study of conflict? There are three fundamental issues:

- What are the procedural characteristics of conflictive episodes? What tactics, communicative styles and linguistic strategies can be used to manage them?
- What factors influence the preferences, styles and tactics that people may choose, and what positive and negative impacts do they have on the outcomes? How may cultural differences impact on the emergence and management of conflict?
- What role does communication play in the emergence and management of conflict?

The following sections explore some of the main approaches that researchers have taken in addressing these questions.

3. Classic Frameworks for Analysing Conflict

3.1. Thomas' (1976) Models of Dyadic Conflict

Kenneth Thomas (1976), in a classic paper, proposed two complementary models of conflict—a process model and a structural model. The process model focuses on the sequence of events within a conflict episode, whilst the structural model focuses on the underlying factors that influence the events.

In his process model, Thomas (1976) proposes that a conflict episode comprises five main events from the viewpoint of one of the parties: frustration, conceptualization, behaviour, other's reaction, and outcome, with the outcome of a given episode setting the stage for subsequent episodes on the same issue. Thomas' specification of the behavioural element in this process is particularly well known. He applied Blake and Mouton's (1964) classic managerial grid to the study of conflict, arguing that people may hold different orientations towards a given conflict, depending on the degree to which they want to satisfy their own concerns and the degree to which they want to satisfy the other's concerns. He identified five orientations: neglect, appeasement, domination, compromise and integration (see Figure 1). Neglect reflects avoidance or indifference, in that no attention is paid to the concerns of either self or other. Appeasement reflects a lack of concern for self, but a high concern for the other, whilst domination represents a desire to win at the other's expense. Compromise is intermediate between appeasement and domination, and is often the least satisfactory for the two parties. Integration represents a problem-solving orientation where there is a desire to integrate both parties' concerns.

A number of different terms are now in widespread use for these five orientations, and these are shown in Table 1. In the rest of this chapter, the terms used are: collaborative, competitive, compromising, accommodative and avoiding.

Thomas and Kilmann (1974) developed the Thomas–Kilmann conflict MODE instrument to measure people's conflict handling orientations. However, Rahim (1983) criticized its validity and reliability, and developed the 'Rahim Organizational Conflict Inventory-II' (ROCI-II Instrument). It achieved higher reliability scores, and this instrument has been widely used by researchers in management studies and intercultural communication. However, Sorenson,

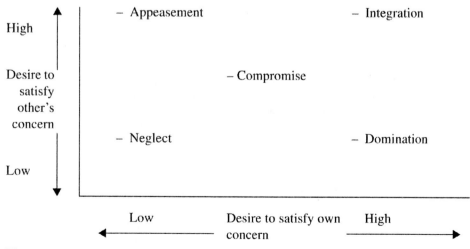

Figure 1. Thomas' 'grid' framework of conflict management orientations (Based on Thomas 1976: 900)

Table 1.   Main terms used as labels for the five conflict management orientations

High self/high other concern	High self/low other concern	Medium self/ medium other concern	Low self/high other concern	Low self/low other concern
—Integrating (Thomas 1976; Rahim 1992) —Collaborative (Thomas 1976) —Problem solving (De Dreu 1997)	—Dominating (Thomas 1976; Rahim 1992) —Competitive (Thomas 1976) —Contending (De Dreu 1997)	—Compromising (Thomas 1976; Rahim 1992) —Sharing (Thomas 1976)	—Appeasing (Thomas 1976) —Accommodative (Thomas 1976) —Obliging (Rahim 1992) —Yielding (De Dreu 1997)	—Neglecting (Thomas 1976) —Avoidant/avoiding (Thomas 1976; Rahim 1992; De Dreu 1997)

Morse and Savage (1999) actually measured the underlying concerns particular to the dual concern model (i.e. self vs. others) and found that only dominating and appeasement strategy choice correlated with these concerns; the more integrative strategies (i.e. problem solving and obliging) shared little variance and seemed subject to other contextual variables.

3.2. Intercultural Perspectives

In his structural model, Thomas (1976) maintains that people's response styles are hierarchically ordered, in that they have a dominant style, a back-up style, a least-preferred style and so on. He suggested that this hierarchy could be influenced by factors such as personality, motives and abilities. Could culture, therefore, influence this hierarchy, with some orientations being more prevalent in certain societies than in others? Many cross-cultural researchers have explored this question, and a widespread finding (e.g., Bond and Hwang 1986; Morris et al. 1998; Ohbuchi and Takahashi 1994; Trubinsky, Ting-Toomy and Lin 1991) is that a neglect style (that is also labeled avoidance) is more common among East Asians than among Americans. Yet, van Meurs (2003) found there were also differences between British and Dutch managers in this respect. Her results showed that although managers preferred a collaborative approach, the British managers were more avoiding than the Dutch managers, both in their own eyes and in those of the Dutch. While Britain and the Netherlands are often grouped together in terms of cultural values, they differ in terms of their need to avoid uncertainty, with the Dutch having a greater aversion to uncertainty and ambiguity (Hofstede 1991, 2001). This is a value that could have a major impact on preferences for handling conflict.

These findings could be regarded as conceptually problematic, because according to Thomas' orientation framework, neglect is an ineffective orientation, in that it reflects a lack of concern for the interests of either self or other and entails withdrawal. In fact, other researchers have found that avoiding is motivated by a concern for the relationship with the people involved (e.g., De

Dreu 1997; Leung et al. 1990; Markus and Kitayama 1991; Morris et al. 1998). Fried-man, Chi and Liu (2006) proposed that far from reflecting lack of concern, an avoiding style could result from concern for others. They hypothesized that it could reflect three possible concerns: (a) concern that a direct approach will damage the relationship, (b) concern that a direct approach will be more costly in cost–benefit terms, and (c) genuine concern for others based on personal values. They also hypothesized that the hierarchical status of the people involved in the conflict would have an impact. Using respondents from Taiwan and the USA, their results show a greater tendency for Taiwanese to use avoidance than Americans do. They found that this was explained by higher Taiwanese expectations that direct conflict will hurt the relationship with the other party, and by greater intrinsic concern for others. They found that it was not explained by differences in expected career costs/benefits of good/bad relations with others. In addition, their Taiwanese respondents showed more sensitivity to hierarchy than their American respondents did, in that avoidance behaviour was even more important for them when the other party was of higher status.

Superficially these studies suggest that Thomas' (1976) grid framework has limited cross-cultural validity. In fact, however, it is important to distinguish people's orientations (i.e. the degree to which they want to satisfy their own desires and those of the opposing party) and the tactics that people use to pursue them. This is a distinction that Thomas himself originally made, and Friedman, Chi and Liu's (2006) qualitative data illustrate its importance. They found that their Chinese respondents often displayed a long-term orientation, reporting tactics such as 'do nothing right now, but draw a lesson for future actions' and 'say nothing but collect more data on my own'. In other words, they found that avoidance was a tactic for achieving a satisfactory resolution of the conflict in the longer-term.

Van Meurs (2003) wanted to assess the motivations for conflict styles by measuring individual's concern for clarity, control and inconvenience without the focus on self vs. other. She found that managers were equally concerned about clarity but that British managers were more concerned than Dutch managers about inconvenience (i.e., to prevent awkward and uncomfortable situations from happening or difficult questions from being asked). They are unlikely to do so because they care for the other party, so it may be that the Dutch managers are extremely unconcerned about inconvenience, mainly because they care more about clarity and control regardless of harmony. Indeed, a concern for inconvenience significantly predicted managers' use of avoiding.

From an intercultural point of view, it is vital, therefore, to explore the tactics that people use, as well as people's desired outcomes for a particular conflict episode and their generally preferred style or orientation for handling it. Lytle (1999), for example, in her study of Chinese conflict management styles, reports several categories of behaviour that cannot easily be linked with the grid framework, because they are tactics rather than orientations or styles. They include group-oriented behaviour (such as consulting with the group to solve a problem, reframing the problem as a group problem and appealing to the group for help) and relational behaviour (including building up the relationship with the other party, and building up 'guanxi' or social connections with others).

3.3. Brown and Levinson's Face Model

A second classic study that has had a major impact on studies of conflict is Brown and Levinson's (1987) face model of politeness. These authors start with the basic assumption that "all competent adult members of a society have (and know each other to have) 'face', the public self-image that every member wants to claim for himself" (Brown and Levinson 1987: 61). They further propose that face consists of two related aspects: negative face and positive face. They define negative face as a person's want to be unimpeded by others, the desire to be free to act as s/he chooses and not be imposed upon. They define positive face as a person's want to be appreciated and approved of by selected others, in terms of personality, desires, behaviour, values, and so on. In other words, negative face represents a desire for autonomy, and positive face represents a desire for approval. The authors also draw attention to another important distinction: the distinction between self-face and other-face.

Brown and Levinson (1987) point out that face is something that is emotionally invested; it can be lost, maintained or enhanced in interaction, and so interlocutors constantly need to pay attention to it. They assume that people typically cooperate with each other in maintaining face in interaction, because people are mutually vulnerable to face attack: if one person attacks another person's face, the other is likely to retaliate. Moreover, they argue that some speech acts (such as criticism and directives) are inherently face-threatening, and that conflict can be avoided by managing those speech acts in contextually appropriate ways. They claim that there are five super-strategies for handling face-threatening acts:

- bald on-record performance (clear, unambiguous and concise speech)
- positive politeness (language that is 'approach-based' and treats the hearer as an in-group member)
- negative politeness (language that is 'avoidance-based' and respects the hearer's desire for freedom and autonomy)
- off-record performance (indirect and comparatively ambiguous speech)
- non-performance of the face-threatening act.

People choose which super-strategy to use by assessing the 'weightiness' of the speech act. According to Brown and Levinson (1987) this entails assessing the power differential between the interlocutors, the distance–closeness between them, and the degree of imposition (or face-threat) of the message itself.

3.4. Limitations of Brown and Levinson's Face Model

Brown and Levinson's (1987) face model has been hugely influential. Numerous studies have used it as an analytic framework and many others have investigated one or more of its elements. Nevertheless, there have also been widespread criticisms of it, and here we consider those that are most pertinent to the study of conflict.

As explained in section 3.3, Brown and Levinson's (1987) framework starts with the assumption that harmony is the desired option, because we all want our own face needs to be upheld. Culpeper (2005, Culpeper, Bousfield and Wichmann 2003), on the other hand, argues that people may sometimes want to be deliberately offensive or face-threatening, and that Brown and Levinson's (1987) framework is not broad enough to cater for this. He therefore proposes a set of 'impoliteness' super-strategies that are mirror images of Brown and Levinson's politeness super-strategies. When speakers use these strategies, their intention is to attack the hearer's face, rather than to uphold it. Culpeper (2005, Culpeper, Bousfield and Wichmann 2003) draws on a variety of data sources to provide authentic examples of the use of these various super-strategies.

Other researchers have questioned whether Brown and Levinson's (1987) focus on the performance of (face-threatening) speech acts provides a broad enough basis for analysing the complexities of (dis)harmony in interaction. Spencer-Oatey (2005), for example, argues that rapport is dependent on the participants' dynamic management of three main factors: interactional wants (both task-related and relational), face sensitivities, and perceived sociality rights and obligations. She maintains that relational conflict is likely to emerge if the various participants' expectations over each of these factors are not handled appropriately, and that a pre-requisite for maintaining positive rapport is thus for each of the participants to be aware of and/or sensitive to the interactional wants, face sensitivities, and perceived sociality rights and obligations that they each hold. Spencer-Oatey (2000: 29–30) also proposes that people may have different orientations towards positive rapport:

1. Rapport-enhancement orientation: a desire to strengthen or enhance harmonious relations between interlocutors;
2. Rapport-maintenance orientation: a desire to maintain or protect harmonious relations between the interlocutors;
3. Rapport-neglect orientation: a lack of concern or interest in the quality of relations between the interlocutors (perhaps because of a focus on self);
4. Rapport-challenge orientation: a desire to challenge or impair harmonious relations between the interlocutors

She points out that people's motives for holding any of these orientations could be various.

3.5. A Synthesized Summary

Building on the theorizing of Thomas (1976), Brown and Levinson (1987), Spencer-Oatey (2000), along with Friedman, Chi and Liu's (2006) and van Meurs' (2003) findings, it seems that the motivations underlying these conflict-handling tactics can be multiple, and can include the following (interrelated) concerns:

- Cost–benefit considerations (the impact of the handling of the conflict on the instrumental concerns of self and/or other)
- Rapport considerations (the impact of the handling of the conflict on the smoothness/harmony between the parties)
- Relational considerations (the impact of the handling of the conflict on the degree of distance–closeness and equality–inequality between the parties)
- Effectiveness considerations (the impact of the handling of the conflict on the degree of concern for clarity, control, and inconvenience between parties)

Thomas' five conflict-handling orientations or styles cannot be mapped in a straightforward manner onto these underlying concerns, and thus cannot be explained simply in terms of concern for self versus concern for other, as Thomas's (1976) and Rahim's (1983, 1992) frameworks suggest. Similarly, styles and tactics do not have a one-to-one relationship. Let us take avoidance as an example. If I avoid handling a conflict, it could be that I want to withdraw from the problem (as indicated by Thomas' grid), but there could also be several other possibilities. It could be that I want to maintain or build rapport with the other person; it could be that I want to show respect for the superordinate status of the other person; or it could be that my long-term goal is to dominate my opponent, and that I feel the best way of achieving this is to initially avoid conflict whilst I muster my arguments and/or gain support from elsewhere. Alternatively, I may feel uncomfortable avoiding the problem, because I have a low tolerance for uncertainty, and prefer to maintain clarity and control. Finding an effective solution may be more important to me, even if it risks damaging the relationship, because I believe I can amend that at a later date. Or I may feel that by NOT avoiding the problem, I will be able to resolve it and thus maintain good relations.

Brown and Levinson's (1987) politeness super-strategies, and Culpeper's (2005, Culpeper, Bousfield and Wichmann 2003) impoliteness super-strategies are potential verbal tactics that primarily relate to rapport considerations (although naturally they can have a knock-on effect on both relational and cost– benefit considerations). Analysis of the verbal tactics that people use in conflict episodes is an area where applied linguistics can make a valuable contribution to the study of conflict (see section 5.2).

The studies discussed in section 3.2 highlight the importance of considering culture in the Bermuda Triangle of conflict, and we explore this in detail in the next section.

4. Conflict and Culture

4.1. Conflict and Cultural Values

Hofstede (1991, 2001) identified five dimensions of cultural values (individualism–collectivism, high–low power distance, masculinity–femininity, high–low uncertainty avoidance, and long/short-term orientation), and many researchers have focused on the impact of individualism–collectivism on conflict management styles and preferences. Hofstede defines this dimension as follows:

> Individualism stands for a society in which the ties between individuals are loose: everyone is expected to look after him/herself and her/his immediate family only. Collectivism stands for a society in which people from birth onwards are integrated into strong, cohesive in-groups, which throughout people's lifetime continue to protect them in exchange for unquestioning loyalty.
>
> Hofstede 2001: 225

Leung (1987) found that respondents from an individualist society (the USA) differed in their conflict-handling preferences from those from a collectivist society (China), although he also found some culture-general results. Ting-

Table 2. Cultural values, self-construals and the conflict process (Derived from Ting-Toomey 1999: 211–212)

Individualist values and independent self-construals	Collectivist values and interdependent self-construals
1. Conflict is perceived as closely related to the goals or outcomes that are salient to the respective individual conflict parties in a given conflict situation.	1. Conflict is weighted against the face threat incurred in the conflict negotiation process; it is also interpreted in the web of ingroup/ outgroup relationships.
2. Communication in the conflict process is viewed as dissatisfying when the conflict parties are not willing to deal with the conflict openly and honestly.	2. Communication in the conflict process is perceived as threaten-ing when the conflict parties push for substantive discussion before proper facework management.
3. Conversely, communication in the conflict process is viewed as satisfying when the conflict parties are willing to confront the conflict issues openly and share their feelings honestly (i.e. assertively but not aggressively).	3. Communication in the conflict interaction is viewed as satisfying when the conflict parties engage in mutual face-saving and face-giving behaviour and attend to both verbal and nonverbal signals.
4. The conflict process or outcome is perceived as unproductive when face issues are not addressed and relational/group feelings are not attended to properly.	4. The conflict outcome is perceived as unproductive when no tangible outcomes are reached or no plan of action is developed.
5. The conflict outcome is perceived as productive when tangible sol-utions are reached and objective criteria are met.	5. The conflict process or outcome is defined as productive when both conflict parties can claim win–win results on the facework front in addition to substantive agreement.
6. Effective and appropriate man-agement of conflict means individual goals are addressed and differences are dealt with openly, honestly, and properly in relation to timing and situational context.	6. Appropriate and effective management of conflict means that the mutual 'faces' of the conflict par-ties are saved or even upgraded in the interaction and they have dealt with the conflict episode strategically in conjunction with substantive gains or losses.

Toomey (1999: 211–212) argues that individualist and collectivist values are reflected in independent and interdependent self-construals respectively, and that these can impact on conflict as shown in Table 2.

Not all studies have completely supported the link between individualism–collectivism and conflict-handling preferences. For example, Gire and Carment (1992) investigated Canadian (individualist) and Nigerian (collectivist) preferences and found there were various similarities. Moreover, others have explored the influence of other values. Leung et al. (1990), for instance, investigated the impact of masculinity–femininity using respondents from Canada and The Netherlands (masculine and feminine societies respectively but both highly individualistic, according to Hofstede's data), and found that their Dutch respondents preferred more harmony-enhancing procedures than their Canadian respondents did.

Other researchers have used Schwartz's (1992; Schwartz et al. 2001) framework of cultural values to examine the interrelationship between values and conflict management styles. Schwartz's framework has the advantage that it can be measured easily and reliably at the individual level, whereas Hofstede's figures are culture level measures; moreover, the other main individual level measure, independent–interdependent self-construal (as referred to by Ting-Toomey 1999), may be too broad and also of dubious validity (Kim 2005: 108).

In Schwartz's (1992; Schwartz et al. 2001) individual-level framework, there are ten universal value constructs, and they fall into four main groupings: Self-Enhancement, Self-Transcendence, Openness to Change, and Conservation. Morris et al. (1998) analysed the extent to which Schwartz's cultural values could predict two of the grid framework conflict handling styles: avoidance and competition. In a study of Chinese and US managers in joint venture firms, they predicted that the Chinese managers would have a greater preference for avoidance than the US managers, and that the US managers would have a greater preference for competition than the Chinese managers. These predictions were confirmed. They also hypothesized that (a) an avoiding style would reflect an individual's orientation towards Conservation values, and that any Chinese–US differences in avoiding style would be mediated by country differences in preference for Conservation; and that (b) a competition style would reflect an individual's orientation towards Self-Enhancement, that any Chinese–US differences in competition style would be mediated by country differences in preference for Self-Enhancement. Both of these hypotheses were confirmed.

Bilsky and Jehn (2002), in a study using German students, found that avoiding behaviour was negatively correlated with Self-Direction (a component value of Openness to Change), and since Schwartz (1992) argues that Openness to Change and Conservation (with the latter comprising the component values Security, Conformity and Tradition) are polar opposites, this fits in with Morris et al.'s (1998) findings. In other words, the studies found that Conservation was important to Chinese MBA students and this was linked with a preference to avoid conflict, whereas the polar opposite value Openness to Change was important to German students and this was linked with a preference NOT to avoid conflict.

Van Meurs (2003) suggests that the role of Uncertainty Avoidance needs to be researched further, as Germanic clusters have been found to be more uncertainty avoidant than Anglo clusters (Ashkanasy, Trevor-Roberts and Earnshaw 2002; House et al. 2002) and this could affect, these groups' preferences for avoiding conflict. Unfortunately, to date, Uncertainty Avoidance is not adequately represented by individual-level value measures.

4.2. Conflict, Culture, and Context

One of the weaknesses of this macro level research is that it ignores a lot of contextual variation. Although there may be differences (such as between Americans and Chinese) in preferred styles for managing conflict, such generalizations can gloss over the rich complexity and variation that exists in real-life situations. Davidheiser's (2005) study of mediation practices in southwestern Gambia illustrates this point very vividly. He observed and recorded 121 live conflict mediation events, conducted 54 ethnographic interviews and 39 semi-structured interviews, and held panel sessions with Gambian mediation experts. He draws the following conclusions:

> Shared values have a profound effect both on how mediation is practiced and on the nature of the process itself. However, this impact is multi-dimensional and resists easy generalization. . . . Whilst it is true that there appear to be meta-level normative differences in orientations to mediation in the West and elsewhere, there is also great heterogeneity in both of these areas. Dichotomizing mediation praxis according to whether the practitioners are Western or non-Western, traditional or modern, high- or low-context communicators, glosses over the multiplicity of practice found outside the realm of theory and dramatically over-simplifies a complex picture.
>
> Mediation practices can be described as 'embedded', or linked to macro- and micro-level influences and varying according to the specific context and characteristics of each case. Peacemaker behaviour was influenced by numerous factors, including the sociocultural perspectives of the participants and situational variables such as the type of dispute in question, the nature of the social relations between the parties, and the participants' personalities.
>
> Davidheiser 2005: 736–7

If we are to gain an in-depth understanding, therefore, of intercultural conflict in real-life situations, it is vital to consider contextual variability. In fact, as Bond, Žegarac and Spencer-Oatey (2000) point out, culture can be manifested in a variety of ways, in addition to cultural values, including perception of contextual variables. Spencer-Oatey's (2005) rapport management framework identifies some features that can be subject to cultural variation yet that are also contextually sensitive. These include (but are not limited to) the behavioural norms, conventions and protocols of given communicative events (e.g., how formal they 'should' be), the 'scripts' as to how given communicative events should be enacted; the rights and obligations associated with given role relationships; and the contractual/legal agreements and requirements (written and unwritten) that apply to a given organization, profession or social group. When people's expectations are not fulfilled, they may perceive this as 'negatively eventful' (Goffman 1963: 7), and this can (but, of course, need not necessarily) be a source of interpersonal conflict. Many cross-cultural and intercultural pragmatic studies aim to unpack and illuminate these processes through careful analysis, as section 5.2 reports.

5. Conflict and Communication

5.1. Communicative Conflict Styles

Much of the argumentation on conflict and cultural values (see section 4.1) touches on the role of communication. Directness–indirectness is seen as having a particularly important impact on both the instigation and the management of conflict. It has been found that different cultures may endorse the same conflict management orientation (e.g., collaborative) yet vary in the way they handle it verbally. Pruitt (1983) found that both direct and indirect information exchange correlated with socially desirable, collaborative agreements. Similarly, Adair, Okumura and Brett (2001) showed that Americans achieve collaborative integration of ideas through direct communication but that Japanese do so through indirect communication which allows people to infer preferences. They concluded that "facility in direct or indirect communications may not lead to joint gains if parties do not also have a norm for information sharing", and that collaborative behaviour is based on different motivations, dependent on the culture (Adair, Okumura and Brett 2001: 380). Similarly, van Meurs (2003) found that Dutch managers equated directness with being consultative, whereas the British preferred to use indirectness and be consultative.

In much intercultural research, directness–indirectness is assumed to be associated with individualism–collectivism and/or independent–interdependent self-construal, and it is linked with concern for face. Unfortunately, however, the majority of studies (in management, cross-cultural psychology and in communication studies) conflate the measurement of the two, using, for example, a questionnaire item on directness both as a measure of Individualism/ Independence and as a measure of communicative directness–indirectness. This, of course, is circular and unsatisfactory. In addition, there is a need to consider whether other communicative styles are important.

Hammer (2005) proposes two fundamental dimensions (directness–indirectness, emotional expressiveness–restraint), and four types of conflict styles: Discussion Style (direct but emotionally restrained), Engagement Style (direct and emotionally expressive), Accommodation Style (indirect and emotionally restrained), and Dynamic Style (indirect and emotionally expressive). Hammer has developed an Intercultural Conflict Styles Inventory [ICSI] in relation to this, and has used it, along with his four-quadrant model, in a variety of applied contexts. He reports that it has been of practical benefit in his mediation sessions.

> In one mediation I conducted, both parties completed the ICSI prior to the initial mediation session. After reviewing the mediation process with the parties, I then reviewed with them their ICSs. One of the disputants–' style was 'engagement' while the other was 'accommodation.' A large part of the conflict between these individuals had involved misperceptions each held of one another, based on differences in intercultural conflict resolution style. For example, the accommodation style individual felt the other party was 'rude and aggressive' while the engagement individual characterized the accommodation style person as deceptive and lacking in commitment. After discussing these misperceptions in terms of differences in conflict resolution styles (rather than personal traits), the disputants were better able to address their substantive disagreements.
>
> Hammer 2005: 691–2

However, one very major weakness of virtually all the research into the role of communication in conflict processes that is carried out in management, cross-cultural psychology and communication studies is that it is nearly always based on self-report data, using Likert-style responses to questionnaire items. There is a very great need for discourse-based research, of the kind reported in the next section.

5.2. Conflict and Discourse Research

One very significant contribution that applied linguistics can make to our understanding of conflict processes is the identification of the types of linguistic tactics that people may use to implement the conflict management styles that Thomas (1976) identified. For example, how may people avoid conflict? What insights does applied linguistic research offer on this question? Most linguistic research does not attempt to draw any explicit links with frameworks in business and communication studies, but an exception is Holmes and Marra (2004). Using their New Zealand workplace data (see Marra and Holmes in this volume), these researchers explored the role that leaders may play in managing conflict in meetings. They argue that the effective management of conflict begins well before any actual conflictual episodes occur, and demonstrate how 'assertion of the agenda' is one effective technique that skillful leaders use to avoid conflict. They provide several examples of actual discourse to illustrate ways in which chairpersons achieve this, including moving talk on to the next agenda item, and directing people's attention back to a key point, when disparate views begin to be expressed. They also identify a second tactic that could be regarded as an avoidance strategy: diverting a contentious issue to another venue for discussion. Saft (2004) also found that the ways in which meetings are chaired has a major impact on conflict behaviour. He analyses two different sets of university faculty meetings in Japan, in which arguments were frequent in one set but rare in the other. Saft demonstrates how the chairpersons' control and organization of turn-taking in the meetings was crucial, in that it either constrained the expression of opposition or enabled it.

In both of these studies, the researchers demonstrate how conflict can be avoided through skillful management of meetings. This data thus indicates that far from being a negative strategy that shows lack of concern both for self and for other (see Figure 1 above), promoting conflict avoidance can be a very effective and positive management strategy. This applied linguistic research thus supports other work in organizational behaviour and cross-cultural psychology (e.g., De Dreu 1997; Gire and Carmet 1992; Leung et al. 1990; Markus and Kitayama 1991; Morris et al. 1998; Ohbuchi and Takahashi 1994) that maintains that conflict avoidance in fact can be motivated by a concern (rather than lack of concern) for others.

Context is important in terms of the choice of strategy (Rahim 1992). A crisis situation may need a dominating strategy, whereas a complex problem may require an integrating (i.e. problem solving) approach, and a relational issue may require people to avoid each other for the short term. Holmes and Marra's (2004) study of workplace discourse confirmed the impact that context can have on conflict management tactics. They found the following factors to be important in influencing leaders' choices of strategy:

- Type of interaction (e.g., workplace meeting), its level of formality, number of participants, and so on;
- Workplace culture, including organizational culture and community of practice culture;
- Importance/seriousness of the issue;
- Leadership style.

In relation to avoidance, they point out that the seriousness of the issue is a key contextual factor. They found that, in their data, good chairpersons and effective leaders tended to encourage 'working through conflict' when a decision was serious or when it was an important one, such as one that set a precedent for subsequent decisions.

Much linguistic research focuses on analysing the detailed linguistic strategies that occur in conflictive discourse, and does not attempt to link them to the macro styles identified in business and communication studies. For example, Günthner (2000) analyses the ways in which German participants in a German– Chinese conversation maximize the expression of dissent, and ways in which the participants end a confrontational frame. She identifies three strategies in her discourse data that the German participants used for signaling dissent in a focused and maximized way:

- 'Dissent-formats': the speaker provides a (partial) repetition of the prior speaker's utterance and then negates it or replaces parts of it with a contrasting element.
- 'Dissent-ties': the speaker latches her disagreeing utterance to the prior turn, and thus produces a syntactic and lexical continuation of the preceding utterance, but then in continuing it demonstrates consequences which contradict the argumentative line of the first speaker.
- Reported speech: the speaker reproduces the opponent's prior utterance (maybe several turns later) in order to oppose it.

She also identifies three strategies that the participants use to (try to) end a confrontational frame:

- Concession, when one participant 'gives in'.
- Compromise, where a speaker moves towards the other party's position and proposes a possible 'middle ground'.
- Change of activity, where a speaker introduces a new verbal activity, such as focusing on the situation at hand (e.g., by enquiring 'what kind of tea is this?')

These last three strategies could, in fact, be linked with the macro styles of avoiding, obliging, competing, sharing and problem solving. Concession is an obliging strategy, compromise is a sharing strategy, and change of activity could be regarded as an avoiding strategy.

Another example of the detailed analysis of linguistic strategies in conflictive encounters is Honda (2002). She analyses Japanese public affairs talk shows, and examines the ways in which oppositional comments are redressed or down-played. Table 3 shows the classification of strategies that she identifies.

Honda (2002) also demonstrates how some confrontations in her data initially proceed in an unmitigated fashion, but later the opposing parties take restorative action and end their argument in a seemingly cooperative fashion. In other words, as with Gunthner's study, different tactics were used at different points in the conflict. This suggests once again that context (in this case, discourse context) can influence choice of strategy, and that macro designations

Table 3. Redressive strategies identified by Honda (2002) in her analysis of Japanese public affairs talk shows

Redressive strategy	Gloss	Example
Mollifiers	Remarks that precede the expression of opposition, and downplay its directness	—Initial praise —Initial token agreement —Initial acceptance of the opponent's point of view —Initial denial of disagreement or one's own remark
Mitigators	Features within the expression of opposition that downplay its directness	—Pauses —Discourse markers that show hesitation —Minimizers such as a little, maybe
Untargeted opposition	Expression of opposition that does not make it clear whether or not it is targeted at a specific person or viewpoint	—Remark that contradicts or differs from the opponent's view but the opposition is attributed as being with a third party rather than with the opponent —Remark that contradicts or differs from the opponent's view but is not directed at the opponent, or made in response to the opponent's previous remarks

of people's conflict management styles will only be able to provide indicative generalizations of their normative preferences.

A second major contribution that applied linguistics can make to our understanding of conflict processes, especially in intercultural contexts, is to reveal how conflicts may arise by carefully analysing authentic interactions. Bailey (1997, 2000), for example, analyses service encounters between Korean retailers and African-American customers to help throw light on the longstanding conflict between these two groups that had been widely reported in the media. Analysing video recordings of the service encounters, he found that there were noticeable differences in the ways that Korean and African-American customers interacted with the Korean retailers, such as in terms of length of the encounter, overall quantity of talk, inclusion of personable topics and small talk, and the amount of affect displayed. Follow-up interviews with the customers and the retailers indicated that both the Korean retailers and the African-American customers evaluated the other negatively, interpreting the other's behaviour as disrespectful, and as racist (in the case of the Korean retailers) and as intimidating (in the case of the African-American customers). Bailey draws the following conclusion:

> ... divergent communicative patterns in these everyday service encounters simultaneously represent (1) an on-going *source of tensions*; and (2) a *local enactment of pre-existing social conflicts.*
>
> Bailey 2000: 87 (italics in the original)

Another example is Spencer-Oatey and Xing (2003). These researchers compare two Chinese–British business welcome meetings which were very similar in many respects, yet were evaluated very differently by the participants. One of them was part of a very successful business visit, whilst the other led to a very problematic visit which came to a climax on the final day when there was a heated dispute that lasted for nearly two and a half hours. The authors analyse the reasons for the differences in outcomes, and identify the following: the role of the interpreter, the role of the chairperson, mismatches between British and Chinese culturally-based and contextually-based assumptions and expectations, confusion over the roles and relative status of the participants, and a confounding effect between all of these factors.

6. Concluding Comments

The various approaches to studying and analysing conflict reported in this chapter each have their own strengths and weaknesses. In terms of research methodology, most organizational psychological and communication researchers use either simulated role play in experimental-type conditions, or self-report questionnaire items. Whilst these approaches are useful in many respects, they have some serious limitations and need to be complemented by studies of authentic conflictive encounters and situations. In such studies various types of research data need to be collected including ethnographic, discourse and/or post-event interview data, in order to improve the validity and granularity of research findings on conflict. Applied linguists have a major role to play here. However, it needs to be acknowledged that much applied linguistic research is impenetrable for people from other disciplines. The analyses are often so detailed and so full of linguistic technical terms, that they are difficult for non-linguists to follow. Moreover, it is hard for people (such as intercultural trainers) to pick out the practical relevance of the findings.

Up to now there has been very little interchange of conceptual frameworks and research findings between applied linguistic researchers of conflict and those working within organizational behaviour and communication studies. Findings are typically published in different journals, and people may be unaware of each other's work. We hope that this chapter will help to start breaking down this divide, and that there will be greater interdisciplinary sharing and discussion of ideas, concepts and findings, even if some conflict is a concomitant part of the process!

References

Adair, Wendi L., Tetsushi Okumura and Jeanne M. Brett, 200,1 Negotiation behaviors when cultures collide: The U.S. and Japan. *Journal of Applied Psychology* 86: 371–385.

Ashkanasy, Neal M., Edwin Trevor-Roberts and Louise Earnshaw. 2002. The Anglo cluster: Legacy of the British Empire. *Journal of World Business* 37: 28–39.

Bailey, Benjamin. 1997. Communication of respect in interethnic service encounters. *Language in Society* 26: 327–356.

Bailey, Benjamin. 2000. Communicative behavior and conflict between African-American customers and Korean immigrant retailers in Los Angeles. *Discourse and Society* 11: 86–108.

Bilsky, Wolfgang and Karen A. Jehn. 2002. Organisationskultur und individuelle Werte: Belege für eine gemeinsame Struktur [Organizational culture and individual values: evidence for a common structure]. In: Michael Myrtek (ed.) *Die Person im biologischen und sozialen Kontext*, 211–228. Göttingen: Hogrefe

Blake, Robert R. and Jane S. Mouton. 1964. *The Managerial Grid*. Houston, TX: Gulf Publishing.

Bond, Michael H. and Kwang-Kuo Hwang. 1986. The social psychology of Chinese people. In: Michael H. Bond (ed.) *The Psychology of the Chinese People*, 213–266. Hong Kong: Oxford University Press.

Bond, Michael H., Vladimir Žegarac and Helen Spencer-Oatey. 2000. Culture as an explanatory variable: problems and possibilities. In: Helen Spencer-Oatey (ed.) *Culturally Speaking. Managing Rapport through Talk across Cultures*, 47–71. London: Continuum.

Brett, Jeanne M. and Tetsushi Okumura. 1998. Inter- and intra-cultural negotiation: U.S. and Japanese negotiators. *Academy of Management Journal* 41: 410–424.

Brown, Penelope and Stephen C. Levinson. 1987. *Politeness. Some Universals in Language Usage.* Cambridge: CUP. Originally published as Universals in language usage: politeness phenomenon. In: Esther Goody (ed.) 1978 *Questions and Politeness: Strategies in Social Interaction.* New York: CUP.

Culpeper, Jonathan. 2005. Impoliteness and entertainment in the television quiz show: *The Weakest Link. Journal of Politeness Research* 1: 35–72.

Culpeper, Jonathan, Derek Bousfield and Anne Wichmann. 2003. Impoliteness revisited: with special reference to dynamic and prosodic aspects. *Journal of Pragmatics* 35: 1545–1579.

Davidheiser, Mark. 2005. Culture and mediation: a contemporary processual analysis from southwestern Gambia. *International Journal of Intercultural Relations* 29: 713–738.

De Dreu, Carsten K.W. 1997. Productive conflict: The importance of conflict management and conflict issue. In: Carston K.W. De Dreu and Evert van de Vliert (eds.) *Using Conflict in Organizations*, 9–22. London: Sage.

Friedman, Ray, Shu-Cheng Chi and Leigh Anne Liu. 2006. An expectancy model of Chinese–American differences in conflict-avoiding. *Journal of International Business Studies* 37: 76–91.

Gire, James T. and D. William Carment. 1992. Dealing with disputes: The influence of individualism-collectivism. *Journal of Social Psychology* 133: 81–95.

Goffman, Erving. 1963. *Behavior in Public Places.* New York: Free Press.

Günthner, Susanne. 2000. Argumentation and resulting problems in the negotiation of rapport in a German–Chinese conversation. In: Helen Spencer-Oatey (ed.) *Culturally Speaking. Managing Rapport through Talk across Cultures,* 217–239. London: Continuum.

Hammer, Mitchell R. 2005. The intercultural conflict style inventory: a conceptual framework and measure of intercultural conflict resolution approaches. *International Journal of Intercultural Relations* 29: 675–695.

Hofstede, Geert. 1991. *Cultures and Organizations: Software of the Mind.* London: HarperCollins-Business. Hofstede, Geert 2001 *Culture's Consequences. Comparing Values, Behaviors, Institutions, and Organizations across Nations.* London: Sage.

Holmes, Janet and Meredith Marra. 2004. Leadership and managing conflict in meetings. *Pragmatics* 14(4): 439–462.

Honda, Atsuko. 2002. Conflict management in Japanese public affairs talk shows. *Journal of Pragmatics* 34: 573–608.

House, Robert, Mansour Javidan, Paul Hanges and Peter Dorfman. 2002. Understanding cultures and implicit leadership theories across the globe: an introduction to project GLOBE. *Journal of World Business* 37: 2–10.

Kim, Min-Sun. 2005. Culture-based conversational constraints theory. Individual- and culture-level analyses. In: William B. Gudykunst (ed.) *Theorizing about Intercultural Communication,* 93–117. Thousand Oaks: Sage.

Leung, Kwok. 1987. Some determinants of reactions to procedural models for conflict resolution: a cross-national study. *Journal of Personality and Social Psychology* 53(5): 898–908.

Leung, Kwok, Michael H. Bond, D. William Carment, Lila Krishnan and Wim B.G. Lie-brand. 1990. Effects of cultural femininity on preference for methods of conflict processing: A cross-cultural study. *Journal of Experimental Social Psychology* 26: 373–388.

Lytle, Anne L. 1999. Chinese conflict management styles: an exploratory study. Paper presented at the Twelfth Conference of the International Association for Conflict Management, San Sebastian, Spain, 20–23 June 1999.

Markus, Hazel R. and Shinobu Kitayama. 1991. Culture and the self: implications for cognition, emotion, and motivation. *Psychological Review* 98: 224–53.

Morris, Michael W., Katherine Y. Williams, Kwok Leung, Richard Larrick, M.Teresa Mendoza, Deepti Bhatnagar, Jianfeng Li, Mari Kondo, Jin-Lian Luo and Jun-Chen Hu. 1998. Conflict management style: Accounting for cross-national differences. *Journal of International Business Studies* 29(4): 729–748.

Ohbuchi, Ken-Ichi and Yumi Takahashi. 1994. Cultural styles of conflict management in Japanese and Americans: passivity, covertness, and effectiveness of strategies. *Journal of Applied Social Psychology* 24(15): 1345–1366.

Pruitt, Dean G. 1983. Achieving integrative agreement. In: Max H. Bazerman and Roy J. Lewicki (eds.) *Negotiating in organizations,* 35–50. Beverly Hills, CA: Sage.

Rahim, M. Afzalur. 1983. A measure of styles of handling interpersonal conflict. *Academy of Management Journal* 26: 368–376.

Rahim, M. Afzalur. 1992. *Managing Conflict in Organizations.* Westport, CT: Preager Publishers. Saft, Scott 2004 Conflict as interactional accomplishment in Japanese: arguments in university faculty meetings. *Language in Society* 33: 549–584.

Schwartz, Shalom H. 1992. Universals in the content and structure of values: theoretical advances and empirical tests in 20 countries. In: Mark P. Zanna (ed.) *Advances in Experimental Social Psychology* (Vol. 25), 1–65. San Diego: Academic Press.

Schwartz, Shalom H., Gila Melech, Arielle Lehmann, Steven Burgess, Mari Harris and Vicki Owens. 2001. Extending the cross-cultural validity of the theory of basic human values with a different method of measurement. *Journal of Cross-Cultural Psychology* 32(5): 59–542.

Sorenson, Ritch L, Eric A. Morse and Grant T. Savage. 1999. What motivates choice of conflict strategies? *International Journal of Conflict Management* 10: 25–44.

Spencer-Oatey, Helen. 2000. Rapport management: a framework for analysis. In: Helen Spencer-Oatey (ed.) *Culturally Speaking. Managing Rapport through Talk across Cultures*, 11–46. London: Continuum.

Spencer-Oatey, Helen. 2005. (Im)Politeness, face and perceptions of rapport: unpacking their bases and interrelationships. *Journal of Politeness Research* 1: 95–119.

Spencer-Oatey, Helen and Jianyu Xing. 2007. The impact of culture on interpreter behaviour. In Helga Kotthoff and Helen Spencer-Oatey (eds.), *Handbook of Intercultural Communication*, 219–236. Berlin: Mouton de Gruyter.

Thomas, Kenneth W. 1976. Conflict and conflict management. In: Marvin Dunnette (ed.) *The Handbook of Industrial and Organizational Psychology*, 889–935. Chicago: Rand McNally.

Thomas, Kenneth W. and Ralph H. Kilmann. 1974. *The Thomas–Kilmann Conflict Mode Instrument*. Tuxedo, NY: Xicom.

Thomas, Kenneth W. and Warren Schmidt. 1976. A survey of managerial interests with respect to conflict. *Academy of Management Journal* 19: 315–318.

Ting-Toomey, Stella. 1999. *Communicating across Cultures*. New York: The Guilford Press.

Trubinsky, Paula, Stella Ting-Toomey and Sung Ling Lin. 1991. The influence of individualism–collectivism and self-monitoring on conflict styles. *International Journal of Intercultural Relations* 15(1): 65–84.

van Meurs, Nathalie. 2003. Negotiations between British and Dutch managers: Cultural values, approaches to conflict management, and perceived negotiation satisfaction. Unpublished doctoral dissertation, University of Sussex, Brighton, East Sussex, UK.

5 ——————————————————————————

Discrimination in Discourse

Martin Reisigl

1. Introduction

Discrimination has become an issue that discourse analysis increasingly focuses on, especially critical discourse analysis and the research on intercultural communication. "Discrimination" means to put individuals, who are considered to be different from others, at a disadvantage. The word prototypically refers to "negative discrimination" and relates to an ethical, normative dimension, to a political as well as legal evaluation and judging against the background of democratic principles of justice and the conviction of the validity of human rights. In this respect, "discrimination" means to treat a specific social group or single members of the group, who are set apart from other groups or members of other social groups, unfairly, unjustly, for example by repressing or suppressing them, decrying them, discrediting them, debasing them, degrading them, defaming them, keeping political rights from them and establishing unjustifiable social, political, economic, educational or other inequalities, by segregating them, excluding them, etc.

In my article, I will primarily be concerned with various forms of verbal discrimination, i.e. with discrimination by language use, and with visual discrimination. Apart from this introduction, the chapter is divided into five sections. Section 2 aims to explain the concept of "social discrimination" from a general and a disciplinary point of view. Section 3 offers an overview of different types of social discrimination. Section 4 contains a brief delineation of various concepts of "discourse" that are relevant for the issue in question. Section 5 presents a discourse analytical framework that allows the approach to discursively realized social discrimination in a methodical way. Furthermore, section 5 considers various strategies of discrimination in the area of visual communication. In the final section, I argue that a critical analysis of verbal and visual discrimination is best accomplished from an interdisciplinary approach and can be an important means of anti-discrimination policy and politics.[1]

---

[1] I would like to thank Helga Kotthoff and Ingrid Piller for constructive comments on an earlier version of the article and Maura Bayer for correcting my English.

2. Concepts of "Social Discrimination"

The action verb "to discriminate" originates from the Latin "discriminare". The Latin verb derives from the noun "discrimen", which means "distinction", "difference", "separating" and "sorting out". Accordingly, "discriminare" originally denotes "distinguish", "differentiate", "separate", "set apart", and this is—so to say—the "harmless" original meaning of the word which does not yet automatically represent negative social exclusion and segregation. The English expression is first recorded to assume the negative denotation of "debasement" and "disadvantaging" in 1866, when the word related to the making of distinctions prejudicial to people of a different "color" or "race" in the USA (The Oxford English Dictionary 1989: 758).

The notion of social discrimination is connected with the infringement of justice. Thus, it serves first and foremost as a legal and political concept, although it has, among others, also been adopted by sociology, social-psychology and discourse analysis. It follows from the concept's social-ethical implications that a discourse analysis and analysis of intercultural communication concerned with the linguistic and visual realization of discrimination should become social analysis.

In discourse analytical studies and analyses of intercultural communication, the term "discrimination" is at times applied in a rather undifferentiated way, as an unquestioned term of scientific everyday language. A close look brings to the fore that "social discrimination" is a relational concept which includes at least five elements. The concept's three main constituents can be explicated as: "Someone discriminates against somebody else by doing something". "Doing something" (including "omitting doing something" and "letting something happen") stands for the discriminating action or process, which includes the two further conceptual components of "on the basis of a specific feature" and "in comparison to somebody else". In other words: "Discrimination" implies (1) social actors as perpetrators that belong to a specific social or cultural group, (2) specific persons or groups of persons affected by the discrimination (i.e. victims or beneficiaries), (3) the discriminating action or process, (4) the "distinguishing feature" or peg on which to hang the discrimination (for example "race", "gender", "language" or "sexual orientation"), and (5) a comparative figure or group in comparison to which or to whom somebody is discriminated.

(1) "Discriminators" are social actors who commit—as perpetrators—the social action of discrimination. Discriminators generally have the power to discriminate against others, or empower themselves (at least temporarily) to discriminate against others, often by the discriminatory action itself. Power asymmetry normally prevents the less powerful to discriminate against the more powerful, except for situations in which the more powerful are absent and cannot exert their power (discrimination *in absentia* is sometimes called "indirect discrimination"; see Graumann and Wintermantel 1989: 199, and see below, section 3). A differentiated analysis has to take into account that social beings adopt very different social roles and can, thus, be discriminators in a specific situation and respect (e.g. as "white" against "black" people, as men against women, as heterosexuals against homo- and bisexuals, as citizens

against noncitizens or "foreigners", as adults against children, as young people against seniors, as healthy people against the disabled or those with special needs), whereas they may become victims of discrimination in another situation and respect. Even though some forms of discrimination (like racism, nationalism and sexism) are kept alive by rather stable social structures in specific social, political and historical contexts, and are thus rather permanent in kind, discrimination is never an absolute, but always a relative matter.

(2) Victims or beneficiaries of discrimination are very often (members of) minorities or socially marginalized groups, and minoritization as well as marginalization themselves are frequently the result of discrimination. Sometimes, as in the case of sexism, in which the victims of discrimination are usually women, discriminated individuals do not belong to a numerical minority, but to a socially widely suppressed group. In certain social contexts, victims of a specific form of social discrimination can sometimes themselves become discriminators, and some victims often turn out to be manifold victims of different forms of discrimination. This latter fact has been neglected in social research for some time. Since the late 1980s and in the beginning of the 1990s, however, feminist African American scholars introduced the concepts of "multiple discrimination" and "intersectional discrimination" into the debate about particular forms of discrimination of African American women, which both differed from discrimination against other groups of women (e.g. "white" women) and from discrimination against African American men (see Fredman and Szyszak 1993: 221; Makkonen 2002: 57, 2003: 14).

"*Multiple discrimination*" is conceived of as complex discrimination on the basis of different distinguishing features and for different (e.g. racist, sexist, ageist, religious fundamentalist) reasons, which operate separately and subsequently, i.e. independently, in different social fields and situations at different times: "A disabled woman may be discriminated against on the basis of her gender in access to highly skilled work and on the basis of her disability in a situation in which a public office building is not accessible to persons with wheelchairs." (Makkonen 2002: 10).

"*Intersectional discrimination*", in contrast, is considered to be a complex discrimination on the basis of different distinguishing features and for different (e.g. racist, sexist or religious fundamentalist) reasons, which operate simultaneously and concurrently in one and the same social field and situation: "One example of such discrimination would be unjustified subjection of disabled women to undergo forced sterilization, of which there is evidence around the world: this kind of discrimination is not experienced by women generally nor by disabled men, not at least anywhere near to the same extent as disabled women." (Makkonen 2002: 11).

Makkonen also distinguishes a third form of complex discrimination, which he terms "*compound discrimination*" (Makkonen 2002: 11). According to him, "compound discrimination" relies on several grounds of discrimination which add to each other *in a particular situation*: "An illustrious example would be, to continue along the intersection of origin and gender, a situation in which the labor market is segregated on multiple basis: some jobs are considered suitable only for men, and only some jobs are reserved particularly for immigrants. In such a situation, the prospects of an immigrant woman to find a job matching her merits are markedly reduced because of compound discrimination." (Makkonen 2002: 11).

The recognition of complex discriminatory phenomena such as multiple, intersectional and compound discrimination should prevent analysts of inter-cultural communication from explaining discrimination simplistically by tak-ing "culture" or "subculture" as an essentialized and homogenous category. Only a multi-factorial analysis becomes aware of the many different facets of discrimination.

(3) The third conceptual component is the discriminating action or process itself, by which justice or human rights are infringed. It is realized in various social sectors or fields (such as legislation, work, education, housing, public services, mass media, sports) and can take the form of a (physical) action or non-action, of an active exclusion and segregation, a denial of opportunities and equal rights, different treatment, an act of ignoring, an omission, etc. It may be realized verbally or in writing (e.g. by a degrading insult, a derision or a banning) or visually (e.g. by a humiliating depiction). It can be direct or indirect, explicit or implicit, etc.

(4) The concept of discrimination always includes a "distinguishing fea-ture" or peg on which to hang the discrimination. The distinguishing features that are taken for the dissimilation and separation are frequently related to social identity markers, for instance to gender, "race", skin colour, birth, hereditary factors, age, disability, the ethnic, national or social background, the membership of a (for example national) minority, language, religion or belief, ideology, political affiliation, sexual orientation and economic situa-tion. The distinguishing criteria on the basis of which people are treated dif-ferently, negatively and adversely are often interpreted as stigmata that are considered to indicate a negative deviancy from a positive "normality" (see Goffman 1963).

Unfortunately, the reasons for discrimination are very often identified by exclusive reference to these real or fictitious features, and this is rather mis-leading, since it is not "race" which is the reason for the discrimination against a specific group of persons, but racism, which lies behind the social construc-tion of "race" categories (see Reisigl and Wodak 2001: 2–5). In most legal texts, be it on a national or an international level, one reads about "discrimination on the grounds of 'race', gender, age, etc." Such "grounds" are often conflated with "reasons", the phrase "on the grounds of" being interpreted as "for the reasons that." At this point, linguistic critique should ask for a more accurate language use that does not risk a fallacious inversion, that is to say, the identification of the reasons for discrimination on the side of the victims, instead of identify-ing the reasons on the side of the perpetrators. Nationalism and not nation or nationality, sexism and not sex or gender, ageism and not age are the reasons for the respective forms of discrimination.

(5) The concept of discrimination finally comprises a comparative element or figure, strictly speaking, a person or group of persons, in comparison to whom someone is considered to be discriminated against. The comparison with another person in a similar situation like the one in which discrimina-tion is carried out, but with different identity markers as distinguishing fea-tures (e.g. a different skin colour, ethnic origin, age, gender, religion, sexual

orientation), is required to clearly prove an unequal, less favourable treatment. Such a comparison is most important in legal conceptions of discrimination. To draw a comparison is uncomplicated, if "direct discrimination" is in question, and rather difficult, if discrimination is "indirect". Sometimes, persons serving as comparative figures are taken from the past (e.g. previous tenants, lodgers or employees), sometimes they are participating investigators (who control, for instance, the accessibility of a restaurant or pub for different social groups remaining incognito), and in cases in which direct comparison is impossible, they can be hypothetical figures employed in comparisons by analogy.

There are no clear-cut terminological distinctions of different forms of social discrimination, nor are there homogeneous conceptualizations on an international level and across the disciplines of legal studies, political science, sociology, social-psychology and discourse analysis. Just to mention two diverse attempts of differentiation:

In his socio-cognitive approach to prejudices in discourse, Teun A. van Dijk differentiates mnemotechnically among "seven Ds of discrimination". They are dominance, differentiation, distance, diffusion, diversion, depersonalization or destruction and daily discrimination. Van Dijk considers them to be general and specific action plans which are part of so-called "ethnic situation models" and which, as such, pre-shape consciously or unconsciously social interactions and the organization of social interests of ingroups. Van Dijk's heterogeneous list encompasses phenomena which do not mutually exclude each other. "Daily discrimination", for instance, is a category which runs across the other "Ds of discrimination" (see Van Dijk 1984: 40).

Cross-cutting categories are a characteristic of the social-psychological approach proposed by Graumann and Wintermantel (see Graumann and Winter-mantel 1989: 184–194) too, whose model is discussed in works on "intercultural communication" (see, for instance, Lüsebrink 2005: 106–108). Graumann and Wintermantel distinguish among five major functions or sub-functions of discrimination and of the perception of others: separating, distancing, accentuating differences, devaluating, and fixating (by assigning traits or by (stereo)typing). Their typology is insightful, although it could probably be re-organized more systematically. Actions or processes of accentuating differences, of devaluating and of (stereo)typing are realized by the explicit or implicit assignment of traits. In this respect, assigning traits—which I call "predication" in section 5.2.—is a more basic operation than accentuating differences, devaluating and stereotyping. On the other hand, assigning traits presupposes the discursive construction of social actors who can be endowed with attributes. This construction—which I discuss in my own approach in section 5.1. under "nomination"—may, among others, be realized by typing. Separating and distancing—two operations which I subsume under "perspectivation" in section 5.4.—also presuppose that there are social actors, i.e. someone who can be separated from someone else.

In the given context I deliberately refrain from trying to offer a unifying proposal that aims to put an end to the terminological muddle across and within the different disciplines, since such a suggestion can only, if it can at all, be successful if it is elaborated in a differentiated interdisciplinary discussion. Given that the terminological difficulties related to the concept of "discrimination" have not yet been appreciated in most of the disciplines concerned with the problem, the explication of terminological differences gets more space in the present chapter than most readers of a handbook of applied linguistics and intercultural communication would probably expect. Both the previous section and the following section are designated to increase the awareness of conceptual distinctions, dissimilarities and similarities.

3. Types of Social Discrimination

Among the—mostly binary—differentiations of "discrimination" are "intended" versus "non-intended discrimination", "direct" versus "indirect discrimination", "explicit" versus "implicit discrimination", "active" versus "passive discrimination", and "individual" versus "structural" or "institutional discrimination". Some of these categories cross-cut, overlap and are thus not neatly separable from each other.

The theoretical distinction between "intentional" and "unintentional discrimination"—which is especially relevant in legal discussions—as well as between "active" and "passive discrimination" seem to be rather palpable differentiations that need no long explications, although it is often difficult to prove concretely that someone discriminates against somebody else purposely. The other three binary distinctions, however, are characterized more inconsistently and disputed more controversially in the relevant literature.

As for the distinction between "direct" and "indirect" as well as "explicit" versus "implicit discrimination", conflicting suggestions are to be found in different disciplines. The psychologists Graumann and Wintermantel propose to speak of *"direct discrimination"* in the realm of verbal discrimination if the discriminated individuals are communication partners of the producers of "discriminatory speech acts", whereas they consider a *"nondirect discrimination"* to be a verbal discrimination of a person who is not present in the situation of discrimination. In this respect, the form of interpersonal relationship is their distinguishing criterion, whereas they further distinguish between "explicit" and "implicit discrimination" according to the form of verbal expression. They regard verbal discrimination as being explicit, if the discriminatory function can be identified with the utterance taken out of the speech situation. In contrast, Graumann and Wintermantel judge verbal discrimination to be implicit, if the discriminatory function cannot be understood without knowing the conditions of the situation, the presuppositions and contextual implications of the utterance (see Graumann and Wintermantel 1989: 199).[2]

The concepts of "direct" and "indirect discrimination" play an important role in legal contexts too. Legal approaches consider an act of discrimination to be *"direct"*, if a person is treated less favourably than another person in a comparable situation has been or would be treated on the basis of a legally prohibited "ground" of discrimination, i.e. of a distinguishing feature such as sex/gender, "race", age, ethnic origin, religion, sexual orientation, etc. Examples

---

[2] See Wagner (2001: 12–13) for a slightly different terminological distinction of "direct" and "indirect" as well as "explicit" and "implicit discrimination".

of "direct discrimination" are an employer's categorical refusal to hire immigrants due to foreign nationality or to hire women due to potential pregnancy or motherhood (see Makkonen 2002: 4). Discrimination is legally considered to be "indirect", if an apparently equal treatment or a neutral provision, decision, criterion, procedure or practice is discriminatory in its effects, that is to say, if it puts a person having a particular characteristic at a particular disadvantage without legal justification. If an employer hires employees on the condition of their perfect fluency in the official language of the state, although the work does not in itself necessitate such fluency, many immigrants are faced with "indirect discrimination" in the labour market (see Makkonen 2002: 4–5). In cases of "indirect discrimination" in the legal sense, it is often difficult, if not impossible (and, thus, legally not necessary) to prove that there is or has been an intention to discriminate against somebody, whereas in many cases of direct discrimination such a proof is legally required.

"Institutional discrimination" is conceptualized as practices or procedures in a company or an institution, which have been internally structured in a way that they tend to have discriminatory effects. This form of discrimination is often unintentional. If it is deliberate, as in the case of the former Apartheid regime in South Africa, Makkonen proposes to call it "institutionalized discrimination" (Makkonen 2002: 4; see also Makkonen 2003: 12). A special case of "institutionalized discrimination", strictly speaking of "positive institutionalized discrimination", is "affirmative action" or "positive discrimination" (the latter term is sometimes rejected as being inappropriate and, thus, replaced by "positive action"; see Makkonen 2002: 5). It aims to arrive at equality via temporary unequal, i.e. preferential treatment. For this purpose, distinctions on "grounds" of the above-mentioned social features are legally justified.

"Structural discrimination" is considered to be a type of intersectional discrimination (see Makkonen 2002: 14). It can take the form of "institutional discrimination" and is frequently not deliberately produced, though it can sometimes be intentionally effectuated by a short-sighted policy or institutional practice. It usually concerns members of groups in vulnerable social positions—in many societies, for example, women—and is often rendered invisible by naturalization and backgrounding. To give just one example taken from Crenshaw and referred to in Makkonen: "Structural discrimination" is actuated in states with immigration laws that try to prevent marriage fraud and require an immigrant to stay in the new state for several years and to remain "properly married" before she or he can apply for a permanent status. This legal regulation has the consequence that immigrant women who have married a national and become a victim of domestic violence have either the option to divorce and get subsequently deported or to suffer continuing violence (see Crenshaw 1991: 1247; Makkonen 2002: 15–16; see also Piller in this volume).

As the above explanations of the disciplinarily distinct concepts of "direct" and "indirect" as well as "explicit" and "implicit" discrimination show, we have to be aware of the problem that different disciplines and analytical approaches only seemingly speak about the same things when they use the same words. This problem has scarcely been recognized in the relevant literature on social discrimination until now. Thus, it is explicated rather extensively in the present chapter, without jumping to a one-sided terminological proposal. My overview leads to at least four conclusions, which could be taken as a basis for further attempts to elaborate conceptual distinctions which could possibly be interdisciplinarily valid: (1) Discrimination in the negative sense of the word represents an infringement of principles of justice. (2) Discrimination can either be committed by unequal treatment, where equal treatment would be just, or by equal treatment, where differentiation would be fair. (3) The distinction between "direct" and "indirect" links up with the relationship between discriminators and discriminated. (4) The distinction between "explicit" and "implicit" relates to the way discrimination is semiotically realized.

4. Concepts of "Discourse" in Approaches to Verbal Discrimination

The analytical focus of the following sections lies on verbal forms of discrimination. Whereas Graumann's and Wintermantel's (1989) as well as Wagner's (2001) approach to verbal discrimination are primarily "speech act" oriented and therefore try to analyse "discriminating as speech acting" and to identify "discriminatory speech acts" (see Graumann and Wintermantel 1989: 193–201), the approaches to be presented in the following are first and foremost discourse oriented. If one speaks about "discrimination in discourse", however, "discourse" can assume different meanings. Here, I want to focus on five approaches to discourse relevant for the analysis of discrimination.

I personally take a "discourse" as a complex topic-related unity of semiotic action, which, among others, involves argumentation about validity claims such as truth and normative validity. In contrast to mono-perspectivist conceptualizations of "discourse" (e.g. Fairclough 1995: 14), I consider pluri-perspectivity, i.e. different points of view, to be a constitutive feature of a "discourse" (Reisigl 2003: 92). In this sense, "discourses" are pluri-perspective semiotic bundles of social practices that are composed of interrelated, simultaneous and sequential linguistic as well as other semiotic acts and that are both socially constitutive and socially constituted. In this view, discursive practices manifest themselves within, and across, social fields of action as thematically interconnected and problem-centred semiotic (e.g. oral, written or visual) tokens that belong to particular semiotic types (i.e. communicative action patterns, genres or textual types), which fulfil specific social purposes (see Reisigl and Wodak 2001: 36). Following Girnth (1996), I conceive "fields of action" as institutionalized frameworks of social interaction structured to serve specific social aims (for more details, see Reisigl 2003: 128–142). Discourses cross between fields, overlap, refer to each other, or are in some other way sociofunctionally linked with each other (Reisigl and Wodak 2001: 36–37).

Although this concept of "discourse" is taken as a basis of the present chapter, there are several other concepts of "discourse" which have been introduced into the discussion about "discrimination in (intercultural) discourses". At least four of them must be mentioned:

Teun A. van Dijk was one of the first critical discourse analysts who dealt with the relationship between social discrimination (especially racist and ethnicist discrimination) and discourse (see van Dijk 1984; Smitherman and van Dijk 1988). His socio-cognitive approach conceives "discourse" as part of a conceptual triangle formed by cognition, discourse and society (see van Dijk 2001a: 98). Van Dijk understands "discourse" in a broad sense as a "'communicative event', including conversational interaction, written text, as well as associated gestures, facework, typographical layout, images and other 'semiotic' or multimedia dimensions of signification". For van Dijk, one of the most urgent tasks of critical research on discourse is the study of and fight against various forms of discrimination—first and foremost of discriminatory gender inequality, ethnocentrism, antisemitism, nationalism and racism—in discourses (see van Dijk 2001b: 358–363). In his numerous studies on discrimination, he especially focuses on the socio-cognitive, discursive and social conditions of the production, reproduction and transformation of prejudices and stereotypes that link up with discrimination (see, e.g., van Dijk 1984, 1987, 1993).

Researchers studying "intercultural communication" usually presuppose a very general understanding of "discourse". The interactional sociolinguist John J. Gumperz was one of the first to connect discourse analysis and intercultural communication (see Scollon and Scollon 2001: 540; see also Hinnenkamp 1991, 2001, 2003). He adopts a rather broad understanding of "discourse" and regards it as language (first and foremost, as spoken language) used in social contexts. Gumperz discussed early on the relationship between intercultural misunderstanding and social discrimination. He found out that various breakdowns in intercultural communication are due to inferences based on undetected differences in contextualization strategies (see Gumperz 1982: 210; see also Gumperz and Cook-Gumperz 2007), and that cultural misunderstandings can lead to discrimination, or are sometimes read as discrimination, even though they may be misinterpretations resulting from unrecognized cultural differences (see Gumperz 1982: 174). Gumperz draws the conclusion that if more people begin to understand culture- and language-bound differences in contextualization cues, discrimination will be lessened. He further concluded that conversation analysis can serve as the diagnostic tool to determine whether there are communicative differences among members of different cultures.

The results of Gumperz' investigations are less relevant for the analysis of "overt discrimination" against minorities, which in western industrialized societies has significantly decreased (see Gumperz 2001: 226), than for the analysis and assessment of "covert", non-intentional, indirect, implicit or structural discrimination associated with unobserved linguistic diversity which causes difficulties in social interactions. An explanation exclusively concentrating on this cultural or linguistic diversity would, however, sometimes be too simplistic, as critics of Gumperz' approach state (see, for instance, Singh, Lele and Martohardjono 1996; see also Scollon and Scollon 2001: 540), and as Gumperz himself notes in more recent works (see, e.g., Gumperz 2001: 225, where he also focuses on factors such as language ideology).

Rajendra Singh, Jayant Lele and Gita Martohardjono (1996: 238) argue that beyond the uncovering of and training to recognize cultural and linguistic differences there is a need to take into consideration economic, political and historical factors and the related structures of power asymmetry, hegemony and dominance when analysing discrimination in intercultural encounters.

They maintain that miscommunications in multiethnic, industrialized societies is often based on institutionally encouraged violations of principles of cooperation, charity and humanity. This observation goes beyond the analytical scope of Gumperz' approach. It is especially important for the study of "institutional discrimination", but also of "intersectional discriminations" characterized by the simultaneous and concurrent intersection of different discriminating factors in one and the same social field and situation.

Ron and Suzie W. Scollon, who have also extensively worked on intercultural communication, distinguish among different ways to use the word "discourse". In their introductory textbook on "intercultural communication", they differentiate among three meanings of the noun (see Scollon and Scollon 2003a: 107). The first and technically most narrow meaning of "discourse" refers to a linguistic unit composed of sentences that are connected by grammatical and other relationships, which constitute cohesion and are reconstructed by inferential processes. The second meaning sees "discourse" as a functional entity relating to the social environment and functions of language use, as situated social practice. The third and broadest meaning of "discourse" is linked to a whole self-contained system of communication with a language or jargon shared by a particular social group, with a particular ideological position and with specific forms of interpersonal relationships among members of the group. This third denotation is more adequately named "discourse system" rather than just "discourse".[3]

Ron and Suzie W. Scollon's approach is known as "interdiscourse communication" approach (see Scollon and Scollon 2001: 544). According to them, language users position themselves in every instance of actual communication multiply within an indefinite number of discourses or, as they prefer to say, of "discourse systems", such as the so-called "gender discourse system", "generation discourse system", "professional discourse system", "Utilitarian discourse (system)" and "voluntary discourse system" (see Scollon and Scollon 2003a). The two discourse analysts assume that each of these "discourse systems" is realized in a complex network of different forms of discourse, face systems, socializations and ideologies—the four basic elements of "discourse systems" (see also Scollon and Scollon 2003a: 108). In contrast to other approaches to intercultural communication, Scollon and Scollon avoid presupposing cultural membership and identity as given concepts. In their "mediated discourse analysis", as they also call their approach, they aim to analyse how, under which circumstances, for which purpose and with what consequences categories such as culture, social identity and social membership are produced in social interactions as relevant categories for the participants. They take social and cultural groups to be outcomes of social interactions and social change and argue against attributing to them the status of direct causal factors (see Scollon and Scollon 2001: 244–245). This implies that social discrimination in

---

[3] In comparison to Scollon and Scollon (2003a), Scollon and Scollon (2003b) mention just two meanings of "discourse". In the narrow sense—they explain—"discourse" means "language in use". In a broader sense, they regard "discourse" as "a body of language use and other factors that form a "social language" such as the discourse of traffic regulation, commercial discourse, medical discourse, legal discourse." (Scollon and Scollon 2003b: 210).

intercultural communication should not only be analysed by plain reference to categories of culture, subculture, identity and social group membership as simple explanatory concepts, but that discrimination, just as these culture- and identity-categories, arises in social interactions, which have to be understood as mediated (inter)actions.

One of the most prominent German groups of researchers dealing with discourse and discrimination is the "Duisburg group", directed by Siegfried and Margret Jäger. This team of critical discourse analysts is strongly influenced by Michel Foucault and Jürgen Link. Siegfried Jäger conceives "discourse" as "the flow of knowledge—and/or all societal knowledge stored—throughout all time [. . .], which determines individual and collective doing and/or formative action that shapes society, thus exercising power" (Jäger 2001a: 130, 2001b: 34). Within this approach, "discourses" are understood as historically determined, transindividual, institutionalized and regulated social practices that become material realities *sui generis*. The "Duisburg group" especially focuses on racist, ethnicist, "xenophobic" and nationalist discrimination against foreigners since the unification of West and East Germany in 1989 and 1990 until now. A specific research interest of this approach relates to the linking up of discourses or "discourse strands". The latter are conceptualized as thematically interrelated sequences of "discourse fragments" (i.e. texts or parts of texts that deal with a specific topic) which manifest themselves on different "discourse levels" (e.g. science, politics, the media, education, everyday life, business life, administration). The Duisburg discourse analysts are also engaged in proposing strategies against discrimination, for instance, against verbal discrimination in the media press coverage (see Jäger, Cleve, Ruth and Jäger 1998; Duisburger Institut für Sprach- und Sozialforschung 1999).

This short overview shows that to speak, write or read about "discrimination in discourse" can imply a variety of things, since "discourse" functions as a broad cover-term for very different meanings, which can at best be inferred from the respective contexts. Researchers on "discrimination in discourses" often are not aware of this conceptual heterogeneity.

The following section will primarily build on my own understanding of "discourse" outlined at the beginning of the section. In accordance with other approaches to discourse sketched out above, I consider "discourse" to be a social-semiotic practice. More precisely than most of the above-mentioned approaches, I take topic-relatedness, problem-centeredness, argumentativity and pluri-perspectivity as basic constituents of a "discourse". Explicitly introducing these constitutive features, I hope to conceptualize "discourse" empirically more comprehensibly than many discourse approaches do.

5. The Realization of Discrimination in Discourses

The relationship between "language and discrimination" (see, e.g., Roberts, Davies and Jupp 1993) can generally be analysed from at least two viewpoints. On the one side, language is employed as a means of social discrimination (see, e.g., Billig 2006). On the other side, language becomes an object of discrimination (see, e.g., Skuttnabb-Kangas and Phillipson 1994; Skuttnabb-

Kangas 2000; Bough 2006). The two forms of discrimination often overlap, as in cases in which discrimination is directed against a language (for example, by language prohibition) and, therefore, also against the group or community of speakers who use this language. However, one difference between the two forms of discrimination just mentioned draws on the distinction between "object language" and "metalanguage": If language is an object of discrimination, the object language becomes a metalinguistic matter of discrimination, especially with respect to language policy or language policies and language planning. In contrast to this, the use of language as a means of discrimination does not normally involve such a straightforward metalinguistic status.

Several discourse studies on racism, antisemitism, nationalism and right-wing populism have been done on the example of Austria by the Viennese group of critical discourse analysts (see, among others, Wodak et al. 1990, 1994, 1999; Gruber 1991; Wodak and van Dijk 2000; Reisigl and Wodak 2001; Reisigl 2002, 2003). The analytical and methodological framework of this approach combines, among others, discourse analysis, argumentation theory, rhetoric and systemic function linguistics. It has been elaborated for the analysis of racist, antisemitic and ethnicist language, but can also be employed in and adapted to the analysis of other forms of social discrimination. In the following, this approach lays the theoretical and methodical foundations for analysing the realization of discrimination in discourses.

5.1. Discrimination by Nomination

The first discourse analytical aspect of verbal discrimination I want to especially focus on relates to the question of how persons are named and referred to linguistically, if they are discriminated against by means of discursive practices (nomination strategies). Discrimination by nomination can take many different forms, some of them being very explicit, as in the case of racist, ethnicist, nationalist, sexist and antisemitic slurs employed in insulting speech acts or verbal injuries, others being more implicit, as is the case of discrimination by simple non-nomination or linguistic deletion.

There are numerous linguistic and rhetorical means and ways to realize discrimination by nomination. These means are not discriminatory as such, but depending on the concrete discursive context in which they are used (the following list being far from complete):

(1) Phonological and prosodic features are sometimes employed as means of intentional prosodic disparagement and slighting alienation of proper names. This is the case if proper names are purposely articulated with a distorting pronunciation (for an example see section 5.6).

(2) Among the potential morphological or morphosemantic means to realize discriminatory nomination are degrading diminutives, depreciatory morphemes and debasing antonomastic semisuffixes (such as German "-heini" in *"Provinz-heini"*, meaning "provincial guy", or "-susi/e" in *"Heulsuse"*, meaning "cry-baby"). A special example for sexist diminutive titulation is the German form

of address *"Fräulein!"* (literally: "little woman"), which refers to an unmarried woman, in contrast to German *"Frau"*, which is used for married women. Here, the discrimination lies in the patriarchal distinction of whether a women is still "free" for marriage or not, whereas an analogous distinction of unmarried and married men has not been lexicalized. Similar examples can be found in languages such as French (*"Mademoiselle!"*), Spanish (*"Senorita!"*) or Italian (*"Signorina!"*). The analysis of intercultural communication has to take into account that such sexist nominations are nowadays judged to be politically incorrect in some speech communities, whereas there is less linguistic sensitivity for this sexism in other speech communities.

(3) Syntactic means relating to discriminatory nomination are passivation and nominalization (see already Sykes 1985: 88–94). They are, strictly speaking, syntactic means of non-nomination. If a politician claims that "immigration must be stopped", those whom the politician wants to be hindered from immigrating, i.e. potential immigrants, are callously backgrounded (see below) by nominalization, and those who the politician wants to reject the immigrants, i.e. those who make, implement and execute a rigid anti-immigration act, are back-grounded by passivation.

(4) Numerous semantic means can potentially serve discrimination against members of specific social groups (see already Sykes 1985: 94–99). Just to mention a few of them: (a) There are various negatively connoted general anthroponyms, e.g. "genderonyms" and "gerontonyms", such as the sexist German *"Weib"*, pejoratively used for "woman", or the ageist German *"Balg"* or *"Göre"* for English "brat". (b) "Ethnonyms" are often employed as debasing antonomasias such as *"Jude"* used in antisemitic idioms like *"So ein Jude!"*, meaning "Such a usurious profiteer!". (c) Synecdochic-metaphoric slurs are frequently based on the names of more or less tabooed body parts and bodily activities, (e.g. sexual practices), for instance "asshole", "cunt", "motherfucker" and "whore". They reduce persons to a socially tabooed part of the body or bodily activity. In many (though not all) contexts, they become discriminatory nominations. (d) Animal metaphors are regularly used as insulting swearwords, for instance, "pig/ swine", "rat", "parasite" (employed, among others, as antisemitic metaphors by the Nazis), cow and dog. (e) Proper names are sometimes employed as generalizing antonomasias, i.e. as appellative nouns. Several examples can be mentioned here: (i) A specific first name is used as a debasing antonomastic epithet for a specific person, for instance, "Heini" or "Susi"; or a specific first name is used as a collective androcentric antonomasias for a whole social group, for instance, English "Fritz" for all Germans, German *"der Ali"* for all Turks, or German *"der Ivan"* for all Russians. (ii) A specific first name is used as antonomastic antisemitic slur, such as "Judas" denoting "traitor"; or a specific first name is used as a discriminating marker of "Jewishness", for instance the two compulsory first names "Sara" and "Israel" prescribed by the Nazis on August 17, 1938 for all female and male Jews in Nazi Germany (see Berding 2003: 177); (iii) Specific surnames are used as antonomastic ethnicist slurs such as "Piefke", a pejorative anthroponym for Germans, especially referring to Germans from the North of Germany.

(5) Among the pragmatic means of discriminatory nomination are deictic expressions. They may relate to personal deixis, such as distancing and debasing "they" and "those", to local deixis such as "down there" or "out there", or to "social deixis" such as condescending asymmetrical personal address with the German *"du"*-form (for instance in "foreigner talk"). Metalinguistic comments or puns on allegedly alien first names or surnames are also potential pragmatic means of discrimination connected with nomination too.

Van Leeuwen's (1996) concepts relating to the representation of social actors allow us to analytically grasp some of the more subtle forms of discriminatorily constructing, identifying or hiding social actors:

The social actors' exclusion from linguistic representation is often employed to veil persons responsible for discriminatory actions. It becomes implicit discrimination by non-nomination in cases such as the sexist non-naming of women (pretending, for example, that the so-called "generic masculine" in languages like German would linguistically include them), or in cases of linguistic under-representation of ethnic minorities by not giving them sufficient access to and voice in mass media and by not reporting about them to an adequate extent. The linguistic exclusion can be a radical, total one which leaves no lexical or grammatical traces in the discursive representation of specific social actors. Van Leeuwen calls this form of linguistic exclusion "suppression" (Van Leeuwen 1996: 38). If the exclusion is partial and leaves some traces that enable readers or hearers to infer the excluded social actors with more or less certainty, van Leeuwen speaks about "backgrounding" (Van Leeuwen 1996: 38). The passive is a syntactic means of backgrounding.

If persons are nominated, i.e. linguistically included, the inclusion is not always an indicator of fair and just representation and treatment, but can sometimes have a disguising, relativizing or averting function. Such is the case, if the linguistic inclusion pretends that there is equal treatment, whereas inequalities and injustices remain in effect. Strategies of linguistic inclusion which can become discriminatory are (according to van Leeuwen):

1. "genericization", i.e. the general nomination of a whole group of persons (e.g. "Germans"),
2. "assimilation", i.e. the reference to social actors as groups, which can be realized by
   a. (a) "collectivization", i.e. the nomination of social actors by collectives or mass nouns (e.g. "the crowd"), or
   b. (b) "aggregation", i.e. the statistical quantification of groups of participants (e.g. "10,000 are too many"), and
3. "impersonalization", i.e. the nomination of persons as if they were not really human beings, which can be realized by
   a. (a) "abstraction", i.e. the representation of social actors by means of a quality assigned to them (e.g. "the unskilled", "illegals"), or
   b. (b) "objectivation", i.e. the nomination of persons by means of reference to a place or object (e.g. by metonymies like "the foreign countries") (Van Leeuwen 1996: 47–59).

There are myriads of lexicalized discriminatory anthroponyms in any language which are employed as discriminatory nominations in different social fields and subfields of action such as policy and politics, economy, religion, military, science, education, sexuality, housing, media, health service, arts, etc. Many of them are tropes, and especially metaphors, metonymies and synecdoches (including antonomasias). They cannot be discussed in the present chapter (for a selection of such anthroponyms, see Reisigl and Wodak 2001: 48–52; for discriminating metaphors, see also El Refaie 2001). Whether a specific anthroponym has a discriminatory effect or not, is, in concrete casas, determined by the pragmatic context or co-text.

5.2. Discrimination by Predication

The second discourse analytical aspect of verbal discrimination I want to selectively focus on relates to predication strategies employed to discriminate against people by ascribing debasing traits, characteristics, qualities and features to them. Such predications are usually connected with social prejudices and stereotypes—the latter being understood as fixed, uniform, reductionist, over-generalizing schemes or schematic modi operandi which are mostly acquired by socialization, are frequently distributed via mass media and show a high degree of recognizability (see Reisigl in print).

Discriminatory predications in discourses are linguistically or visually more or less explicit or implicit and—like nomination and argumentation—specific or vague. Predicational strategies are mainly realized by specific forms of nomination (based on explicit denotation as well as on more or less implicit connotation), by attributes (in the form of adjectives, appositions, prepositional phrases, relative clauses, conjunctional clauses, infinitive clauses and participial clauses or groups), by predicates or predicative nouns/adjectives/pronouns, by collocations, by explicit comparisons, similes, metaphors and other rhetorical figures (including metonymies, hyperboles, litotes, euphemisms) and by more or less implicit analogies, allusions, evocations, and presuppositions or implications. The visual predication of discriminatory stereotypes is realized by strategies characterized below in section 5.5.

Two short examples must suffice for illustrating discriminatory predications ascribed to social groups who are often discriminated against in discourses with an intercultural dimension.

Among the most frequent discriminatory traits explicitly or implicitly predicated to so-called *"Ausländer"* ("foreigners") in the discourse about migrants and migration in countries such as Austria and Germany, we find the predications that "foreigners" would be bad, uncooperative work colleagues and workmates, "socio-parasites", unwilling to assimilate and integrate, different in culture and religion, culturally immature, less civilized and more primitive, careless, dirty, infectious, backward, conspicuous, loud, inclined to sexual harassment, sexism and patriarchal oppression, physically different, aggressive, criminal, etc. (see Karl-Renner-Institut 1990; Reisigl and Wodak 2001: 55). And discourses about gypsies, for example in Germany and Austria, contain discriminatory predications against gypsies such as being tattered and ragged, roguish and wicked, thieving, vagrant, unreliable and antisocial, false and mendacious, superstytrous, inclined to cursing and witchcraft, and so on.

Empirical discourse studies lead to analogous overviews of corresponding discriminatory stereotypes directed against other social minorities and marginalized groups (e.g. against Jews, see Wodak et al. 1990; Gruber 1991; Reisigl and Wodak 2001: 91–143).

A potent discursive resource for fighting such stereotypes and the related prejudices is argumentation. Argumentation, however, also represents a widespread technique of discrimination.

5.3. Discrimination by Argumentation

Social discrimination against others is often justified and legitimized by means of arguments and argumentation schemes (argumentation strategies). In discourses containing arguments for and against discrimination, argumentation does not always follow rules for rational dispute and constructive arguing such as the freedom of speech, the obligation to give reasons, the correct reference to previous utterances by the antagonist, the obligation to "matter-of-factness", the correct reference to implicit premises, the respect of shared starting points, the use of plausible arguments and schemes of argumentation, logical validity, the acceptance of the discussion's results and the clarity of expression and correct interpretation (see van Eemeren and Grootendorst 1992). Numerous violations of these rules, i.e. many fallacies, can be identified in discourses on ethnic or intercultural issues, where racist, ethnicist or nationalist legitimizing strategies are employed in order to justify unequal treatment and the violation of basic democratic principles and human rights.

Among these fallacies are the *argumentum ad baculum* (a verbal threat or intimidation instead of using plausible and relevant arguments), the *argumentum ad hominem* (a verbal attack on the opponent's personality and character instead of trying to refute the opponent's arguments), the *argumentum ad populum* (an appeal to "masses" of people, often aiming to justify prejudiced emotions and opinions of a social group, instead of relevant arguments), the *argumentum ad verecundiam* (the misplaced appeal to deep respect and reverence for—allegedly—competent, superior, sacrosanct or unimpeachable authorities, instead of relevant arguments), the *argumentum ad nominem* (a fallacious argumentation scheme based on the conclusion rule that the literal meaning of a person's name, a thing's name or an action's name applies to the person, thing or action themselves, just in the sense of "nomen est omen"), the *post hoc, ergo propter hoc* (this fallacy consists in mixing up a temporally chronological relationship with a causally consequential one, in the sense of "A before B, therefore B because of A"), the *argumentum ad consequentiam* (a fallacious causal argumentation scheme that stresses the consequences of a (non-)decision or (non-)action, without these consequences being plausibly derivable from the (non)-decision or (non)-action), the hasty generalization (an argumentation scheme based on an empirically, statistically unconfirmed overgeneralization; in fact, many racist, ethnicist, nationalist and sexist prejudices rely on this fallacy, which takes a part for the whole), etc. (for more details and examples of these fallacies, see Reisigl and Wodak 2001: 71–74).

In discourses related to problems of social discrimination it is sometimes difficult to distinguish between fallacious and more or less plausible argumentation schemes, which, in argumentation theory, are designated as "topoi". "Topoi" are those obligatory parts of argumentation which serve as "conclusion rules". They link up the argument or arguments with the concluding claim (see Kienpointner 1992: 194). A typical topos in the discourse about migrants and migration is the topos of danger or topos of threat. It means that if a political action or decision bears dangerous, threatening consequences, one should not perform or do it, or if there is a specific danger and threat, one should do something against it. This topos is often fallaciously realized, if immigrants are "xenophobically" depicted as a threat to national identity and culture against which the government should proceed. This and other content-related topoi and the respective content-related fallacies to be found in the discourses about migrants and asylum seekers (e.g. the discourse about migration and the discourse about asylum) are, among others, analysed in Kienpointner and Kindt (1997), Wengeler (1997), Reeves (1983) and Reisigl and Wodak (2001: 75–80).

5.4. The Perspectivation, Intensification, and Mitigation of Discrimination

Two further types of discursive strategies closely linked with argumentation strategies and thus to be taken into consideration in the analysis of social discrimination are *perspectivation strategies* and *intensification* or *mitigation strategies*. The one group of strategies relates to the position or point of view a speaker or writer assumes with respect to discriminating language, i.e. to the perspective from which discriminating arguments—but also nominations and predications—are expressed, and to the method of framed discriminatory language. Discriminatory nominations, predication and argumentations, can, for instance, be realized from an I-perspective, she-/he-perspective or we-perspective; they can be framed by direct quotation, indirect quotation or free indirect speech, and so on. The other group of strategies links up with the question of whether utterances containing discriminating nominations, predications and argumentations are articulated overtly or covertly, whether the respective speech acts are intensified or mitigated. The former can, among others, be realized by hyperboles or amplifying particles like "very" and "absolutely". The latter can be realized by questions instead of assertions or by procataleptic concessions like "yes, but" (for more details on these two types of discursive strategies, see Reisigl and Wodak 2001: 81–85; Reisigl 2003: 214–237).

5.5. Visual Discrimination

Social discrimination is not just realized in the multiple semiotic modes of verbal language, but also in other semiotic modes, including visual modes. Theo van Leeuwen (2000) approaches "visual racism" with the help of two complementary methods, combining (a) the method of analysing the "grammar of visual design" (see Kress and van Leeuwen 1996), which, among others, allows to grasp the imaginary relationship between visually represented individuals and viewers, with (b) his functional-systemic model of the representation of social actors (see van Leeuwen 1996). Although van Leeuwen focuses on the problem of "racism" (although he does not explicate his concept of "racism"), his approach offers a far more general framework, which enables the analysis of diverse forms of social discrimination (especially of implicit discrimination).

Without any claim of completeness, van Leeuwen distinguishes among eight strategies of "visual racism", which, taken more generally, represent eight strategies of various forms of visual discrimination. They are (1) symbolic distanciation, (2) symbolic disempowerment, (3) symbolic objectivation, (4) exclusion, (5) representation as agents of negatively valued actions, (6) homogenization, (7) negative cultural connotation and (8) discriminatory stereotyping.

The first three strategies are differentiated on the basis of criteria such as distance, angle and gaze, which constitute three key factors that are involved in each visual representation and can be integrated into a system network.

Different degrees of distance are visually represented within a continuum of close shots and long shots. Visual discrimination by *symbolic distanciation* means to depict specific persons or groups of persons in relation to the viewers as if they were not "close" to the viewers, as if they were "strangers" far from the observers (see van Leeuwen 2000: 339). Such a representation entails an undifferentiated, de-individualizing portrayal without any details. Long shots, however, are not a means of visual discrimination per se, but—since any form of discrimination is a relational issue that involves a comparative figure—become discriminatory against specific persons or social groups only if there are other persons or groups, which, in comparison to those preferentially depicted by long shots, are preferentially represented by close-ups, which imply greater nearness, differentiation and the possibility to perceive more individual characteristics. Kress and Van Leeuwen discovered in a case study on the Australian school book *Our Society and Others*, that in the chapter on Aboriginal people, all Aborigines except one were represented by long shots, whereas the book's depictions of non-Aboriginal people did not follow this pattern (see van Leeuwen 2000: 337). Comparisons like this one permit a diagnosis of whether there is discrimination at work or not. Such a comparison of the representation of in-and outgroups has to draw on representative empirical findings, since symbolic distanciation is predominantly part of a pattern or syndrome not recognizable at first glance, and thus part of implicit discrimination.

The angle from which a person is depicted can tell both (a) about the relation of power between the viewer and the represented person (this aspect regards the vertical angle from above, from below or on eye level), and (b) about the relation of involvement between the viewer and the represented person (this aspect concerns the horizontal angle, i.e. the frontal or oblique representation). Presupposing that looking up at someone from a low angle in many social contexts means to be less powerful, that looking at someone from eye-level denotes a symmetric power relationship or equal social position, and that social superordination or domination is related to a relatively high, more elevated point of view (one may just think of the "boss's chair"), to visually represent somebody as below the viewer, as "downtrodden" (van Leeuwen 2000: 339), can mean to symbolically disempower the depicted person. *Symbolic disempowerment* becomes implicit discrimination, if specific social groups and their members (e.g. outgroup and minority members) are systematically more often "objects" of a perspectivation from above or a bird's eye view than other social groups (e.g. in-group and majority members).

The relation of involvement and detachment, which concerns the apparent social interaction between depicted figures and viewers, is visually expressed on the horizontal axis and by the gaze. If a visually represented person looks at the picture's viewer and the depicted body is angled towards the viewer, this bodily orientation suggests a high degree of interactional involvement, since both the frontal posture and the direct gaze are highly phatic and sometimes also conative (e.g. demanding). If the gaze and the posture of a depicted figure are not directed at the viewer, but represented from an oblique angle, the appellative quality is rather low, and the viewers assume the roles of "voyeurs" who are looking at somebody who is not aware of being looked at (see van Leeuwen 2000: 339). It is within such relational contexts that *symbolic objectivation* can become visual discrimination. Such is the case if persons of specific social groups are—in contrast to other social groups—systematically represented "as objects of our scrutiny, rather than as subjects addressing the viewer with their gaze and symbolically engaging with the viewer in this way" (van Leeuwen 2000: 339). We are faced with such a form of discrimination if women are shown as available sexual commodities.

The other five strategies of discrimination distinguished by Theo van Leeuwen do not primarily relate to the interpersonal metafunction, but to the ideational metafunction. They generally correspond to the above-mentioned strategies of verbal discrimination, if one disregards the differences of semiotic modes.

5.6. An Example of Indirect and Implicit Discrimination

In the present context, I just analyse one concrete example of indirect and implicit discrimination in order to illustrate a specific discriminatory argumentation strategy in connection with discriminatory nomination, predication, perspectivation and intensification strategies.

The example gives an idea about coded antisemitism in the Austrian postwar era (see Wodak and Reisigl 2002 for a detailed analysis of the example). It documents how Jörg Haider, the former leader of the far-right Austrian Freedom Party, employs the fallacious topos of name-interpretation in order to attack the head of Vienna's Jewish community, Ariel Muzicant, during a polemic "beer hall speech" on February 28, 2001. The primary audience of Haider's speech were mostly party followers and party sympathizers. The secondary audience was composed of those who saw and heard the speech extract transmitted in the radio and TV news. The tertiary audience consisted of those who read the transcribed speech (extract) in print media and the internet. Haider uttered his discriminatory attack against Muzicant in the campaign period preceding the regional elections in Vienna in March 2001, and in a political and historical situation in which, among others, two discourses were intensely present in public: the discourse about the so-called "sanctions" of the 14 EU member states against the participation of the Austrian Freedom Party in the coalition government and the discourse about the restitution of Jewish spoils robbed by Austrian National Socialists. Ariel Muzicant was engaged both in the critique and warning of the FPÖ's participation in the government and in the negotiations about the restitution. In his polemic speech, Haider insulted Muzicant as follows:

> Mister Ariel ((0.5 sec)) Muzicant. ((*1.0 sec*)) I don't understand at all <u>how</u> ((*1.0 sec*)) if <u>some</u>one is <u>called</u> Ariel [he] can have so much <u>dirt</u> sticking to him ((*fervent applause and beginning laughter*)) this I really don't understand, but ((*Haider looks below at his manuscript*)) I mean ((*2 sec of applause and laughter*)) this is an<u>other</u> <u>thing.</u> ``7 sec of applause, during which Haider seizes a beer mug standing at the desk before him and takes a swig*))

> ((Transcript of an extract of the TV news *Zeit im Bild 2* (*Time in Pictures 2*) of March 1, 2001; underlining stands for stressing))

> [Der Herr Ariel ((*0.5 sec*)) Muzi<u>cant.</u> ((*1.0 sec*)) I versteh überhaupt net, <u>wie</u> ((*1.0 sec*)) wonn <u>a</u>na Ariel <u>haßt</u>, so viel <u>Dreck</u> am Steckn haben kann ((*starker Applaus und Lachen setzen ein*)) des versteh i <u>über</u>haupt <u>net</u>, oba ((*Haider blickt nach unten auf das Manuskript*)) i man ((*2 sec langer tosender Applaus und Lachen*)) des is a <u>on</u>dere <u>So</u>che. ((*7 sec lang anhaltender Applaus, während dessen Haider zum Bierkrug greift, der vor ihm auf dem Podium steht, und einen Schluck Bier trinkt*))]

For those among the primary, secondary and tertiary audience who have a respective historical background knowledge, Haider's criminalizing insult of Muzicant bears high allusive potential of coded antisemitism. Within the specific context, Haider's slur alludes to at least four prejudiced predications discriminating against Jews, viz. (a) the stereotype of "the Jewish traitor to the Fatherland.", (b) the stereotype of "the Jew as criminal world conspirator against Austria", (c) the stereotype of "the dirty, impure Jew" and (d) the stereotype of "the business-minded, tricky, fraudulent, criminal Jew". In addition, some of the Jewish listeners and readers of the secondary and tertiary audience associated Haider's offense with the historically unproven assertion that National Socialists processed bodies of murdered Jews in order to make soap. These recipients argued that Haider metaphorically transformed Jews once again into soap.

Haider expresses the stereotypes (a) and (b) in the speech sequence immediately preceding the quotation. He claims in this "pre-sequence" that Muzicant had a share of the responsibility for the so-called "sanctions" against Austria and sent a letter with the World Jewish Congress "throughout America" (please note the exaggerating intensification) in which he stated that Jews were again in dire straits and had to leave Austria. In order to vividly and persuasively construct his insinuating assertion that Muzicant would complain about a growing antisemitism in Austria, Haider makes use of pseudo-authentic direct speech. He puts the following words into Muzicant's mouth: "Now we must already collect, because our fellow citizens are again being badgered and must leave Austria. [Jetzt müssen wir schon sammeln, weil unsere Mitbürger sind wieder bedrängt und müssen Österreich verlassen.]" A syntactic indicator for the fact that this perspectivation strategy recurs to fictitious quotation is the word order in the subordinate causal clause: a verb-second position after the German subjunction *"weil"* ("because") would be typical for spoken language, but is not for a letter like the one Haider ascribed to Muzicant (apart from the fact that such a letter would have been written in English).

The third and fourth stereotypes are implicitly verbalized in the allusive predication of criminality contained in the quoted extract. Among the discursive features which support discriminating associations with these two antisemitic prejudices are four peculiarities: (1) The first one relates to nomination and perspectivation. Haider phonetically distorts the surname of the Jewish president, articulating "Muzicant" with [ts] instead of [s]. This distancing perspectivation by alienating nomination is combined with the syntactic realization of *"Der Herr Ariel Muzicant"* as an isolated "free topic" that is segmented by two relevance pauses. Both of these features are suited to open for the audience a potential space of associations with the name of the Jewish president, all the more since the determining article *"der"* in Austrian German suggests that the person named "Ariel Muzicant" is well-known. This nomination is followed (2) by the allusive homonymic and antithetic play on words based on a fallacious topos of name interpretation, i.e. *argumentum ad nominem*. In a syntactically not well-formed conditional formulation, Haider plays with the contrast between the proper name "Ariel", which is both a male Jewish first name and the name of a detergent (i.e. an ergonym) that connotes cleanness, purity, and the criminalizing German idiom *"Dreck am Stecken haben"* meaning "to have dirt (sticking) on the stick", with the implication of having a shady, criminal past. The implicit fallacious argumentation scheme can generally be explicated by the conditional paraphrase: If a person carries a specific proper name, the (denotative or connotative) meaning of this proper name also applies to the person her- or himself. In the concrete case, the *argumentum ad nominem* means: If a male's name is "Ariel", he should be a person with a pure, clean character. (3) The third linguistic particularity of the quoted passage is the strategic intensification of the criminalizing predication by "so much". In the given context, the deictic expression "so" points to an undefined, sensually not perceptible aspect in the speaker's and listeners' mental "space of imagination". If the listeners' space of imagination" contains allusive paths leading to antisemitic prejudices, the allegedly large amount of dirt ("much") is de-coded in a way as to be associated with the stereotypes of "the dirty, impure Jew" and "the business-minded, tricky, fraudulent, criminal Jew". (4) The fervent applause as an indicator of agreement with the content of Haider's insult and the laughter of the primary audience as a sign of being amused by Haider's utterance show that the speaker's message well reaches his first addressees in the room. In view of the fact that these listeners are first and foremost followers and sympathizers of the far-right party which is the successor organization of the "Verband der Unabhängigen" (VdU; "Association of Independents"), a political melting pot for former National Socialists in Austria, it is reasonable to suspect that many of the primary auditors associated Haider's insult with the two discriminatory stereotypes. Several additional factors (both linguistic and contextual ones) which further increased the probability of Haider's primary audience to develop discriminatory antisemitic associations are discussed in Wodak and Reisigl (2002).

6. Conclusion

Many supplementary questions and aspects of social discrimination in discourses cannot be dealt with in the present chapter, for example the relationship between discrimination and propaganda, instigation and ridiculation, the question of whether there are specific "genres" or "text types" (e.g. transgressive inscriptions in public space, jokes, caricatures and satires) which are more frequently employed for discrimination than other "genres" or "text types", and the question of whether there are culture-dependent and legal norms that variably delimit the boundaries between verbal discrimination and joking, caricaturing and lampooning backed by freedom of speech. A critical analysis must also take them into consideration.

Such a critical analysis of discursive practices that aim at discriminating against specific social groups or at disguising discrimination has both theoretical as well as practical relevance. Linguistic critique or language critique can be a means of anti-discrimination policy and politics (see Reisigl and Wodak 2001: 263–271). Its controlling and sensitizing contributions consist (1) in the narrow text- and discourse-related reconstruction and description of the use of semiotic means of discrimination (e.g. in the accurate linguistic and interactional analysis of Haider's utterance and the reactions of the primary audience); (2) in the sociodiagnostic integration of the linguistic analysis into a broader, trans- or interdisciplinarian framework that uncovers socio-political functions of discriminatory discursive practices that are performed at a specific time in a specific place, i.e. in a specific historical situation (e.g. in the analytical embedding of Haider's speech in the actual political situation of the election campaign and of the controversial discussions about the so-called "sanctions" and the restitution of Jewish spoils, as well as in the embedding in the historical context of coded antisemitism in the Austrian post-war era); and (3) in prospective practical critique which aims to contribute to the solution of discrimination-related social problems, for example, by attempting to improve the communicative relations between different (sub)cultural groups within the political system of a democracy, by attempting to sensitize speakers and writers of a specific society with respect to discriminating semiosis, and by offering, for example, discourse analytical knowledge in the area of anti-discriminating argumentation and media coverage (e.g. in writing a specialist linguistic report for the legal proceedings started by Muzicant against Haider).

As the article and especially the analysis of the example in section 5.6. have shown, the problem of social discrimination in discourses is far too complex to be grasped comprehensively by an exclusive analysis of intercultural communication in a strict sense. Verbal and visual discrimination are topics which are best approached in interdisciplinary analyses that combine the analysis of intercultural communication with critical discourse analysis and, possibly, also with politological analysis, social-psychological analysis, legal analysis and economic analysis.

References

Berding, Dietz. 2003. Gutachten über den antisemitischen Charakter einer namenpolemischen Passage aus der Rede Jörg Haiders vom 28. Februar 2001. In: Anton Pelinka and Ruth Wodak (eds.), *Dreck am Stecken: Politik der Ausgrenzung*, 173–186. Vienna: Czernin.

Billig, Michael. 2006. Political rhetorics of discrimination. In: Keith Brown (ed.), *The Encyclopedia of Language and Linguistics*, Volume 9, 2nd edition, 697–699. Oxford: Elsevier.

Bough, John. 2006. Discrimination and language. In: Keith Brown (ed.), *The Encyclopedia of Language and Linguistics*, Volume 3, 2nd edition, 694–696. Oxford: Elsevier.

Crenshaw, Kimberlé. 1991. Mapping the margins: intersectionality, identity politics, and violence against women of color. *Stanford Law Review* 43 (6): 1241–1299.

Van Dijk, Teun A. 1984. *Prejudice in Discourse*. Amsterdam: Benjamins.

Van Dijk, Teun A. 1987. *Communicating Racism. Ethnic Prejudice in Thought and Talk*. Newbury Park, CA: Sage.

Van Dijk, Teun A. 1993. *Elite Discourse and Racism*. Newbury Park, CA: Sage.

Van Dijk, Teun A. 2001a. Multidisciplinary CDA: a plea for diversity. In: Ruth Wodak and Michael Meyer (eds.), *Methods of Critical Discourse Analysis*, 95–120. London et al.: Sage.

Van Dijk, Teun A. 2001b. Critical discourse analysis. In: Deborah Schiffrin, Deborah Tannen and Heide Hamilton (eds.), *Handbook of Discourse Analysis*, 352–371. Oxford: Blackwell.

Duisburger Institut für Sprach- und Sozialforschung (eds.). 1999. *Medien und Straftaten. Vorschläge zur Vermeidung diskriminierender Berichterstattung über Einwanderer und Flüchtlinge*. Duisburg: DISS.

Van Eemeren, Frans H. and Rob Grootendorst. 1992. *Argumentation, Communication, and Fallacies. A Pragma-Dialectical Perspective*. Hillsdale, NJ et al.: Laurence Erlbaum Associates.

El Refaie, Elizabeth. 2001. Metaphors we discriminate by: naturalized themes in Austrian newspaper articles about asylum seekers. *Journal of Sociolinguistics* 5/3: 352–371.

Fairclough, Norman. 1995. *Critical Discourse Analysis. The Critical Study of Language*. London, New York: Longman.

Fredman, Sandra and Erika Szyszak. 1993. The interaction of race and gender. In: Bob Hepple and Erika M. Szyszak (eds.), *Discrimination: The Limits of Law*, 214–226. London: Mansell Publishing.

Girnth, Heiko. 1996. Texte im politischen Diskurs. Ein Vorschlag zur diskursorientierten Beschreibung von Textsorten. *Muttersprache* 1/1996: 66–80.

Goffman, Erving. 1963. *Stigma: Notes on the Management of Spoiled Identity*. Englewood Cliffs, NJ: Prentice Hall.

Graumann, Carl Friedrich and Marget Wintermantel. 1989. Discriminatory speech acts: A functional approach. In: Daniel Bar-Dal, Carl Friedrich Graumann, Arie W. Kruglanski and Wolfgang Stroebe (eds.), *Stereotyping and Prejudice: Changing Conceptions*, 183–204. New York/ Berlin: Springer.

Gruber, Helmut. 1991. *Antisemitismus im Mediendiskurs: Die Affäre "Waldheim" in der Tagespresse*. Wiesbaden/ Opladen: Deutscher Universitätsverlag/Westdeutscher Verlag.

Gumperz, John J. 1982. *Discourse Strategies*. Cambridge: Cambridge University Press. Gumperz, John J. 2001 Interactional sociolinguistics: A personal perspective. In: Deborah Schiffrin, Deborah Tannen and Heidi Hamilton (eds.), *The Handbook of Discourse Analysis*, 215–228. Malden, MA/Oxford, UK: Blackwell.

Gumperz, John and Jenny Cook-Gumperz. 2007. Discourse, cultural diversity and communication: a linguistic anthropological perspective. In: Helga Kotthoff and Helen Spencer-Oatey (eds.), *Handbook of Intercultural Communication*, 13–30. Berlin: Mouton de Gruyter.

Hinnenkamp, Volker. 1991. Talking a person into interethnic distinction: A discourse analytic case study. In: Jan Blommaert and Jeff Verschueren (eds.), *Intercultural and International Communication: Selected Papers from the 1987 International Pragmatics Conference (Part*

III) and the Ghent Symposium on Intercultural Communication, 91–109. Amsterdam/Philadelphia: John Benjamins.

Hinnenkamp, Volker. 2001. Constructing misunderstanding as a cultural event. In: Aldo di Luzio, Susanne Günthner and Franca Orletti (eds.), *Culture in Communication: Analyses of Intercultural Situations*, 211–243. Amsterdam/Philadelphia: John Benjamins.

Hinnenkamp, Volker. 2003. Misunderstandings: Interactional structure and strategic resources. In: Juliane House, Gabriele Kasper and Steven Ross (eds.), *Misunderstanding in Social Life: Discourse Approaches to Problematic Talk*, 57–81. Harlow, UK: Longman/Pearson Education.

Jäger, Siegfried. 2001a. *Kritische Diskursanalyse: Eine Einführung*. Duisburg: DISS.

Jäger, Siegfried. 2001b. Discourse and knowledge: Theoretical and methodological aspects of a critical discourse and dispositive analysis. In: Ruth Wodak and Michael Meyer (eds.), *Methods of Critical Discourse Analysis*, 32–62. London: Sage.

Jäger, Margret, Gabriele Cleve, Ina Ruth and Siegfried Jäger. 1998. *Von deutschen Einzeltätern und ausländischen Banden: Medien und Straftaten: Mit Vorschlägen zur Vermeidung diskriminierender Berichterstattung*. Duisburg: DISS.

Karl-Renner-Institut (eds.). 1990. *Fremdenangst und Ausländerfeindlichkeit—Gegenargumente*. Vienna: Karl-Renner-Institut.

Kienpointner, Manfred. 1992. *Alltagslogik: Struktur und Funktion von Argumentationsmustern*. Stuttgart-Bad Cannstatt: Frommann-Holzboog.

Kienpointner, Manfred and Walther Kindt. 1997. On the problem of bias in political argumentation: An investigation into discussion about political asylum in Germany and Austria. *Journal of Pragmatics* 27: 555–585.

Kress, Gunther and Theo van Leeuwen. 1996. *Reading Images*. London: Routledge.

Van Leeuwen, Theo 1996 The representation of social actors. In: Carmen Rosa Caldas-Coulthard and Malcom Coulthard (eds.), *Texts and Practices: Readings in Critical Discourse Analysis*, 32–70. London/New York: Routledge.

Van Leeuwen, Theo. 2000. Visual racism. In: Martin Reisigl and Ruth Wodak (eds.), *The Semiotics of Racism: Approaches in Critical Discourse Analysis*, 333–350. Vienna: Passagen.

Lüsebrink, Hans-Jürgen. 2005. *Interkulturelle Kommunikation*. Stuttgart/Weimar: Metzler.

Makkonen, Timo. 2002. Multiple, Compound and Intersectional Discrimination—Bringing Experiences of the Most Disadvantaged to the Fore. *Institute for Human Rights Research Reports* No. 11 (April 2002): ⟨http://www.abo.fi/instut/imr/norfa/ timo.pdf⟩.

Makkonen, Timo. 2003. Hauptursachen, Formen und Folgen von Diskriminierung. In: Internationale Organisation für Migration (IOM) und Regionalbüro für die Baltischen und Nordischen Staaten (eds.), *Handbuch zur rechtlichen Bekämpfung von Diskriminierung*, 8–31. Helsinki: International Organisation for Migration (IOM).

The Oxford English Dictionary. 1989. *The Oxford English Dictionary*. Volume IV, *Creel–Duzepere*. Second Edition. Prepared by J.A. Simpson and E.S.C. Weiner. Oxford: Clarendon Press.

Piller, Ingrid. This volume. Cross-cultural communication in intimate relationships. Chapter 14.

Reeves, Frank. 1983. *British Racial Discourse: A Study of British Political Discourse about Race and Race-Related Matters*. Cambridge: Cambridge University Press.

Reisigl, Martin. 2002. "Dem Volk aufs Maul schauen, nach dem Mund reden und angst und bange machen"—Von populistischen Anrufungen, Anbiederungen und Agitationsweisen in der Sprache österreichischer PolitikerInnen. In: Wolfgang Eismann (ed.), *Rechtspopulismus. Österreichische Krankheit oder europäische Normalität?*, 149–198. Vienna: Cernin.

Reisigl, Martin. 2003. *Wie man eine Nation herbeiredet. Eine diskursanalytische Untersuchung zur sprachlichen Konstruktion der österreichischen Nation und österreichischen Identität in politischen Fest- und Gedenkreden*. Vienna: unpublished PhD.

Reisigl, Martin. In print. Stereotyp. In: Gert Ueding (ed.), *Historisches Wörterbuch der Rhetorik (HWRh)*. Volume 8, Tübingen: Niemeyer. Reisigl, Martin and Ruth Wodak 2001 *Discourse and Discrimination: Rhetoric of Racism and Antisemitism*. London/New York: Routledge.

Roberts, Celia, Evelyn Davies and Tom Jupp. 1993. *Language and Discrimination: A Study of Communication in Multi-Ethnic Workplace*. London/New York: Longman.

Scollon, Ron and Suzie Wong Scollon. 2001. Discourse and intercultural communication. In: Deborah Schiffrin, Deborah Tannen and Heide Hamilton (eds.), *Handbook of Discourse Analysis*, 538–547. Oxford: Blackwell.

Scollon, Ron and Suzie Wong Scollon. 2003a. *Intercultural Communication: A Discourse Approach.* Malden, MA/Oxford, UK: Blackwell.

Scollon, Ron and Suzie Wong Scollon. 2003b. *Discourses in Place.* London/New York: Routledge.

Singh, Rajendra, Jayant Lele and Gita Martohardjono. 1996. Communication in a multilingual society: some missed opportunities. In: Rajendra Singh (ed.), *Towards a Critical Sociolinguistics*, 237–254. Amsterdam: Benjamins.

Skuttnabb-Kangas, Tove and Robert Phillipson (eds.). 1994. *Linguistic Human Rights: Overcoming Linguistic Discrimination.* Berlin/ New York: Mouton de Gruyter.

Skuttnabb-Kangas, Tove. 2000. *Linguistic Genocide in Education—Or Worldwide Diversity and Human Rights?* Mahwah, NJ/London: Lawrence Erlbaum Associates.

Smitherman, Geneva and Teun A. van Dijk (eds.). 1988. *Discourse and Discrimination.* Detroit: Wayne State University Press.

Sykes, Mary. 1985. Discrimination in Discourse. In: Teun A. van Dijk (ed.), *Handbook of Discourse Analysis. Volume 4: Discourse Analysis in Society*, 83–101. London et al.: Academic Press.

Wagner, Franc. 2001. *Implizite sprachliche Diskriminierung als Sprechakt: Lexikalische Indikatoren impliziter Diskriminierung in Medientexten.* Tübingen: Narr.

Wengeler, Martin. 1997. Argumentation im Einwanderungsdiskurs: ein Vergleich der Zeiträume 1970–1973 und 1980–1983. In: Matthias Jung, Martin Wengeler and Karin Böke (eds.), *Die Sprache des Migrationsdiskurses: Das Reden über "Ausländer" in Medien, Politik und Alltag*, 121–149. Stuttgart: Westdeutscher Verlag.

Wodak, Ruth and Teun A. van Dijk (eds.). 2000. *Racism at the Top: Parliamentary Discourses on Ethnic Issues in Six European States.* Klagenfurt-Celovec: Drava.

Wodak, Ruth and Martin Reisigl. 2002. "Wenn einer Ariel heißt"—Ein linguistisches Gutachten zur politischen Funktionalisierung antisemitischer Ressentiments in Österreich. In: Anton Pelinka and Ruth Wodak (eds.), *"Dreck am Stecken". Politik der Ausgrenzung*, 134–172. Vienna: Czernin Verlag.

Wodak, Ruth, Johanna Pelikan, Peter Nowak, Helmut Gruber, Rudolf de Cillia and Richard Mitten. 1990. *"Wir sind alle unschuldige Täter!" Diskurshistorische Studien zum Nachkriegsantisemitismus.* Frankfurt am Main: Suhrkamp.

Wodak, Ruth, Florian Menz, Richard Mitten and Frank Stern. 1994. *Die Sprachen der Vergangenheiten: öffentliches Gedenken in österreichischen und deutschen Medien.* Frankfurt am Main: Suhrkamp.

Wodak, Ruth, Rudolf De Cillia, Martin Reisigl and Karin Liebhart. 1999. *The Discursive Construction of National Identity.* Edinburgh: Edinburgh University Press.

6

Power and Dominance in Intercultural Communication

Winfried Thielmann

1. Introduction and Overview

The treatment of non-native speakers within legal proceedings, linguistic expansion of indigenous languages in post-colonial societies, and science transfer to developing countries—these quite heterogeneous phenomena have two things in common: they are, somehow, matters of intercultural communication and they are, somehow, linked to the issues of power and dominance. Linguistic analysis of these phenomena faces a serious difficulty: Best linguistic evidence available consists of authentic *speech* and authentic *texts*. Hence there is a tendency to interpret elements of the linguistic surface as manifestations of, say, power and dominance—much in the way of text-immanent literary interpretation (e.g. Fairclough in print). Any attempt to go beyond the linguistic surface implies, however, that one has to make assumptions about people's intentions—for which there is no ultimate evidence in the material (McIlvenny 1992: 89–91).

In the first section of this chapter I shall argue that one can get out of this conundrum if one acknowledges that *extralinguistic phenomena* play a crucial role in societal interaction. Societal interaction consists in routine pursuits of systems of purposes. These routines are results of societal problem-solving processes and manifest themselves in *institutions* and in *interactional patterns* such as the *question-answer-pattern*—a specific, non-universal, purpose-driven structure for knowledge-processing (Ehlich and Rehbein 1979). In a pragmatic sense, these routine pursuits are already "cultural". Thus, intercultural issues systematically arise when people interact who—as a matter of societal routine—do things differently, even though they may speak the same language (Redder and Rehbein 1987). Issues of power and dominance within intercultural communication come into play when, for instance, institutional asymmetries such as the agent-client relationship are compounded by asymmetries of knowledge (Günthner and Luckmann 1995, Günthner 2007). Hence for an understanding of power and dominance in intercultural communication, societal organization and actants' knowledge are crucial factors to be considered in the analysis. If linguistics takes these matters seriously, analysis of authentic intercultural discourse—or of texts and concepts from

the intercultural sphere—may be able to dissolve issues of power and dominance into the question of how and in which systematic way people deal with
asymmetrical situations while pursuing their purposes. Such analyses may be
able to expose the pivots of such communication and thus provide the basis for
concrete suggestions of improvement.

In the second section of this chapter I shall attempt to examine—with due
brevity—three authentic situations of intercultural communication occurring
under the constraints of particular asymmetries:

- Intercultural communication within legal proceedings (Mattel-Pegam
  1985)
- Conceptual aspects of intercultural science and knowledge transfer
  that inspired the "grassroots" Grameen banking system in Bangladesh
  (Yunus and Jolis 1998)
- Linguistic expansion of an indigenous language in a post-colonial situation (Kummer 1985). All translations are mine.

2. Language, Cultural Knowledge, and Extralinguistic
Reality—Some Theoretical Reflections on Intercultural
Communication and Power

In this section I intend to unfold, motivate and exemplify the notion of *cultural
apparatus* developed in Redder and Rehbein (1987), as this concept has proven
to be a helpful analytical tool in dealing with intercultural communication
phenomena.

2.1. The Concept of Culture and Its History

The concept of culture has a complex history of which I shall only mention a
few crucial stages. For a critical discussion see Redder and Rehbein (1987:
7–8) and Ehlich (1996).

The Latin verb *colere* 'to farm', its past participle *cultus* and the noun *cultura* are initially almost exclusively tied to the agricultural sphere (e.g. Cato:
De agricultura). Through *colere*, Romans differentiated themselves from
other societies that did not farm, for instance nomadic tribes. It appears that
the discriminating potential of the concept was the driving force for Cicero's
metaphor of the *cultura animi* (Tusculanae disputationes) through philosophy—the 'farming of the mind' to overcome the state of "barbarism". Despite
its discriminatory aspects, the Roman concept is essentially dynamic. It is
the concept of an *activity*. During enlightenment, the concept—while maintaining its dynamic aspects—was expanded to also comprise other activities
through which human societies can overcome the *status naturalis* and gain
comfort: crafts, technology as well as politeness. Herder, for instance in his
reflections on the origin of language ([1772] 1997: 120), then links the concept to the development and improvement of nations and thus provides the
basis for a more static interpretation: culture as a *way of being*. Promulgated

by highly influential scholars such as Humboldt, this static concept of culture dominates in the 19th century and also remains powerful throughout the twentieth century: Culture is understood not as an activity, but as a product of activity, a system of achievements through which a society defines itself. The contradiction between *activity* and *entity*, however, never completely disappears: The change from assimilationism to multiculturalism in post-war Australian immigration policy may be taken as evidence of a recognition of the dynamic elements of the culture concept, yet the actual results of this change remain doubtful. In their sceptical but sympathetic history of post-war Australian immigration, Bosworth and Wilton (1984: 36–37) suggest that even modern Australian multiculturalism is hardly more than a public celebration of a multiplicity of cultural icons whilst immigrants' different ways remain unrecognized.

2.2. The Cultural Apparatus and Its Role in Intercultural Communication

Is it possible to scientifically instrumentalize and bring to fruition a concept that is—because of its complex tradition—rather an *explanandum* than an *explanans*? Drawing on Gramsci (1983), who reinstated the dynamic aspects of the culture concept and conceived of it as the practice of critical awareness of societal processes, Redder and Rehbein (1987) advocate a *pragmatic* concept of culture. They conceive of culture as an *apparatus*, a "functional aggregate of essentially different action paths determined by certain purposes". Punctuality, for instance, is part of the cultural apparatus, an "organised ensemble of societal [and therefore transindividual; W.T.] experience, ways of thought, forms of representation and practices" (Redder and Rehbein 1987: 16). The cultural apparatus is the basis for the societal reproduction of the respective domain (for instance punctuality). At the same time, however, it is the basis for criticism and change when actants become aware of its structure. Because of its importance for societal reproduction, a cultural apparatus may also be externalized. Then it takes the form of a *societal apparatus*, an *institution*.

Intercultural communication occurs when the differences between two people's cultural apparatus become apparent to them (Redder and Rehbein 1987: 18). Due to the aggregate nature of the cultural apparatus, these differences can lie in the areas of societal experience, practice and language. Intercultural communication in a *narrow sense* occurs when actants of the same society who speak the same language encounter a problem that results from differences in their cultural apparatus. Intercultural communication in a *broader sense* occurs when this kind of problem is encountered by actants from different societies who speak different languages.

What is the systematic place of the cultural apparatus within our daily activities ? Consider this quasi-empirical example:

> *Helga* (five years old, looking into the fridge): Mum, where's the juice?
> *Mother:* It's still on the table where you left it.

Helga has a need and tries to use her own resources to locate the item that ful-fils the need. But she encounters an obstacle. She can categorize this obstacle as a specific *knowledge* deficit ("where") within what she already knows ("that the juice must be somewhere"). She also knows that her mother usually knows where things are. She asks her mother a question, and her mother supplies the knowledge element Helga needs. This exchange of words will have conse-quences in extralinguistic reality: juice will be consumed.

The *question-answer-pattern* (Ehlich and Rehbein 1979) is a societal problem solution for the purpose of knowledge management the child has already learned. At school, however, she will encounter an unfamiliar usage of this pattern: It is usually the teachers who ask questions, and they do not do so because they want to know something, but because they want to know if one knows. Helga will have to make the transition from a child to a student within an *institution* and will have to learn how to handle an institutional transformation of the question-answer pattern that serves a completely dif-ferent kind of knowledge management. She will have to modify and expand her *cultural apparatus*.

2.3. Intercultural Communication in a Narrow Sense: Power and Dominance Within Intercultural Communication at School

School is a cultural apparatus turned institution: Schools exist in societies that—to ensure their reproduction—need to pass on a complex ensemble of *standard problem solutions* to the next generation (Ehlich and Rehbein 1986: 11, Scherr in this volume). Because of this very purpose, schools suffer from an inherent contradiction. They have to pass on standard solutions to problems that are not problematic for their clientele. As Ehlich and Rehbein demon-strate (1986: 11–13), the core of problem-solving consists of an *interest-driven lack of understanding*, the productive bafflement arising from a blockage of an action path. Schools, however, have to pass on a great number of standard problem solutions very quickly. Because of this, they have to:

1. leave out crucial stages of the actual problem-solving process (especially the stage of productive bafflement)
2. as a consequence of a), abstract from the "reality out here" and gener-ally pass on knowledge through language only.

To overcome these inherent contradictions, schools have developed specific solutions, for instance the *task-solution pattern* (Ehlich and Rehbein 1986: 14) and the *teacher's presentation with parts assigned to students*, during which the teacher elicits parts of knowledge from the class in order to ensure that stu-dents maintain involvement and participate in the presentation of new knowl-edge (Ehlich and Rehbein 1986: 81–87).

By the time children go to school, they have developed a cultural appa-ratus that allows them to manage their lives in the social situations they have encountered so far. Once they are at school, they become *clients* of an institution. There they encounter teachers, institutional *agents* with a very different cultural apparatus. Communication between students and teachers at school is, to a certain degree, *intercultural communication* in the narrow sense outlined above, i.e. it is intercultural communication whenever students and teachers encounter a problem that is due to a difference in their cultural apparatus.

Within the institution, the onus is on the students to modify—via intercultural communication in an *asymmetrical* situation—their cultural apparatus in a way that they become "proper" clients. The following admonition is a typical authentic example of this type of intercultural communication:

> T[eacher]: People who are wriggling are not looking.
>
> (Thwaite 2004: 83)

From the perspective of the institution, students are not expected to use the critical potential of their cultural apparatus (except for institutionally provided valves such as school newspapers), but rather its potential for adaptation and expansion.

This not only comprises the acquisition of, say, punctuality, but also the ability to manage the client-side of institution-specific interactional patterns such as the task-solution pattern, the exam-question or the teacher's presentation with parts assigned to students. In terms of knowledge management, students' institutional survival is virtually guaranteed when they can memorize the linguistic side of knowledge regarding standard solutions to problems that are not their own. Kügelgen (1994), an empirically based study of school discourse, paints a dark picture of what actually arrives in students' minds apart from mere words to be uttered at the right time.

Students' expanded cultural apparatus also comprises a cultural sub-apparatus, so to speak, of institutional survival consisting, for instance, of tactical questions (to pretend interest and thus escape the teacher's attention for a while) and maxims ("Cheat where you can but don't get caught!") (Ehlich and Rehbein 1977: 66), etc.

To sum up: Communication between agents of an institution and their clients has—because of their different cultural apparatus—*per se* an intercultural dimension whenever a problem occurs that points to these differences. Since the communicative situation in institutions is asymmetrical, the onus is usually on the clients to adjust, modify and expand their cultural apparatus to make this communication work. As we have seen, the very fact of institutionalization of areas essential to a society's reproduction may lead to intrinsic contradictions the institution can only partially overcome: Knowledge acquired at school cannot have the same quality as knowledge acquired through the individual, interest-driven solution of an authentic problem, even though pedagogical refinement of, say, the task–solution pattern may give students the illusion that they have done so. While the institutional agents have developed routines to at least partially overcome the institution's inherent contradictions on their part, clients have to absorb the interactional consequences of these contradictions into their cultural apparatus.

Of course, these issues can be discussed in the terms of power and dominance. Students are in the teacher's *domain of power* (Ehlich and Rehbein

1977: 22), they have to do—within the institutional limits, of course—what the teacher wants. Students and teachers are at the bottom of a hierarchy topped by, say, a minister—a hierarchy that, frequently in mysterious ways, decides on the content of what is being taught. Power is also—somehow—embodied in the *ideological knowledge* (i.e. a representation of society's structure that is inadequate but necessary for the society's reproduction as it is [Ehlich and Rehbein 1986: 167–168]) schools have to pass on by virtue of being schools.

I hope that I have been able to demonstrate, however, that it is the structure and dynamics of institutions themselves that require the most crucial—and often painful—changes on the part of the individual. And institutions are something no complex society can do without.

3. Asymmetrical Intercultural Communication in a Broader Sense

In this section I shall examine three very different authentic examples of asymmetrical intercultural communication in a broader sense, i.e. with actants belonging to or deriving from different societies.

3.1. Ethnocentrism—The Failure of Intercultural Communication in Prison

The particular asymmetries of legal institutions and their impact on communication have for some time been in the focus of linguists' attention (Hoffmann [1989] offers a collection of mostly empirically based studies from various perspectives). Aspects investigated include discourse types and strategies in the court room (Hoffmann 1983, 2002), the impact of class on legal proceedings (Wodak 1985), and problems of understanding resulting from the disfunctionality of discourse types within the institution (Hoffmann 1980). Koerfer's study of interpreter-mediated discourse in the court room (1994) deals explicitly with intercultural communication in the broader sense (for an account of the state of research in this area see Schröder 2000 and also Eades 2007 and Meierkord 2007).

The following reflections are based on the material and analysis in Mattel-Pegam (1985). The material consists of a transcription of the discourse at a German prison between an Italian prisoner, his German lawyer and an interpreter of German nationality. The Italian has been sentenced to seven years in prison for robbery. The lawyer is preparing an appeal. The consultation occurs at the client's request. In the following section of the transcript, the Italian client is-for about the third time—trying to get across the reason for which he wanted to see his lawyer: As the appeal is not looking too good, the Italian wishes to inquire whether there is the possibility of a *provvedimento*, an extra-judicial means that could be used in his favour. (I: Interpreter; L: Lawyer; C: Client):

> (39) I: Un altro avvocato non/
> *Another lawyer, not/*

(40a) C: Ma io non ho detto altro avvocato
           but I haven't said different lawyer
(40b) C: di prendere <u>provvedimento</u>
           use a means
(40c) C: Capisce provvedimento.che signific/
           Do you understand provvedimento.what that mean/
(41)   I: No.
           No.
(42a) C: Di fare ancora qualcosa.
           To do something else.
(42b) C: Di scrivere a qualche pubblico ministero più interessante
           To write to some public ministry that's more interested
(43)   I: I see . . . a mediator.
(44)   L: The only one to decide about this is the Fourth Panel of the Federal
           Court and nobody else, isn't it?
(45)   I: C'è soltanto la corte suprema . . . nessun altro.
           There's only the Supreme Court . . . nothing else.

The interpreter—whose performance throughout the exchange is not impressive—does not understand the crucial term *provvedimento* (see Spencer-Oatey and Xing 2007 on interpreter behaviour). This has—prior to the section quoted here—already caused some annoyance on the lawyer's part, who came to believe that his client wanted a *second* lawyer. In this section, the client can finally identify the problem, raise it *as a problem* (40c) and provide some knowledge to make the term less problematic (42a–42b). The interpreter begins to understand (43), but the lawyer, who has got some Italian too, cuts the conversation short by stating that there is only the institutionally provided path and no other. Mattel-Pegam writes (1985: 312; her emphasis):

The prisoner clearly has some idea about the meaning of the term [i.e. *provvedimento*]. But in his view *it is up to the expert to give the term precise meaning*, i.e. up to the lawyer, whom the prisoner not only sees as a legal expert, but also as a helper. Hence it would have been necessary for the interpreter to give some explanation.

Within the framework of Redder and Rehbein (1987), this is an example of failed intercultural communication in a *broader sense*: The prisoner on the one side, and the lawyer and the interpreter on the other not only belong to different groups of actants, but also to different societies. They encounter a problem that points to differences in their cultural apparatus (here: knowledge about institutional paths and alternatives as well as about the function of institutional agents). The actants on the institutional side and their client act *ethnocentrically* in that they assume mutual validity of their presuppositions. Otherwise the client would not have readily assumed the existence of a *provvedimento*, and the lawyer and the interpreter would have expected some reference to alternative remedies. The three interactants make no use of the critical potential of their cultural apparatus. None of them reaches their goal: The client, instead of a proper explanation, receives what can only be called a *rebuff* in illocutionary terms (44). The lawyer and the interpreter are not quite sure why the client wished to consult them in the first place.

Since all interactants act ethnocentrically, why does the transcript seem to transmit a strong sense that the client is being treated unfairly? This is due to the institutional asymmetry: The agents can afford to act ethnocentrically. Their client, however, cannot. As he does, the agents can make him "[. . .] accept what he has not understood" (Mattel-Pegam 1985: 322). Mattel-Pegam aligns herself with Gumperz (1978) when she concludes that because of institutional power structures and role-specific behaviour institutional agents usually do not all become aware of the failure of intercultural communication (Mattel-Pegam 1985: 322, Gumperz and Cook-Gumperz 2007). In the light of the discussions above, I feel that this point can be elaborated: Even when agent and client belong to the same society and speak the same language, institutional communication is already intercultural communication in the narrow sense. And because of this it has a similar potential of failure. Research into institutional communication (e.g. Ehlich 1980; Rehbein 1985b; Löning and Rehbein 1993; Redder and Wiese 1994) reveals that agents have a very strong tendency to act "ethnocentrically" also with clients belonging to their own society—i.e. with the majority who considers this as "normal". An (ethnic) minority, however, is *qua se* not yet part of societal normality—otherwise it would not be perceived as such. Hence it is more likely that institutional change is, in the long run, brought about by the ramifications of intercultural communication failure in the broader sense. Ironically, society as a whole is likely to profit from the pain its institutions cause (ethnic) minorities.

3.2. Dominant Knowledge—A Productive Failure of Intercultural Science Transfer

The relationship between first world donor countries and third world recipients of foreign aid is—for obvious reasons—highly asymmetrical. Foreign aid can be used as an instrument of power (for the complex interrelation between political and economic interests behind foreign aid see Schmidt [2003]). It is even more disturbing, however, when measures undertaken "within a responsible and constructive approach to the question of development aid" (Schmidt 2003: 507) seem to backfire. The steel plant at Rourkela, India, which was built with German aid, is a case in point: While this technology transfer has generated growth and employment, its impact on the region has resulted in substantial environmental and social problems such as the displacement of tribal populations (Meher 2003).

Science and knowledge transfer to developing countries is technology transfer's silent companion. Science transfer appears to be devoid of the interests behind foreign aid, and—because it involves scientists on both sides—to be somehow even immunized against intercultural communication problems. Yet the following brief case study may show that intercultural science transfer has the potential of being a silent instantiation of dominance in intercultural communication.

In the late 1960s, Muhammad Yunus from Bangladesh—on whose book (Yunus and Jolis 1998) this section is based—completed his doctorate in Economics at Vanderbilt University in Nashville, Tennessee. In 1972 he returned to Bangladesh as a lecturer for economics at the University of Chittagong. The great famine of 1974 made him aware of the limits of his knowledge: "I remember very well the enthusiasm with which I taught my students the solutions economic theories provided for all sorts of economic problems. I was enthralled by the beauty and elegance of these theories. But all of a sudden I realised the futility of my efforts. What was their point when everywhere, on the pavements and in front of the doors, people were dying from starvation?" (Yunus and Jolis 1998: 17). Yunus stopped teaching equations of economic theory. Instead, he and his students began to study empirically the reasons for poverty in their country. They soon found out three things: Most of the poor of their country ran small businesses. They stayed poor because in order to set up their businesses they had to borrow money from money lenders who charged ursurious rates. The poor would not be eligible for a bank loan, however, because they had nothing to offer as a material collateral. Yunus realized that the concept of "collateral" could be reinterpreted: "Collateral" did not have to be anything material, it could also consist of the clients' economic potential within their social network. This was the principle upon which Yunus developed his—profit making—Grameen bank, which meanwhile operates successfully in more than fifty thousand villages in Bangladesh.

The conceptual implications of this productive failure of intercultural science transfer are very intricate (for a detailed analysis see Thielmann [2004: 296–302]). Here I shall focus on the intercultural dimension, which—on a large scale—displays parallels to what has been said in Section 2.3. about power and dominance within intercultural communication at school.

Yunus studied economics in a Western country. In the terms of the previous analyses, he started out as a client of a foreign university and returned as a lecturer, as an institutional agent. As a client, he did not act ethnocentrically. On the contrary, he embraced the new knowledge. He willingly expanded his cultural apparatus. As an agent, being "enthralled by the beauty and elegance" of the theories he had studied, he passed this knowledge on. He acted as a multiplier within global science transfer—and he, unknowingly, was instrumental in imposing Western societal problem solutions on a society that worked differently. I shall argue that Yunus' initial ethnocentrism was due to the tacit assumptions behind the theories he studied in America.

As Toulmin (2001: 47–66) demonstrates in his insightful chapter "Economics or the physics that never was", Western economic theory formation was highly influenced by early modern physics, especially by Newton's theory of planetary motion. Yet by the beginning of the 19th century, physicists already knew that the solar system is much less stable than Newtonian law suggests. Economists of the 20th century, however, were still modelling their theories in the tradition of their predecessors, i.e. after a physics "that never was". In accordance with an early interdisciplinary science transfer gone sour without their knowledge, they expected their theories to hold, like a natural law, everywhere at any point in time. They did not expect them to be subject to variations of societal makeup. This had major consequences for intercultural science transfer: The knowledge that economic laws possess a status close to natural laws formed an integral part of economists' cultural apparatus. They tended to conceive of economic laws as universally applicable problem solutions, as a *set of recipes* that could be readily passed on as such.

Within intercultural science and knowledge transfer, the ethnocentricity that lies in passing on knowledge based on such a presupposition is, however, not likely to reveal itself: The appeal of recipes that supposedly hold for any society makes multipliers uncritically reproduce their inbuilt ethnocentricity—with potentially disastrous consequences for the society that imports solutions to problems that are not its own.

The powerful corrective of 1974's famine made Yunus fall back on another part of his education: empirical methodology. His studies yielded economic laws specific to his society, on the basis of which concrete measures for improvement could be put into place.

I have conducted this discussion without any reference to powerful institutions such as the World Bank or interest-driven policies of donor countries, etc. The reason why I could do so is, I believe, quite evident: Even if these players had behaved genuinely altruistically, they would still have been prone to act on the basis of a knowledge the ethnocentricity of which they were not aware of.

3.3. Linguistic Expansion (Sprachausbau) Under Postcolonial Duress

santa Maria   nijéit—chu
               fuck   neg.

(*virgo intacta* in Shuara; from Kummer 1985: 127)

Nowhere perhaps are power and dominance in intercultural communication felt more strongly about than in the area of—to put it neutrally—language maintenance. "Languages differ in their linguistic devices and purposes. Beyond this they differ in the forms of representation and practices, i.e. in the cultural apparatus, tied to them." (Redder and Rehbein 1987: 19). This complex interrelation is the basis for nation building via aggressive language policy (e.g. Hill 2002; Mikula 2002), maintenance of minority languages (e.g. Aklif 1999; Clyne 2004; Hatoss 2004) and issues of language planning and "ecology" (e.g. Gundara 1999; Mühlhäusler 2000; Liddicoat and Muller 2002b). As can be seen from most of these studies, linguists and policy makers alike make frequent use of the concept of *identity*—which is unfortunate, as this concept is as much of an *explanandum* as the culture concept. For if one just takes "identity" in a minimalist sense, say, "that which holds out against another", the concept can be applied to the major part of the material world as well as to mental entities such as thoughts in the sense of Frege (1967). Also the ecological metaphor tends to lose its descriptive merits very quickly when it is used to re-introduce, after the Darwinist speculations of the 19th century, biological notions to societal and linguistic processes (Finke 1996).

I therefore believe that an understanding of these issues is facilitated by trying to look at the purposes that generate them:

Nation building usually occurs amongst societies that are very similar. Its purpose is territorial and is best achieved by making political and linguistic borders coincide in people's minds (Auer 2004). Dragosavljevic˘ (2002) illustrates how aggressive language policy instrumentalizes the tiny differences between Ijekavian and Ekavian to ultimately create different countries within former Yugoslavia.

The issue of language maintenance frequently arises in postcolonial societies that comprise—very different—indigenous societies. Tradition and communication in these societies are mostly oral. If they lose their languages, they do not lose "identity", they lose their cultural apparatus. They lose society as such. "If people don't have their land and language, they will be lost. They won't know the names of the hills or waterholes, the trees or the animals. They won't know the dreaming stories for their country." (Deegan 1999: v).

For an indigenous society within a postcolonial environment there are three principal paths of further development:

1. It survives intact, i.e. its members can survive in the traditional way.
2. Part of the tradition is lost, the rest is maintained. The truncated indigenous society is supported as a resource (e.g. for tourism) by the postcolonial society and/or by members who are also integrated in the postcolonial society.
3. The indigenous society is completely absorbed by the postcolonial society.

I shall now focus on a society that has taken a fourth, alternative route of *linguistic expansion* ('Sprachausbau'): the Shuar of the Ecuadorian Amazon. My reflections are chiefly based on Kummer (1985).

After the Shuar had successfully resisted colonization attempts until the late 19th century, Salesian missionaries succeeded in establishing schools and administration, which in turn brought more and more colonists to the Shuar territory. While the major part of the acephalous Shuar society retained its language and traditional ways, a smaller part was integrated in the colonial society. Further change occurred when the Ecuadorian government required land for more colonists during the 1960s. The missionaries, whose contract with the government was cancelled in 1966, ensured their institutional survival by assisting the Shuar in setting up their own administration: the *Federación de los Centros Shuar*. The Shuar language, whose status had suffered during the first colonization period, became an important instrument to unify the Shuar against the new colonists. It was also made a language of instruction in the Federation's bilingual school system. Missionaries and their former Shuar students designed lessons in accordance with Ecuador's curriculum. These lessons were then radio broadcast to the remote *Centros*. There they were passed on to children by assistant teachers. According to Almeida (2004), the Catholic influence has been meanwhile reduced and the Bi-cultural Shuar Radio Education System (SERBISH) "provides education for about 7,500 children—out of a Shuar population of 70,000—in 297 schools teaching from primary to the end of the secondary level". During this process, the Shuar language had to be linguistically expanded to render concepts of the modern, Spanish speaking postcolonial society.

As can be seen from the brief example at the beginning of this section, first attempts at the linguistic expansion of Shuara were made by missionaries—who were also the first to write the language. "Holiness" and "virginity" were not part of the Shuar's cultural apparatus; thus *santa* was left as part of the name and "virginity" was rendered via the neutral concept of intercourse, *nijéit*—for which there does not seem to be a neutral term in Western languages (Kummer 1985: 127).

The modern linguistic expansion of Shuara occurred within a few decades. Kummer discusses various sections from Shuar school books, from which I have compiled a small word list to show some examples of expansion of the lexicon (the numbers in brackets refer to the pages of Kummer's article):

Table 1. Expansion of the lexicon in Shuara

Shuar word	Literal translation	Intended meaning	Reference
tuntui	drum	radio	(131, 133)
tsuramta	fit, seizure	electricity	(132, 133)
uunt kunkuim	big turtle	truck	(132, 133)
chikich kunkuim	small turtle	car	(132, 133)
irun-mia-yi	there lived	there were	(136, 137)
jiru (from Span. 'hierro')	iron	iron	(145, 146)
mahin	machine	machine	(145, 146)
mahin tante	machine that turns	turbine	(145, 146)
entsa kya aaniun katsurman	something strong that is similar to a rock in water	dam	(145, 146)
takamtiktai	a means that is made work	slave	(140, 142)
nekainiachiat (for Span. 'inculto')	someone who knows nothing	uneducated person	(140, 142)

Apart from the loan words *jiru* and *mahin*, the linguistic devices employed to render new concepts are exclusively Shuar. The strategies include metaphorization ("drum" for "radio") and paraphrase ("something strong that is similar to a rock in water" for "dam"). These terms and phrases are *motivated* (Ricken 1995) in that the new concept is, however vaguely, linked to knowledge already there—which facilitates recollection. The form *takamtiktai* 'slave' is the result of word formation: "(. . .) the suffix -tai (. . .) designates a person or a thing that is used as a means for an action. This suffix is one of the most important productive elements to derive terms for appliances that are new to the culture from the activities characteristic for these appliances." (Kummer 1985: 143). Another structural device used frequently by the translators is the verbal suffix -iti which allows the attribution of processes to entities. This new and frequent usage of structural devices "leads to new syntactic registers that—to ensure accessibility of the new text types—need to remain close to the traditional registers." (Kummer 1985: 147).

At a first glance none of the linguistic expansion strategies discussed here is in any way surprising. When European vernacular languages were expanded for the purpose of doing science, all of these strategies were used in one way or another (for German see Wolff [1733] 1973, [1713] 1978; Ricken 1995; Ehlich 1995; for Italian Thielmann 2003). But these expansions were not only a slow process, they also occurred on the basis of concepts that were already known to the scientific community by their Latin terms.

Yet the Shuar language was expanded within a few decades to accommodate the complete cultural apparatus of postcolonial Ecuador as it is represented by the National Curriculum. New concepts were rendered by new terms in a language of instruction stretched to the limits. The language was made "do the splits". So were—presumably—the students when in this language they learned about societal solutions to problems alien to their society. As for the linguistic difficulties during the process of linguistic expansion, Kummer writes (1985, 141): "Within the analytical sections of the school book texts, the shift in the frequencies of certain syntactic connection devices and their unusual combination results in a syntax the average speaker of Shuar cannot decode. (. . .) Even teachers who have to work with these texts can only reproduce the parts of a complex sentence, but not the complex sentence as a whole. As a result, students taught by these teachers do not understand these complex sentences either. It would require a larger study to determine whether the new syntactic registers created in the school book language are gradually going to be accepted by the ethnic community, or whether education in their own language is going to fail for reasons such as the large distance between traditional syntax and the new register."

According to Almeira (2004) the experiment has worked and enjoys the Shuar's full support: "In the search for an alternative to modernization imposed from above, the Shuar have managed to reduce semi-illiteracy to seven per cent and total illiteracy to two per cent." "Relying on their organizational strength, they now have some very ambitious projects, including one for an educational television station, for which they are seeking foreign technical assistance and funding."

The Shuar survived as a society because they codified, institutionalized and expanded their language. Stretched to its very limits, this language at least partially mediates and reconciles two extremely different cultural apparatus in a way that gives the society a genuine opportunity to determine its own future within postcolonial Ecuador.

Even in the light of this, it is still possible to argue that the linguistic expansion of Shuara is equivalent to the Shuar's final colonization and that the society's traditional ways will suffer. But such a view would presuppose authenticity as desirable for indigenous societies in a postcolonial context. It would neglect the fact that the only authentic indigenous societies are those still unknown. The only way to preserve the "authenticity" of a known indigenous society is to limit contact and to make sure they cannot communicate their own interests in a world that to them will never be the same nevertheless.

4. Conclusion

Power and dominance within intercultural communication are due to asymmetrical constellations within three different instances of reality: societal structure, actants' knowledge and language. I have discussed three particular asymmetries with regard to these instances: the agent-client asymmetry of institutions; tacit ethnocentrism of knowledge within intercultural science transfer; and linguistic expansion of an indigenous language under postcolonial duress.

Interaction within institutions is paradigmatic for intercultural communication in a narrow sense: Even when agents and clients speak the same language, their cultural apparatus differ. School, which is concerned with the expansion of its clients' cultural apparatus, is an extreme example of an institution whose intrinsic contradictions make it perpetuate its permanent intercultural communication failure. Institutional asymmetries compound the difficulties for intercultural communication in a broader sense: As agents can get away with behaving ethnocentrically, their clients may not find advice, but encounter a rebuff.

Intercultural science transfer is a complex process in institutional terms, as multipliers are former clients turned agents. If the knowledge they are meant to spread is based on ethnocentric presuppositions, they will act ethnocentrically in spreading it—which will have ramifications for the society intended to profit from this knowledge.

Indigenous languages are usually not equipped to render the cultural apparatus of the postcolonial administrative languages they are in competition with. This puts them in a fragile position.

The problems of power and dominance in intercultural communication thus analysed cannot be resolved by "removing" power and dominance. As far as institutions can at all reconcile their intrinsic contradictions, ethnocentric behaviour of agents can be overcome by intercultural training and guidelines. Intercultural science transfer should, on principle, be perceived as intercultural communication in a broader sense, i.e. the knowledge transferred should be conceived of as a problem solution specific to the society that solved the problem for itself. On principle, indigenous languages can be expanded to mediate and reconcile the cultural apparatus of both the indigenous and the postcolonial society, so that the indigenous society has a genuine opportunity to determine its own future. As the case of the Shuar has shown, this necessitates circumstances and prerequisites that enable the indigenous society to design its own language policy.

References

Aklif, Gedda. 1999. *Ardiyooloon Bardi Ngaanka. One Arm Point Bardi Dictionary.* Halls Creek,WA: Kimberly Language Resource Centre.

Almeida, Marcos. 2004. Shuara, a language that refused to die. In: *UNESCO Courier* 2004: 4 (http://www.unesco.org/courier/2000_04/uk/doss23.htm, 7. 12. 04).

Auer, Peter. 2004. Sprache, Grenze, Raum. *Zeitschrift für Sprachwissenschaft* 23(2): 149–179.

Bosworth, Richard and Janis Wilton. 1984. *Old Worlds and New Australia. The Post-War Migrant Experience.* Ringwood (Australia): Penguin.

Brünner, Gisela and Gabriele Graefen (eds.). 1994. *Texte und Diskurse. Methoden und Forschungsergebnisse der Funktionalen Pragmatik.* Opladen: Westdeutscher Verlag.

Clyne, Michael. 2004. Languages taken at school and languages spoken in the community—a comparative perspective. *Australian Review of Applied Linguistics* 27(2): 1–17.

Deegan, Bonnie. 1999. Foreword to the One Arm Point Bardi Dictionary. In: Gedda Aklif (ed.), *Ardiyooloon Bardi Ngaanka. One Arm Point Bardi Dictionary*. Halls Creek, WA: Kimberly Language Resource Centre.

Dragosavljevic˜, Andjelija. 2002. Language and politics in the Republika Srpska. In: Anthony Liddicoat and Karis Muller (eds.), *Perspectives on Europe. Language Issues and Language Planning in Europe*, 141–152. Melbourne: Language Australia.

Eades, Diana. 2007. Understanding Aboriginal silence in legal contexts. In: Helga Kothoff and Helen Spencer-Oatey (eds.), *Handbook of Intercultural Communication*, 285–302. Berlin: Mouton de Gruyter.

Ehlich, Konrad (ed.). 1980. *Erzählen im Alltag*. Frankfurt a. M.: Suhrkamp.

Ehlich, Konrad. 1995. Die Lehre der deutschen Wissenschaftssprache: sprachliche Strukturen, didaktische Desiderate. In: Leo Kretzenbacher and Harald Weinrich (eds.), *Linguistik der Wissenschaftssprache* (Akademie der Wissenschaften zu Berlin. Forschungsbericht 10), 325–352. Berlin: de Gruyter.

Ehlich, Konrad. 1996. Interkulturelle Kommunikation. In: Hans Goebl and Peter H. Nelde (eds.), *Kontaktlinguistik. Ein internationales Handbuch zeitgenössischer Forschung*, 920–931. Berlin/New York: de Gruyter.

Ehlich, Konrad and Jochen Rehbein. 1977. Wissen, kommunikatives Handeln und die Schule. In: Herma C. Goeppert (ed.), *Sprachverhalten im Untericht. Zur Kommunikation von Lehrer und Schüler in der Unterrichtssituation*, 36–114. München: Fink.

Ehlich, Konrad and Jochen Rehbein. 1979. Sprachliche Handlungsmuster. In: Hans Georg Soeffener (ed.), *Interpretatorische Verfahren in den Sozial- und Textwissenschaften*, 243–274. Stuttgart: Metzler.

Ehlich, Konrad and Jochen Rehbein. 1986. *Muster und Institution. Untersuchungen zur schulischen Kommunikation*. Tübingen: Narr.

Fairclough, Norman (in print) Critical discourse analysis in researching language in the new capitalism: Overdetermination, transdisciplinarity and textual analysis. In: Claire Harrison and Lynne Young (eds.), *Systemic Functional Linguistics and Critical Discourse Analysis*. London/New York: Continuum.

Finke, Peter. 1996. Sprache als *missing link* zwischen natürlichen und kulturellen Ökosystemen. Überlegungen zur Weiterentwicklung der Sprachökologie. In: Alwin Fill (ed.), *Sprachökologie und Ökolinguistik*, 27–48. Tübingen: Stauffenburg.

Frege, Gottlob. 1967. Begriff und Gegenstand. In: Ignacio Angelleli (ed.), *Gottlob Frege, Kleine Schriften*, 167–178. Hildesheim: Olms.

Goeppert, Herma C. (ed.). 1977. Sprachverhalten im Unterricht. Zur Kommunikation von Lehrer und Schüler in der Unterrichtssituation. München: Fink.

Gramsci, Antonio. 1983. Marxismus und Kultur. Ideologie, Alltag, Literatur (transl. and ed. by Sabine Kebir). Hamburg: VSA.

Gumperz, John. 1978. The conversational analysis of interethnic communication. In: E. Lamar Ross (ed.), *Interethnic Communication*. Proceedings of the Southern Anthropological Society, 305–325. University of Georgia Press.

Gumperz, John and Jenny Cook-Gumperz. 2007. Discourse, cultural diversity and communication: a linguistic anthropological perspective. In: Helga Kothoff and Helen Spencer-Oatey (eds.), *Handbook of Intercultural Communication*, 13–30. Berlin: Mouton de Gruyter.

Gundara, Jagdish. 1999. Linguistic Diversity, Globalisation and Intercultural Education. In: Joe Lo Bianco, Anthony J. Liddicoat and Chantal Crozet (eds.) *Striving for the Third Place. Intercultural Competence through Language Education*, 23–42. Melbourne: Language Australia.

Günthner, Susanne and Thomas Luckmann. 1995. *Asymmetries of Knowledge in Intercultural Communication: The Relevance of Cultural Repertoire of Communicative Genres*. Konstanz: Fachgruppe Sprachwissenschaft der Universität Konstanz, Arbeitspapier Nr. 72.

Günthner, Susanne. 2007. Intercultural communication and the relevance of cultural specific repertories of communicative genres. In: Helga Kothoff and Helen Spencer-Oatey (eds.), *Handbook of Intercultural Communication*, 127–152. Berlin: Mouton de Gruyter.

Harrison, Claire and Lynne Young. 2004. *Systemic Functional Linguistics and Critical Discourse Analysis*. London/ New York: Continuum.

Hatoss, Anikó. 2004. Mother tongue maintenance and acculturation in two vintages of the Hungarian diaspora in Queensland. *Australian Review of Applied Linguistics* 27(2): 18–31.

Herder, Johann Gottfried. 1997. [1772] *Abhandlung über den Ursprung der Sprache*. Stuttgart: Reclam.

Hill, Peter M. 2002. Language and national identity. In: Anthony Liddicoat and Karis Muller (eds.), *Perspectives on Europe. Language Issues and Language Planning in Europe*, 11–20. Melbourne: Language Australia.

Hoffmann, Ludger. 1980. Zur Pragmatik von Erzählformen vor Gericht. In: Konrad Ehlich (ed.), *Erzählen im Alltag*, 28–64. Frankfurt a. M.: Suhrkamp.

Hoffmann, Ludger. 1983. *Kommunikation vor Gericht*. Tübingen: Narr.

Hoffmann, Ludger (ed.). 1989. *Rechtsdiskurse*. Tübingen:
Narr. Hoffmann, Ludger. 2002. Rechtsdiskurse zwischen Normalität und Normativität. In: Ulrike Haß-Zumkehr (ed.), *Sprache und Recht*, 80–100. Berlin/New York: de Gruyter.

Koerfer, Armin. 1994. Interkulturelle Kommunikation vor Gericht. Verständigungsprobleme beim fremdsprachlichen Handeln in einer kommunikationsintensiven Institution. In: Gisela Brünner and Gabriele Graefen (eds.), *Texte und Diskurse. Methoden und Forschungsergebnisse der funktionalen Pragmatik*, 351–373. Opladen: Westdeutscher Verlag.

Kügelgen, Rainer v.. 1994. *Diskurs Mathematik. Kommunikationsanalysen zum reflektierenden Lernen* (Arbeiten zur Sprachanalyse 17). Frankfurt a. M.: Lang.

Kummer, Werner. 1985. Probleme der Funktionserweiterung von Sprachen: Der Sprachausbau bei den Shuara in Ecuador. In: Jochen Rehbein (ed.), *Interkulturelle Kommunikation*, 166–174. Tübingen: Narr.

Liddicoat, Anthony and Karis Muller (eds.) 2002a *Perspectives on Europe. Language Issues and Language Planning in Europe*. Melbourne: Language Australia.

Liddicoat, Anthony and Karis Muller 2002b Language issues and language planning in Europe. In: Anthony Liddicoat and Karis Muller (eds.), *Perspectives on Europe. Language Issues and Language Planning in Europe*, 1–10. Melbourne: Language Australia.

Lo Bianco, Joe, Anthony Liddicoat and Chantal Crozet (eds.). 1999. *Striving for the Third Place. Intercultural Competence through Language Education*. Melbourne: Language Australia.

Löning, Petra and Jochen Rehbein (eds.). 1993. *Arzt-Patienten-Kommunikation. Analysen zu interdisziplinären Problemen des medizinischen Diskurses*. Berlin/New York: de Gruyter.

Mattel-Pegam, Gesine. 1985. Ein italienischer Strafgefangener konsultiert einen deutschen Rechtsanwalt. In: Jochen Rehbein (ed.), *Interkulturelle Kommunikation*, 299–323. Tübingen: Narr.

McIlvenny, Paul. 1992. Missing an important transition relevance point: Towards a critical conversation analysis. In: Leena Kuure and Paul McIlvenny (eds.), *Text and Talk. Proceedings of the 4th Discourse Analysis Seminar*, Oulu, October 1992, 87–112. Oulu (Finland): University of Oulu.

Meher, Rajkishor. 2003. The social and ecological effects of industrialisation in a tribal region: The case of the Rourkela Steel Plant. *Contributions to Indian Sociology* 37(3): 429–457.

Meierkord, Christiane. 2007. Lingua franca communication in multiethnic contexts. In: Helga Kothoff and Helen Spencer-Oatey (eds.), *Handbook of Intercultural Communication*, 199–218. Berlin: Mouton de Gruyter.

Mikula, Maja. 2002. Croatia's independence and the language politics of the 1990s. In: Anthony Liddicoat and Karis Muller (eds.), *Perspectives on Europe. Language Issues and Language Planning in Europe*, 109–123. Melbourne: Language Australia.

Mühlhäusler, Peter. 2000. Language planning and language ecology. *Current Issues in Language Planning* 1(3): 306–367.

Redder, Angelika and Jochen Rehbein. 1987. Zum Begriff der Kultur. *Osnabrücker Beiträge zur Sprachtheorie (OBST)* 38: 7–21.

Redder, Angelika and Ingrid Wiese (eds.). 1994. *Medizinische Kommunikation: Diskurspraxis, Diskursethik, Diskursanalyse*. Opladen: Westdeutscher Verlag.

Rehbein, Jochen. 1997. *Komplexes Handeln. Elemente zur Handlungstheorie der Sprache*. Stuttgart: Metzler.

Rehbein, Jochen (ed.) 1985a *Interkulturelle Kommunikation*. Tübingen: Narr.

Rehbein, Jochen 1985b Medizinische Beratung türkischer Eltern. In: Jochen Rehbein (ed.), *Interkulturelle Kommunikation*, 349–419 Tübingen: Narr.

Ricken, Ulrich. 1995. Zum Thema Christian Wolff und die Wissenschaftssprache der deutschen Aufklärung. In: Leo Kretzenbacher and Harald Weinrich (eds.), *Linguistik der Wissenschaftssprache* (Akademie der Wissenschaftssprachen zu Berlin. Forschungsbericht 10), 41–90. Berlin: de Gruyter.

Scherr, Albert. 2007. Schools and Cultural Difference. In: Helga Kothoff and Helen Spencer-Oatey (eds.), *Handbook of Intercultural Communication*, 303–322. Berlin: Mouton de Gruyter.

Schmidt, Heide-Irene. 2003. Pushed to the front: The foreign assistance policy of the Federal Republic of Germany. *Contemporary European History* 12(4): 473–507.

Schröder, Hartmut. 2000. Sprachliche Aspekte der Kommunikation von Ausländern vor Gerichten. In: Gerhard Wolf (ed.), *Kriminalität im Grenzgebiet. Bd. 3: Ausländer vor deutschen Gerichten*, 269–284. Berlin/Heidelberg/New York: Springer.

Spencer-Oatey, Helen and Jianyu Xing. 2007. The impact of culture on interpreter behaviour. In: Helga Kothoff and Helen Spencer-Oatey (eds.), *Handbook of Intercultural Communication*, 219–236. Berlin: Mouton de Gruyter.

Thielmann, Winfried. 2002. The problem of English as the *lingua franca* of scholarly writing from a German perspective. In: Anthony Liddicoat and Karis Muller (eds.), *Perspectives on Europe. Language Issues and Language Planning in Europe*, 95–108 Melbourne: Language Australia.

Thielmann, Winfried. 2003. Wege aus dem sprachpolitischen Vakuum? Zur scheinbaren wissenschaftskulturellen Neutralität wissenschaftlicher Universalsprachen. In: Konrad Ehlich (ed.), *Mehrsprachige Wissenschaft—europäische Perspektiven. Eine Konferenz im Europäischen Jahr der Sprachen*. www.euro-sprachenjahr.de/.

Thielmann, Winfried. 2004. Begriffe als Handlungspotentiale—Überlegungen zu einer Klärung des Phänomens der 'Bedeutung' einiger fach- bzw. wissenschaftssprachlicher Symbolfeldausdrücke. *Linguistische Berichte* 199: 287–311.

Thwaite, Anne. 2004. Classroom discourse of an experienced teacher of indigeneous children. *Australian Review of Applied Linguistics* 27(2): 75–91.

Toulmin, Stephen. 2001. *Return to Reason*. Cambridge, MA: Harvard University Press. Van Dijk, Teun (ed.). 1985. *Handbook of Discourse Analysis*. Volume 4. *Discourse Analysis in Society*. London: Academic Press.

Wodak, Ruth. 1985. The interaction between judge and defendant. In: Teun A. Van Dijk (ed.), *Handbook of Discourse Analysis*. Volume 4. *Discourse Analysis in Society*, 181–191. London: Academic Press.

Wolff, Christian. 1978. [1713] *Ausführliche Nachricht von seinen eigenen Schriften, die er in deutscher Sprache heraus gegeben* (Facsimile of the edition from 1733; Gesammelte Werke 1. Abt. Bd. 9). Hildesheim: Olms.

Wolff, Christian. 1973. [1733] *Vernünfftige Gedanken von den Kräften des menschlichen Verstandes und ihrem richtigen Gebrauch in Erkenntniß der Wahrheit* (Deutsche Logik). Hildesheim: Olms.

Yunus, Muhammad and Allan Jolis. 1998. *Grameen—eine Bank für die Armen der Welt*. Bergisch Gladbach: Lübbe.

7

Communicating Identity in Intercultural Communication

Janet Spreckels and Helga Kotthoff

When studying intercultural communication, the question automatically arises of the identities through which individuals encounter each other and how this encounter can be analyzed. When an Italian and a Swedish surgeon jointly perform an operation in Zurich, their national identities are not necessarily important. What is relevant under the given circumstances is that both are surgeons, can communicate with each other, and who has more experience in performing particular surgical procedures. In order to discuss, in the second part of the article, the various procedures which set cultural categorization as relevant, in the first part the conceptualization of "identity" will be outlined.[1]

1. Social Identity

The concept of *social identity* arose in social psychology and was, among others, developed by the social psychologists Henri Tajfel, Joseph Forgas and Jim Turner. Tajfel (1982: 2) defines the concept of social identity as follows:

> Social identity will be understood as that *part* of the individuals' self-concept which derives from their knowledge of their membership of a social group (or groups) together with the value and emotional significance attached to that membership.

Social identity is thus the part of an individual's self-concept that is derived from her/his knowledge of her/his membership in social groups and from the emotional significance with which this membership is endowed. Tajfel's emphasis on "part" can be understood if one considers the other part of the self-concept, 'personal' identity. The concept of this division of the 'self' into two parts goes back to the social psychologist George Herbert Mead. In his major work, *Mind, Self and Society* (1934), he developed an interactionist paradigm

---

[1] This first part is based on Janet Spreckels's discussion of identity concepts in her book *Britneys, Fritten Gangschta und wir*: Identitätskonstitution in einer Mädchengruppe. Eine ethnographisch-gesprächsanalytische Untersuchung (2006).

of identity that contains the reflexive ability of the subject to behave toward himself and toward others. Identity accordingly has two components:

1. a social component, the so-called 'me' and
2. a personal component (also the personal, individual, subject or self) component, the 'I'

Mead thereby paved the way for the later concept of the 'social' vs. the 'personal' identity, without, however, himself using these terms. The social component of identity worked out by Mead develops through the growth of the individual into his socio-cultural surroundings and is derived from identification with various social collectivities, such as, e.g., a family, sport association or peer group of which the individual understands himself to be a part. Social identity is thus a part of the self worked out in the socio-cultural life context. Personal identity, to the contrary, refers to the uniqueness of the individual in connection with his unmistakable life history (Hillmann 1994: 350–53) and is "something like the continuity of the I" (Habermas 1968). Krappmann (1978: 39) summarizes this dichotomy as follows:

> Obviously, identity is both simultaneously: the anticipated expectations of the other and the individual's own answers. G.H. Mead took this dual aspect of identity into account in his concept of the self, which contains a "me" that is the adopted attitudes of the other, and an "I," the individual's answer to the expectations of the others.

Although most authors usually speak of 'identity' in the singular, "each social identity is just one among many [. . .] which each individual possesses" (Schwitalla & Streeck 1989: 237), because "the uniqueness of individuals lies in their blend of multiple social and personal identities" (Meyerhoff 1996: 215). We all take various roles in everyday life (as daughter, girlfriend, member of a sport club, etc.), affiliate with various social groups and thereby mark out a variety of social identities. Individuals construct their social identities on the basis of various socially and culturally relevant parameters, such as nationality, gender, age, profession, lifestyle, etc. (Duszak 2002: 2 and Keupp et al. 2002: 68). The concept of social identity must therefore be understood as multi-sided and very dynamic.

Today it is commonplace in social psychology to think of identity as the processual and never-ending task of each person (see Brabant, Watson and Gallois in this volume), but this was not always the case. In the older literature there were occasionally static concepts which portrayed biography and identity "as something stable, permanent and unchangeable" (Keupp et al. 2002: 22). Such approaches, which portray identity as a sort of goal to be achieved, can however not be upheld in view of empirical studies and an increasingly multi-facetted society. Already Mead (1934) pointed in his interactionist approach to the constructive and negotiated character of social identity and emphasized that identity is by no means a quantity that is set once and for all, but rather is constantly being negotiated in interaction. More recently, this important aspect has often been emphasized, thus, e.g., Duszak (2002: 2) has written, "social identities tend to be indeterminate, situational rather than permanent, dynamic and interactively constructed."

1.1. Modern Patchwork Identities

If the construction of identity, as described above, is a lifelong process, this dynamism and changeability simultaneously pose the danger of an inconsistent identity. Our modern world is marked by accelerated processes of change, greater geographic and social mobility, freedom to form attachments, the pluralization of life forms and worldviews, and progressive individualization. Thereby each individual's possible identity spectrum has considerably increased: "While earlier the development of identity was much more strongly marked by the position into which one was born, modern man is forced to choose among many possibilities, and this struggle of youth with the required choice of a self-definition is [. . .] referred to as an identity crisis" (Oerter and Dreher 1995: 348; Baumeister 1986; Luckmann et al. 1981).

A key term in the contemporary process of finding an identity is 'possibility of choice': "modernity confronts the individual with a *complex diversity of choices* and . . . at the same time offers little help as to which options should be selected" (Giddens 1991: 80, emphasis added). Where previously there was little possibility of choice, today individuals face a life-world variety of experiences that on the one side frees them, but on the other side leaves them deeply insecure and partly overtaxed. Schäfers (2001: 92) points out that identity problems only arise in social systems like the present ones. Giddens (1991: 81) aptly describes this situation with the insight: "[W]e have no choice but to choose."

Certain basic, self-evident aspects of our society are being put in question and shaken by new alternatives. Today there are, e.g., various models of the most important social group upon which society is based: the family. The emancipation movement brought about the possibility for the classical role models of the devoted mother and housewife and the father as family breadwinner to be challenged and revised. Certainly there are still a large number of families with traditional role assignments, but besides this, today there are also some families where the wife 'brings home the bacon' while the husband takes a parental leave of absence. In addition, there are single mothers and fathers, commuter families, homosexual couples with children, so-called 'patchwork families' that result from the founding of families after respectively terminated partnerships, etc. Family relationships are today anything but clearly defined and therefore no longer serve to the same degree as previously as stable references for identity. The family is only one area of societal life that has lost stability in the course of socio-cultural change; besides it one can name class membership, nation, professional world, religion, gender and generational relationships, sexuality and many others. Keupp et al. (2002: 87) therefore speak of the "dissolution of guarantees of coherency" and affirm that "even the core stocks of our identity constructions—national and ethnic identity, gender and body identity [have lost] their quasi-'natural' quality as guarantors of identity."

In the 1960s James Marcia, a student of Erikson, developed the identity model of his teacher, by constructing a differentiated model with four different identity states, the "identity status model" (Marcia 1966). He distinguishes among a) "achievement," i.e., an earned or developed identity, b) the "moratorium," a currently ongoing struggle with various value questions, c) "foreclosure," the adopted identity, mostly through the adoption of the value conceptions of the parents, and finally d) "identity diffusion," a state in which individuals have not yet reached a firm position on values. In order to grasp a person's current identity status, Marcia posed youthful subjects a series of questions in the frame of an "identity status interview" (concerning professions, religion, politics, etc.). His empirical studies (Marcia 1989) showed that the share of youth with diffuse identities had increased after ca. 1984 from 20 % to ca. 40 %. Marcia thereby offered an early proof that youth are becoming less inclined to "commit themselves to stable, binding and obligating—and in this sense identity-giving—relationships, orientations and values." (Keupp et al. 2002: 81).

This tendency has increased in recent years. In the so-called 'fun society' of today hedonistic, media-, experience- and consumer-oriented values play a commanding role, which simultaneously entails a large number of new possible identifications. Penelope Eckert (2000: 14) describes the situation of youth in modern times as a "marketplace of identities," and Baacke (1987) describes the life worlds of youths as "surfing between various experiential worlds." The result of these expanded possibilities of choice are modern identities that Elkind (1990) refers to as "patchwork identities." Such an identity is, as the metaphorical concept reveals, pieced together from individual "patches," namely partial-identities, and possesses no unified identity core. Oerter and Dreher (1995: 354) point out that persons with patchwork identities can be very successful, but no longer fulfill "the 'classical' criteria of a worked-out, integrated identity." In a patchwork-self, "value attitudes and customs are juxtaposed with no ties and in part contradict each other." (ibid.) The classical question of identity research, namely of how the individual succeeds in achieving a consistent identity from a variety of possibilities and thereby experiences herself, despite all the differences, as not torn, but rather coherent, thus is becoming increasingly important in modern times. Keupp and other psychologists take up Elkind's concept in a study entitled *The Patchwork of Identities in Late Modernity* and come to the conclusion that in many situations individuals by no means achieve a unified self (2002: 196). This is, however, neither possible nor necessary, since, "the constancy of the self does not consist in resolving all differences, but rather in enduring the resulting tensions and mastering constantly recurring crises." Modern identities are thus, on the one side, marked by more possibilities, to which the virtual communities of the internet have made a not inessential contribution, and, on the other side, however, also by more uncertainties. The construction of identity in youth can therefore take the form of an "open and often chaotic process of search." (Eckert et al. 2000: 17).

1.2. Social Categorization

Besides the so far presented complexity and changeability of social identity, the meaning of the 'other' forms the second central aspect for the constitution

of the 'self'. As the initially formulated definition of social identity by Tajfel
and others and the discussions above have made clear, this part of individual identity is derived from simultaneous membership in specific groups and
demarcation from other groups: the development of a person's identity must
be understood as "interdependent and inter-subjective" (Keupp et al. 2002:
138). We develop our identity not in a vacuum, but rather in and through the
constant comparison of the self with other individuals and groups: "Only by
comparing ourselves with others can we build up our affiliations and our non-
alignments" (Duszak 2002: 1). Turner (1982: 17) therefore brings the concept
of social identity together with a further central concept of identity research,
social categorization:

> Social identification can refer to the process of locating oneself, or another
> person, within a system of social categorizations or, as a noun, to any social
> categorization used by a person to define him- or herself and others. [. . .]
> The sum total of the social identification used by a person to define him- or
> herself will be described as his or her *social identity*. Social categorizations
> define a person by systematically including them within some, and exclud-
> ing them from other related categories. They state at the same time what
> a person is and is not.

Identity can thus only be grasped in a social context. Anyone who wants to do
research on the social identities of individuals must therefore of necessity also
take into account the relationships of these individuals to other persons and
groups (Keupp et al. 2002: 67, Oerter and Dreher 1995: 361, Strauss 1969: 44),
for from an "anthropological perspective identity is a *relationship* and not, as
everyday language supposes, an individual characteristic" (Goussiaux cited
in Keupp et al. 2002: 95). Identity and alterity are inseparably bound to one
another, and hence Goussiaux formulates the question of identity not as 'Who
am I?', but rather as "[W]ho am I in relationship to the others, who are the
others in relationship to me?" Tajfel & Forgas (1981: 124) express this relationship with the intuitive formula: "We are what we are because they are
not what we are." This fundamental aspect of relationships of social identity
is constantly being emphasized in identity and categorization research. Since
creating affinity with or respectively demarcation from others is often achieved
using linguistic means, it is especially linguistic studies that have been dedi-
cated to these processes (recently, e.g., Duszak 2002, Hausendorf and Kesselheim 2002, Androutsopoulos and Georgakopoulou 2003). Already in 1959,
Anselm Strauss asserted: "Central to any discussion of identity is language"
(1969: 15). Articles with titles like: "We, They and Identity" (Sebba and Wootton 1998), "Us and Others" (Duszak 2002), and "Us and Them" (Zhou 2002)
point to the fact that without the 'they' no 'we' can exist.

  Representations of self and other are embedded in processes of social categorization. Already Goffman (1963: 2) linked the term social identity and
the concept of social category together: "When a stranger comes into our presence, then, first appearances are likely to enable us to anticipate his *category*
and attributes, his '*social identity*'." He thus refers to the individual's category
membership as social identity. In every interaction individuals consciously and
unconsciously place themselves in relation to others and thereby perform a

stranger- and self-categorization. Duszak (2002: 2) even speaks of the "impossi-bility of *non-othering*" (emphasis in original) and refers to social identities as the products of categorization processes "that fulfill the human needs of organ-izing experience for future access and use."

The concept of social categorization goes back to the sociologist Harvey Sacks. In the mid-1960s Sacks studied interaction processes, which he referred to as *social* or *membership categorization*. His *Lectures on Conversation* (and related topics from the social sciences), held in the 1960s and 1970s at the University of California, were first published by Gail Jefferson in 1992, after Sacks's death, and thereby stimulated new interest in categorization research. Sacks defines "membership categories" very broadly (but also very statically) as "known things," as units of societal knowledge.

1.3. Category Variety

There are a great variety and number of categories. Sacks (1992) refers to a small number of category collections that are applicable to everyone, such as gender, age/generation, confession, nation, etc., as basis collections. Some cat-egories are more persistent than others: for example, individuals, other than transsexuals, usually retain their congenital biological gender for their entire lifetime, and we usually never change our nationality. Besides this, there are many categories to which people belong for only short periods of their lives. Between the ages of ca. 13 and 19 years persons belong to the age category "teenager," which, however, only constitutes a transitional stage and is fol-lowed by other age-related categories. Unlike such transitional categories, there are permanent ones which people keep for a lifetime, e.g., ethnic mem-bership ("Asian"). In everyday life we encounter special categories that can be traced back to lifestyle preferences, as for example, heavy metal fan, environ-mentalist, inline-skater, and sexual preferences (heterosexual, homosexual, transvestite) and many others (Spreckels 2006).

There are categories that, without contextual knowledge, are neutral or at least can be (Portuguese, student, barber) and those whose designation can by definition contain an evaluation, thus, e.g., derogatory designations and invectives like Wog, Pollack or suck-up, idiot, slut, etc. This type of category, in which societal evaluations are anchored, are of particular interest to Jayyusi (1984) in her study *Categorization and the Moral Order*.

Often it makes a difference whether it is a matter of a self- or strangers' categorization. The category *greenie* (*Öko*), which is often named in the group communication of the girls in Spreckels's study (2006), is more of a strang-ers' categorization. Even if a dictionary merely refers to this short word as a 'humorous' term for a 'supporter of the ecology movement', the particular des-ignation is often used in a derogatory sense. Members of the category would therefore probably not categorize themselves as *greenies*. The politically incor-rect word 'nigger', if used by a white, is an expression of racism, while the same word, if used by a black, is a playful adaptation of the racist expression and a conscious profession of his ethnic origin (see chapter 5 by Reisigl in this vol-ume). A jocular adoption of a strangers' attribution observed from outside was also studied by Schwitalla & Streeck (1989: 249) in a group of working-class youth who are viewed by adults as bothersome and unpleasant. By identifying with this strangers' attribution ("mir falle iwwerall uff"—"we stand out everywhere") they are performing an inversion of values. Categories can thus be used for discrimination, but they can also be played with.

1.4. Social Categories Versus Social Groups

It is important to differentiate between the two concepts of 'social category' and 'social group', which are sometimes used as synonymous. Sacks himself emphasizes this difference (1979: 13).

> We're dealing [. . .] with a category. They're not groups. Most of the categories (women, old people, Negroes, Jews, teenagers, etc.) are not groups in any sense that you normally talk about groups, and yet what we have is a mass of knowledge known about every category, any member is seen as a representative of each of those categories; any person who is a case of a category is seen as a member of the category, and what's known about the category is known about them [. . .].

Besides Sacks, other researchers point to the important distinction between groups and categories. Thus, e.g., Turner writes (1982: 169): "In general . . . [a] group has been conceptualized as some (usually) small collection of individuals in face-to-face relations of interaction, attraction and influence [. . .]" and demarcates from it social categories that he, drawing on Tajfel, refers to as the result of "discontinuous divisions of the social world into distinct classes" (Turner 1982: 17).

Often it cannot be determined to what extent categories coincide with reality, for in a certain sense we only create reality through categorization (Kesselheim 2003: 72). But this is exactly where we confront the danger of social categories. Kesselheim (p. 72) points out that categories are not completely arbitrary just because they are "created," "for they must prove themselves in societal action."

Each category is related, according to the respective circle of usage, to various "category-bound activities" (Sacks 1992: 568), thus 'typical' activities for all members of the category. We expand the Sacksian concept to the term "category-bound features," proposed by Jayyusi (1984: 35), thus category-bound characteristics that besides activities and modes of behavior also include aspects such as category-bound external appearance (clothing, hairstyle, political symbols, etc.), convictions, competencies, rights, etc.

Besides such categories, which refer back to a societal knowledge stock, there are also categories that are only understood by a narrow circle of persons (e.g., a community of practice, see Meyerhoff and Marra 2007). Such categories that are accessible only to a limited extent arise in the frame of common experiences. Hausendorf (2000: 14) points out that making links with existing categories and creating one's own categories are often closely linked.

Tajfel (1959) has pointed out that categorization processes can occur not only inductively, but also deductively, i.e., "the assignment to a category of some attribute perceived to characterize an exemplary member." The categorization thus occurs deductively, if one knows that an individual belongs to a specific category and on the basis of this knowledge imputes to him certain 'typical' attributes. Conversely, it occurs inductively, if one assigns a person to a category on the basis of certain category-typical attributes. Both sequence directions of categorization often unavoidably include stereotyping.

1.5. Stereotyping as Part of Categorization

Whether we want to categorize or not: Categorization processes are unavoidable in our everyday interactions. We continually and automatically categorize our environment, i.e., we assign persons, animals or also objects to larger units in order to structure the complexity of our experiences: "There is nothing more basic than categorization to our thought, perception, action, and speech. Every time we see something as a *kind* of thing, for example, a tree, we are categorizing." (Lakoff 1987: 5) In his study *Women, Fire and Dangerous Things*, George Lakoff goes even further when he asserts that, "without the ability to categorize, we could not function at all, neither in the physical world nor in our social and intellectual lives" (1987: 6). That means that we must categorize in order to make the world understandable, for categorization means simplification. But it is precisely in this simplification that we find a danger of stereotyping and thereby as a consequence the danger of developing prejudices.

Categories are often very large units that of necessity entail reducing individuals to one or a few attributes, equating them with other representatives of the category and thereby robbing them of their individuality. Such a large category as, e.g., 'women' or 'blacks' or 'Italians' makes it clear how problematic it can be to subsume individuals under a unit on the basis of an individual attribute, even though they differ from one another on the basis of countless other attributes. By categorizing we decide which attributes of persons are to be set as relevant and which are not: "The way in which things [or respectively persons] are classed together reveals, graphically as well as symbolically, the perspectives of the classifier" (Strauss 1969: 20).

Categorizations are especially problematic when persons are refused certain rights merely on the basis of their membership in a specific category, when, e.g., women receive lower salaries for the same work merely on the basis of their biological sex, or when people are treated as potential criminals on the basis of their skin color. Lakoff (1987: 85) writes in this regard: "[. . . social stereotypes] are used in reasoning and especially in what is called 'jumping to conclusions'. [. . .] Stereotypes are used in certain situations to define expectations, make judgements, and draw inferences." If social categories are linked with stigmata, these are automatically transferred to each individual member. But just as categorization is unavoidable in human interactions, so is stereotyping: "it is useless to talk of trying to eradicate from the human mind the tendency to stereotype, to designate nastily, and to oversimplify," writes Anselm Strauss (1969: 21). With Lakoff, he regards this tendency, however, as typically human: "This is not to say that humans are brutish, but that they are thoroughly human".

Harvey Sacks himself linked his concept of "category-bound activities" with that of "stereotypes" (1992: 568). With both concepts it is a matter of the generalizing ascription of behavioral modes to individuals as representatives of specific larger units. Although Sacks sees the dangers that such a generalization can entail, he emphasizes a certain value of categorizations (1992: 577). Many other scientists besides Sacks have emphasized the connection between categories and stereotypes and offered various definitions, of which a few will be briefly summarized.

Thus, e.g., Allport writes (1979: 191): " . . . *a stereotype is an exaggerated belief associated with a category.* [. . .] A stereotype is not identical with a category; it is rather a fixed idea that accompanies the category". This means that Allport also sees the proximity of both concepts, but separates them. Two other definitions of 'stereotype' neglect the concept of 'category' and instead introduce other central concepts. Schwarz and Chur (1993: 52) conceive the term "stereotype" as "a mental representation in which aspects of an area of reality are crudely generalized and strongly reduced to a few (in part not even applicable) attributes."

After a critical discussion of various approaches, Quasthoff formulates a definition that shifts the linguistic realization of stereotypes to the center of attention:

> A stereotype is the verbal expression of a conviction applied to social groups or individual persons as their members that is widespread in a given community. It has the logical form of a judgment that in an unjustifiably simplifying and generalizing way, with an emotionally valuing tendency, ascribes or denies to a class of persons certain qualities or modes of behavior. Linguistically it is describable as a sentence (1973: 28).

According to this definition, a stereotype therefore represents a verbal form of stating a conviction. Thereby the first important step was taken to making a formerly entirely social-psychological concept of stereotype for the first time understandable from a linguistic perspective. Twenty-five years later the author herself criticized her concept, however, insofar as it was presumably too static, and demanded the "dynamization of stereotype research" (Quasthoff 1998). Since she, similar to Sacks, understands "stereotypifications as components of social categorizations" (1998: 47), this more dynamic approach likewise applies to categorization research. The goal of more recent categorization research has been to work with a process-oriented concept of stereotypes that makes it possible to empirically understand stereotypes and categories with the aid of conversation analysis as interactively produced constructs.

In categorization it is always a matter of more than a pure assignment of persons to larger units and of the thereby achieved structuration, or respectively simplification, of the world. Interactants often categorize with a specific intention, which can be conversation-organizationally conditioned. Thus Sacks (1992: 40) already stated that categorization questions often appear at the beginning of a conversation, because they are suitable, as an important component of everyday knowledge, for starting conversations with strangers. Categorizations can, however, be employed beyond the discourse level for the purpose of social organization. Quasthoff (1998: 47), e.g., points out that connected with stereotypifications and social categorizations are "processes of alliance formation or respectively of the demarcation and exclusion of those present or absent." Categorization processes thus crucially determine the social framework of a group; they are a possibility for 'social positioning' (Davies and Harré 1990; Wolf 1999). Interactants can categorize cooperatively or dissent from categorizations. The cooperative negotiation of a negatively connotated 'other category' usually leads to alliance formation against it. Simultaneously, these processes influence the interactive formation of group identity.

Kesselheim (2003: 57) names two essential lines of tradition that pursue such a more dynamic conceptualization of categorization: For one thing, he mentions the British Manchester School, which has further developed the concept from a sociological (and social-psychological) perspective. As representatives of this research approach he names, among others, Antaki, Edwards, Hester, Jayyusi, Widdicombe. On the other hand, he names linguistic work on categorization in the German-speaking countries, such as the Bielefeld "National Self- and Other Images in East-European States—Manifestations in Discourse" project and the "Communication in the City" project of the Institute for the German Language (IDS) in Mannheim (Kallmeyer 1994). From the first research strand arise concepts such as "identity-in-interaction" (Antaki & Widdicombe 1998), which, in the frame of linguistic research on social identity, has proved to be an extremely fruitful instrument.

"The student of identity must necessarily be deeply interested in interaction for it is in, and because of, face-to-face interaction that so much appraisal—of self and others—occurs," writes Anselm Strauss (already in 1969: 44). If one wishes to study a complex phenomenon like identity with the aid of conversation analysis as an interactively produced phenomenon, identity must be conceptualized differently than was for a long time the case in social psychology. Deppermann and Schmidt point out that earlier social scientific concepts of identity cause great problems for the empirical study of identity in conversations, because they often refer to "abstracting constitutional dimensions of identity which can not or can only in a highly rudimentary form be drawn into the study of everyday action episodes" (2003: 27). "The current concepts of identity thus seem to have too many assumptions, to be too macroscopic and too much weighted with empirically irredeemable implications to offer a foundation appropriate for the subject-matter to use in the study of everyday interactions" (2003: 28).

For this reason, ethnomethodological conversation analysis and discursive psychology (Edwards and Potter 1992; Potter and Wetherell 1987) developed an interactionist concept of identity that can be much better grasped empirically. Stuart Hall points out that identities are positions that interactants take in discourse (1996: 6). Identities are accordingly understood as everyday world resources with the help of which individuals can better position themselves. Already in 1990 Davies and Harré introduced the concept of "positioning" as a more dynamic representation of identities in conversation. They define "positioning" as "the discursive process whereby selves are located in conversations as observably and subjectively coherent participants in jointly produced story lines" (1990: 48). In conversations we assign various positions to ourselves and to others, and from them we observe and evaluate the world. "Position" appears to the authors as "the appropriate expression to talk about the discursive production of a diversity of selves" (1990: 47) and they therefore propose this term as an alternative to more static models such as that of the 'role', or Goffman's concepts of "frames" and "footing" (Goffman 1974, 1981).

Like Davies and Harré, the social psychologists Antaki and Widdicombe (1998) emphasize in their concept of 'identity-in-interaction' the importance of discourse or respectively interaction in doing research on identities. Already the title of their collection *Identities in Talk*, which gives an overview of various constructivist theories of identity, points to the discursive negotiation of identity. Widdicombe summarizes, "the important analytic question is not [. . .] whether someone can be described in a particular way, but to show *that* and *how* this identity is made relevant or ascribed to self or others" (1998: 191). Thus it is not a matter of studying who conversational partners are in terms of their demographic data, but rather of studying locally identifiable, discursively produced identities which interactants select from a broad spectrum of possibilities and set as relevant. At the center of this new concept of identity is who or what conversational participants locally identify each other as being in the microcosm of the interaction, why and in what manner (with what linguistic means) they do this. Identity is thereby "regarded as an everyday world resource with which societal members themselves perform identity work, categorize and interpret their social world and thereby also construct their own identity" (Deppermann and Schmidt 2003: 28).

A source of orientation for identity research from a linguistic viewpoint is in addition the concept of 'acts of identity' of Le Page and Tabouret-Keller (1985), which up to the present has been widely received. This approach, developed in the frame of (socio-linguistic) Creole research, regards linguistic practice as 'acts of identity' and thereby produces the important connection between speech variation and identity (P. Eckert 2000). According to this, individuals adopt linguistic patterns as an expression of their identification with specific reference groups. Youths can thus express their membership in specific youth cultural groups and scenes by employing the appropriate vocabulary. In a newer study, Auer and Dirim (2003) show how non-Turkish youth perform various 'acts of identity' by acquiring Turkish.

2. Communicating Identity in Intercultural Encounters

Intercultural scenarios have a variety of effects on the communication of identity. Ethnic and national identities can be set as relevant simply because the way a behavioral mode is marked by culture first becomes clear in a foreign culture. Whereas, for example, for many Germans punctuality represents an inconspicuous aspect of normality, in a foreign cultural context it suddenly becomes a characteristic of one's own 'being German'. Besides that, there is the influence of specific national stereotypes that belong to active knowledge stocks. The ethno-comedies that are currently popular in some Western countries play with the knowledge of such stereotypes by humorously exaggerating them (Kotthoff 2004).

Many identity categories are interwoven in their cultural typification. Thereby the space-time scope of the categories is in each case hard to determine. What is regarded today as the typical manner of a young woman lawyer from Munich will not differ in many contexts from that of a woman lawyer in London, Stockholm or Chicago. Gender, class, profession, age, and style influence each other and together with nationality and ethnicity produce a context-dependent type. The young urban professionals who serve as an example here can show their individual identity through a specific styling as more or less fashion-conscious, more or less status-conscious and much more. In Russia such a woman will possibly be immediately identified as coming from the West. Wearing low-heeled shoes and not using much makeup can, for example, become symbolic difference markers for this type of woman, indices of a cultural membership that is not in a strict sense national. West-East could become a flexible demarcation line for the female yuppie. Such habitus phenomena of clothing and body presentation are sometimes divested of their status as normality in the foreign culture. Something that does not attract attention at home suddenly indicates elsewhere cultural difference. The space in which normalities go unchallenged can range from a close 'community of practice' to diffuse communities with comparable consumption habits, lifestyles, attitudes and values (e.g. 'Asian cultures' or 'the West').

In this section we wish to go into the communication of national and ethnic identity. Language plays a role in the attribution of ethnic and national identity. As was pointed out in the first part of this chapter, we do not view identity as something constructed through institutions, individuals and 'discourse' within an 'imagined community', but as situated in the life world. In many sciences, national identity is utilized as a category for causal and/or variable analysis, often generating important statistical data for various policy requirements and institutional actors. As Hester and Housley (2002: 2) point out, the emergence of national identities has been located within important social and economic transformations, developments and historical fissures. They regard the work of Billig (1995) on the everyday routines and practices of 'banal nationalism' as the most notable attempt to move beyond the theoretical matrix surrounding the social reproduction of nationalism and identity. The two authors also recommend Bechhofer, McCrone, Kiely and Steward (1999) as a study which investigated national identity among Scottish landowners and the Scottish cultural elite. Bechhofer et al. (1999: 530) state:

> It is relatively straightforward to argue that national identities are not essentially fixed or given. This is usually taken to mean that such identities are open to manipulation, most obviously by the state and its institutions so that people come to think of themselves as 'nationals' in a fairly unproblematic way [. . .] Our argument, on the other hand, is that national identities depend critically on the claims which people themselves make in different contexts at different times. But the processes of identity work rest not simply on the claims made, but on how such claims are received, that is validated or rejected by significant others.

Nationality and ethnicity can overlap. Often there are political disputes about which ethnic group can imagine itself as bearing the state. Right-wing circles often avail themselves of such slogans as 'France for the French' and thereby contribute to the marginalization of immigrants (see chapter 5 by Reisigl in this volume).

Below we attempt to further illuminate a few linguistic and non-linguistic forms of communicating cultural identity and alterity.

2.1. Formations of "Us" and "Them" by National Identity Categorization

Koole and Hanson (2002) examine the display and use of national identity categories in classroom interaction in the Netherlands. 'Moroccan' is the teacher's membership categorization (outlined above), which is challenged by the pupils. The teacher adopts the position of a knowledgeable actor in discussions of topics from the everyday experience of her students. Koole and Hanson in particular show how the teacher employs the national identity category 'Moroccan' in a deterministic, deductive manner. In response, Moroccan students challenge not so much the national identity category as such, but its meaning in terms of category-bound activities. They also show how difficult it can be for a teacher to participate successfully in the student-centered approach that is advocated for multi-ethnic classes today. The interactional practices and competencies required for such participation appear to be largely incompatible with the teacher's acting as the one who knows (2002: 212). The authors show in detailed transcriptions that even when all participants recognize a category such as 'Moroccan', this does not imply that they agree on all the attributes of this category. In one lesson, the class discusses the practice of bathing and taking showers, and the teacher claims that, in contrast to Dutch children, Moroccan and Turkish children are taught that boys and girls should do this separately. A Moroccan girl challenges the teacher's category predicate that Moroccan boys and girls never bathe together. She tells about her family in which she (seven years old) had a bath together with her eight year old brother. The teacher sets her counterexample apart as an exception to the rule. Her family is more liberal.

In another case (2002: 221), the teacher works with a category that links wearing headscarves to religion. This category knowledge allows the teacher to select an answer from the children that is in line with her knowledge, and to neglect answers ("we wear them at home") that are potentially, or actually, not in agreement with this knowledge. She seems to aim at having her category knowledge confirmed, rather than at having the students relate their experiences with headscarf practices, as the authors discuss. Teachers such as the one presented by Koole and Hanson have often been trained from a transfer perspective and have received their education from knowledge-transferring teachers, not from a construction model of learning and education. The authors conclude that they faced a problem of interactional competence in the school environment (see chapter 12 by Scherr in this volume).

2.2. Formations of "Us" and "Them" by Communicative Style

Communicative style (see Kotthoff 2007) is another possibility to index and/or symbolize a certain social identity. There are many studies of how young people in urban settings use vernacular, linguistic creativity, playfulness, polyphony, and bricolage as resources for "acts of identity" (Le Page and

Tabouret-Keller 1985, Irvine 2001). Distinctive patterns of bilingual speech among adolescents frequently make use of stylized immigrant speech varieties that function as group consolidating resources (Androutsopoulos and Georgakopoulou 2003). In contemporary multi-ethnic urban environments 'language crossing' can be observed, i.e. the use of minority languages or language varieties which do not belong to the speaker, e.g. German youths using English or Turkish (Auer and Dirim 2003), Anglo youths using varieties of Jamaican Creole in England or African-American vernacular English in the USA (Rampton 1995, Cutler 1999). As an interactional practice, language crossing foregrounds ethnic group relations and at least partially challenges traditional conceptions of ethnicity.

As an example of the development of a socio-cultural identity through a communicative style, we summarize an ethnographic and interaction analytic study of a group of Turkish girls made by Keim (2003, 2004, forthcoming). The girls, who grew up in a typical Turkish migrant neighborhood in the inner city of Mannheim, Germany, categorize themselves as 'power-girls'. On the basis of biographical interviews with group members and long-term observation of group interactions, Keim reconstructs the formation of an ethnically-defined ghetto clique and the group's development into educated, modern German-Turkish young women. She describes a change in the stylistic repertoire of the girls that is closely related to key experiences of their social life relevant to the group's changing socio-cultural identity.

Keim (forthcoming) summarizes that many migrant families have been living in Germany for over 30 years, and most of their children view Germany as their home country. In the course of time, migrant 'ghettos' emerged and stabilized in many inner city districts. Preschool institutions and schools were and still are badly equipped for the instruction of children from various cultural and linguistic backgrounds (see chapter 12 by Scherr in this volume). Many teachers in Germany saw, and still see, migrant children as double semi-linguals with serious deficits. A high percentage of migrant children are not successful in school and have few opportunities in the German job market. Out of frustration with their children's educational and professional failure and out of fear that they would become more and more estranged from 'their culture', many Turkish parents tried to educate their children with increasing rigidity in their own traditional norms and values. One of the central problems for young migrants has been coming to terms with their parents' traditional demands and, at the same time, experiencing failure in and exclusion from more advanced educational and professional worlds in Germany. Keim shows the children's ability to cope with often contrasting traditions and demands from different social worlds as fundamental in the process of forming their own socio-cultural identity.

Ghetto children who, at the age of ten, have the chance to go to the *Gymnasium* or the *Realschule* (only 10–20 % of an age-group attend these prestige schools) develop quite different social orientations. Since both types of schools are situated outside the ghetto, the children have to enter German educational worlds where migrants are a small minority. They experience the negative image of the Turkish migrants in terms of abuse such as *scheiß Ausländer* ('damn foreigner') and *dreckiger* ('filthy') or *dummer Türke* ('stupid Turk'). In these schools they have to cope with new educational, linguistic, and social standards for which they are usually not prepared. A typical reaction to these experiences is the organization of an ethnically-defined peer group, along with dissociation from or the upgrading of ethnic features.

Keim observed the stylistic development of the 'power-girls' in two processes of differentiation: the girls' emancipation from the traditional Turkish female role and their opposition to the German school world. The 'power-girls' created a specific style that contrasted on all stylistic dimensions with the Turkish style of their parents and of the 'traditional young Turkish woman', as well as with that of the German *Gymnasium*. Both contrasts made the girls fall back on features taken from the behavior of young Turkish males in their surroundings in their early phase. They used many vulgar expletives, a German-Turkish language mixture, and pidginized morphosyntax, for example.

The 'power-girl' style was rigorously rejected by German educational institutions. These experiences led them to transform their style in order to become socially and professionally successful in German society. Stylistic elements that had been evaluated by the peer-group as 'not belonging to us' were accepted in later biographical phases when the processing of new experiences effected a change in social orientations and aspirations.

In the case of the 'power-girls', a mixing of German and Turkish was preferred in in-group communication, especially in everyday interactions, such as in narration and argumentation. In mixing, the girls use their bilingual competence for discursive and socio-symbolic functions, as Keim shows. Turks of the parental generation, as well as Germans (the girls' teachers and German peers), were excluded from mixing. Since Keim could not find another group that had developed such a highly elaborate mixing style, she assumes that mixing, as well as its discursive functions, are part of the 'power-girls'' peer-group style.

Those 'power-girls' who had to leave the ghetto early in the course of their educational careers had—when Keim met them—already acquired a high level of competence in mono-lingual German. But in in-group communication, mixing was their preferred code of interaction. The mixing of these girls differed slightly from that of the others in the higher proportion of German structures and elements. In some interactions—for example, discussions about their school affairs—German was their dominant language. This shows, according to Keim, that in the course of their educational careers outside the ghetto, the girls' linguistic competences and preferences had changed: in specific constellations, together with specific topics, the relevance of mixing had decreased, and the relevance of German had increased.

When all girls attended schools outside the ghetto, they acquired a high competence in mono-lingual German. For the oldest girls, who had just started university study, German had become the central means of expression in all professional domains. But in in-group communication, all the girls still preferred mixing. At this later time of Keim's study, it had become a means of symbolizing their affiliation with the category of the 'German-Turk' and their dissociation from the Turkish-speaking world, as well as from the German-speaking majority. When Keim asked them about their ideal life-partner, they spontaneously answered that they would only marry a German-Turk, a man who could mix languages. Thus, the formation of German-Turkish mixing, as well as the use of monolingual German, are closely related to the speakers' processing of social experiences and to their construction of a genuine socio-cultural identity.

Besides language, clothing is also an important resource for indexing or symbolizing cultural identity.

2.3. Non-Verbal Formation of "Us" and "Them"

2.3.1. WOMEN'S HEADSCARVES AS A BOUNDARY MARKER. We deal in this section with the symbolic discourse about the headscarves worn by Muslim women and their potential to arouse controversy. Clothing is one of the cultural signs that have an effect at first glance and convey meaning in a variety of ways. Clothing can mark the boundaries of age, sex/gender, status, religion and many other dimensions. Its symbolic significance is thus "multivocal" (Korff 1990). Schöning-Kalender (2000) shows Islamic discourse as significant in two regards: for one thing, as a body of religious rules and regulations that does or does not prescribe the clothing of confessing Muslims, for another, as a political ideology that is symbolized by specific forms of clothing. If Turkish, German or French state and school authorities point out that Islam does not absolutely prescribe that women wear veils, they can thereby draw on a rich literature of Islamic experts (Mernissi 1989 Bilgin 1997). On the basis of the Turkish constitution, there are strict clothing requirements for public institutions that are oriented to basic secular principles (i.e. prohibition of wearing headscarves). As a second dimension, Schöning-Kalender (2000: 191) describes political Islam, for which the veiling of women has become a public symbol on the basis of a veiling requirement in some countries. In its various and especially in its radical forms, political Islam in Iran, Afghanistan and Algeria is very present in Western media. As well in Turkey a conflict is smoldering over university attendance for women students wearing headscarves.

In 1998, a teacher named Fereshta Ludin was forbidden to wear a headscarf when teaching in German schools. She insisted that wearing a headscarf was just an expression of her personality. Schöning-Kalender points out that thereby a sign was also selected that in the meantime has come to be seen almost everywhere in the world as a sign of political Islamization. The type of scarf and especially the way of tying it, as well as generally all the other clothing worn by Ludin in public indicated that it was not a matter of the traditional headscarf worn, e.g., by her grandmother. In Turkey a variant consisting of a long coat and headscarf that falls over the shoulders, leaves the face free but covers all the hair and the neck, has since the early 1980s been referred to as *Türban*. With this reinterpretation, according to Schöning-Kalender, this way of wearing a headscarf is also set apart from all traditional ways of wearing a headscarf. In the course of the dispute in Turkey this has resulted in the concept of *Türban* itself becoming a symbol of political Islam.

Another discursive context for Ludin's headscarf is constituted through the perception of cultural difference as an instrument for codifying social inequality. The critique points to the fact that Turkish women wearing a headscarf were allowed for decades to do janitorial work in German schools, but a woman wearing a headscarf is not suitable as a teacher. Young Turkish women of the second or third generation living in Germany suspect that the prohibition of the headscarf expresses a fear of the majority society of the rise of the minority. Some of them wear a headscarf with pride: "Look here, you Germans. Someone who wears a headscarf is not born to be a cleaning lady." Schöning-Kalender introduces as a third perspective gender discourse. A few young women wear headscarves in Turkey and in Western countries not due to pressure from their fathers, but rather reinterpret it as a confession of the Muslim significance of physicality and feminine identity against Western gender ideals that favor particularly for young women the maximal display of sexual attributes. With the headscarf they demonstrate that a female identity continually focused on selferoticization is not their ideal. The multi-vocality of such symbols makes it necessary to trace their location in different contexts. The dispute does not end there; the voices of the dispute are, however, better recognizable.

2.3.2. SYMBOLS OF NATIONAL IDENTITY. In conclusion, we will take a look at newly arising national identities and their symbolization. Although ethnic labeling had never been entirely absent in postwar Europe, its status was relatively modest. The collapse of the communist regimes in Eastern Europe in the late 1980s, however, saw the resurgence of ethnicity in an unsuspected and brutal way. Also, the process of globalization invokes or stimulates certain strategies for constructing and managing one's 'own' national, regional, local or non-territorially bound identities.

As an example of newly arising national identities we take a look at a former Republic of the Soviet Union: Lithuania. Cepaitiene (2000) studied the creation and meaning of Lithuanian national symbols in the press and memoirs of Lithuanian national revival leaders in the first half of the 20th century and at the end of 20th century. Flags as well as crests, currencies, monuments, mottoes, etc. are seen as carefully constructed and projected images of identity that result from a conscious decision-making process. The intention to create the Lithuanian national flag emerged during the First World War, when the political independence of Lithuania was becoming a reality. In the summer of 1988, after almost half a century of Soviet occupation, the Lithuanian national flag, which was banned by the Soviet Union, appeared openly at demonstrations organized by political movements. Cepaitiene describes (2000: 466) how the banned national symbol, displayed in public, implied the idea of a recovering nation and an independent state. The publicity of the national flag crystallized previously disseminated national feelings. The legalization of the national flag was initiated by authorities who were influenced by Gorbachev's *perestroika*. But people could perceive and experience different meanings of the banned national symbol—and such was the case. When it was proclaimed as a Lithuanian national flag by the Lithuanian Communist party authority at one of the first rallies, the Sajudis press reported the next day: "That evening in the Vingis park we finally experienced our power. Sajudis (political mass movement for a restoration of Lithuania) and all Lithuanians are awakening to the new moral life" (p. 469).

More and more the flag became an icon of pride in a new state and nation and emotional affiliation with the ethnic community. In conclusion and finally, the flag also became a symbol of demarcation from Russia.

2.4. Conclusion: Identity in a Globalized World

Intercultural encounters make it clear that identity constitutes itself in relationships rather than being merely a characteristic of individuals. Even when we grant that modern identities are patchwork constructions and that a complex communicative management is needed to make a certain identity accountable, it is all the same evident that these identities also need a certain stability and coherence within their respective cultures. For persons, groups or larger social configurations like states it is often the case that the respective identities have to be asserted in the face of external opposition. Thus, for any unity, a part of the associated politics of identity will consist in the search for an environment in which the social identity can solidify and assert itself, secure from outside incursion. In this age of globalization we must bear in mind that the construction of identity is no longer bound to locality (Giddens 1990). The essence of globalization is the intensification of world-wide social relations, at the expense of formerly local activities and relations. Along with economic and cultural globalization, the globalization of social relationships has far reaching consequences for individuals' life goals and identity formation. "The advent of modernity increasingly tears space away from place by fostering relations between 'absent' others, locationally distant from any given situation of face-to-face interaction." (Giddens 1990: 18). Appadurai (1995) posits that modern configurations of space, time and culture overlap with 'imagined worlds' and 'imagined communities'. Each of these landscapes is assembled by social actors on the basis of the cultural images and possibilities for identity that are presented to them. Tourists, migrants and refugees produce new 'ethnoscapes' that, in turn, overlap with the 'technoscapes' of transnational enter-prizes and the 'mediascapes' of globalized sources of information, images and symbols.

Identity and otherness are still driving forces between social conjunctions and disjunctions, and in a globalized world ever more social knowledge is required to understand their manifestations. Not only for this reason will the field of study called 'communicating identity' remain interdisciplinary, drawing together sociology, linguistics, psychology, political science and anthropology, as this article has attempted to show.

References

Allport, Gordon W. 1979. *The Nature of Prejudice*. Reading MA et al.: Addison-Wesley.
Androutsopoulos, Jannis K. and Alexandra Georgakopoulou (eds.). 2003. *Discourse Constructions of Youth Identities*. Amsterdam/ Philadelphia: Benjamins.
Antaki, Charles and Sue Widdicombe (eds.). 1998. *Identities in Talk*. London: Sage.
Appadurai, Arjun. 1995. The Production of Locality. In: Richard Fardon (ed.), *Counterworks: Managing the Diversity of Knowledge*, 204–225. London: Routledge.
Auer, Peter and Inci Dirim. 2003. Socio-cultural orientation, urban youth styles and the spontaneous acquisition of Turkish by non-Turkish adolescents in Germany. In: Jannis K.

Androutsopoulos and Alexandra Georgakopoulou (eds.), *Discourse Constructions of Youth Identities*, 223–246. Amsterdam/ Philadelphia: Benjamins.

Baacke, Dieter. 1987. *Jugend und Jugendkulturen.* Weinheim: Juventa.

Baumeister, Roy F.. 1986. *Identity: Cultural change and the struggle for self.* New York: Oxford University Press.

Bechhofer, Frank, David McCrone, Richard Kiely and Robert Steward. 1999. Constructing National Identity: Arts and Landed Elites in Scotland. *Sociology* Volume 33, N° 3, 515–534.

Bilgin, Beysa. 1997. Das emanzipatorische Potential des Islams. In: Claudia Schöning-Kalender, Ayla Neusel and Mechthild Jansen (eds.), *Feminismus, Islam, Nation: Frauenbewegungen im Maghreb, in Zentralasien und in der Türkei*, 199–216. Frankfurt: Campus.

Billig, Michael. 1995. *Banal nationalism.* London: Sage.

Brabant, Madeleine, Watson, Bernadette and Gallois, Cindy this volume Psychological perspectives: social psychology, language and intercultural communication. Chapter 2.

Cepaitine, Auksule. 2000. Lithuanian national symbols. In: Decker, Ton/Helslot, John/Wijers, Carla (eds.), *Roots & Rituals. The Construction of Ethnic Identities*, 465–476, Amsterdam: Het Spinhuis.

Cutler, Cecilia. 1999. Yorkville Crossing: White teens, hip hop, and African American English. *Journal of Sociolinguistics 3:4,* 428–442.

Davies, Bronwyn and Rom Harré. 1990. Positioning: The Discursive Production of Selves. *Journal for the Theory of Social Behaviour 20:1,* 43–63.

Deppermann, Arnulf and Axel Schmidt. 2003. "Vom Nutzen des Fremden für das Eigene: Interaktive Praktiken der Konstitution von Gruppenidentität durch soziale Abgrenzung unter Jugendlichen. In: Hans Merkens and Jürgen Zinnecker (eds.), *Jahrbuch Jugendforschung 3/2003,* 25–56. Opladen: Leske und Budrich.

Duszak, Anna. 2002. Us and Others: An introduction. In: Anna Duszak (ed.), *Us and Others: Social Identities across languages, discourses and cultures,* 1–28. Amsterdam/ Philadelphia: Benjamins.

Eckert, Penelope. 2000. *Linguistic Variation as Social Practice.* London: Blackwell.

Eckert, Roland, Christa Reis and Thomas Wetzstein. 2000. *"Ich will halt anders sein wie die anderen": Abgrenzung, Gewalt und Kreativität bei Gruppen Jugendlicher.* Opladen: Leske und Budrich.

Edwards, Derek and Jonathan Potter. 1992. *Discursive Psychology.* London et al.: Sage.

Elkind, David. 1990. *Total verwirrt: Teenager in der Krise.* Bergisch Gladbach: Bastei Lübbe.

Giddens, Anthony. 1990. *The Consequences of Modernity.* Cambridge: Polity Press.

Giddens, Anthony. 1991. *Modernity and self-identity: Self and society in the later modern age.* Oxford: Polity Press.

Goffman, Erving. 1963. *Stigma: Notes on the Management of Spoiled Identity.* Englewood Cliffs NJ: Prentice-Hall.

Goffman, Erving. 1974. *Frame Analysis.* New York: Harper and Row.

Goffman, Erving. 1981. *Forms of Talk.* Oxford: Blackwell.

Habermas, Jürgen. 1968. *Erkenntnis und Interesse.* Frankfurt a.M.: Suhrkamp.

Hall, Stuart. 1996. Introduction: Who Needs Identity? In: Stuart Hall and Paul du Gay (eds.), *Questions of Cultural Identity*, 2–17. London: Sage.

Hausendorf, Heiko. 2000. *Zugehörigkeit durch Sprache: Eine linguistische Studie am Beispiel der deutschen Wiedervereinigung.* Tübingen: Niemeyer.

Hausendorf, Heiko and Wolfgang Kesselheim. 2002. The communicative construction of group relationships: A basic mechanism of social categorization. In: Anna Duszak (ed.), *Us and Others: Social identities across languages, discourses and cultures,* 265–289. Amsterdam/ Philadelphia: Benjamins.

Hester, Stephen and William Housley (eds.). 2002. Language, Interaction and National Identity: Studies in the social organisation of national identity in talk-in-interaction. Burlington: Ashgate.

Hillmann, Karl-Heinz. 1994. Wörterbuch der Soziologie. Stuttgart: Alfred Kröner.

Irvine, Judith. 2001. "Style" as distinctiveness: the culture and ideology of linguistic differentiation. In: Penelope Eckert and John Rickford (eds.), Style and sociolinguistic Variation, 21–43. Cambridge: University Press.

Jayyusi, Lena. 1984. *Categorization and the Moral Order.* Boston et al.: Routledge and Kegan Paul.

Kallmeyer, Werner (ed.). 1994. *Kommunikation in der Stadt: Teil 1*. Berlin/ New York: de Gruyter.

Keim, Inken. 2003. Social style of communication and bilingual speech practices: Case study of three migrant youth groups of Turkish origin in Mannheim/ Germany. *Turkic Languages* 2003, Vol. 6/2, 284–298.

Keim, Inken. 2004. Linguistic variation and communication practices in migrant children and youth groups. In: C.B. Dabelsten and N.J. Jorgensen (eds.), *Languaging and Language Practices. Copenhagen Studies in Bilingualism*, Vol. 36, 78–94. Copenhagen.

Keim, Inken forth-Socio-cultural identity and communicative style: a case study of a group of coming German-Turkish girls in Mannheim/ Germany. In: Peter Auer (ed.), *Social identity and communicative styles—An alternative approach to linguistic variability*. Berlin: de Gruyter.

Kesselheim, Wolfgang. 2003. Prozesse der Gruppenkonstitution: Die konversationelle Herstellung von Gruppen im aktuellen argentinischen Einwanderungsdiskurs. Bielefeld: unpublished dissertation.

Keupp, Heiner, Thomas Ahbe, Wolfgang Gmür, Renate Höfer, Beate Mitzscherlich, Wolfgang Kraus and Florian Straus. 2002. *Identitätskonstruktionen: Das Patchwork der Identitäten in der Spätmoderne*. Reinbek: Rowohlt.

Koole, Tom and Mylène Hanson. 2002. The Category 'Moroccan' in a Multi-ethnic Class. In: Stephen Hester and William Housley (eds.), *Language, Interaction and National Identity: Studies in the social organisation of national identity in talk-in-interaction*. Burlington: Ashgate.

Korff, Gottfried. 1990. Rote Fahnen und Bananen: Notizen zur politischen Symbolik im Prozess der Vereinigung von DDR und BRD. *Schweizerisches Archiv für Volkskunde* 86, 130–160.

Kotthoff, Helga. 2004. Overdoing culture: Über Typenstilisierung bei Kaya Yanar. In: Karl Hörning and Julia Reuter (eds.), *Doing culture*, 184–201. Bielefeld: Transcript.

Kotthoff, Helga. 2007. Ritual and style across cultures. In: Helga Kotthoff and Helen Spencer-Oatey (eds.), *Handbook of Intercultural Communication*, 173–198. Berlin: Mouton de Gruyter.

Krappmann, Lothar. 1978. *Soziologische Dimensionen der Identität*. Stuttgart: Klett.

Lakoff, George. 1987. *Women, fire and dangerous things: What categories reveal about the mind*. Chicago: Chicago University Press.

LePage, Robert B. and André Tabouret-Keller. 1985. *Acts of Identity: Creole-based approaches to language and ethnicity*. Cambridge: Cambridge University Press.

Luckmann, Thomas et al. 1981. Anonymität und persönliche Identität. In: Franz Böckle, Franz-Xaver Kaufmann and Karl Rahner (eds.), *Christlicher Glaube in moderner Gesellschaft*, Volume 25, 6–38. Freiburg i.B. et al.: Herder.

Marcia, James E. 1966. Development and validation of ego identity status. *Journal of Personality and Social Psychology 3*, 551–558.

Marcia, James E. 1989. Identity diffusion differentiated. In: Mary Ann Luszcz and Ted Nettelbeck (eds.), *Psychological development: Perspectives across the life-span*, 289–295. North Holland: Elsevier Science Publishers.

Mead, George Herbert. 1934. *Mind, Self and Society*. Chicago et al.: Chicago University Press.

Mernissi, Fatema. 1989. *Der politische Harem*. Frankfurt: Campus.

Meyerhoff, Miriam. 1996. Dealing with gender identity as a sociolinguistic variable. In: Victoria Bergvall, Janet Bing and Alice Freed (eds.), *Rethinking language and gender research: theory and practice*, 202–227. New York: Longman.

Oerter, Rolf and Eva Dreher. 1995. Jugendalter. In: Rolf Oerter and Leo Montada (eds.), *Entwicklungspsychologie*, 310–395. Weinheim: Beltz.

Potter, Jonathan and Margret Wetherell. 1987. *Discourse and Social Psychology: Beyond attitudes and Behaviour*. London et al.: Sage.

Quasthoff, Uta. 1973. *Soziales Vorurteil und Kommunikation—eine sprachwissenschaftliche Analyse des Stereotyps*. Frankfurt a. M.: Athenäum Fischer.

Quasthoff, Uta. 1998. Stereotype in Alltagskommunikationen: Ein Beitrag zur Dynamisierung der Stereotypenforschung. In: Margot Heinemann (ed.) *Sprachliche und soziale Stereotype*, 47–72. Frankfurt/M.: Lang.

Rampton, Ben. 1995. *Crossing: Language and ethnicity among adolescents*. London: Longman.

Reisigl, Martin this volume *Discrimination in intercultural communication*. Chapter 5.

Sacks, Harvey. 1979. Hotrodder: A Revolutionary Category. In: George Psathas (ed.), *Everyday Language—Studies in Ethnomethodology*, 7–14. New York: Irvington.

Sacks, Harvey. 1992. *Lectures on Conversation*. Edited by Gail Jefferson. Cambridge MA: Blackwell.

Schäfers, Bernhard. 2001. *Soziologie des Jugendalters*. Opladen: Leske und Budrich.

Scherr, Albert. This volume. *Schools and cultural difference*. Chapter 12

Schöning-Kalender, Claudia. 2000. Textile Grenzziehungen: Symbolische Diskurse zum Kopftuch als Symbol. In: Judith Schlehe (ed.), *Zwischen den Kulturen—zwischen den Geschlechtern*, 187–198. Munich: iudicium.

Schwarz, Monika and Jeannette Chur. 1993. *Semantik—ein Arbeitsbuch*. Tübingen: Narr.

Schwitalla, Johannes and Jürgen Streeck. 1989. Subversive Interaktionen: Sprachliche Verfahren der sozialen Abgrenzung in einer Jugendlichengruppe. In: Volker Hinnenkamp and Margret Selting (eds.), *Stil und Stilisierung: Arbeiten zur interpretativen Soziolinguistik*, 229–251. Tübingen: Niemeyer.

Sebba, Mark and Tony Wootton. 1998. We, they and identity: Sequential versus identity-related explanation in code-switching. In: Peter Auer (ed.), *Code-switching in conversation: Language, interaction and identity*, 262–286. London: Routledge.

Spreckels, Janet. 2006. *Britneys, Fritten, Gangschta und wir*: Identitätskonstitution in einer Mädchengruppe. Eine ethnographisch-gesprächsanalytische Untersuchung. Frankfurt, Bern, New York: Lang.

Strauss, Anselm L. 1969. *Mirrors and Masks: The Search for Identity*. Mill Valley CA: Sociology.

Tajfel, Henri. 1959. Quantitative judgement in social perception. *British Journal of Psychology 50*, 16–29.

Tajfel, Henri (ed.). 1982. *Social Identity and Intergroup Relations*. Cambridge: Cambridge University Press.

Tajfel, Henri and Joseph Forgas. 1981. Social categorization: cognitions, values and groups. In: Joseph Forgas (ed.), *Social Cognition: Perspectives on everyday Understanding*, 113–140. London: Academic.

Turner, John C.. 1982. Towards a cognitive redefinition of the social group. In: Henri Tajfel (ed.), *Social Identity and Intergroup Relations*, 15–40. Cambridge: Cambridge University Press.

Wolf, Ricarda. 1999. Soziale Positionierung im Gespräch. *Deutsche Sprache 27: 1*, 69–94.

Zhou, Minglang. 2002. Us and Them in Chinese: Use of *lai* (come) and *qu* (go) in the construction of social identities. In: Anna Duszak (ed.), *Us and Others: Social Identities across languages, discourses and cultures*, 51–68. Amsterdam: Benjamins.

8

Multilingual Forms of Talk and Identity Work

Benjamin Bailey

1. Introduction

Language is our primary semiotic tool for representing and negotiating social reality, including social identity categories. Through talk we position ourselves and others relative to co-present interlocutors, the communicative activities in which we are engaged, and various dimensions of the wider world, including social identity categories and their relative value. This positioning of selves is intertwined with the achievement of intersubjective understanding. We speak and interpret language from subject positions (Davies and Harré 1990), i.e., social identities, that are simultaneously a product and contextual frame of our talk.

Some identity negotiations through language are conscious, intentional, and referentially explicit, but most are not, and aspects of social identities are established, reproduced, or contested in even the most fleeting, instrumental, and seemingly trivial social encounters. In the exchange of greetings, for example, we choose the words, timing, and prosody of our utterances—along with facial and corporeal demeanor—to mark our relationship to our interlocutor, thus positioning ourselves and our addressees. This positioning is contingent and interactively negotiated across turns: the people we greet may provide a response to our greeting that positions them as more or less intimate or higher or lower in social hierarchies (Irvine 1974) or they might ignore our greeting entirely. Terms of address in such greetings—*Miss, Ms., Mrs., Dr., Mary*, or none at all—similarly position both speaker and addressee, as do the second-person pronouns, e.g. *tu* versus *vous*, of many European languages (Brown and Gilman 1960) or the multiple status-relationship marking verb endings of such languages as Korean (Lee 1989).

Even the absence of speech positions participants in an encounter. A momentary delay in producing a response to an assessment (Goodwin and Goodwin 1992) can signal disagreement with an interlocutor or something else problematic about the phenomenon or stance invoked by the prior turn. More extended silent co-presence (re)constitutes particular relationships among those who are co-present or displays stances toward widely recognized social categories and who is an authentic member of them (Basso 1972; Wieder and

Pratt 1990). To speak—or even not to speak in a social encounter—is always an act of identity (cf. Le Page and Tabouret-Keller 1985).

Turn-by-turn analysis of naturally occurring language and interaction is a means to understanding how individuals, as social actors, socially position themselves and are positioned by others. Interlocutors publicly display and continuously update for each other their on-going understandings of talk—including such positioning. Because they must make these negotiations visible to each other to achieve a degree of intersubjectivity, analysts can 'look over their shoulders' to gain a window onto the understandings that interlocutors, themselves, display of these processes (cf. Heritage and Atkinson 1984: 11).

Compared to monolingual, monocultural individuals, multilingual individuals have an expanded set of linguistic resources for the omnipresent task of positioning self and other, and often a broader range of social categories that can be made relevant through talk. On the linguistic level, bilinguals can draw forms from two languages as well as hybrid forms resulting from language contact. On the social and cultural level, many are familiar with relatively diverse cultural frameworks for interpreting and evaluating the world and positioning themselves and others within it.

Take the following example, in which two Dominican American high school students in a northeastern US city switch languages to negotiate a local meaning of the term *hick*. The use of multiple languages both facilitates coming to a common understanding of the word *hick* and highlights facets of speakers' identities as youthful, relatively acculturated, female Dominican Americans. Their bilingualism is a key to expressing social identity distinctions that are relevant in their multilingual, multicultural immigrant community.

Example 1. [(JS #212:40:58) Janelle (US-born) and Isabella (arrived in US at age 6) are sitting outside of their school and have just referred disparagingly to some male, immigrant students staring in their direction as 'hicks'.][1]

Janelle: What do you call a hick? Cause Jose says a hick is someone ridiculous, somebody stupid. Isn't a hick someone who just came back from

---

[1] Transcription conventions are as follows:

Janelle:	The speaker is indicated with a name or abbreviation on the left of the page.
loca	Italics indicate words spoken in languages other than English.
['Jerk.']	Text surrounded by single quotation marks and brackets indicates a translation of the immediately preceding language.
( )	Empty parentheses indicate material that couldn't be heard clearly enough to transcribe.
((smiling))	Double parentheses surround nonverbal, visual, prosodic, or other contextual information.
//I don't- //He said	Text after double slashes that is directly above or below other text after double slashes indicates words spoken in overlap.
(1.5)	Numerals in parentheses indicate periods of time, in seconds, during which there is no speech.
Da::mn	A colon indicates that the preceding sound was elongated in a marked pronunciation.
if I- I	A hyphen indicates that speech was suddenly cut-off during or after the word preceding the hyphen.
stabbin'	A single apostrophe indicates the elision of a single letter.

the country and they can't really dress, they can't speak English? And they, you know,

Isabella: They be like *loca, loca, //e:::::: pa, epa:::, huepa*: (high pitched and nasal) ['honey, honey, he:::::::y, alright!, alri::::ght!, alri:ght!']

Janelle: //Yeah, right?

Janelle offers a candidate understanding of a *hick* in referential terms: as someone who just came from the (Dominican) countryside, is not acculturated to urban American youth clothing fashions, and can't speak English. Isabella confirms Janelle's candidate understanding of 'hicks' not through reference but by giving a representative direct quotation of their speech: *loca, loca, e:::::, epa, epa, huepa*. She squints and scrunches her face, using a nasal, slightly high-pitched register. She introduces this direct quote with the African American English habitual *be* (Rickford 1999), meaning that this category of person *habitually* and *repeatedly* says things of this sort. Janelle displays immediate agreement with this characterization of 'hicks' with an affirmative, overlapping *Yeah, right?*, even before the characterization is completed.

Janelle and Isabella mockingly use these Spanish words and this way of speaking Spanish—associated with a stereotyped island Dominican male style—to position certain recent immigrant male identities and ways of speaking as undesirable in an American urban youth context. *Loca, loca, e:::::, epa, epa, huepa* is associated with the relative directness and intensity of heterosexual Dominican males from the island in approaching females, a style that is being constructed as inappropriate for this US context. 'Hicks' not only know little English and fail to dress according to urban US youth styles, they also fail to adhere to appropriate local cultural frameworks and practices for heterosexual interaction. This code switched characterization of 'hicks' contributes to both a) the achievement of intersubjectivity between Isabella and Janelle, and b) the construction of a desirable category for them to inhabit, even though the category and associated characteristics are not explicitly named.

The relatively indirect linguistic means by which Isabella and Janelle constitute their common, desirable social position is typical of identity work, which is seldom achieved through direct, propositional statements of identity (e.g., 'I am a relatively acculturated Dominican American female teen-ager who would like to distance herself from certain recent immigrant male ways of being'). Much more commonly, speakers exploit non-referential social associations of ways of speaking to position themselves and others. Linguistic forms always include a dimension of social associations or *indexical* meanings (Peirce 1955; cf. "voice" in Bakhtin 1981) in addition to their propositional, or denotive, meanings. Particular ways of speaking, for example, are associated with particular geographic regions, socioeconomic statuses, genders, vocations, etc. These associations, or indexical meanings, vary much more with context than denotive meanings do. In the above example, speaking Spanish is used to disparage a fellow Dominican, but in many other contexts, Janelle and Isabella associate speaking Spanish with a highly valued Dominican identity. Both are bilingual, speak Spanish to monolingual relatives, and regularly code switch in intragroup peer interaction.

The indexical meanings, or active social associations, of linguistic forms are both "brought along" to the interaction as well as "brought about" in the interaction itself (Auer 1992). They are brought along to the interaction in that codes, and specific forms within codes, have social associations that pre-exist particular interactions. They are brought about within interactions in that codes and forms have *multiple* social associations, and interlocutors creatively exploit particular associations in situationally specific ways.

Because they involve both received and negotiated meanings, social identity negotiations provide a means of linking meaning—making processes in interactions at the local level with larger social and historical processes, e.g., racial formation, acculturation, and social stratification, that both inform, and are informed by these social interactions. At a general level, identity work is a perspective from which to examine the encounter of individual social actors with meanings and structures accrued from history. Individuals use language to both resist and reproduce existing meanings and structures, making identity work a lens for viewing the on-going constitution of society in the present (Giddens 1984).

In this chapter, I first define *identity* as I use the term, emphasizing the socially constructed and processual nature of identity negotiations and achievement. I then analyze an example of identity negotiations in monolingual talk. This example illustrates key principles of identity negotiations through language—that they are interactional, indexical, and contingent—that are applicable to both monolingual and multilingual contexts. In the next section, I give four examples of code switching to illustrate the metaphorical implications that some such switches can have for identity, and I situate such metaphorical switches among functional categories of code switching and broader categories of metaphorical language use. In the final section, I argue that what is distinctive about identity negotiations in multilingual contexts is not so much linguistic as social and political, i.e., that the distinctive salience of multilingual talk in Western societies is a function of social and linguistic ideologies rather than the nature of the forms themselves. To analyze identity work in multilingual contexts is thus to analyze the larger social and political systems in which identity options and the value attributed to associated linguistic forms are created, contested, and maintained (Pavlenko and Blackledge 2004).

2. What is Identity?

I use the term *identity* in a specific sense that contrasts with popular psychological and biological uses of the term. In popular psychology terms, identity refers to an individual's subjective sense of self, which is perceived as an enduring quality or essence lodged in that individual. In popular biological terms, identity refers to overlapping essential social, behavioral, and phenotypic qualities that are seen as fixed and heritable, such as ethnicity or race (cf. Carbaugh 1996; Tracy 2002). In both cases, identity is treated as relatively fixed, as located in the individual, and as an analytical prime that affects or explains social behavior and meanings.

This popular notion of identity contrasts sharply with the social constructionist perspective that has been dominant in the humanities and interpretive social sciences since the 1970s. From this social constructionist perspective, social identities are a function not of static attributes of individuals or groups, but rather of on-going processes of social differentiation. The fact that social identity categories have different configurations and meanings across time and space is evidence that they are socially constructed, rather than reflections of essential nature. Even racial categories, which are popularly perceived as biologically-based and thus fixed, can be shown to be a function of time and place rather than attributes of individuals or group members. An individual who counts as White in the Dominican Republic, for example, may count as Black upon immigrating to the United States (cf. Hoetink 1967; Bailey 2002), and the Jewish, Italian, and Slavic immigrants to the United States in the early 1900s who were commonly seen as members of distinct races lost this "racial" distinctiveness over time, becoming White Americans after two to three generations (Waters 1990; Brodkin 1998). From an analytical perspective, social identity is not what one *is*, but what one *counts as* in a particular time and place.

Two subjective processes of ascription serve to constitute social identities: "self-ascription"–how one defines oneself—and "ascription by others"–how others define one (Barth 1969: 13). These two subjective processes, often under other names, are at the core of identity definitions across many academic fields. Discursive psychologists refer to self- and other-ascription as "reflective positioning" and "interactive positioning" respectively (Davies and Harré 1990); in cultural studies, Stuart Hall refers to identity as "the names we give to the different ways we are positioned by, and position ourselves within, the narratives of the past" (1990: 225); and sociocultural linguists Bucholtz and Hall (2005: 586) define identity as "the social positioning of self and other." Individuals typically make reference to empirical attributes of group members in these processes of ascription or positioning, but the membership categories themselves are not based on the sum of objective similarities and differences among individuals or groups. Minor features can be treated as emblems of difference or similarity among groups, for example, and radical differences among group members can be downplayed or denied.

While this conceptualization of identity highlights the subjective, contingent nature of identity constitution and the agency of individuals as social actors, identity construction is fluid only within certain parameters. Our phenomenological understandings develop in an historical world in which history is omnipresent in embodied form, as *habitus* (Bourdieu 1990: 56). Individuals only ascribe identities to themselves, for example, that are imaginable and available in a particular social and historical context, and they are only ratified in identities (through other-ascription) that social history makes available to them. The relative degree of individual agency versus structural constraint experienced by individuals in identity negotiations varies with the specific social histories through which particular categories have been constituted as meaningful. In the US, for example, 3rd or 4th generation Italian or Irish Americans can situationally choose whether to invoke their symbolic ethnicity (Waters 1990; Gans 1979), while members of non-White racial groups or

linguistic minorities have much less control over whether those facets of identity are treated as relevant by others (Mittelberg and Waters 1992). Negotiations of identity thus take place within specific parameters that history has
imposed in a particular time and place.

3. The Interactional, Indexical, and Contingent Negotiation of Identity

In this section, I present and analyze a segment of monolingual interaction
among young Korean Americans in which identity negotiations are salient.
This monolingual example illustrates a number of principles, common to both
monolingual and multilingual contexts, for relating language use to identities:
identities are constituted in talk; identity work is interactional; the indexical
dimension of linguistic forms is central to identity constitution; and achieved
identities are partial, multiple, contingent, and shifting (cf. Bucholtz and Hall
2005). The continuities between this monolingual example and the multilingual examples in the next section lay a foundation from which to argue, in
the final section of this chapter, that the salience of identity negotiations in
multilingual contexts is a function of politics and ideology rather than formal
linguistic difference.

In this example, adapted from Chun (2001: 60), 1.5[2] and 2nd generation
Korean American males in their early 20s negotiate shared and overlapping
position for themselves through naming and characterizing the social category
'White people'.

Example 2.
1 Jin: I think white people just don't keep it real and that's why
2 Dave: That is- that's true man?
3 Jin: Cause that's why they always back stabbin', like my roommate who
        wasn't gonna pay the last month's rent
5 JH: white
6 Jin: He kicks us out // of
7 Eric: //the prototypical whitey
8 Jin: Ye:::ah ma::n?
9 JH: No social skills.
10 Jin: But that's not true for everyone, I don't think.
11 EC: Uh huh
12 Jin: Cause all those ghetto whiteys in my neighborhood, I think they're
        cool.

In line 1, Jin explicitly names a category *white people* and states a stance
toward them, that they *just don't keep it real*, i.e., that they are insincere or
dishonest. David, Eric, and JH respond to this initial assessment with various

---

[2] Second-generation Korean Americans are US-born of Korean immigrant parents. The term
'1.5 generation' is used to refer to Korean-born individuals who come to the US before adulthood,
typically before the end of primary school, thus receiving much of their socialization in the US.

second assessments (Goodwin and Goodwin 1992) of agreement in lines 2, 7, and 9. By displaying this congruent understanding of White people, they position themselves as similar in some respect(s) to Jin and to each other, but different from White Americans.

Jin uses a phrase *keep it real* and a grammatical structure, zero copula *they always back stabbin'*, that are strongly associated with African American identities, in characterizing both White Americans as a group and a particular White individual whose insincerity was characteristic of his social group. While these language forms do not constitute a claim by Jin of being African American, they suggest commonalty of his perspective with African American perspectives on White Americans. This interpretation of these non-referential indexical usages is highly context specific, as the use of forms popularly associated with African American English can have many possible connotations, e.g., such forms can be used by outsiders to mock African Americans.

In line 7, Eric makes the sharing of an African American-like perspective more explicit by referring to Jin's insincere roommate as *the prototypical whitey*. *Whitey* is a disparaging term that African Americans sometimes use to refer to White Americans as well as the privileged, hierarchical social position inhabited by White Americans. In using this term, Eric is positioning himself and, implicitly, his interlocutors, as sharing some dimensions of the experience of African Americans as non-Whites in a racially organized society. This proposed positioning of selves vis-à-vis White and Black Americans is ratified by Jin in line 8, *Yeah man*.

The constitution of identities through talk is always contingent and partial. While these five Korean Americans have initially collaborated in differentiating themselves from a disparaged White identity, the positioning of self and other becomes more complicated in lines 9 and 11 when Jin qualifies the group's criticisms of White Americans *that's not true for everyone* and cites examples of White Americans who do not share the negative attributes that Jin and others have been attributing to them. Jin is thus modifying his subject position as one that can be defined in part through opposition to *certain* White American subject positions, but not all of them. His positive evaluation of *ghetto whiteys* may reflect class solidarity—inhabitants of ghettos being relatively poor and powerless, regardless of color—or an alignment with Whites who live in ghettos and who have adopted hip hop practices and ideologies.

While the identity work in this talk highlights opposition to certain White identities, aspects of gender and age are also being implicitly performed in this segment. The adoption of African American youth, or hip hop, language is much more common among teen-agers and young adults than among older adults, and the adoption of such language by young non-African Americans has been documented primarily among males, for whom it is a resource for enacting masculinity (Bucholtz 1999; Cutler 1999; Kiesling 2001; Zentella 1997). Identities that we claim or enact are always at the intersection of multiple social categories, e.g., race, age, gender, ethnicity, and class, even though only one such dimension may be focal in a given interaction or analysis.

Identities in this short segment of talk are partial, multiple, interactionally negotiated and constituted, and rapidly shifting. The specific social position that is being claimed, 'young Korean American males who see White

Americans as disingenuous and inhabiting a position of privilege that excludes non-Whites' does not have a specific category name. This example of social positioning relies almost entirely on indexical meanings. Neither the social positions being enacted—Korean American, male, and young—nor a social identity perspective that informs much of their talk—African American—is explicitly named in this talk.

By their nature, indexical meanings are highly context bound, both in terms of the local interaction and the particular social history that infuses linguistic forms with particular social connotations (Bakhtin 1981). The interpretation of any indexical meaning depends not just on the form and context, but crucially on the interpreter's subject position. While these young Korean American males treat their uses of language and their positioning of themselves as desirable, outsiders might interpret it very differently. Their Korean-raised parents, for example, might find their use of African American English—and their implied solidarity with African American perspectives—undesirable, for example. Many first-generation immigrants to the United States make great sacrifices so that their children can achieve socioeconomic mobility. Aligning oneself with African Americans, who face great obstacles to socioeconomic mobility in the United States, can be directly counter to this desired trajectory (Bailey 2001, 2000; Waters 1994; Chang 1990).

4. Negotiating Identities Through Metaphorical Code Switching

Research over the last 35 years has highlighted local meanings and functions of code switches in ways that can be subsumed under three broad headings: situational switching, discourse contextualization switching, and metaphorical switching. Such categories serve as a heuristic for highlighting particular functions of code switching and should not be understood as representing discrete or manifest types. Many switches simultaneously serve more than one of these functions. In this section, I briefly describe these three functional emphases of switches and then give four examples of multilingual talk that highlight identity work through metaphorical switches. While any instance of multilingual speech has implications for identity in Western contexts dominated by monolingual ideologies, I focus here on cases in which speakers exploit local social associations of codes to position themselves vis-à-vis each other and local categories.

In *situational* switching, distinct codes are employed in particular settings and speech activities and with different categories of interlocutors, i.e. there is a direct relationship between code use and observable features of the situation (Blom and Gumperz 1972). Codes are switched as observable changes in the context occur, e.g. to accommodate a monolingual speaker who joins the group or as interlocutors move to a different institutional setting associated with a distinct code. In switching characterized as *discourse contextualization*, individual switches do not necessarily co-occur with external changes in the context or significant shifts in sociocultural framework. Individual switches serve instead as contextualization, or framing, cues to mark off quotations, changes in topic, repair sequences, etc. from surrounding speech (Auer 1984; Auer 1988, 1995; Alfonzetti 1998; Wei 1998; Milroy and Wei 1995; Bailey 2000). These functions in monolingual speech are typically filled through prosody, word choice, and visual cues. In such unmarked discourse contextualization switching, conventionalized associations between particular codes and social worlds are not treated as relevant by participants (although non-member bystanders may see them as relevant), and the act of code switching itself, rather than the particular social associations of given codes, is what helps to organize the interaction.

In the following example, from Bailey (2002: 239), a code switch into Spanish by Dominican American Janelle coincides with a change in footing, a temporary re-framing of talk (Goffman 1979; cf. Zentella 1997: 93):

Example 3.   [(JS #210:50:10) Discussing whether she needs new immunizations to do her summer job at a hospital.]

Janelle: I don't know if I- I don't know if I have to go again cause*dizque no es verdad que* ['supposedly isn't it true that'] after a certain time- after a certain time you have to do it again? You gotta get shots again?

Janelle is unsure whether she needs new immunizations before beginning her summer job. She moves from *reporting* this uncertainty in the first part of her turn, to directly *asking* her interlocutor to confirm that one needs to be re-immunized after a certain period of time. This switch from a statement to a question coincides with a cut-off of *cause*- a shift in pitch and tempo, and a change of code, from English to Spanish. Code switching is a linguistic resource—like prosody or body alignment—that can be activated to highlight this shift in footing, or communicative activity, but it is not being treated here by interlocutors as having any greater metaphorical meaning related to identities than the corresponding monolingual change of footing would have.

Neither situational nor discourse contextualizing switching necessarily has *locally* salient implications for identity. Such switching can simply be a means of speaking appropriately to people in ways that they can understand and of managing and organizing conversational sequences.

Metaphorical switches, in contrast to situational switches, partially *violate* conventionalized associations between codes and context, activity, or participants. Elements of setting, participants, activities, or perspectives that are conventionally associated with a code can be invoked by a switch into that code when such elements are not otherwise present or active in the conversation. Changes in language can thus constitute alternative cultural frameworks for interpreting experience and constructing social reality. The switch in Example 1, above, has such a metaphorical import in that Isabella's *loca, loca, epa* brings to life a Dominican male persona and cultural framework for male-female relations that are associated with certain Dominican Spanish ways of speaking but not with American English ways of speaking. This switch simultaneously serves a discourse contextualizing function, i.e. marking off directly quoted speech from the surrounding talk.

Such metaphorically constitutive uses of language can also be monolingual, of course. In Example 2, above, the use of African American English forms by young Korean Americans constitutes them as young non-Whites who see parallels between their racial exclusion and the racial exclusion of African Americans. In both cases, aspects of a sociocultural world that were not demonstrably active in prior talk are invoked and made relevant through use of linguistic forms associated with that particular world.

The following four examples of metaphorical code switches generate meanings about identities, perspectives, and sociocultural frameworks for understanding the world that would not be generated in the same way through continued monolingual speech. In each case, the metaphorical meanings generated depend on specific social and historical associations of language forms and their situated use by speakers.

The first two examples are drawn from Kroskrity's (1993) study of the Arizona Tewa, a small Native American group who are officially members of the Hopi tribe, but who maintain a distinct Tewa language in addition to speaking Hopi. This distinct Tewa language and identity have been maintained despite nearly 300 years of closest proximity to the Hopi.

In Example 4, two middle-aged Tewa men have been discussing, in Hopi, a recent, favorable court ruling on a land dispute between the Hopi and the larger Navajo tribe whose land surrounds Hopi land. The conversation has been proceeding in Hopi, which is common among Arizona Tewa, who live among the numerically dominant Hopi and are always fluent in Hopi. In this particular conversation, their use of Hopi also coincides with their larger tribal interest in confronting the outside Navajos.

Example 4.   (Kroskrity 1993: 196–197. In these examples, Hopi language is represented in italics, e.g. *Hopi*, while Arizona Tewa is represented in underlined italics, e.g. *Arizona Tewa*.)

A: *Tenatyava. Tenatyava. Pay-sen 'ita-m nanami pihi:k'yani.*
    ['It's come true. It's come true. Maybe now we will live peaceably among each other.']
B: *'u to'o wi' he:yu-bí-'í'i-dí han ankhyaw 'u-mu:.*
    ['You are one among the few who think so.']

While *A* expresses optimism about the ruling, *B* suggests that many people are not so optimistic about the eventual outcome. The metaphorical meanings generated by *B*'s switch into Arizona Tewa are a function of the local social connotations of Tewa language, which are directly linked to Arizona Tewa ideologies of identity. Arizona Tewa folk histories position the Tewa as inheritors of a warrior tradition, and the Arizona Tewa view themselves as more pragmatic and realistic regarding issues of conflict than their Hopi brethren, whom they sometimes position as strong in spiritual matters but possibly naïve in more worldly affairs. By switching to Tewa in the above exchange, *B* communicates that he is not just speaking as an individual disagreeing with *A*. He is also positioning himself as representing a more realistic position in such political matters, a position associated with distinctively Tewa perspectives.

The following Arizona Tewa code switch occurs at a *kachina* dance in Tewa village that includes both Hopi and Tewa. The speaker sits among several observers of the dance.

Example 5. (1993: 199–200)

A: *Hi:wo'i díbí-hí-'ó! Loloma, loloma, lomahin-yin^{w}a.*
[((*in Arizona Tewa*)) 'They are dancing good!'
((*in Hopi*)) 'Beautiful, beautiful, they look good!']

Kroskrity's native consultants found this specific sequence of assessments of the dancing to be highly complimentary. Arizona Tewa see Hopi as highly accomplished in ceremonial, spiritual, and ritual realms. By using Hopi language, the speaker invokes the (implicitly) higher standards of the Hopi for evaluating the dance, and his compliment is thus perceived as communicating relatively greater acclaim than the corresponding Tewa utterances would.

The achievement of intersubjectivity is intertwined with the positioning of selves in these examples. With each of these code switches, there is a shift in sociocultural frameworks for interpreting both the specific words as well as the position from which the words are spoken. In both cases, speakers constitute their identities as both Tewa and Hopi in the process of everyday communicative activities: discussing politics and praising a performance.

Example 6 is one of many instances of Spanish-English code switching in the documentary film *My American Girls* (Matthews 2000), a film about a Dominican immigrant family in New York City. In this segment, Sandra, who immigrated from the Dominican Republic to New York as an adult, confronts her 14-year-old, US-raised daughter Mayra over Mayra's failure to do her homework. Mayra is hanging out in front of her house with a peer, Wendy, when Sandra addresses her.

Example 6.

 1 Sandra: *Yo te dije que tú fueras arriba para que hacieras algo pero tú dijistes*
 2 *que no podías porque tenías muchas tareas. //Métate inmediate-*
    mente.
 3 ['Mayra, when I told you to do something upstairs you said you
 4 couldn't because you had too much homework. Get in there right
    now.']
 5 Mayra: *//Yo lo hice.* ['I did it.']
 6 Sandra: I don't care. *Vete a estudiar. Tú tienes examenes la semana entera.*
 7 ['Go and study. You have tests all week.']
 8 Mayra: Wendy *vamo'* ['let's go']
 9 Sandra: [   ]
10 Mayra: I'm going. Wendy *vamo'* ['let's go']
11 Sandra: *Vete!* ['Go']
12 Mayra: I'm going!
13 Sandra: *Vete!* ['Go']
14 Mayra: Hold on, I'm going!
15 Sandra: *Mira, yo te quiero abajo ni para un segundo Oístes?*
16 ['Hey, I don't want you down here for even a second. You hear
    me?']
17 Mayra: I'm going!

Both Mayra's switch into English *I'm going* (line 10) to address her mother, and Mayra's and Sandra's non-reciprocal code use (lines 10 to 17) generate metaphorical meanings in this exchange. While it is not unusual for bilingual Latino children in the US to respond to their parents' Spanish with English (Zentella 1997: 57), Mayra initially responds to her mother in Spanish and even addresses her peer Wendy in Spanish (while maintaining an English pronunciation of Wendy's name). It is only after her mother reprimands her and uses the imperative *Vete* that Mayra responds to her mother in English, a pattern that is repeated across the final four turns.

The non-reciprocal code choice in these six turns reflects negotiations about the sets of rights and obligations between speakers (Myers-Scotton 1993). Differing sets of rights and obligations are implied by Spanish and English in this context. In a Latin American cultural framework, parents have significant authority over teen-age children, and parent-child interactions are to be guided by respect for the hierarchical relationship between children and adults. In mainstream US culture, there is much less hierarchy between parents and children, and teen-agers are given considerable individual choice in pursuing friends, interests, and activities. The individualistic nature of US society and the seductive freedoms offered to US youth are a near universal source of tension between first-generation immigrants to the US and their US-raised children.

In this case, the use of Spanish by Sandra represents an effort to constitute a Dominican world, in which parents have authority in the family and children are obedient. It conjures the world of first-generation labor migrants, a world in which children are obligated because their parents work long hours in low-paying, dead-end jobs so that their children, through education, can have a better life. Sandra thus positions herself as a Dominican immigrant mother of a Dominican child.

Mayra's use of English, in contrast, constitutes an assimilated US world in which teen-agers readily talk back to parents and make personalistic choices about activities and work habits, even if such choices undermine opportunities for socioeconomic mobility. She thus positions herself as an American teenager.

Competing visions of the world are thus juxtaposed through the juxtaposition of codes across these turns. Neither Sandra nor Mayra accommodates to the other by switching codes because accommodation would be tantamount to acceding to the other's position. It would be difficult for Mayra to talk back to her mother so brazenly in Spanish, because such behavior would constitute a grave offense in Dominican worlds. Sandra does not switch to English, because in the American world thus constituted, children can be relatively disrespectful to parents with impunity.

The final multilingual example in this section is drawn from the same conversation as in Example 1, between Dominican American high school students Janelle and Isabella. In both examples of their talk, code switches into Spanish serve to position them as particular types of Dominican American teen-age females who are different from more recent immigrants. In both examples, Isabella uses direct quotes of a recently immigrated Dominican teen-age male's speech to display negative stances toward the category(ies) of people who talk in such a way. Isabella and Janelle collaborate in coming to a shared perspective on a disparaged category, thus constituting themselves, as interlocutors in the here-and-now, as occupying similar identity positions.

Example 7.   [(JS #211:56) Isabella and Janelle are sitting outside of their high school and have been discussing their weekend plans. Isabella has been dating a boy named Sammy for about 10 days, and she is now explaining why she is going to break up with him despite the fact that he is physically attractive. This segment of talk occurs about 40 minutes before the segment in Example 1.]

```
 1 Isabella: He's like- I don't kno:w. He's- he's so jealous.
 2 Janelle:  Oh
 3 Isabella: This kid is sickening! He- he tells me to call him before I go to the
 4           club. He- I'm like, I don't have time to call you, pick up the phone,
 5           call you while my friends are outside beeping the horn at me so I
 6           can jet with them to the club. And he's like- I don't know, he talks-
 7           he's like a hick, he talks so much Spanish!
                             And he //( )
 8 Janelle:                           //O::h! ((looks away))
 9 Isabella: No, but he speaks Spanish, but- I- the reason- I talk to him- when he
10           talks on the phone he speaks English a lot because I speak English.
11           More. I tell him, speak English, speak English.
12           ((wrinkled face)) Y que, lo::ca ['What's up, honey']). He goes,
13           you know, ni:na ['girl'], and you know, and I don't want to hear it.
14 Janelle:  You should have found that out before you went out with him.
15 Isabella: I know, he's rushing into it. . . . . .
```

Isabella is explaining why she was breaking up with Sammy, a recent immigrant whom she had been briefly dating. She specifies a particular personality deficiency from which Sammy suffers (*he's so jealous*), gives an example of his jealous behavior, and specifies that he's *like a hick* and *talks so much Spanish*.

Janelle responds (lines 2 and 8) to these assessments (Goodwin and Goodwin 1992) of Sammy with *oh*'s and vertical head nods, suggesting a shared understanding of the undesirable nature of a male who is jealous, like a hick, and speaks so much Spanish. Isabella, however, treats some aspect of Janelle's displayed understanding of this as problematic, by initiating a repair *No, but he . . .* (line 9). As in Example 1, there are initial, referential descriptions of an undesirable Other, but Janelle and Isabella only treat the characterization as adequate when there is a code switched performance of the speech of this Other. The use of code switching to set off quotations from surrounding talk has often been noted as a function of code switching, and many have noted that the code used for the quotation is not necessarily the same one that the speaker originally used (e.g. Gumperz 1982: 75–76). In this case, the code match between the quoted speech and the antecedent speech is important because the Spanish forms carry social associations for Janelle and Isabella that would not be carried by corresponding English forms. It is only when Isabella enacts Sammy, through a code switched direct quotation of particular Spanish forms—*Y que lo:ca* ('What's up, honey') and *ni:na* ('girl')–that she treats her characterization of Sammy as complete and definitive, and she and Janelle can proceed to speak about the break up from other perspectives. For Isabella, Sammy's addressing her as *loca* and *nina* may invoke a traditional Dominican social framework for their romantic, male-female relationship, a framework that she wishes to avoid. In establishing the undesirable qualities of Sammy, Janelle and Isabella constitute their own identities—as relatively acculturated, urban, Dominican American teen-age females—as desirable.

While Spanish language can be a unifying emblem of Spanish or Dominican identity in US contexts involving non-Latinos, it can be a key index of difference in local, intra-Latino contexts. The fact that such intra-group boundaries can be situationally highlighted through Spanish use shows that there is not a fixed, one-to-one correspondence between use of a linguistic code and the social affiliation that it expresses. While a notion of 'we-code' versus 'they-code' (Gumperz 1982: 82–95) is appealing from a macrosocial perspective, situated language use reveals no such stable dichotomy, as social meanings and identity associations of particular forms are constituted in specific local contexts.

While language is popularly seen as a referential system for labeling or communicating propositional information, the six examples of talk given in this chapter suggest that direct reference plays only an indirect and often minor role in the enactment of identity. *None* of the social identity positions being claimed by speakers in the six examples in this chapter is referentially named. In three of the examples, a category of Other, who is not present–'hicks' in Example 1, 'white people' in Example 2, and Sammy (as hick) in Example 3–is referentially named. The use of explicit category names and a marked style of speaking for constituting an Other against which one defines oneself may be characteristic of relationships between linguistic forms and social identities more generally. One's own identity and ways of speaking are generally treated as normal, natural, and unmarked, so it can be difficult to call attention to them. Identities, like linguistic styles (Irvine 2001) are constituted through meaningful opposition to other identities, so it is through the highlighting of boundaries—through naming and disparaging of an Other or exaggeration of linguistic features seen as emblematic of other identities—that one's own identities and associated ways of speaking are constituted as distinct and discrete (e.g. Basso 1979; Mitchell-Kernan 1972).

5. Multilingualism as a Social and Political Phenomenon

The examples of metaphorical code switching that I presented in the previous section illustrate the power of multilingual ways of speaking to constitute sociocultural world and position selves within them. Although I have tried to highlight the partial, contingent, and situated nature of such identity work through talk, the power of language to reflect and (re)constitute identities in these examples can inadvertently reinforce essentialist beliefs about the relationships between language and identity. The assumption of an essential language-identity link is misleadingly reinforced by Western ideologies in which language, race, and nation are seen as forming a natural unity. Westerners tend to see *being* ethnically French, *speaking* French, and inhabiting a French *nation-state* as more or less the same thing, for example, and individuals who fit one or two of these criteria but not all three—e.g. French speaking inhabitants of Paris who are of sub-Saharan African descent—are seen as something other than 'just French'.

This ideology is a function of European nation building projects of the last several centuries, in which links among language, nation, and identity were essentialized and naturalized as parts of political projects. This monolingual ideology informs both popular and academic approaches to multilingualism. The fact that social and cultural linguists have focused so much attention on the meanings and functions of code switching, for example—while paying relatively less attention to corresponding monolingual speech—reflects the monolingual ideology that code switching is not an entirely natural form, but something that is in need of explanation (Woolard 2004).

In the following sections of this chapter, I tease out some of the implications of this ideology for understanding identity work in multilingual contexts. I first show that privileging formal definitions of multilingualism and assuming an essential language-identity link distract attention from a number of multilingual-like forms of talk that have important implications for social identities. I then argue that the distinctiveness of multilingual talk in Western societies has more to do with monolingual ideologies and politics than with the formal distinctiveness of such ways of speaking, and that perceptions of distinctiveness are rooted in particular subject positions and ideologies. At the local, in-group level, for example, most instances of multilingual speech in Western societies do not generate local metaphorical meanings, and for many multilingual speakers, the two (or more languages) they use in some situations do not form a relevant, or meaningful opposition (which undermines the notion of multilingualism as a discrete phenomenon). At the same time, however, such talk is always marked and consequential for identities in the larger context of Western societies. Finally, I argue that the social implications of multilingual ways of speaking are not a function of the formal linguistic distance between forms but of the social histories that have infused forms with particular meanings and varying levels of prestige. The value of analyzing identity negotiations in multilingual contexts is not so much in the details of linguistic forms but in the perspective that such analysis gives on social and political processes and meanings. The notion of 'multilingual' thus becomes a more useful social-analytical construct if it is approached as a socially, rather than formally, based concept.

5.1. Multilingual-Like Ways of Speaking

Starting from formal definitions of multilingualism or code switching, e.g. the use of two or more grammatical systems in a single speech exchange (Gumperz 1982), distracts attention from the uses to which language is put. From the functional perspective of identity work, multilingual speech is simply one way among many of positioning self and other. A more functional approach to talk can encompass a broader range of multilingual, or multilingual-like phenomena that have implications for social identity but that may or may not meet analysts' more formal criteria for what constitutes multilingualism. If one's starting point is social identity, it may not be central whether a speaker is switching languages, alternating between a dialect and a national standard, register shifting, or speaking monolingually in a variety that highlights language contact. If one starts from a more functional perspective, one is relieved, to a degree, of the questions of what exactly constitutes a language (Alvarez-Caccamo 2001, 1998), and what constitutes the competence level in a second or third language that allows one's speech to count as multilingual (Meeuwis and Blommaert 1998). The focus can thus shift to individuals as social actors using heteroglossic (Bakhtin 1981) sets of linguistic resources to negotiate the social world.

From the perspective of social identity, language alternation may be socially meaningful and worthy of analysis regardless of whether a speaker is a competent speaker of a second language. Rampton (1995), for example, has shown how teen-agers in England use short segments of speech in languages of which they know only a limited number of words or phrases to socially position themselves vis-a-vis their peers and the wider society. Such instances of "crossing" involve the use of language that is strongly associated with an ethnic or racial category to which the speaker does not belong. Thus an Anglo British youth may situationally use words or phrases from Caribbean Creole English or Panjabi to position himself relative both to interlocutors (who may or may not be members of categories popularly associated with those forms), and to the wider, racially organized society.

Similarly, from the perspective of identity work, there is no *a priori* reason why switching among what count as discrete languages should be privileged over switching among what count as dialects. What counts as a language and what counts as a dialect is typically a political question, as captured in the widely-circulated aphorism that a language is a "dialect with a navy." It is not formal or genetic linguistic distance or issues of mutual comprehensibility that differentiates a dialect from a language, but rather the links of a variety to political power, institutions, and states. Varieties, such as Spanish and Portuguese, which are linked to nation states thus count as languages, while varieties that are not at the center of national power typically count, at least popularly, as dialects.

Finally, a more functional perspective can encompass identity work in monolingual speech that has been affected by multilingualism or multilingual situations. Even monolingual speakers may reproduce contact phenomena in their speech from having learned a language in a situation that was formerly multilingual. Thus the English pronunciation of monolingual New York Puerto Ricans, for example, may include a degree of syllable-timing, a feature of Spanish, as opposed to the stress-timing of dominant varieties of Anglo American English (Zentella 1997: 45). Such pronunciation distinguishes the speech of many second- and third-generation US Latinos from more institutionally prestigious varieties and can be used by both in-group and out-group members to constitute a social boundary.

In addition to phonetic effects of language contact, there can also be persistent discourse level patterns inherited from ways of speaking in languages that have been lost through language shift to monolingualism. In such communities, distinctive rhetorical styles can serve as an emblem of social distinction and a locus of both misunderstanding and political struggle in intergroup encounters (Philips 1983; Scollon and Scollon 1981; Tannen 1982).

5.2. To Whom Do the Languages of Multilingual Talk Represent a Socially Meaningful Opposition?

The social meaningfulness of multilingualism is a phenomenological question. While the languages of multilingual contexts are popularly seen as distinct by dominant groups in Western societies, in some contexts multilingual speakers do *not* treat the languages involved in such a way. A growing body of literature since the early 1980s has challenged the assumption that the languages used in code switching are essentially distinct and that code switching necessarily involves social meanings that are different from ones communicated in monolingual talk (Meeuwis and Blommaert 1998; Heller ed. forthc.; Poplack 1980; Woolard 2004). The multilingual practice that most forcefully undermines assumed distinctions among languages is the relatively frequent, intrasentential code switching that has been widely documented in intra-group peer interaction among the children of international labor migrants to Western societies and in many urban, African contexts (e.g. Myers-Scotton 1993; Swigart 1992). When language alternation functions as a discourse mode it its own right (Poplack 1980), it undermines the assumed opposition between languages, and the assumed unity of a single language with identity.

When languages are not compartmentalized and strictly associated with particular social domains (Fishman, Cooper, and Newman 1971), the search for a function of a particular switch may be akin to trying to explain why a monolingual speaker selects one synonym or phrasing over another (Zentella 1997: 101). In a corpus of 1,685 switches among young New York Puerto Rican girls, Zentella (1997: 101) assigns fewer than half of her switches to specific conversational strategies, or functions, arguing that the motivations and meanings of such switches were no different at the local level than the motivations and meanings of monolingual speakers' choices among synonyms in monolingual speech. Similarly, Meeuwis and Blommaert (1998: 76) argue that the multilingual talk among Zairians in Belgium can represent "one code in its own right," and that the insistence on two distinct languages as the frame of reference for this form of speech is an ideologically-motivated *a priority* that is not useful in terms of interpreting it.

While languages may have lost their distinctiveness to multilingual speakers in particular local contexts, in larger contexts such as Western nation-states where monolingualism is considered normal and natural, multilingual talk is always salient and seen as requiring explanation in ways that monolingual speech is not. The meanings that one finds in such switching vary with one's subject position and analytical perspective. For many adults, including first-generation immigrant parents, code switching is a haphazard jumble of linguistic elements that is emblematic of the inability to speak what those adults see as the correct language, i.e. the ideological standard that is prestigious in institutional contexts (Lippi-Green 1997; Milroy and Milroy 1985; Silverstein 1996). Right-wing nativist groups typically point to immigrant multilingualism as a form of mongrelization and a threat to prosperity and the social fabric (Piatt 1990). Many academics since the 1970s, in contrast, have celebrated the linguistic sophistication displayed in code switching (McClure 1977; Sankoff and Poplack 1981; Lipski 1985) and the social 'strategies' that some forms of it imply (cf. Myers-Scotton 1993: 74; Gumperz 1982; cf. Woolard 2004). For more politically oriented analysts, such code switching can be seen as a form of resistance to dominant discourses of unquestioning assimilation (Gal 1988: 259) and a means to constructing a positive self in a political and economic context that disparages immigrant phenotypes, language, class status, and ethnic origins (Zentella 1997). The meanings and implications of particular forms for identity work are a function of the interpreter's subject position in a larger sociopolitical field.

5.3. Multilingualism as a Dimension of Social and Political Practice

Linguistic approaches to multilingualism can veil the social and political history of which multilingualism is part-and-parcel. The social and political conditions, such as migration and social stratification, that afford the on-going co-existence of multiple languages are the same ones that afford on-going inequality and construction of social difference among groups. In cases of labor migration or refugee streams to Western societies that result in multilingualism, immigrant groups commonly assume lower positions in power hierarchies and their degree of assimilation is a political and contested issue. Often the language, culture, religion, and/or phenotypes of such immigrants are devalued by members of dominant groups, so any expression of identity must engage discourse about the worthiness of those identities. Assimilationist practices are discouraged by group solidarity among oppressed groups, while maintenance of immigrant language and cultural practices are seen by dominant groups as an explanation and justification for on-going inequality. More generally, identity categories and language choice and attitudes are inseparable from power hierarchies and related ideologies about the relative value of identity categories and ways of speaking.

The increased flow of people, goods, and ideas around the world in the last century has made multilingualism and identity negotiations in Western urban centers increasingly visible to Western elites and academics. In relatively stable social and linguistic situations of monolingualism, the social and linguistic categories favored by dominant groups are seen as natural through processes of hegemony or symbolic domination (Bourdieu 1991; Heller 1995). Speakers tend to be relatively unaware of the ways in which their ways of speaking represent performances of identity because speech in stable social situations reproduces what are assumed to be natural, or normal identities. When a member of an ethnic group speaks in a manner popularly associated with that ethnic group, the talk is simply seen as a reflection of a natural, essential, independently pre-existing identity rather than a social negotiation process. The multilingual identity work that is characteristic of more rapidly changing social contexts, in contrast, destabilizes assumptions about an essential unity of language, nation, and identity.

Formal definitions of multilingualism also veil the range of practices and meanings that multilingualism encompasses. The occurrence, form, distribution, and meanings of multilingual talk vary across and within communities, contexts, and interactions. This variation is not random, but rather follows patterns that can be linked to specific questions of power and the construction of social difference. What are relevant social boundaries in a particular context and how did they arise? What are groups' relative and situational interests in boundary-maintenance versus boundary-leveling? How much access to cross-boundary social roles and domains do members of a society have (Heller 1988)?

Patterns and meanings of multilingual talk at the local level can thus be linked to larger sociohistorical questions. Poplack (1988), for example, shows that contrasting patterns of code switching between two communities—a New York Puerto Rican one and a Ottawa-Hull French Canadian one—correlate to contrasting social positions of the two groups. Even though the genetic relationship between French and English is virtually identical to the genetic relationship between Spanish and English, both the form and interpretation of the switching are very different in the two communities. Bilingual New York Puerto Rican switches tend to be smooth and seamless, i.e. unmarked, while French-English switches tend to be highlighted, or marked, through repetition, hesitation, intonational highlighting, and even explicit metalinguistic commentary.

Whereas bilingualism is seen to be emblematic of New York Puerto Rican identity—differentiating members from island Puerto Ricans and non-Puerto Rican Anglophones—Ottawa-Hull French Canadian bilingualism is not associated with a social identity distinct from that of local monolingual French Canadians. For New York Puerto Ricans, use of two languages is both an emblem of a distinctive identity and a practice that draws in immigrant newcomers. In the French Canadian situation, there is no stream of newcomers to incorporate and no distinctive identity bridging disparate communities that needs to be enacted or maintained through language.

Gal (1988: 247) argues that particular code switching ideologies and practices can be linked to even broader political economic and historical contexts. Thus, groups with similar structural positions in the world system—e.g., second-generation labor migrants to Western, industrialized states—will display similarities in code switching meanings and practices. Thus Italian-German switching among the children of Italian labor migrants to German will be similar to that of Spanish-English code switching among second-generation Puerto Ricans in the US, both in terms of patterns and local functions.

Within particular communities, code switching practices and meanings shift over time in conjunction with shifting identity politics. Heller (1992), for example, demonstrates how francophone political mobilization in Quebec destabilized conventional patterns of multilingual speech, resulting in significant negotiations and metacommentary on which language, French or English, to speak and what it means to speak one or the other. In Brussels, where relatively frequent, and intra-sentential code switching was once common, younger generations are switching less than the older generations, in part because of the political polarization between French and Flemish speakers in the country. This polarization makes a joint-French-Flemish Brussels identity—as expressed through frequent French-Flemish switching—less tenable (Treffers-Daller 1992).

The implications of multilingual talk for identity negotiations are thus a function of the history that gives rise to constellations of differently valued identity options and infuses ways of speaking with social meanings and perspectives. If historical social relations among groups are particularly coercive and stratified, ways of speaking associated with those groups will be particularly infused with related social associations, and those ways of speaking will symbolize and reconstitute social difference particularly starkly.

The salience and persistence of distinctions between African American and other varieties of American English illustrate the political and historical bases of social meanings of language. These distinctions have persisted for centuries, despite long-term close contact between speakers of African American and other American varieties of English. It is the distinctively coercive and unjust nature of historical social relations in the US—slavery, systematic Jim Crow laws, segregation, and on-going social and economic inequality—that have both a) sustained African American and other American English as distinct varieties, and b) made African American English salient as a social marker. In contexts of discrimination and inequality, different ways of speaking will tend to persist as markers of social identity, just as the identities themselves are made to persist. In contexts of relative equality, in contrast, identities and ways of speaking assimilate to each other relatively rapidly, as has occurred among European immigrants to the US across three generations.

5.4. Multilingualism as Social Construction

While the notion that identity categories such as race or ethnicity are socially constructed is now an academic commonplace, multilingualism, as both a popular and analytical category, is not generally seen as a social construction. There are fundamental parallels, however, in the social and political processes through which difference is constructed among social identity categories and the linguistic forms that count as separate languages. Both, for example, are popularly seen as having self-evident, empirical bases, and both form parts of the highly naturalized assumption of a language-race-nation unity. In both cases, however, the conceptualizations, salience, and social significance of the categories are a function of social and political processes rather than inherent, or essential characteristics of members of the categories. The fact that multilingual speech draws both popular and academic attention may tell us relatively little about the nature of code switching or linguistic forms, and relatively more about popular and academic language ideologies of Western nation-states.

Conceptualizing bilingual speech as a social construction does not minimize its on-the-ground social implications. An example from social identity categories can help make this clear: the fact that Black-White race in the United States is a social construction, for example, does not make race an illusion or socially insignificant (Omi and Winant 1994). Race has been, and remains, a central organizing principle in the United States and a way of representing, rationalizing, and reproducing tremendous social inequality. Approaching race as a social construction allows one to see, however, that race is not about essential biological difference (which is how race is popularly construed) but about social history. What is socially significant about race is a distinctively violent history of coercion and inequality, not details of hair texture, skin shade, or other morphological features. The social constructionist perspective directs attention to the political and historical processes through which race has been constituted and given such significance in the US.

Similarly, approaching monolingualism and multilingualism as socially constructed does not change their social force at the level of lived experience, but it does show that this social force is not a function of formal, or inherent linguistic differences among what count as languages. If multilingual talk is an especially meaningful mode of speaking, it is not the nature of the forms that make it so but rather particular social and political histories.

Studying identity work in multilingual talk can be a route to understanding society not because of formal linguistic distinctions among languages, but because of the inherent social and political nature of language. In contexts such as Western societies where code switching or multilingual talk has been made to count as particularly socially meaningful, insights into identity negotiations can come from attention to the social and political processes that have made monolingual-versus-multilingual speech a meaningful opposition. The value of analyzing identity negotiations in multilingual contexts is not in the details of linguistic forms but in the perspective that such analysis gives on social and political processes and meanings. Identity work is thus a perspective from which to examine the encounter of individual social actors with history as they resist and reproduce historical meanings and structures in the present.

References

Alfonzetti, Giovanna. 1998. The conversational dimension in code-switching between Italian and Dialect in Sicily. In: P. Auer (ed.), *Code-Switching in Conversation: Language, Interaction, and Identity*, 180–211. London/New York: Routledge.

Alvarez-Caccamo, Celso. 1998. From 'switching code' to 'code-switching': Towards a reconceptualisation of communicative codes. In: P. Auer (ed.), *Code-Switching in Conversation: Language, Interaction, and Identity*, 29–48. London/New York: Routledge.

Alvarez-Caccamo, Celso. 2001. Codes. In: A. Duranti (ed.), *Key Terms in Language and Culture*, 23–26. Malden, Massachusetts: Blackwell.

Auer, Peter. 1984. *Bilingual Conversation*. Philadelphia/Amsterdam: John Benjamins.

Auer, Peter. 1988. A conversation analytic approach to codeswitching and transfer. In: M. Heller (ed.), *Codeswitching: Anthropological and Sociolinguistic Perspectives*, 187–213. New York: Mouton de Gruyter.

Auer, Peter. 1992. Introduction: John Gumperz's approach to contextualisation. In: P. Auer and A. Di Luzio (eds.), *The Contextualisation of Language*, 1–38. Amsterdam: Benjamins.

Auer, Peter. 1995. The pragmatics of code-switching: A sequential approach. In: L. Milroy and P. Muysken (eds.): *One Speaker, Two Languages: Cross-disciplinary Perspectives on Code-Switching*, 115–135. Cambridge: Cambridge University Press.

Bailey, Benjamin. 2000. Communicative behavior and conflict between African-American customers and immigrant Korean retailers in Los Angeles. *Discourse and Society* 11 (1): 86–108.

Bailey, Benjamin. 2000. Social/interactional functions of code switching among Dominican Americans. *IPrA Pragmatics* 10 (2): 165–193.

Bailey, Benjamin. 2001. Dominican-American ethnic/racial identities and United States social categories. *International Migration Review* 35 (3): 677–708.

Bailey, Benjamin. 2002. *Language, Race, and Negotiation of Identity: A Study of Dominican Americans.* New York: LFB Scholarly Pub.

Bakhtin, M. M. 1981. *The Dialogic Imagination:* Four Essays. University of Texas Press Slavic series; no. 1. Austin: University of Texas Press.

Barth, Frederik. 1969. Introduction. In: F. Barth (ed.), *Ethnic Groups and Boundaries: The Social Organization of Culture Difference,* 9–38. Boston: Little Brown and Co.

Basso, Keith H. 1972. "To give up on words": Silence in western apache culture. In: P. P. Giglioli (ed.), *Language and Social Context,* 67–86. Harmondsworth: Penguin Books.

Basso, Keith H. 1979. Portraits of "the Whiteman": Linguistic Play and Cultural Symbols Among the Western Apache. Cambridge [Eng.]/ New York: Cambridge University Press.

Blom, Jan-Peter and J. J. Gumperz. 1972. Code-switching in Norway. In: J. Gumperz and D. Hymes (eds.), *Directions in Sociolinguistics,* 407–434. New York: Holt, Rinehart and Winston.

Bourdieu, Pierre. 1990. *The Logic of Practice.* Stanford, Cal.: Stanford University Press.

Bourdieu, Pierre. 1991. *Language and Symbolic Power.* Cambridge, MA: Harvard University Press.

Brodkin, Karen. 1998. *How Jews Became White Folks and What that Says About Race in America.* New Brunswick N. J.: Rutgers University Press.

Brown, Roger and Albert Gilman. 1960. The pronouns of power and solidarity. In: T. Sebeok (ed.), *Style in Language,* 253–276. Cambridge, MA: MIT Press.

Bucholtz, Mary. 1999. You da man: narrating the racial other in the production of white masculinity. *Journal of Sociolinguistics* (3-4): 443–460.

Bucholtz, Mary and Kira Hall. 2005. Identity and interaction: A sociocultural linguistic approach. *Discourse Studies* 7 (4-5): 585–614.

Carbaugh, Donal A. 1996. *Situating Selves: The Communication of Social Identities in American Scenes.* Albany, NY: State University of New York Press.

Chang, Edward. 1990. *New Urban Crisis: Korean-Black Conflicts in Los Angeles.* Dissertation, Ethnic Studies, University of California Berkeley, Berkeley.

Chun, Elaine. 2001. The construction of White, Black, and Korean American identities through African American Vernacular English. *Journal of Linguistic Anthropology* 11 (1): 52–64.

Cutler, Cecilia. 1999. Yorkville crossing: White teens, hip hop and African American English. *Journal of Sociolinguistics* (3-4): 428–442.

Davies, Bronwyn, and Rom Harré. 1990. Positioning: The discursive production of selves. *Journal for the Theory of Social Behavior* 20 (1): 43–63.

Fishman, Joshua A., Robert Leon Cooper and Roxana Ma Newman. 1971. *Bilingualism in the barrio, Indiana University publications. Language science monographs,* vol. 7. Bloomington: Indiana University.

Gal, Susan. 1988. The political economy of code choice. In: M. Heller (ed.), *Codeswitching: Anthropological and Sociolinguistic Perspectives,* 245–264. Berlin/ New York/ Amsterdam: Mouton de Gruyter.

Gans, Herbert. 1979. Symbolic ethnicity: the future of ethnic groups and cultures in America. *Ethnic and Racial Studies* 2 (1): 1–20.

Giddens, Anthony. 1984. *The Constitution of Society: Outline of the Theory of Structuration.* Berkeley: University of California Press.

Goffman, Erving. 1979. Footing. *Semiotica* 25: 1–29.

Goodwin, Charles and Marjorie Harness Goodwin. 1992. Assessments and the construction of context. In: A. Duranti and C. Goodwin (eds.), *Rethinking Context: Language as an Interactive Phenomenon,* 147–190. Cambridge/ New York: Cambridge University Press.

Gumperz, John Joseph. 1982. *Discourse Strategies.* Cambridge/New York: Cambridge University Press.

Hall, Stuart. 1990. Cultural identity and diaspora. In: J. Rutherford (ed.), *Identity: Culture, Community, Difference,* 222–237. London: Lawrence and Wishart.

Heller, Monica. 1988. Introduction. In: M. Heller (ed.), *Codeswitching: Anthropological and Sociolinguistic Perspectives,* 1–24. New York: Mouton de Gruyter.

Heller, Monica. 1992. The politics of code-switching and language choice. In: C. Eastman (ed.), *Codeswitching,* 123–142. Cleveland/Avon: Multilingual Matters.

Heller, Monica. 1995. Language Choice, Social Institutions, and Symbolic Domination. *Language in Society* 24 (3): 373–406.

Heller, Monica (ed.). (Forthc.). *Bilingualism: A Social Approach.*

Heritage, John, and J. Maxwell Atkinson. 1984. Introduction. In: J. M. Atkinson and J. Heritage (eds.), *Structures of Social Action: Studies in Conversation Analysis,* 1–15. Cambridge: University of Cambridge Press.

Hoetink, Harry. 1967. *Caribbean Race Relations: A Study of Two Variants.* New York: Oxford University Press.

Irvine, Judith T. 1974. Strategies of status manipulation in the Wolof Greeting. In: R. Bauman and J. Sherzer (eds.), *Explorations in the Ethnography of Speaking,* 167–191. London: Cambridge University Press.

Irvine, Judith T. 2001. "Style" as distinctiveness: the culture and ideology of linguistic differentiation. In: P. Eckert and J. R. Rickford (eds.), *Style and Sociolinguistic Variation,* 21–43. Cambridge/New York: Cambridge University Press.

Kiesling, Scott. 2001. Stances of Whiteness and hegemony in fraternity men's discourse. *Journal of Linguistic Anthropology* 11 (1): 101–115.

Kroskrity, Paul V. 1993. *Language, History, and Identity: Ethnolinguistic Studies of the Arizona Tewa.* Tucson: University of Arizona Press.

Le Page, R. B. and Andrée Tabouret-Keller. 1985. *Acts of Identity: Creole-Based Approaches to Language and Ethnicity.* Cambridge/ New York: Cambridge University Press.

Lee, Hyon-Bok. 1989. *Korean Grammar.* Oxford/ New York: Oxford University Press.

Lippi-Green, Rosina. 1997. *English With an Accent: Language, Ideology, and Discrimination in the United States.* London/ New York: Routledge.

Lipski, John M. 1985. *Linguistic Aspects of Spanish-English Language Switching.* Tempe, Ariz.: Center for Latin American Studies Arizona State University.

Matthews, Aaron (ed.). 2000. *My American Girls.* New York: Filmmakers Library.

McClure, Erica. 1977. Aspects of code-switching in the discourse of bilingual Mexican-American children. In: M. Saville-Troike (ed.), *Linguistics and Anthropology,* 93–115. Washington, D.C.: Georgetown University Press.

Meeuwis, Michael and Jan Blommaert. 1998. A monolectal view of code-switching: Layered code-switching among Zairians in Belgium. In: P. Auer (ed.), *Code-Switching in Conversation: Language, Interaction and Identity,* 76–98. London/ New York: Routledge.

Milroy, James, and Lesley Milroy. 1985. *Authority in Language: Investigating Language Prescription and Standardisation.* London/ Boston: Routledge and K. Paul.

Milroy, Lesley and Li Wei. 1995. A social network approach to code-switching: The example of a bilingual community in Britain. In: L. Milroy and P. Muysken (eds.), *One Speaker, Two Languages: Cross-disciplinary Perspectives on Code-Switching,* 137–157. Cambridge: Cambridge University Press.

Mitchell-Kernan, Claudia. 1972. Signifying and marking: Two Afro-American speech acts. In: J. Gumperz and D. H. Hymes (eds.), *Directions in Sociolinguistics: The Ethnography of Communication,* 161–179. New York: Holt, Rinehart and Winston.

Mittelberg, David, and Mary C. Waters. 1992. The Process of Ethnogenesis among Haitian and Israeli Immigrants in the United-States. *Ethnic and Racial Studies* 15 (3): 412–435.

Myers-Scotton, Carol. 1993. *Social Motivations for Codeswitching: Evidence from Africa.* Oxford: Clarendon Press.

Omi, Michael, and Howard Winant. 1994. *Racial Formation in the United States: From the 1960s to the 1990s.* 2nd ed. New York: Routledge.

Pavlenko, Aneta and Adrian Blackledge. 2004. Introduction: New theoretical approaches to the study of negotiation of identities in multilingual contexts. In: A. Pavlenko and A. Blackledge (eds.), *Negotiation of Identities in Multilingual Contexts,* 1–33. Clevedon/ Buffalo/Toronto: Multilingual Matters LTD.

Peirce, Charles S. 1955. Logic as semiotic: The theory of signs. In: J. Buchler (ed.), *Philosophical Writings of Peirce,* 98–119. New York: Dover Publications.

Philips, Susan Urmston. 1983. *The Invisible Culture: Communication in Classroom and Community on the Warm Springs Indian Reservation.* New York: Longman.

Piatt, Bill. 1990. *Only English: Law and Language Policy in the United States.* Albuquerque, NM: University of New Mexico Press.

Poplack, Shana. 1980. Sometimes I'll start a sentence in Spanish y termino en espanol—toward a typology of code-switching. *Linguistics* 18 (7–8): 581–618.

Poplack, Shana. 1988. Contrasting patterns of codeswitching in two communities. In: M. Heller (ed.), *Codeswitching: Anthropological and Sociolinguistic Perspectives,* 215–244. Berlin/ New York/ Amsterdam: Mouton de Gruyter.

Rampton, Ben. 1995. *Crossing: Language and Ethnicity Among Adolescents.* London/New York: Longman.

Rickford, John R. 1999. *African American Vernacular English: Features, Evolution, Educational Implications.* Malden, Mass.: Blackwell Publishers.

Sankoff, David and Shana Poplack. 1981. A formal grammar for code-switching. *Papers in Linguistics* 14: 3–46.

Scollon, Ronald and Suzanne B. K. Scollon. 1981. *Narrative, Literacy, and Face in Interethnic Communication.* Norwood, N.J.: Ablex Pub. Corp.

Silverstein, Michael. 1996. Monoglot "Standard" in America. In: D. L. Brenneis and R. K. S. Macaulay (eds.), *The Matrix of Language: Contemporary Linguistic Anthropology,* 284–306. Boulder, Col.: Westview Press.

Swigart, Leigh. 1992. Two codes or one? The insiders's view and the description of codeswitching in Dakar. *Journal of Multilingual and Multicultural Development* 13: 83–102.

Tannen, Deborah. 1982. Ethnic style in male-female conversation. In: J. Gumperz (ed.), *Language and Social Identity,* 217–231. New York: Cambridge University Press.

Tracy, Karen. 2002. *Everyday Talk: Building and Reflecting Identities.* New York: The Guilford Press.

Treffers-Daller, Jeanine. 1992. French-Dutch codeswitching in Brussels: Social factors explaining its disappearance. *Journal of Multilingual and Multicultural Development* 13 (1–2): 143–156.

Waters, Mary. 1994. Ethnic and racial identities of second-generation Black immigrants in New York City. *International Migration Review* 14 (1): 57–76.

Waters, Mary C. 1990. *Ethnic Options: Choosing Identities in America.* Berkeley: University of California Press.

Wei, Li. 1998. The 'why' and 'how' questions in the analysis of conversational codeswitching. In: P. Auer (ed.), *Code-Switching in Conversation: Language, Interaction, and Identity,* 156–176. London/ New York: Routledge.

Wieder, Larry, and Stephen Pratt. 1990. On being a recognizable Indian among Indians. In: D. Carbaugh (ed.), *Cultural Communication and Intercultural Contact,* 45–64. London /Hove: Lawrence Erlbaum.

Woolard, Kathryn Ann. 2004. Codeswitching. In: A. Duranti (ed.), *A Companion to Linguistic Anthropology,* 73–94. Malden, MA: Blackwell.

Zentella, Ana Celia. 1997. *Growing up Bilingual: Puerto Rican Children in New York.* Malden, MA: Blackwell.

9

Crossing–Negotiating Social Boundaries

Pia Quist and J. Normann Jørgensen

1. Introduction

Several recent studies have focused on speakers' spontaneous acquisition and fragmentary use of out-group minority and non-standard language varieties. Such linguistic behavior was for a long time unexpected and not given serious attention in linguistic and sociolinguistic studies. However, the spontaneous acquisition and use of languages "that are not generally thought to belong to" (Rampton 1995: 280) a particular person or group seems to be common in local negotiations of ethnic, social and linguistic boundaries. These sociolinguistic processes can be termed 'crossing' (Rampton 1995). Although crossing as a metaphor—that connotes "a step over a heavily fortified and well-guarded linguistic border" (Auer 2003: 74)—is disputable, we will for the sake of convenience use it as a cover-term for the processes we are dealing with in this chapter.

Crossing is related to code-switching, stylization, and double-voicing—terms which we will explain in the following. In the first part of our chapter we approach the phenomenon of crossing in relation to processes of (ethnic) identity and solidarity construction. We refer to studies that examine negotiations of in- and out-group relations and mention a few studies that discuss adolescent use of crossing as a strategy against adults in institutional settings. In the second part we look at studies of crossing as mocking and joking in processes involving stereotyping and stigmatization. In connection to this we discuss the stylization of minority languages and varieties in the media. In the third part we shall look at two examples of crossing in more detail and see how the meanings of crossing, among other things, are related to the local organization of peer network relations. We end our chapter by briefly considering the consequences crossing can have for our understanding of language and speakers in general.

2. Language Crossing and Negotiations of (Ethnic) Categorizations and Solidarity

In the 1980s Roger Hewitt conducted ethnographic studies among inter-racial groups of friends in two areas of London (Hewitt 1986, 1992). In his pioneering study of white speakers' use of London Jamaican Creole, Hewitt observed how local cross-linguistic behavior is connected to wider patterns of race and ethnicity in society. He described how the use of Creole by whites in inter-racial groups sometimes functioned to "neutralize" stigmatized racial differences (Hewitt 1986: 163–164). Whites talking like blacks sometimes achieve "the substitution of a relation to language for the more complex relation to the black community. By temporarily freeing themselves from constraints of their respective groups, the friends can achieve in language a fictive social relation over and above their personal relationship of friendship" (Hewitt 1986: 164). Hewitt distinguished between different strategic modes of outsiders' use of Creole—modes that, if placed on a continuum, would range from a collaborative inter-racial friendship mode, over a public cultural mode to a hostile competitive mode of derision. Such an approach to language use in inter-racial groups was very different from the ways sociolinguistics had thus far treated white speakers' use of Black English Vernacular. Labov (1980), for instance, studied the degree to which white speakers were able to acquire more than just a subset of the vernacular of the black community (see also Le Page 1980 and Sweetland 2002). Hewitt's perspective was also quite different from Gumperz's (1982a and b) approach to inter-ethnic communication. Gumperz (and his associates) were mostly concerned with institutionalized interactions, typically between an applicant and a gate-keeper (interviews with local authorities, job interviews etc.)—situations with clearly defined roles and power relations. The focus was on how speakers acted according to their affiliation with predefined social and ethnic categories, rather than on the (re)construction and (re)negotiation of these affiliations. Hewitt's interest in the use of a language variety that was not generally accepted as belonging to the speaker, and resulting in the neutralization of racial and ethnic hostility, was indeed something new.

Hewitt found that the out-group use of Creole was always somewhat delicate. Blacks were normally sensitive to "the use of creole in derisive ways, and even just the possibility of its use to serve those ends, [is what] sensitises some blacks to *any* uses of creole by whites" (Hewitt 1986: 135). The delicacy—or potential social danger—connected to crossing seemed to be the very basis for how and why the different modes of conduct resulted in renegotiations of ethnic and racial positions, i.e. the very transgression sometimes achieved temporary, new social meanings and positionings. This aspect of crossing was of special interest to Rampton in his study of language crossing in a multiethnic youth club in London. When defining crossing, he writes:

> Crossing [. . .] focuses on code alternation by people who are not accepted members of the group associated with the second language they employ. It is concerned with switching into languages that are not generally thought to belong to you. This kind of switching, in which there is a distinct sense of movement across social or ethnic boundaries, raises issues of social legitimacy that participants need to negotiate (Rampton 1995: 280).

Hewitt's analyses of the political, strategic modes of cross-linguistic practices were an important source of inspiration for Rampton (1995: 4). Since Rampton introduced the term 'crossing' scholars have taken it up and analyzed crossing phenomena in different languages and contexts. The term quickly gained

popularity, perhaps due to its immediate and intuitive appeal. It seems to provide the analyst with a theoretic and practical tool for dealing with complicated social and linguistic processes in multilingual communities. However,
as Rampton's own complex analyses confirm, crossing is a multifaceted phenomenon that takes form and meaning in locally situated interactions and has
a different legitimacy and different effects depending on who, where, how, and
into which language variety the crossing is done.

2.1. Ritual and Liminality

It is a major point in Rampton's work that *ethnicity* is not a sufficient explanatory category for crossing (1995, 2001). Crossing practices involving the use of
Punjabi, Creole, and stylized Indian English by out-group speakers do not correspond with traditional sociolinguistic treatments of ethnicity, since these are
profoundly linked to assumptions about 'system', 'coherence' and 'community'
(2001: 265)—something which does not make sense when we focus on adolescent language practices in multilingual and multicultural settings. Instead of
acting according to the normal expectations of the ethnic group, the adolescents in Rampton's study seemed to be attracted to and aligned with shifting
out-group norms and cultural forms. Rather than fitting into or representing
one ethnic category, speakers used language to negotiate these affiliations and
to challenge them in ways that sometimes made new meanings or "new ethnicities" possible (1995: 297). Instead of approaching the crossing practices with
ethnicity as the analytic tool, Rampton found that the sociological and anthropological concepts of ritual and liminality were useful. Ritual is linked to the
symbolic conduct in interaction. It "displays an orientation to issues of respect
for social order and [. . .] emerges from some sense of the (actual or potential)
problematicity of social relations" (1995: 19). In the case of e.g. stylized Asian
English, Rampton found that three different situations or activities involving
crossing resulted in different ritual conducts. (1) When adults were the direct
or indirect recipients (1995: 141–62), stylized Asian English seemed to serve
as an anti-rite—"a small destabilising act counterposed to the categories and
conduct that the adult would normally be orienting to" (2001: 281). (2) In more
informal interactions among peers, crossing seemed to serve "as a differentiating ritual, focussing on transgression and threatening the recipient with isolation in the marginal zones that AE [Asian English] conjured if the offender did
not return to the norms of proper adolescent conduct" (2001: 282–83). Finally,
(3) during play or game activities, crossing into stylized Asian English seemed
to be a "consensual ritual [. . .] highlighting the ideals and rules of play rather
than their disruption" (2001: 283). Hence, crossing into one language variety,
here stylized Asian English, served quite different ritual functions depending
on the status of the interlocutors and the types of activities they engaged in.
It is not enough for the analysis of crossing, then, to reveal the attitudes and
stereotypes connected to Asian English. It is the concrete, local employment of
the variety that tells us how the crossing should be interpreted.

   In anthropology the notion of ritual (or rite) is sometimes connected to
that of liminality. Rampton borrows the term *liminality* from Victor Turner
(1974) and defines it as characterizing a ritual period of transition *"outside*

normal social structure", where interlocutors "occupy neither their former nor their future statuses" (Rampton 1995: 19–20). Rampton found that crossing was most likely to occur in such liminal situations when normal routines and structures were temporarily loosened (1995: 192–97). Also, liminality some-times seemed to be a consequence of language crossing: "Although crossing was often inserted into moments and settings where a breach of the taken-for-granted patterns of ordinary life had arisen independently of ethnic lan-guage use, it was also used productively to enhance or create such loosenings" (1995: 196). Hence, crossing was often born out of liminal situations, but it also sometimes led to a liminal situation with temporarily loosened or even reversed social roles and structures. As Auer notes (2003: 75), this is a point where crossing is clearly different from code-switching. Auer and Dirim (2000, 2003) find that Turkish is rarely used by non-Turkish adolescents in limi-nal situations. Rather, adolescents' shifts between German and Turkish can be described as discourse- and participant-related code-switching (e.g. Auer 1998) which normally do not involve the social risk of transgression which is implied in Rampton's definition of crossing.

2.2. The Spontaneous Acquisition of Turkish by Non-Turkish Adolescents

Auer and Dirim studied the spontaneous acquisition of Turkish by non-Turk-ish adolescents who grew up in Turkish-dominated neighborhoods in Ham-burg. The acquisition of Turkish was "spontaneous" in the sense that the speakers had never taken classes or learned Turkish from their parents or families. Instead, they had picked it up among their Turkish-speaking peers in kindergartens, schools, and during leisure time activities. In order to gain access to the friendship groups in their neighborhood, they used Turkish as an "entry ticket" (Auer and Dirim 2003: 228)—"it seems to be essential to acquire at least a minimum of knowledge of Turkish in order to be accepted in their surroundings" (Auer and Dirim 2000: 160). Although an almost instrumen-tal motivation for acquiring and using Turkish was common, the adolescents diverged substantially with regard to their Turkish cultural orientations and affiliations. Placed in a sociocultural space, the adolescents with non-Turkish backgrounds who used Turkish differed greatly on the dimensions 'main-stream vs. subcultural orientation' and 'youth-cultural vs. anti-youth cultural orientation'. The following finding by Auer and Dirim is of particular interest: according to the common stereotype, adolescents who grow up in immigrant-dense areas and use ethnically coded language markers (such as Turkish) are identified with marginal (street gang) cultures, face difficulties in school and other state institutions and are involved in criminal acts. This stereotype—as represented in the media (Auer and Dirim 2003: 223)—does not capture the diverse social landscape in which the adolescents who use Turkish position themselves. 13 out of the 25 informants in their study oriented more towards German mainstream culture than towards marginal subculture, i.e. they attended and engaged in school and education and seemed to accept "the rules and regularities of the 'official market'" (2003: 227). Some of the informants oriented themselves towards an adult lifestyle, i.e. they displayed explicit affiliation with their parents' way of living and tried to distance themselves from other adolescents their age. Many of the adolescents had a neutral rather than overtly positive attitude towards what they see as Turkish culture. They did not seem to have acquired Turkish because they valued or praised the Turks and Turkish ways of living. Their motivation seemed more instrumental than symbolic (Auer and Dirim 2003: 227–229). However, other informants explained their motivations with an almost romanticized positive appreciation of Turkish culture. Auer and Dirim conclude that the adolescents' stances and affiliations within socio-cultural space are very diverse. Thus, they argue that the various "ethnic, 'subcultural' and youth cultural affiliations (and, therefore, acts of identity) should be kept analytically distinct" (2003: 223).

Some of the informants with non-Turkish ethnic backgrounds were surprisingly fluent in Turkish (e.g. Hans and Thomas, both of German descent, who even spoke Turkish together without the presence of their Turkish friends), while others seemed to know only a few words and chunks of the language. It is not always clear whether the mixing of German and Turkish should be characterized as code-mixing or code-switching. Auer and Dirim found both in their data. There was evidence that a mixed speaking style involving the alternating use of German and Turkish was common and widespread. Also, partly due to the varying degrees of competence in the involved languages, code-switching was typical. However, Auer and Dirim did not find any qualitative difference between the ethnic groups in their switching behavior—native as well as nonnative Turkish speakers code-switched and code-mixed in more or less the same ways (Auer 2003: 84).

2.3. The Spontaneous Acquisition of Turkish by Non-Turkish Adolescents—A Case of Crossing?

Auer (2003) discusses whether or not the use of Turkish by the non-Turks can be characterized as a type of crossing, i.e. as the use of an out-group language. In a broad sense the use of Turkish by adolescents of e.g. Polish, Iranian and German descent is a type of crossing. The speakers employ a language which is associated with an ethnic group that they are normally not considered to belong to. However, the use of Turkish did not have the trespassing character which is implied in Rampton's definition of crossing. The code-mixing was rather part of "an unmarked speaking style" which was "detached from its Turkish roots and [had] instead become part of a general, ethnic, but not Turkish, and sometimes not even ethnic but just fashionable, streetwise youth style" (Auer 2003: 77). Auer's data further includes cases where the alternations could be characterized as code-switching. The switching serves pragmatic and competence-related functions (this resembles the findings in other studies of code-switching, see ch. 11), rather than symbolic, ritual functions in liminal situations. Hence, Auer concludes that crossing in the sense of Rampton is not common among the adolescents in this large immigrant neighborhood of Hamburg. However, Auer claims that crossing occurs among young mainly male speakers with German ethnic backgrounds who usually are not in peer contact with immigrants: "these adolescents do not cross the boundary into Turkish, but rather, they cross into a stereotyped ethnic variety of mock-German (sometimes called Kanaksprak) ascribed to Turkish and other migrant speakers" (Auer 2003: 90). We will discuss the mocking use of stereotype varieties in the next section. Crossing in Auer and Dirim's study seems to be different from that in Rampton's study with regard to its symbolic and transgressing meanings. The reason might be found in the specific type of environment studied in Hamburg. Ethnic hostility and racism do not appear to be at stake to the same extent as in the London immigrant communities. In Hamburg, the adolescents (at least the 25 informants in the study) have positive attitudes towards Turks and Turkish culture (Auer and Dirim 2003: 241). Only one of the informants (Daniel of Capverdian origin) displayed explicitly negative feelings towards Turks. In this generally positive atmosphere where Turkish language and culture seem to be accepted, normal, and unmarked, the use of Turkish by non-Turks is likely to be less problematic. In contrast, in the areas of London where Rampton and Hewitt carried out their studies, racism and ethnic segregation were part of the everyday life of the adolescents (cf. Rampton 1995: 27–30, and Hewitt 1986: ch. 1, especially his "area A" friendship groups were clearly divided between blacks and whites).

2.4. Crossing and School

It is sometimes argued that the schools' institutional categorizations and reactions to bilingual speakers in multilingual settings neglect speakers' abilities to handle and make creative use of their linguistically and culturally heterogeneous resources (Evaldsson 2002; Hewitt 1989; Rampton 1995: ch 13; Jørgensen 2003; Hinnenkamp 2003). There is a contradiction between the schools' official appraisal of linguistic diversity on the one hand, and their (also often official) monolingual educational policy on the other. The school as an institution often categorizes speakers according to linguistic or ethnic origin, ignoring among other things the fact that many bilinguals in urban, western communities grow up in mixed families with different linguistic and ethnic backgrounds (Evaldsson 2002: 6; Quist 2005).

Evaldsson (2002) describes this categorization of individual speakers as e.g. 'Spanish' or 'Turkish' as a means of controlling and predicting students' behavior and their needs for special teaching. This, she argues, can be described as "ethnic absolutism" (referring to Gilroy 1987). Ethnic categories become exclusive and explanatory at the cost of other possible categories (e.g. gender, age or peer group status). Of course, peer group interaction is not unaffected by these broader institutional framings. In a Swedish school setting investigated by Evaldsson, they make relevant ethnic and linguistic categorization for the activities that take place within the school. This is because (1) they determine which students are grouped together at different times and places (in normal classes as well as classes of special training) and (2) they shape explicit discourses about (what the school thinks to be a lack of) linguistic competence. Evaldsson found that the students challenged and renegotiated the social organization and the monolingual norms of the school. Strategic code-crossing and mixing was one of the ways in which students did so (Evaldsson 2002: 11).

The institutional framing was also decisive for some types of crossing in Hewitt's and Rampton's studies. Hewitt found that the use of Creole by white speakers in London was easier for their black peers to accept when the crossing was used as a sort of anti-language against adults: "A common use of creole by white secondary school children, and one which excites no objections from their black friends, is where it is used deliberately to exclude and mystify teachers and other adults in authority" (Hewitt 1986: 154). Rampton also reports on crossing used strategically in opposition against adult authorities, and he interprets Asian English *I no understand* stylizations within the analytic framework of 'ritual' (Rampton 1995: ch. 3). Especially stylized Asian English was often employed as a ritual contesting the pupil–teacher or youngster–adult power imbalance:

> They switched into an exaggerated Asian English at the threshold of activities like detention or basketball; when they were asking white adults for goods or services; when teachers tried to institute question-answer exchanges; and [. . .] when interviewers asked for more concentrated attention. These switches seemed to operate as a kind of probe, saying 'if I'm this, then how will you respond?' They conjured awkward knowledge about intergroup relations and in doing so, the purpose seemed to be to disturb transition to the activity being expected (Rampton 2001: 270).

A common feature of these studies (Evaldsson, Hewitt and Rampton) is that crossing does not only challenge (institutionalized) ethnic categorizations, but is also part of the speakers' constructions of youth identities in opposition to adults. This point has been emphasized elsewhere as well (e.g. Auer and Dirim 2003; Cutler 1999; Jørgensen 2003, 2004; Quist 2005). Code-crossing and mixing among adolescents often has to do more with the speakers' constructions of themselves as young people than with displaying specific ethnic identities.

3. Stylization, Mocking, and Stereotyping

As mentioned above, Auer (2003) found crossing (in the sense of transgressing a social and linguistic boundary) among speakers of German ethnic background. These speakers stylize 'ethnic' German speech, often in ways that are obviously taken from media stereotypes. Some of these instances of crossing can be characterized as mocking, for which there are various examples in the literature. Some studies report on its occurrence in face-to-face interaction (e.g. Hewitt 1986: 170; Hinnenkamp 2003; Quist 2005), others examine mock-type crossing in public media (e.g. Hill 1995; Androutsopoulos 2001; Andersen 2004). Androutsopoulos (2001) demonstrates that these crossing patterns can be followed "from the streets to the screens and back again", i.e. "from their community of origin ('the streets') over mediated discourse ('the screens') to face-to-face-communication of native speakers ('back again')" (Androutsopoulos 2001: 1).

In face-to-face interaction, we can roughly distinguish between out-group mocking, typically performed by members of a majority group who imitate a minority groups' styles of speaking, and in-group mocking, for instance sons and daughters mimicking the non-native accent of their immigrant parents.

Hewitt reports the former. When whites use Creole in conversations with other whites, they usually do so with a parodistic and mocking stance (1986: 148), and sometimes for racist purposes (1986: 135). The use of stylized Asian English by speakers of Indian or Pakistani descent is sometimes also used parodistically (Rampton 1995: 142–153). The Bangladeshi adolescents in Rampton's study rank lowest in the peer hierarchy in the youth club. A mocking, stylized use of their language by the others is one way in which the adolescents establish and display this hierarchy.

In-group mocking is mostly based on stylizations of a non-native command of the majority language. Hinnenkamp (2003: 27–33) shows how such stylizations are incorporated by the children of immigrants into their Turkish-German mixed speaking styles (which he calls "code-oscillation"). But the mimicking of "Gastarbeiterdeutsch" is not only used by the second and third generation speakers. Hinnenkamp discusses a conversation between a mother of Turkish descent and her son, who was born and raised in Germany. He shows that the boy *and* the mother stylize the first generation's way of speaking German.

According to Hinnenkamp, "its function is purely phatic: a We that reassures itself of its own identity via an exaggerated and caricatured use of voices that are not their own (anymore) but which become re-appropriated in play [. . .] stripped of any threatening connotations" (Hinnenkamp 2003: 33). Thus, there is not always a straightforward relationship between the stylized voice and the (ethnic) group which is imitated. Local positions and statuses are also constructed through stylization—something we will find again in the examples in the next section.

Hinnenkamp borrows terminology from Bakhtin for whom language use is always "half someone else's" (Bakhtin 1981: 293): when employing words in interactions, the speaker "appropriates the word, adapting it to his own semantic and expressive intention" (ibid.). However,

> not all words for just anyone submit equally easily to this appropriation, to this seizure and transformation to private property: many words stubbornly resist, others remain alien, sound foreign in the mouth of the one who appropriated them and who now speaks them; they cannot be assimilated into his context and fall out of it; it is as if they put themselves in quotation marks against the will of the speaker (Bakhtin 1981: 294).

Crossing might be characterized as a very clear and deliberate case of the re- or ex-appropriation of the words of others. In dealing with crossing, Quist (2005) found it useful to use Bakhtin's distinction between uni- and vari-directional double-voicing (Bakhtin 1984: 193–94). In instances of vari-directional double-voicing, voice and speaker are clearly separated (e.g. irony, parody, joking), whereas in uni-directional double-voicing the voice of the other is integrated into the speaker's own voice (see also Rampton 1995: 221–24).[1]

There are also various examples of stylizations of minority varieties in the media. Androutsopoulos (2001) lists a series of instances of stylized "Türkend-

---

[1] We will refer to the notions of uni- and vari-directional double-voicing in our analyses of the examples of crossing in the next section.

eutsch" (Turkish German) from movies, TV and radio. Interviews reveal that these stereotyped stylizations are well known among German adolescents, and that fragments of the stylized voices are often quoted and imitated. In Denmark most adolescents are familiar with *Mujaffa*—a stereotyped young male character with an immigrant background (Turkish or Arabic). Mujaffa was originally a computer game launched by Radio Denmark's youth targeted web-page as *Perkerspillet* (*perker* is the derogatory term for immigrants in Denmark). Due to public complaints and debates about the use of the word *perker*, the name was changed to *Mujaffaspillet* (The Mujaffa Game).[2] The Mujaffa web-page and the Mujaffa game are based on the stereotype of a young male immigrant who is attracted to street gang culture, who wears heavy golden chains and his baseball cap backwards. In the computer game the player takes on the identity of Mujaffa and cruises through the streets of Nørrebro and Vesterbro (the immigrant-dense areas of Copenhagen). The car is a 'top tuned' and heavily decorated BMW (according to a stereotype, the preferred car among young male second generation immigrants). During the cruise, Mujaffa scores points when he collects gold chains, when he crashes into passing police cars and when he succeeds in picking up a blonde girl (a stereotypical 'bimbo'). The Mujaffa game was launched in 2000 and is still a popular site. A quick Google search shows that it has circulated (and is subject to debates) on various Danish web-sites. The attraction seems to be based on the comic representation of 'Mujaffa' alone. Besides serving as an example of the vulgar, stereotyped portrayal of young male immigrants (and young Danish girls), there are two further details which are interesting for our discussion. First, the name Mujaffa has come to serve as a cover-term for this specific stereotype. Andersen (2003) argues that *Mujaffa* is about to assume the state of a noun in Danish, in the same way as *Brian*,[3] and she traces this back to the Mujaffa game web-site. Andersen (2003: 15) reports an example from an interview with a Muslim boy in Denmark who says: "One is forced to pay attention to the effect one has on other people. I try not to look like a Mujaffa" (our translation). In another example taken from Andersen (2003: 15), a reader of the newspaper 'Jylland-sposten' complains in a letter to the editor that the taxis in the town of Århus drive much too fast: "one is not supposed to drive through the Bus Street like Brian or Mujaffa" (our translation).

By coining a noun, *mujaffa*, it becomes possible—with one word—to index 'the whole package', i.e. everything that is associated with and implied in the stereotyped representations of young immigrant males. Part of this 'package' is the speech style of these males (referred to as multiethnolect by Quist 2000). This is the second point of interest in the Mujaffa game: it is a good illustration of the life-circle of crossing which Androutsopoulos (2001) describes. In the first stage, an ethnolectal vernacular is created among speakers of minority

---

[2] http://www.dr.dk/skum/mujaffa/#.
[3] In Danish *en brian* ('a brian') is used as a general metaphor for a person with working class background who has little or no education, who is not very smart, and who typically solves his problems through violence instead of talk. To the best of our knowledge this derogatory stereotyping of unskilled working class males has never been an issue in public debate. There are, interestingly enough, more than 19,000 persons in Denmark with the name Brian—who are probably not keen on having their name associated with the stereotype of 'a brian'.

backgrounds (Quist 2000; Auer and Dirim 2003; Hinnenkamp 2003). In the second stage, the ethnolect is taken as a source of inspiration for a stereotyped character in the media. In the Mujaffa game the Mujaffa character repeats the same phrase *wolla, min fætter* again and again. It literally means 'vallah, my cousin', with *vallah* derived from Arabic and Turkish and meaning 'by God'. It is a frequent term in immigrant Danish, used as a swearword and intensifier (see examples in the next section). The expression *wolla, min fætter*, however, is not a commonly used phrase among minority youth. *Min fætter* connotes the Danes' stereotype of immigrants' close family relations. In the Mujaffa game 'cousin' is used as a cover-term for all family members (and also evokes the close-knit, family-like organization of gangster and gang culture), and apparently 'Mujaffa' always runs into his 'cousins'. Adolescents who are not familiar with the speech of young second and third generation immigrants in Denmark pick up this phrase (probably assuming that this is what minority youth actually say), and quote and employ it in their conversations. This, then, is the third stage of Androutso-poulos' life-circle. The linguistic source of crossing is not direct communication with the people portrayed, but their stereotyped representation in the media.

The stylized variety 'Mujaffa' speaks can be called mock immigrant Danish. Hill (1995) has investigated Mock Spanish which involves little pieces of Spanish (e.g. *adios, hasta la vista, mañana*) and is used, mostly jokingly, by Anglo-Americans. It can be found in real conversations as well as in movies, on postcards, bumper stickers, mugs, etc. The Spanish-speaking population is—through the use of mock-Spanish—portrayed "with gross sexual appetites, political corruption, laziness, disorders of language and mental incapacity" (Hill 1995: 2). Hill argues that such uses of Spanish in the USA are part of an "elite racist discourse" which is rarely acknowledged as such beause the mocking is only indirect, "in fact [racism] is actively denied as a possible function of their usage, by speakers of Mock Spanish, who often claim that Mock Spanish shows that they appreciate Spanish language and culture" (Hill 1995: 2). Instead, by crossing into Mock Spanish, speakers "signal that they possess desirable qualities: a sense of humour, a playful skill with a foreign language, authentic regional roots, an easy-going attitude toward life" (Hill 1995: 1).

A closer look at the public debate about the Mujaffa web-page (in 2000, when the name was changed from *Perkerspillet* to *Mujaffaspillet*) is likely to reveal a discourse parallel to the one Hill analysizes for Mock Spanish. In fact, the creators of 'Mujaffa' argued that through their 'friendly' comic portrayal, they are promoting the inclusion of young immigrant males in the media representations of society. They saw this as a part of the process of integrating foreigners into Danish society. However, it could be characterized as a racist act as well—Hill's argument being that "the speakers and hearers can only interpret utterances in Mock Spanish insofar that they have access to the negative residue of meaning" (Hill 1995: 2). In other words, crossing into mock immigrant Danish, e.g. in a high school class, would not make sense if it was only connected to knowledge about the classmates with an ethnic minority background. In order to interpret 'Mujaffa's' speech the listener needs to be familiar with (and connect this specific speech style to) the criminal, girl-hunting, etc. stereotype of a young immigrant boy. This is one of the ways in which the stereotype is reproduced and kept alive.

4. Crossing and Peer Networks

We shall now look briefly at two examples of crossing. As Rampton points out, organized games involve "an agreed relaxation of the rules and constraints of ordinary behaviour" (1995: 193)—a situation that is likely to trigger language crossing. This was indeed the case in a study of language variation in an ethnically heterogeneous high school in Copenhagen. Quist (2005) analyzes instances of crossing in conversations recorded during a game called *Matador* (a board game, a type of *Monopoly*). In the two examples shown below, 'ritual' and 'liminality' are relevant analytic notions in the description of the situations in which crossing occurs. Furthermore, besides 'ritual' and 'liminality', Quist finds that the roles and positions of the speakers in the local peer network are crucial for (1) who is allowed to do the crossing, and (2) how crossing is interpreted and accepted by the peers.

Extract 1.

	Danish		English
Amina:	hahaha det er min fød-selsdag jeg skal have to hundrede kroner af jer alle sammen	*Amina:*	hahaha it's my birthday I shall have two hundred kroner from all of you
Phillip:	fuck dig	*Phillip:*	fuck you
Olav:	hold din kæft mand hvad snakker du om	*Olav:*	shut up man what are you talking about
Amina:	to hundrede (.) wallah jeg sværger jeg sværger det er Deres fødselsdag	*Amina:*	two hundred (.) wallah I swear I swear it is your birthday
→ Phillip:	og jeg sagde wallah jeg s:	→ *Phillip:*	and I said wallah I s:
Amina:	modtag af [hver spiller to hundrede] kroner	*Amina:*	receive from [each player two hundred] kroner
→ Phillip:	[wallah jeg sværger]	→ *Phillip:*	[wallah I swear]

Extract 2.

	Danish		English
Ali:	hvad er nu det for noget?	*Ali:*	now what is this?
Johan:	nej du skal i fængsel mand	*Johan:*	no you are going to prison man
Kristoffer:	næh det er kun hvis han	*Kristoffer:*	no that's only if he
Johan:	du skal være der de næste ti ture uden noget	*Johan:*	you have to stay there for the next ten turns without anything
Kristoffer:	ja og så skal du betale Naweds madpakke	*Kristoffer:*	yeah and then you have to pay for Nawed's lunch box
Johan:	jamen der sker ikke noget du holder der bare	*Johan:*	yes but nothing happens you are just parked there

Ali:	ikke ti ture er du dum eller hvad	*Ali:*	not ten turns are you stupid or what
Johan:	jo ti ture	*Johan:*	yes ten turns
Ali:	det siger den ikke	*Ali:*	it doesn't say that
Johan:	det gør den da	*Johan:*	of course it does
Ali:	you are a liar	*Ali:*	you are a liar
Johan:	skal vi vædde?	*Johan:*	wanna bet?
Ali:	hallo I bliver færdige mand hvad laver du	*Ali:*	hello you are going to finish what are you doing
Kristoffer:	kig i reglerne	*Kristoffer:*	read the rules
→ Johan:	ja jeg siger wallah kig I reglerne	*→ Johan:*	yeah I say wallah read the rules

On the surface, if we look at the linguistic features only, these two examples seem to be similar. The crossings into the multiethnic style (see arrows) are marked by a change of intonation, the use of the intensifier *wallah*, and the phrase *jeg sværger* ('I swear') (cf. Quist 2000: 151–59). From an interactional point of view, however, the two examples are very different. Extract 1 is an instance of mocking, and extract 2 is an example of non-parodistic crossing (i.e. the difference between Bakhtin's notions of uni- and vari-directional doublevoicing). These different meanings of crossing relate to the positions of the speakers in the peer-network. Phillip has a Danish ethnic background, and he mostly hangs out with other boys with a similar background. Johan, however, who also has Danish ethnic background, is one of the few who breaks the general pattern and hangs out with boys with ethnic minority background. The different group affiliations are crucial for a proper understanding of the instances of crossing in these examples.

In extract 1 Phillip makes fun of Amina, and he is a bit hostile. Amina has a minority background and is the only girl playing the board game with four boys. Amina tries to hold her own in a discussion during the game. She picks a 'lucky card' which says that 'it is your birthday' (*det er Deres fødselsdag*), and that the other players must pay her 200 kroner. Olav and Phillip protest. Amina insists (reading aloud from the 'lucky card') *wallah I swear I swear it is your birthday*. She says this with an intonation characteristic of immigrant Danish (as e.g. described by Hansen and Pharao 2004) and not unusual for her. Phillip immediately takes up and repeats the phrase *wallah I swear*, in a loud and mocking voice clearly copying Amina. However, his imitation is exaggerated: he says [æSWeWL] for Amina's [æSVeWL], i.e. instead of a labial dental obstruent he changes [v] to a labial one, which makes it sound exaggerated 'foreign'. This way Phillip manages not only to make fun of Amina and her way of speaking; he also invokes associations of 'foreigners who speak a non-native variety of Danish'—a move which has the effect of positioning Amina as a foreigner, i.e. in a stigmatized position different from Phillip's and Olav's.

Extract 2 is an example of uni-directional double-voiced crossing. Johan uses multiethnic style features to get his way during another disagreement during the game. But Johan does not make fun of the others. On the contrary, although there is a jovial atmosphere, Johan appears rather hostile as he shifts codes. The shift is prosodically signalled by a high rise in intonation, lack of glottal constriction (e.g. omitted 'stød' in the word *reglerne* [æʁɛ.l̩.nə] instead of the standard [æʁɛjʔlnə]), and non-standard stress (cf. Quist 2000: 151–159). Johan does not position himself as Ali's ally (Ali being of a minority background). Rather, he exploits the 'toughness' associated with the minority male youth culture to gain the upper hand in the discussion.

This interpretation is also supported by a look at the sociogram in Figure 1, a graphic representation of the networks of some of the students in the high school. The closer two persons are placed to each other, the more time they spend together in the school during breaks and lessons. The arrows link the students to those of the other students they in the interviews reported to "talk most to", and the gray boxes are the participants of extracts 1 and 2. It is possible for Johan to make use of the style normally associated with Ali as part of his own voice because of his position in the peer network. Johan's friends at school mostly have a minority background. His crossing in this extract, combined with a slightly aggressive tone, seems to borrow from the toughness associated with the group of boys who Johan normally hangs out with, i.e. Mehmet and Ahmet (cf. Quist 2005 for a more detailed analysis of this network). This way Johan also positions Ali as an outsider among the boys who are participating in the game—i.e. as a not-very-tough-guy. Johan is able to do this because of his position in the peer group. In extract 1, however, Phillip would probably not be able to use crossing in this way because of his position in the peer network. Both by themselves and by others, Phillip, Olav, Max, Jakob, and Mads are seen as the 'tough Danish guys', somewhat in opposition to the 'tough foreign guys' ('Danes' and 'foreigners' being the common categorical terms among the students). For instance, Phillip, Olav, Max, Jakob, and Mads drink a lot of alcohol, and they talk a lot about drinking—something Mehmet and Ahmet never do. Phillip never uses double-voicing uni-directionally, but only in a stylized way as in extract 1. Since he does not hang out with boys of a minority background, even a non-stylized crossing would run the risk of being interpreted by his peers as parodistic.

In the case of Johan, one could ask if the multiethnic style is indeed a language "which is not generally thought to belong to Johan". Johan does not use this variety all the time, but often shifts for single utterances, as in extract 2. He does not make fun of his peers, but incorporates their voice into his own. A point we would like to make here is that this practice would not be meaningful if it was *only* connected to ethnicity categories. Arguably, Johan's momentary shifts are a way of performing and presenting himself as a 'Dane-who-is-allowed-to-act like-an-immigrant-boy' and thereby defining his place in the social peer network. Hence Johan's crossing works in two directions. (1) The incorporation of the minority voice into his own voice is possible (i.e. a legitimate act of identity) because of his position in the peer network. And (2) because of his majority background and his traditional Danish appearance, Johan is not automatically a legitimate or accepted

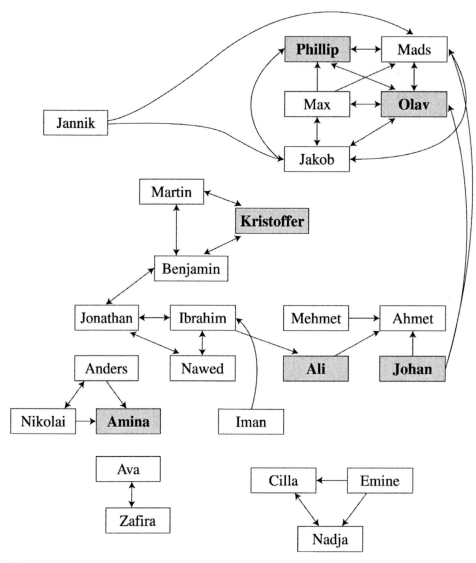

Figure 1.   Sociogram of friendship relations. Gray names appear in extracts 1 and 2.

member of his peer group. Hence, crossing may be one means (among many others) available to him to construct a legitimate identity.

5. Conclusion

In this paper we have used crossing as a cover term for the related but somewhat different processes of crossing, mocking, stylization and double-voicing. These processes of transgression all point to an understanding of language as a human phenomenon which is used by speakers to pursue their goals. Accordingly, we have primarily concentrated on the construction and maintenance of social relations among individual speakers in small groups and networks, but this understanding of language may as well cover any other purpose. The speakers use whatever linguistic means are at their disposal, regardless of the presumed origin of the specific linguistic features. In crossing and mocking, as well as in regular code-switching and code-mixing, speakers use linguistic features which are considered to belong to different sets of linguistic clusters (usually termed *languages* or *varieties*), and the speakers know this. Even to the most 'monolingual' speaker, 'knowing' a word entails not only knowledge of its morphological and syntactic properties, its denotation and connotations. It also involves knowledge of its stylistic value, and its place inside or outside registers and varieties of the 'one' language of the 'monolingual'. The same is true for speakers with access to more than one language. They know where the words belong, and they know the values attached to (the speakers of) each of the involved languages. Furthermore, as we saw in the examples of the last section, speakers in multilingual communities also know about and relate the crossing practices to their local peer group positions and statuses. Transgressing the border between a majority language in a western society and a stigmatized minority language is not in principle different from transgressing the border between a middle class urban standard and a stigmatized rural dialect. Speakers do it all the time, and they do it with a purpose. This is what Jørgensen (2004) terms *languaging*. Crossing and mocking as presented here, i.e. as means to negotiate social relations, are instances of languaging which involve quite separate sets of linguistic features. The transgressions are therefore open and observable *acts* performed with a purpose. This is a fact that makes crossing an ever-interesting source of knowledge about local and global meaning construction and negotiation.

References

Andersen, Margrethe Heidemann. 2003. Om Mujaffaspillet, Mujaffaer og Brianer. In: *Nyt fra Sprognævnet*, 13–15. December. København: Dansk Sprognævn.

Androutsopoulos, Jannis. 2001. From the streets to the screens and back again: On the mediated diffusion of ethnolectal patterns in contemporary Germany. *LAUD Linguistic Agency*, nr. A522. http://www.linse.uni-essen.de/laud/catalogue.htm

Androutsopoulos, Jannis. 2003. Jetzt speak something about italiano. Sprachliche Kreuzungen im Alltagsleben. In: Erfurt, Juergen (ed.), *'Multisprech': Hybridität, Variation, Identität*. *OBST Osnabrücker Beiträge zur Sprachtheorie*. 65. 79–109. Duisburg: OBST.

Auer, Peter. 1998. Introduction: 'Bilingual Conversation' revisited. In: Peter Auer (ed.), *Code-switching in Conversation*, 1–24. London: Routledge.

Auer, Peter. 2003. Crossing the language border into Turkish? Uses of Turkish by non-Turks in Germany. In: Lorenza Mondada and Simona Pekarek Doehler (eds.): *Plurilinguisme—Mehrsprachigkeit—Plurilingualism. Festschrift for Georges Lüdi*, 73–93. Tübingen: Francke.

Auer, Peter and Inci Dirim. 2000. On the use of Turkish Routines by Adolescents of non-Turkish descent in Hamburg. In: Anne Holmen and J. N. Jørgensen (eds.): *Det er Conversation 801 degil mi? Perspectives on the bilingualism of Turkish speaking children and adolescents in North Western Europe*, 159–194. (Copenhagen Studies in Bilingualism. The Køge Series, vol. K7). Copenhagen: The Danish University of Education.

Auer, Peter and Inci Dirim. 2003. Socio-cultural orientation, urban youth styles and the spontaneous acquisition of Turkish by non-Turkish adolescents in Germany. In: Jannis K. Androutsopoulos and Alexandra Georgakopoulou (eds.): *Discourse Constructions of Youth Identities*, 223–246. Amsterdam: Benjamins.

Bakhtin, Mikhail. 1981. *The Dialogic Imagination. Four Essays.* Austin: University of Texas Press.

Bakhtin, Mikhail. 1984. *Problems of Dostoevsky's Poetics.* Minneapolis: University of Minnesota Press.

Cutler, Cecilia A. 1999. Yorkville crossing: White teens, hip hop, and African American English. In: Rampton (ed.), 1999, 428–442.

Evaldsson, Ann-Carita. 2002. Sociala och språkliga gräsdragningar bland elever i en mångkulturell skola. In: *Pædagogisk Forskning i Sverige.* Årg. 7, nr. 1, 1–16. Göteborg: Göteborgs Universitet.

Gilroy, Paul. 1987. *'There ain't no black in the Union Jack': The Cultural Politics of 'Race' and Nation.* London: Hutchinson Education.

Gumperz, John J. (ed.). 1982a. *Language and Social Identity.* Cambridge: Cambridge University Press.

Gumperz, John J. 1982b. *Discourse Strategies.* Cambridge: Cambridge University Press.

Hansen, Gert and Nicolai Pharao. 2004. Prosodic aspects of the Copenhagen Multiethnolect. In: *Proceedings from the 9th Nordic Prosody Conference.* August 8–10, 2004, Lund, Sweden.

Hewitt, Roger. 1986. *White Talk Black Talk. Inter-Racial Friendship and Communication Amongst Adolescents.* Cambridge: Cambridge University Press.

Hewitt, Roger. 1989. Creole in the classroom: political grammars and educational vocabularies. In: Grillo, R. (ed.): *Social Anthropology and the Politics of Language,* 126–144. London: Routlegde.

Hewitt, Roger. 1992. Language, youth and the destabilisation of ethnicity. In: Palmgren Cecilia, Lövgren Karin and Bolin Göran (eds.), *Ethnicity in Youth Culture,* 27–41. Stockholm: Stockholm University.

Hill, Jane. 1995. *Mock Spanish: The Indexical Reproduction of Racism in American English.* http://www.uta.fi/FAST/US8/SPAN/mockspan.html (Reformatted version of original formally at www.language-culture.org/colloquia/symposia/hill-jane)

Hinnenkamp, Volker. 2003. Mixed language varieties of migrant adolescents and the discourse of hybridity. In: *Journal of Multilingual and Multicultural Development.* 24 (1/2): 12–40.

Jørgensen, J. Normann. 2003. Languaging among fifth graders: code-switching in conversation 501 of the Køge Project. In: *Journal of Multilingual and Multicultural Development.* 24 (1/2): 126–148.

Jørgensen, J. Normann. 2004. Languaging and languagers. In: Christine Dabelsteen and J. Normann Jørgensen (eds.), *Languaging and Language Practices.* (Copenhagen Studies in Bilingualism, Vol. 36), 5–22. Faculty of Humanities, University of Copenhagen.

Labov, William. 1980. Is there a Creole Speech Community? In: Albert Valdman and Arnold Highfield (eds.), *Theoretical Orientations in Creole Studies,* 369–388. New York: Academic Press, INC.

Le Page, Robert. 1980. Theoretical aspects of sociolinguistic studies in pidgin and creole languages. In: Albert Valdman and Arnold Highfield (eds.), *Theoretical Orientations in Creole Studies,* 331–367. New York: Academic Press, INC.

Quist, Pia. 2000. Ny københavnsk 'multietnolekt'. Om sprogbrug blandt unge i sprogligt og kulturelt heterogene miljøer. In: *Danske Talesprog.* Vol.1. Institut for Dansk Dialektforskning, 143–212. København: C.A. Reitzels Forlag.

Quist, Pia. 2005. Stilistiske praksisser i storbyens heterogene skole. Ph.D. dissertation, Department of Scandinavian Research, Dialectology. University of Copenhagen.

Rampton, Ben. 1995. *Crossing. Language and Ethnicity among Adolescents.* London: Longman.

Rampton, Ben (ed.). 1999. Theme issue: Styling the Other. *Journal of Sociolinguistics,* 3 (4).

Rampton, Ben. 2001. Language crossing, cross-talk, and cross-disciplinarity in sociolinguistics. In: Nikolas Coupland, Srikant Sarangi and Christopher N. Candlin (eds.): *Sociolinguistics and Social Theory,* 261–296. Essex: Pearson Education Limited.

Sweetland, Julie. 2002. Unexpected but authentic use of an ethnically-marked dialect. *Journal of Sociolinguistics,* 6 (4): 514–538.

Turner, Victor. 1974. Liminal to liminoid in play, flow, and ritual: An essay in comparative symbology. *Rice University Studies* 60 (3): 53–92.

Additional Sources

Auer, Peter (ed.). 1998. *Code-switching in Conversation*. London: Routledge.
Auer, Peter and Aldo di Luzio (eds.). 1992. *The Contextualization of Language*. Amsterdam: John Benjamin.
Le Page, Robert and Andrée Tabouret-Keller. 1985. *Acts of Identity*. Cambridge: Cambridge University Press.
Jørgensen, J. Normann (ed.). 2003. *Bilingualism and Social Relations: Turkish Speakers in North Western Europe*. Clevedon, England: Multilingual Matters.

Journals

International Journal of Bilingualism. Kingston Press Ltd.
Journal of Sociolinguistics. Blackwell Publishing.
Journal of Pragmatics. Elsevier.

10

Silence and Taboo

Sabine Krajewski and Hartmut Schröder

1. Introduction

"One cannot not communicate. Every behavior is a kind of communication. Because behavior does not have a counterpart (there is no anti-behavior), it is not possible not to communicate" (Watzlawick, Bavelas, and Jackson 1980: 48). Originally this axiom implies that everything we do (or don't do) is part of (verbal and non-verbal) communication. With the development of new communication systems, Watzlawick's assertion takes on another dimension: it is, for example, impossible not to react to an SMS or an e-mail, because silence also communicates a message.

However, silence is a phenomenon which is difficult to categorize. No matter how we define it, silence and its meaning have to be sensed and interpreted taking a particular situation into account. According to the Oxford English Dictionary (Soans and Hawker 2005), silence as a noun is 1) complete absence of sound, or 2) the fact or state of abstaining from speech. The result of this would be muteness, reticence, taciturnity. German *schweigen* and Hebrew *shtika* describe this state.[1] The state or condition when nothing is audible, as in complete stillness, can be expressed with different words—*Stille* in German, *dmama* or *dumia* in Hebrew. Their closest equivalent in English is *stillness*. Though silence can be a sort of absence of something, it suggests potential: "[It] may be peculiarly difficult if one's purpose is to objectify the state, that is, to say that it *is* something" (Scott 1993: 11).

In this chapter, silence and its relative, taboo, are in the center. We give an overview of the relevant theorizing and the relevant results achieved in the research on taboos and silence. We include examples to show where this research leads to in practical terms and what the future perspectives are.

---

[1] In his review of the term *Shtika*, Ulrich Struve (1998) points out that, in their book *Shtika*, Bubis and Mehler (1996) illustrate the result of silence in families. Even if the experiences of parents who survived the National Socialist ghettos in the 1940s are not discussed at all, they are always present under the surface. *Shtika* tries to break the taboo, but the authors and most of the interviewees fail to do this on account of depth of silence. Bubis and Mehler (cited in Struve, http://www.literaturcafe.de/bf.htm?/erinnern/teil5.htm; last access: February 10, 2008) arrive at the conclusion that one has to respect the victims' life elixir which is suppression: "The long, silent years between the generations cannot be caught up with through talks in the future."

In Section 2, we introduce the state of the art in linguistic research on silence and taboo. In Section 3, we discuss the concepts and functions of silence and taboo. The interpretation of silence and its function in communication is different from one culture to another (3.1.). Cultural differences shape the meanings of silence across different contexts and individuals. Culture-related silence is connected with *taboo* (3.2.). In the following, we focus on *the meaning and functions of taboo* (3.3.) and, finally, on the interdependence of taboo and taboo violation (*taboo complex*, 3.4.).

Section 4 centers on linguistic means and taboo discourse (4.1.) and analyzes them with reference to their place in different cultures. An example of calculated silence (4.2.) shows how the meaning of communicatively relevant silence is context dependent. We exemplify (universal) *taboo topics* by using representations from hospital drama (4.3.). Taboo-related silence in family therapy (4.4.) characterizes the *pact of silence* which is explained in part 4.5.

Section 5 highlights silence and taboo in intercultural communications and it leads to our conclusions about the significance of taboo and silence for communicative competence in general (6.).

2. State of the Art in Linguistic Research on Silence and Taboo

Both silence and taboo are important and frequent topics of discussion and analysis in recent linguistic research and are considered to be highly dependent on the culture and society in which they occur. This results in a variety of interpretations which can be attached to both phenomena.

Summaries of research on silence and an overview of relevant publications can be found in Knapp (2000) and in Tannen and Saville-Troikje (1985). Jaworski (1997) gives an interdisciplinary perspective on silence and discusses *social and pragmatic perspectives* of the power of silence (Jarowski 1998). The most recent monograph about *Silence in Intercultural Communication* has been written by Nakane (2007) and presents an analysis of silence in intercultural contexts by referring to examples from Japan and Australia.

While linguistic research on silence has predominantly been published in English, research on taboo, particularly studies on linguistic taboo and euphemism, still seems to interest specifically German scholars. This is also reflected in the usage of terminology. The notion of *Sprachtabu* ('linguistic tabu') seems to belong especially to scientific literature written in the German language while equivalents in other languages (English: *linguistic taboo*, French: *tabou linguistique*; Italian: *tabu linguistico*) have either been replaced by different formulations (French: *interdiction linguistique*; Italian: *interdizione linguistica*) or, in some instances, equivalents of *Sprachtabu* are used as a general term, but this phenomenon occurs less frequently than in the German language (cf. Schorch 2000: 6, fn 10).

An analysis of taboo discourse in languages other than German reveals that the usage of euphemisms is just as dominant when topics such as death or bodily functions are concerned. We assume with Balle (1990: 177) that linguistic taboo is inseparable from euphemism: "Where there are euphemisms, there have to be taboos—and vice versa. Euphemisms are the other side of the coin."

A phase of research on linguistic taboo in the German language is represented by Luchtenberg (1985: 35), who develops a pragmatic-semantic view
and shows that euphemisms may realize covering as well as veiling functions,
regardless of the particular subject area. The first, *covering*, is used for communication about terms made taboo for consideration of feelings and values; the
latter, *veiling*, has the task of introducing certain facts to the listener in a way
that is favorable for the speaker who chooses how (s)he is to present the facts
(Luchtenberg 1985: 24). Luchtenberg understands taboos as objects, processes,
or thoughts that are, for various reasons, forbidden to be thought, touched, or
named in a certain society (1985: 24). He also identifies zero-euphemism as
a linguistic tool, namely, when the veiling consists of omission (rather than
replacement) of certain words or expressions, or where dots replace words.

The work of Allan und Burridge (2006) has been published under the
main title of *Forbidden Words*—so only the subtitle refers to taboo: *Taboo and
the Censoring of Language*. Allan und Burrdige offer a thorough overview of
English language literature and focus on topics such as *sweet talking, political
correctness*, and *verbal hygiene*—the readily available literature in German is
unfortunately not taken into account. The reception of the relevant literature
outside the Anglo-Saxon world is also missing in Holden's (2000) *Encyclopedia of Taboos*. It does, however, include perspectives from various disciplines
such as anthropology, psychology, and literary studies and introduces the
most important theories and authors including Sigmund Freud, Mary Douglas, Edmund Leach, and Franz Steiner as well as various taboo areas such as
incest, cannibalism, sex, death, and nourishment taboos.

The earliest scientific writings which explicitly refer to linguistic taboos
within the context of magical words that indicate their relevance for the Indo-
Germanic languages were compiled at the beginning of the 20th century. This
research focuses on name taboos, the denotation of God, animal names, and
circumstances often associated with taboos such as death and dying, illness,
and others. Havers (1946) offers an excellent summary of the status quo of
these studies in his book *Arbeiten zum Sprachtabu* ('Studies on Linguistic
Taboo'). Havers starts from the assumption that the Indo-Europeans were
also aware of linguistic taboo and illustrates this with many examples. He
introduces a typology of replacements which is still being used in more recent
studies on linguistic taboos. Havers connects the beginning of the linguistic
work on taboos with Meillet's essay entitled *Interdictions* (1906).

Apart from the French scholar Meillet, the Swede Sahlgren draws a
connection between the concepts of linguistic taboo and euphemism, as, for
instance, in his study *Blåkulla och blåkullafärderna* ('The witches dance on
the Blocks-berg'; translation from Swedish ours, S.K./H.S.) (1915). Chapter
VI concerning *Taboo och noa* ('Taboo and Noa'; translation from Swedish ours,
S.K./H.S.) is of particular interest to the present study. He uses examples
from Swedish historical-linguistic studies and cultural history to illustrate
their meaning outside of the so-called "primitive people's languages". Sahlgren
introduces the term *noaword*.[2] In the Polynesian language, *noa* is the opposite

---

[2] Noa refers to the opposite of taboo and means *common* or *free from taboo*.

to *taboo*; it describes the ordinary and the everyday, in other words, everything that is not under the influence of the power of a taboo, the *mana*. The mana of a taboo can be so great that the offender will suffer punishment merely through fear of its powers. Without the supernatural power of mana, taboo cannot be established. Mana is created through interaction within groups (Kraft 2004: 15) and is necessary to maintain a taboo. If mana loses strength, the taboo may fade and finally cease to exist. Noa, on the other hand, describes the ordinary and is independent of the powers of mana.

Sahlgren (1915: 132) assumes that there are numerous traces of name taboos in today's modern languages. In Swedish, it was not allowed to use the word *wolf*, but it is acceptable to say *goldfoot* or *the grey*. A noaword, therefore, is a replacement word that enables us to describe the things that are taboo (Sahlgren 1915: 133). Sahlgren (1915: 136) was one of the first to describe examples of the *tabu-euphemism-cycle*: noawords eventually become taboo words themselves and need to be replaced by new noawords.

A widely discussed German dissertation on *Indo-Germanic word taboo* was submitted by Trost at the University of Prague in 1934. Trost concentrates on coping strategies to deal with word taboos. The results of this study are summarized by Trost in his essay on *Bemerkungen zum Sprachtabu* ('Remarks on linguistic taboo', 1936), published in the *Travaux du cercle linguistique de Prague* series. Among other things, Trost (1936: 289) discusses the function of so called "cover words" which he characterizes as words that use a different meaning to denote the same object as a taboo word. Furthermore, he discusses the phenomenon of the taboo-plural and the effects of metaphors and metonyms as linguistic replacements in various areas of the word taboo.

The 1930s mark a fresh start in taboo research. Linguistic work on taboos in language concentrated on the concrete usage of language and culminated in Ullmann's contribution (1962) which is still widely read. In structurally oriented linguistics, it was Bloomfield (1933: 155, 396–401) who was one of the first to become involved with the concept of linguistic taboo. In a chapter about the meaning of words in his introduction to linguistics (*Language*), he describes the usage of euphemisms in connection with name and word taboos. Bloomfield shows examples of homonyms from English and French which are still being avoided because of their phonetic similarity with taboo words. Furthermore, he compares name taboos that often lead to the disappearance of the expressions made taboo with taboo words that are against common decency, but which continue to exist. In this context Bloomfield also refers to the *taboo-euphemismcycle*.

Ullmann (1962: 204–206) describes various causes for semantic change. He expands the (linguistic, historical, and social) causes identified by Meillet by including the category of psychological causes which he divides into emotive factors and taboos. Ullmann differentiates between the categories he refers to as the *taboo of fear, taboo of delicacy*, and *taboo of propriety*. Within these categories, he describes the origin of euphemisms and gives examples for the *taboo-euphemism-cycle*. Ullmann pointedly views the linguistic taboo as a universal phenomenon which does not only concern linguistic history but also the current use of language: "It is a general human tendency to avoid direct reference to unpleasant subjects" (Ullmann 1962: 206).

In the 1980s and 1990s, linguistic taboo was discussed within the framework of discourse- and conversation analysis. A study by Schank on conversation around tabooized subjects triggered more research on the subject. Schank (1981: 36) talks about the phenomenon of "covered speech" which is marked by a more frequent use of metaphors, pro forma, euphemisms, archaisms, etc., and which may be characterized by a certain degree of directness and explicitness.

Pelikan (1987: 77), who also focuses on the the linguistic coping with taboos at the level of discourse, points out that taboo discourse in political debates on television is marked by lack of confidence, fear, aggression, feelings of guilt, and repression. This again manifests itself at various linguistic levels. According to Pelikan, the taboo breach becomes linguistically visible in the choice of termini, in the modus being used, and in certain general speaker strategies at textual level. The way a topic is made taboo is also visible in the text. If the topic is mentioned directly, this part will be different from the rest of the text, and will be indicated by emphasis on the word or an increase of volume, an increased uncertainty, pauses, and stuttering. In mentioning the topic, the speaker may either use clichés and euphemisms, or provocatively direct expressions. The attempt to not address the topic directly also leads to an escape into abstract, generalizing terms with the reference often remaining unclear (cf. Pelikan 1987: 77).

The most recent and more extensive study on linguistic taboo and euphemism is Zöllner's dissertation *Der Euphemismus im alltäglichen und politischen Sprachgebrauch des Englischen* ('Euphemism in everyday and political use of the English language', 1997). Zöllner regards euphemisms as means of glossing over and veiling. Euphemisms are used within conventions of politeness and also in order to prevent loss of face. Zöllner expands Ullmann's categorization by adding the so-called "taboos of social tact" in connection with the US-American "political correctness movement". They are ideologically motivated and, according to Zöllner (1997: 52), appear in societies which claim to have a high degree of civilization. Taboos of social tact are devoted to the idea of progress in societies which recognize the principle of equality of all people.

3. Silence and Taboo—The Concepts

In this section, we examine the functions of silence and taboo in different contexts and in different cultures. To interpret silence, one needs to be aware of cultural differences and of how culture-related silence is connected with taboo. An advertisement for sanitary pads on the internet and other sites for taboo-related products are used to show how taboos go beyond mere silence.

3.1. Silence as a Part of Communication

Depending on the specific situation, silence can be used to express, and be interpreted as expressing, a wide range of meanings. Where in one context silence will cause unease and be uncomfortable for those sharing it, in another context, silence may be experienced as comfortable and intimate. Jensen (1973: 253) outlines the different intentions and functions of silence. His categories are often used in more recent research:

1. A linkage function: silence may bond two (or more) people or it may separate them.
2. An affecting function: silence may heal (over time) or wound.
3. A revelation function: silence may make something known to a person (self exploration) or it may hide information from others.
4. A judgmental function: silence may signal assent and favor or it may signal dissent and disfavor.
5. An activating function: silence may signal deep thoughtfulness (work) or it may signal mental inactivity.

Jaworski (1997) pursues a similar approach to Jensen's in categorizing silence according to its nature and function. He lists an interesting and diverse list of *types of silence* in the index of his book on *Silence: Interdisciplinary Perspectives*: absolute, acoustic, antecedent, anterior, arbitrary, contemplative, displayed, gustatory, inter- and intra-turn, olfactory, spiritual, static, surrogate, tactile, temporal, and visual.

The way silence is intended and read as part of communication does not only depend on the general situational context but also on the cultural context. The values connected to silence may therefore be negative, positive, or neutral, and may express disagreement and anger in one context, affection and respect in another. In educational settings, silence can be a sign of active learning and concentration, as well as of idleness and ignorance (Jaworski 1999). In Western cultures, silence in organizational contexts may signal lack of motivation and interest, while actually originating in stress and ambiguous communication (Jenkins 2000). In Asian cultures, silence is often a sign of respect and affection; but remaining silent is also very common as a means to avoid verbal negation and to show disagreement.

The meaning of silence is strongly tied to cultural conventions. Knapp (2000) distinguishes between *conventional* silence and *significant* silence. The first type refers to silence which is in accordance with the prevailing conventions while the latter is characterized by the non-realization of a verbal act that conventionally is expected to occur. Knapp (2000: 8) categorizes different ways of communication that can be summarized under the label of silence. By means of differentiated analyses of silence, he points out how communicative misunderstandings may arise because of different, culturally rooted functions of silence in various situations. In addition to terminological differentiation of the various forms and functions of silence, Knapp looks at stereotypes created by cultural differences in this context. Investigating the value of eloquence in different cultures, he shows how

> [. . .] forms of behavior related to silence figure prominently as potential sources of intercultural misunderstanding. In view of the metaphor of malfunction it does not come as a surprise that members of cultures or ethnic groups who conventionally communicate with more or longer phases of non-

talk and less talk proper, are perceived negatively, at least by interactants from Western cultures, and that repeated contact with members from cultures that in this sense are "more silent" leads to generalizing individual person-related negative attributions to negative stereotypes of different ethnic groups or cultures (Knapp 2000: 3).

The problem of using *silence* or *being silent* as descriptive categories from an academic point of view, is that these vague concepts are usually used from one's own cultural perspective but are treated as universal with regard to interactive behaviors and the way they are perceived. In order to understand silence, it is essential to be aware of the formal features of face-to-face interaction; the perception of non-talk as pauses, silences or non-communication depends on the cultural conventions that the individual who categorizes the respective communicative functions is familiar with. We can see that silence may be misunderstood if we generalize its meaning or when we attach the meaning a pause has in our own cultural environment to a conversation held in another. In intercultural situations, silence may also have serious implications for the communication act altogether, namely, when it is an indication that a taboo has been touched.

3.2. Taboo—Meaning and Functions

Like *silence*, taboo is a complex concept which has serious implications for intercultural communication. Before we look at the connection between the two concepts, we will analyze the origin of the term and the meanings taboos have in today's modern societies.

It is apparent that the basic meanings of *taboo/tabu* in today's usage have little to do with the original concept from Tonga.[3] The essential meaning the word has in Tonga and that is attached to the word in European languages is known to most users: The Encyclopedia Britannica (2002: DVD Edition) specifies a first meaning, according to which taboo "is a prohibition against touching, saying, or doing something for fear of immediate harm from a supernatural force." In the following discussion, a taboo concept should be developed which follows the second basic meaning mentioned in the Encyclopedia Britannica (2002: DVD Edition) according to which a taboo is "a prohibition imposed by social custom or as a protective measure". The newer colloquial use of *taboo* with a pejorative meaning is not yet considered in dictionaries.[4]

The second meaning of the word *taboo* given in the Encyclopedia Britannica is that taboos in modern societies are a part of the social code, which

---

[3] The word *Tabu*—originally *tapu*—comes from the Polynesian language, Tonga. It is one of the few words, from a language other than Indo-Germanic ones, to have found its way into languages of Western civilizations. James Cook brought this word to England in 1777 from his South Seas trip. From this point onwards, it spread rapidly to other languages and found its way into educated speech.

[4] This is playing an increasingly significant role, particularly in the media where taboos in communication serve as reproachful linguistic acts. Expressions such as *free of taboos, breach* and *to free from taboos* go along with positive connotations in this context.

establishes the actions and behaviors that should not take place (Zöllner 1997: 25–26), and determines what one does not communicate about or what should only be communicated about in a certain way. Thus, we mean by the term—*taboo*—(negative) conventions of actions (what one does not do), non-themes (what one does not speak about), as well as themes which require a certain linguistic etiquette (what one only speaks of in a certain way).

Communication, linguistic taboos, and action taboos have one feature in common. They are normally not explicitly mentioned or codified like grammar rules or laws. In the process of primary language acquisition, language principles, rules, and the lexicon do not need to be codified because they are, like taboos, internalized in the process of growing up. The difference here is that, in the case of grammar rules, there is a right or wrong, but taboos are context-sensitive, and there is no clear definition of what is right and what is wrong.[5]

Taboo has no (visible) features except for silence that may act as an indicator. Only the violation of a taboo makes its existence visible. The quintessence of the term *taboo* in various disciplines, such as sociology, psychology, and linguistics, is that they are usually concerned with something that is forbidden to be done, said, thought, felt, known, and touched, though it is do-able, say-able, feel-able, recognizable, and touchable: otherwise, it need not be protected by a taboo. Taboos mark boundaries of acting, speaking, and thinking (Kraft 2004: 10) and can be understood as negative conventions: certain things, spirits, institutions, subjects, and contexts are not supposed to be touched or have actions performed on them, whereas the symbolic touch is also forbidden, as for example in picture taboos.

Reimann's (1989: 421) concept of taboo is particularly appropriate for the analysis of modern societies (with secularly rather than religiously motivated taboos). According to Reimann, taboos are societal matters of course and thus hold an important social function in the regulation of behavior, the establishment of boundaries, and the recognition of authority, for example, in the protection of property, the position of leaders, and certain social rules (Reimann 1989: 421). *Taboo* can be seen as the recognition of persons and subjects who indicate force and threat and thereby require careful behavior upon the encounter. In general, the role of taboo is to enforce social order.

However, taboos should not be confused with prohibitions. Prohibitions require codification, whereas taboos presuppose that everyone knows what is considered taboo; there are no explicit norms. This also means that, if one breaks a taboo, there will be no discussion of the violation; therefore there is no way of defending oneself. Punishing a violation, in the case of taboos, relies mainly upon feelings of guilt, detestation, and shame: the person committing a taboo violation is isolated, avoided by the society, "made taboo". The person who violates a taboo is stigmatized without discussion (Reimann 1989: 421).

---

[5] There are attempts to provide sets of cultural rules to travelers, for example by offering useful guidebooks such as *KulturSchluessel* (KulturSchluessel Malaysia and Singapur 2003) which include sections such as *Do and Taboo*. The taboo chapters include what to bring (or what not to bring) to a festive event or the advice not to wash your hair during Chinese New Year, because it is believed to mean bad luck. As useful as this advice may be, it is related to customs and superstitious belief and does not cover what we mean by *taboo* in the present chapter.

Taboos are impassioned; they strongly depend on emotional influence and they are beyond all discussion; this phenomenon is known in nourishment taboos and the socialization of the small child. He or she already knows at a very young age that certain actions and contacts are forbidden through statements like "One does not do that", "That is not appropriate", etc. Taboos get internalized by means of these kinds of inarticulate imperatives in the process of raising children. Thus, legal rules and formal sanctions often become superfluous (Reimann 1989: 421).

Taboos are a particularly effective way of control (Reimann 1989: 421) and can be understood as axioms of communication, i.e., as unquestionable basic truths of a society which may not be broached. Certain persons, places, and activities, e.g., nourishment as well as other areas, such as sexuality, desire, poverty, inequality, corruption, violence, death, and certain diseases, are considered taboo (Reimann 1989: 421). These topics are universally burdened with taboos, though the degree to which a topic is taboo varies from one culture to another, and there are differences within societies and across individuals. The younger generation of a society may be more comfortable discussing sexuality than the earlier generations of the same society. Taboos are always context-sensitive.

Apart from the social and political control discussed in this section, there are other important social functions that taboos fulfill: they add to the stability of societies and groups and have protective functions. Taboos secure the survival and the future of a society by simply avoiding or covering things that might be a threat for the positive identity and life perspective of an individual or a group: dark sides of one's own history, death, illness, or the question about the meaning of life. Therefore, taboo can be understood as a coping mechanism, as a strategy to build individual and collective identity (Kraft 2004: 114). Taboos cover the potentially dangerous and painful in a society.

3.3. Culture-Related Silence and Taboo

Culture-related silence is connected with taboos and can lead to misunderstandings and conflicts in intercultural contact situations. Taboo and silence are related, but they are not the same. Taboos are negative conventions and refer to actions and verbal communication. They mark that something should not be touched, while the touching can also be symbolic. Knowledge about taboo grows with the child. Taboos do not need to be explained or justified, and they are a matter of course besides being part of a person's social identity, but they are also culture-bound. If they are being broken, the shame falls on the taboo breaker and disgust on the affected person. This is only the case, of course, if the person touching a taboo is aware of it, which may not be the case in intercultural situations.

Taboos are related, on the one hand, to strategies of omission, avoidance, and concealment, so that certain actions and interactions remain completely avoided. On the other hand, taboos also make possible and require the application of strategies of disguising, covering, glossing over, and circumvention. Taboos go beyond mere silence and make substitutes available for communication. Language always finds new forms of coping, when dealing with taboos.

Like other communication devices, silence can be used as a tool, and can function in contrary ways. It can be empowering or oppressive, indicate interpersonal closeness or anger and hatred. It can also be used (or read) as a means to mislead by concealing something.

To exemplify the relationship between silence and taboo, we will take a look at how the two strategies are purposefully connected in advertisements of certain products. In advertising, the relation between silence and taboo often has to be a well calculated one. Many products that belong to areas of health and hygiene are connected to such taboo areas as bodily functions, sexuality, and therefore become taboo products. This holds true for products for feminine hygiene, for the protection from incontinence, for the treatment of hemorrhoids, or the athlete's foot. Advertisements for these products have to take into account taboos and use appropriate taboo discourse.

Taking into account taboos involves strategies of *hedging* as well as verbal and visual silence. Hedging in this context means to shield oneself against something unpleasant by doing something which will protect you from it. Hedging a problem or question may involve avoidance of giving a definite answer to a question or giving a non-committing answer and postponing a decision. Hedging can be understood as the verbal realization of vagueness which depends on context and situation. The aim of hedging may be the avoidance of conflict, or in any case the avoidance of break-off of communication (cf. Markkanen and Schröder 1997).

Hedging may also be used in non-verbal communication. In online advertising (cf. Wrobel 2003), there are usually pictures involved that demonstrate how a product is supposed to be used or how effective it is. Just as taboos are culture specific, icons and symbols that communicate product information only work within cultural boundaries. Depending on the degree to which a bodily function is taboo, visual hedging may be used.

Online advertising for sanitary pads for example uses soft-focusing or, as on the US-American Websites of Kotex®, "visual silence" (www.kotex.com, last access: January 10, 2008). Information involving the actual use of the product is also "packed away" to a deeper level of the site (concealed) to lead consumers gradually to more detailed information. This careful approach is used to avoid total break-off of communication that may occur if consumers are confronted with taboo topics too abruptly.

Complete silence about bodily functions or potential users of a product is of course also part of verbal hedging. Wrobel (2003) transfers the concept of *exceptional situations*, such as mourners, menstruating women, and women in childbed, from indigenous cultures to people in Western societies. The taboo areas have changed to certain illnesses and ageing processes. In her study, Wrobel compares US and German websites to show that the taboo is stronger and the discourse more vague if the advertisers have less experience with advertising taboo products (Wrobel 2003: 124). Wrobel proves that the high degree of hedging around subjects such as *incontinence* or *hemorrhoids* indicates that though the advertisers claim that these topics are becoming less taboo, this is not the case. The verbal discourse around hemorrhoids is full of metalinguistic signs that indicate that they are not only a sensitive topic but downright taboo, the actual name of the illness only occurs in the third sentence, where it is described as a "sensitive problem" (Wrobel 2003: 157).

Hedging and other strategies such as omission and silence are being used in taboo discourse. Taboos are carefully addressed in a society when there is a need for it (for example, in advertising) to avoid break-off of communication. Where taboo and silence are combined and used as tools, culture specific meanings of both concepts have to be taken into account. This is especially important in intercultural communication where social conventions differ and an ignorance of cultural differences may lead to unintended taboo violations.

3.4. Taboos and Taboo Violations

Within the area of taboo, it is necessary to make a distinction between *object taboos* (taboos on things, institutions, and persons) and *action taboos*, which are accompanied and substantiated by *communication taboos* (taboo themes), *word taboos* (vocabulary taboos), and *picture taboos*, which are in turn supported by *thought taboos* and emotion taboos. Specific functions of verbal taboos (communication taboos), in comparison to non-verbal taboos (taboos of action), include the following:

- Confirmation and support of taboos that fall under an absolute taboo of action ("One does not speak about that, nor does one do that."). An example of this is incest as taboo. It is a taboo to a degree that it is not talked about at all; this way, the verbal taboo confirms the action taboo, thus sanctioning the act of incest. (Kraft underlines his socio-economic approach by indicating that in case of the incest-taboo the aim is also the survival of the individual and his social group (Kraft 2004: 92)).
- Permission for certain tabooed actions—through a thin veil—according to accepted rules of etiquette ("One does not openly speak about that, but one may do that according to the pre-established rules of etiquette."). Examples here include sexuality and other bodily functions and activities that a culture has silenced.
- The veiling of tabooed actions, where general acceptance cannot be presupposed. The actions are made possible through the modification of facts. ("Actually, one does not do that, but if one does it, then one speaks about it in a secretive manner or expresses it another way"). Taboos in politics and economy fit this category, as for example when politicians (and others) speak of "a gift" instead of "a bribe" and of "an operation" instead of "war". Veiling also concerns other euphemisms that may indicate taboo topics. If we have to talk about the fact that someone died, we may use the phrase "he passed away" or, in recent times, "he passed".

Taboos serve as an important relief for every society. Sensitive issues and the way we deal with them need to be self-explicatory, do not have to be justified, and must not be questioned. In this respect, taboos are often more efficient than direct prohibitions, because they seem natural to the involved and have been internalized. Taboos express silent consensus which the concerned may not be aware of at all.

The taboo complex, on the one hand, consists of the taboo and the acceptance of the taboo, i.e. the marking of boundaries, and, on the other hand, the taboo violation or the crossing of the boundaries. The violation of taboos is unthinkable without their existence. Viewed from the opposite perspective, taboos would not be necessary without the danger of a possible violation. Kraft (2004: 211) points out that taboos secure identity but at the same time enable development. Usually, a taboo violation is an attack on personal and social identity: "Taboo violations are indicators for changes in identity" (Kraft 2004: 177). This means that taboo violations are very important for social development, and they fulfill several functions at once: they mark what is taboo in a society, raise consciousness with regard to boundaries, and indicate shortcomings.

One has to differentiate between individual and collective taboo violations, and between permanent and temporary taboo crossings. It can be assumed that ritualized or institutionalized taboo crossings are common in some areas, but they work only temporarily. Such taboo violations are not arbitrary; they have a function in the relevant society. Temporary taboo crossings do not entail the abolition of the taboo, but they temporarily lift the sanctioning mechanism. It is possible for the taboo mechanism on the whole to be strengthened by a temporary taboo lift; humor can be used as comic relief in this context. When we talk about death and dying, there are many humorous expressions that cover how uncomfortable we may feel around the topic (*bite the dust, kick the bucket, buy the farm*, or *cash in one's chips*). The temporary taboo lift occurs in special situations: academic discourse, doctor-patient communication, communication in court, general emergency situations and situations of social change, jokes and satire, curses, religion, and media strategies, such as talk-shows and advertisements. The function of ritualized and institutionalized taboo violations is, that, as part of the order system, they not only actually mark the violation but also serve as an outlet for the pressure and thereby strengthen the taboo itself.

4. Linguistic Means and Taboo Discourse

A discussion about the different functions of linguistically realized taboos needs to include a closer analysis of taboo discourse and a closer look at different degrees of directness. Meaningful silence as part of taboo discourse is closely linked to avoiding directness in addressing a topic. Throughout this section, examples are used to illustrate the scope and complexity of both, silence and taboo, so that the relations between them will become visible.

4.1. Taboo Discourse

In communication, we do not usually have only the choice between speaking or being silent (and refraining completely from addressing a theme). Rather, through the application of certain linguistic means, we can certainly treat delicate topics, without "putting our foot in our mouth". Our language gives us a multitude of possibilities for these cases. We can hint at, circumvent, gloss over, etc., and in these ways communicate about areas with taboos, but without violating conventions. In this context we use the term *taboo discourse*.

Taboo discourse enables communication about things, which one does not actually wish to talk about or even should not talk about. It includes various forms of covering up, which exist in our language and culture but which we are not always aware of. We mean, by the term *taboo discourse*, that in certain situations one can communicate about actions, subjects, institutions, and persons with taboos. However, this can only be done in a very specific way, which does not constitute a (verbal) taboo violation itself.

At the same time, euphemisms are not the only possibility to speak of subjects, actions, and facts with taboos. Apart from the possibility of withdrawing completely from a discussion about taboos (breaking-off of a discussion, spatial distance, etc.), there are also various levels of openness available to the speakers. This can range from the explicit "One does not speak about that" to a thorough discussion. In this range of possibilities, the speakers must develop mechanisms or strategies, which allow them to speak with a "one-quarter", "half", or "three-quarter" openness (Günther 1992: 48–49).

Concerning linguistic substitutes for taboo discourse, Havers (1946) lists the following basic types in his linguistic-historical work on Indo-Germanic languages: pronunciation changes, loan words, antiphrasing (one says the opposite of what is meant; wish names), representative pronouns, euphemistic contamination (word-crossing), stretching meanings, sentence-like descriptions (wish sentences and descriptive relative sentences), *captatio benevolentiae*, ellipsis, subject-instrumental, as well as escape to generalities (generalization, taboo-plural). More recent works on linguistic taboo research go far beyond this typology from Havers (i.e., Balle 1990). At the same time, they extend the formulation and methods of discourse and conversation analysis to "indirect" or "hidden" speech. In particular, Günther (1992) handles linguistic means, which make the veiling of an expression possible. She names metaphor as the best known strategy. Other strategies named by Günther (1992: 52–54, 218–220) are: the use of euphemisms and specialized vocabulary, agent emphasis and omission, rhetorical account and role specification, word avoidance and vagueness, additional information on the limitation of expressions, and the use of pro-forms.

However, taboos can also be used as tools. The degree of directness plays an important role: taboo topics may be openly discussed (explicit taboo), suggested (implicit taboo), or they may be completely avoided (avoided taboo). In this case, a topic would not be tackled at all but kept in verbal and visual silence (Krajewski 2002: 137). Attention is assured by deliberately choosing taboo topics and addressing them straightforwardly, rather than indirectly through socially accepted taboo discourse.

The clothing company *Benetton* has followed this strategy for years. It is part of their communication strategy to shock, to provoke strong reactions by visually presenting taboo topics. The actual product, colorful clothing, is usually absent from their posters. Oliviero Toscani, who is known for his provocative advertising, views advertising as a legitimate tool for social criticism that can do without products. An example is Benetton's campaign "We, on death row" which shows images of death row inmates to address the human side of

death row in several US-prisons. This campaign created considerable problems for the company and its advertising director. In reaction to the campaign,
the US clothing chain *Sears* cancelled the contract with Benetton and removed
all products from its stores, because the killers' victims were not mentioned
at all (Müller 2004: 80). Benetton defended the campaign but withdrew the
ads. By the end of this campaign, Benetton and Toscani separated after many
years of close cooperation.

Niskanen (1999) acknowledges that campaigns that use pictures dealing
with cultural taboos regularly create problems in society.

> Taboos can vary from society and even from subgroup to subgroup and
> include, for example, death, illness, birth, and the human body. Themes
> such as refugees, Mafia, over-population, and pollution might be actual
> phenomena in our society, but they are not always accepted when used in
> advertising commercial products (Niskanen 1999: 370).

The pluralism of values among different societies becomes apparent, especially when cultural taboos are involved. Taboo themes may collide with legal,
political, or social prerequisites. A flag in an advertisement may be banned
for legal reasons; Jews or Blacks protesting against an advertisement presenting representatives of their group is a political issue (Niskanen 1999:
373); and an advertisement presenting people on death row is a cultural,
ethical, and aesthetic taboo. More recent examples of "taboo acts" that are
widely discussed are the cartoons in Danish papers picturing Mohammed: in
the West this counts as a harmless joke, but Muslims are outraged because
depicting God or Mohammed in a mocking way is seen as an attack (on identity) and strictly taboo.

Pop icon Madonna has always enjoyed provocative performances. On her
latest tour, she is suspended from a cross as she performs the song *Live to Tell*.
By deliberately mocking a symbol, she attracts attention and gains publicity,
but also provokes many negative reactions: Vatican Cardinal Ersilio Tonino,
who spoke with the approval of the Pope, called the concert "a blasphemous
challenge to the faith" and a "profanation of the cross" (http://news.bbc.co.uk/2/
hi/ entertainment/5251614.stm; last access: February 08, 2008). He also called
for Madonna, who was raised as a Catholic, to be excommunicated. Not only
Catholics feel offended; Mario Scialoja, the head of Italy's Muslim League
refers to the act as "in the worst taste" and Riccardo Pacifici, vice president of
the Roman Jewish community, said she should have cut the routine because of
the close proximity of the Olympic Stadium to the Vatican.

4.2. Discourse Relevant Silence

Silence is always a relevant part of communication acts and may be a calculated part of taboo discourse. In a personal conversation between two people,
the actual topic may be avoided by remaining silent. The participants get rid
of the uncomfortable task of talking directly. There are numerous studies of
silence that indicate various "meanings". Silence is used to fulfill the interpersonal metafunction and may be used to avoid conflict. It may be a means of

negotiating power relations or a face-saving strategy in impaired communication (Jaworski and Stephens 1998).

One person alone can speak, but to be silent one needs the co-operation of all involved. This means that meaningful silence is only possible in the case of two or more people sharing the situation in which silence takes place and their mutual understanding of the code of silence. An exchange of silence can only take place when all sides accept the rules and do not break them by directly addressing the subject. The relation between taboo and silence is apparent in everyday life situations and sometimes results from small misunderstandings or inconveniences.

4.3. The Representation of Taboo Topics

Subjects such as sexual abuse and incest are classical taboo topics that, by all means, should remain action taboos but not communication taboos. The social convention of avoiding communication about abuse and incest is enhancing the possibilities for abuse to take place. This is why the silence about these taboo areas must be broken.

Television mediated discourse about taboos may actually help facilitate communication about taboo topics in real life. What is seen on television can be discussed just like real-life events but since drama shown on television is mere fiction based on real life, it seems "safer" to discuss taboo topics shown on television. We will look at hospital drama to exemplify the effects television discourse may have on the development of taboos in real life.

Playing with taboo is a key ingredient of this genre. It seems to be natural to have a conglomerate of mental and physical health problems, social dysfunction, and human tragedy in hospital drama. Hospital drama presents a place where body and soul are human and fallible, and taboo topics may be touched with less fear: there are no longer unmentionable illnesses, and taboo topics may be openly discussed. Hospital drama is a television genre that consists of stories around life and death and therefore covers stories around bodily functions and human problems that are often connected to taboo topics, and, last but not least, death itself. The discourse around these taboo topics reflects interpersonal communication about taboo topics in medical drama, but the mediated discussions could and probably do take place in a similar way in real life. Hospital drama is an entertainment product that works with stereotypes; storylines are kept simple and are eventually brought to an end while new ones are developed. Despite the simple structure and many shortcomings, most medical details are well researched and "real doctors" give advice about procedures. They also inform producers about recurring "cases" from their practical experience. The mediated discourse about taboo topics, such as sexual abuse, includes hedging strategies and silence and often could have been taken straight from medical practice. Sexual abuse is a familiar theme within the genre of hospital drama.

In *Life Goes on. And Sometimes it Doesn't*, Krajewski (2002) shows how television drama uses real-life taboo discourse. In a conversation between two nurses (Die Stadtklinik 1995), the head nurse approaches a young colleage and asks her why her behavior has recently changed:

(1)

head nurse: I can tell something is weighing on your mind, you don't talk any more, you withdraw. Your father wants to leave the clinic as soon as possible [music sets in] and your mother remains silent when I ask what is wrong with you. Gabi, what has happened? (translation from German ours; S.K./H.S.).

Finally, Gabi breaks down and tells her that her father has repeatedly raped her (Krajewski 2002: 147). The television show skillfully uses interruption of speech and longer silences when presenting taboo topics, the silence of affected people is verbally referred to and the use of music is an additional device to show just how "sensitive" the topic is.

In another medical drama series (*OP ruft Dr. Bruckner*, Germany 1999), the topic of infibulation (the removal of the female outer genital organs) is part of the story line. Infibulation is a taboo in Western societies, though there are recurring campaigns by women's liberation groups and human rights organizations trying to inform the public about this practice and to organize action against it. The topic provokes heated discussions, but it is not threatening to Western society. The "problem" is far away and will not touch our private sphere. The taboo topic can be dramatized, but there is a picture taboo: we do not see the mutilated body or the books the doctors lose their appetite over, but instead we have to use our imagination. All the gory details in operating theatres are visualized, so that we even see organs accidentally being dropped onto the floor, but there is visual silence about infibulation. The taboo is verbally discussed, but there is no solution. One TV doctor sees infibulation as the utmost degradation of the female, her male colleague claims that this practice is merely a cultural, religious ritual. Another doctor claims that it is men's fear of female sexuality. The topic is far too complex to fit into 50 something minutes, and because of this it becomes farcical and involuntarily creates a humorous effect.

The first example may open a discussion about sexual abuse and incest among viewers. The context of a fictive drama series makes it easier to discuss and voice opinions about a topic that is otherwise taboo (Krajewski 2002: 151). The second example provides different views within the television episode, but infibulation is an action taboo in Western societies, not a communication taboo. In terms of the development of the taboo in real life, the breaking of the silence around sexual abuse as represented in the first example may have an effect on the strength of the communication taboo within a society. Topics such as the ones in our examples were not included in early television drama. This is a development of the 1990s and may be read as a sign that the strength of the communication taboo is gradually fading.

4.4. Taboo-Related Silence in Family Therapy

Significant events, such as the experience of violence, may lead to impaired speech or to complete silence. It is the task of psychologists and psychotherapists to work out the problems behind the symptoms. Psychotherapists who work with refugee children and their families encounter taboo-related silence in different dimensions. In their article about eloquent silence in children and family therapy, Walter, Möller, and Adam (2000) concentrate on the importance of language (and lack thereof) in psychotherapeutical work with refugee children and their families. Loss of language, stuttering, and silence are symptoms of trauma. The ability to express oneself verbally is diminished by experiences of violence. Because of this lack of immediately readable language, there is a chance to avoid superficial understanding and instead develop and find a common language. The aim is to lift the communication taboo, to create contact with the inner self (feelings, imagination, needs) as well as to create contact with the family and society. The authors describe alienated language, language that has been muted, and language that has been mutilated in refugee children. One of their patients is Jussuf who comes from Afghanistan.

> He stutters, but only in his mother tongue, Dari (Afghan Persian). The language has become the symbol of what happened in this language. One night, the family was raided by the Talibani. The father took his son on his arm, tried to flee down a staircase, fell and the son broke off his front teeth. Ever since, he is ashamed and covers his mouth with his hand when he opens it. Pictures of danger, flight, physical injury, having to be silent, and not to be held onto by his father, mix in his memory (Walter, Möller, and Adam 2000: 554; translation ours, S.K./H.S.).

To help Jussuf, his father now speaks only German with him, but this makes a differentiated communication impossible. For both, the traumatic event has had consequences, because they have lost a communication tool and are constantly reminded of the father's inability to protect Jussuf in a critical situation.

Many of the children who go through traumatic experiences *become* silent. Mutism is a sign of social fear.

In their discussion about post-traumatic stress disorder, Walter, Möller, and Adam (2000) address another kind of taboo—the picture taboo. The ability to think in pictures and feel to pictures is often restricted through experiences of violence. Language cannot be used creatively any more, but reflects the numbing caused by trauma. The loss of symbolic thinking, and therefore of creativity and imagination, is especially deleterious to the development of children. While stuttering is a sign of disturbed communication to the outside world, mutism affects the inner language and therefore the ability to build inner cognitive schemes that help predict the outside world (Walter, Möller, and Adam 2000: 557).

4.5. The Pact of Silence

A central concept that has been proven to help traumatized families of the kind described in the previous section is the pact of silence.

The *pact of silence* (Danieli 1980) is a central concept in the work with traumatized families. The *social pact of silence* includes the climate of terror as ruling instrument of dictatorial regimes as well as the societal negation of social violence. The negation refers to the victims who do not want to acknowledge their victimization because that would mean facing feelings of humiliation and shame; but it also refers to the perpetrators who, in order to avoid feelings of guilt, understand their doings as reactive violence or as violence against brutes.

The *family pact of silence* aims at making things undone and reflects the wish to quickly get back to a familiar normality. This non-communication about problems often becomes a model for the children, according to the motto "One does not talk about the most difficult". This makes it hard to get help and often adds to feelings of loneliness. The pact of silence is connected with the hope that the children or the partner may not realize how bad one feels (Walter, Möller, and Adam 2000: 558).

The examples discussed so far have already indicated that taboo areas have an additional dimension. The next section highlights the issues that arise as soon as people from different cultural backgrounds are involved in the communication process.

5. Taboo Topics and Silence in Intercultural Communication

Societies differ in their beliefs and in their rules of propriety and decency. When one enters a foreign culture, therefore, there are, certain matters that one should not talk about. However, one might still have to mention them somehow. Speakers tend to observe the societal decency code, and when the need arises to talk about a tabooed referent, they create new lexical items. Some may be jocular at first, but often they become generally accepted and thus conventionalized. Foreigners who come to England, for instance, are always amazed at what they regard as "fanciful names" for *toilet*. What they are looking for in public buildings, theatres, restaurants, or pubs may be called *cloakroom, Gents, Ladies, lavatory, powder room, public convenience, rest room*, etc. (Quirk and Stein 1990: 131–132).

Taboos almost universally cover the references to sexual and excretory functions, incest, and matricide. As a result of the intimate connection between language and culture, every group of humans assigns offensive or otherwise negative associations with certain sounds, words, names, numbers, figures, shapes, and colors (Aman 1982: 215–216).

An exemplary study on taboos within the context of politeness in communication between Poles and English-speaking foreigners was conducted by Jaworski et al. (1990). They understand taboo topics as "topics which speakers feel to be unsuitable or inappropriate for them to mention in the presence of others" (1990: 1). The aim of the study was to find answers to the following questions:

1. What do the British and Americans feel is inappropriate to say in the presence of Poles?
2. What do the British and Americans feel is an appropriate or safe topic in their home countries but is usually avoided (i.e. tabooed) by Poles?
3. What do the British and Americans feel is inappropriate to say in Britain and in the United States, but Poles do not hesitate to say? (Jaworski et al. 1990: 16)

As an outcome of the study, on the basis of a written questionnaire, with 18 for-eigners who are living in Poland, the following taboo areas were identified to be the most important ones for foreigners staying in Poland: religion, sexuality, bodily functions, politics and Polish history. Furthermore, it was disclosed that the questioned foreigners felt it to be especially complicated to criticize cases of obvious racism by Poles, negative attitudes towards minorities by Poles (homo-sexuals, handicapped, non-Catholics), as well as criticizing authorities who are particularly popular in Poland (Walesa, Reagan, Thatcher). To avoid "topic-based conflicts" in intercultural contact situations, Jaworski et al. (1990: 1) demand "'optimal convergence' between a foreigner and host along the level of topic" based on increased sensitivity for the existing differences between people from different cultures.

While questionnaires and interviews doubtlessly lead to revealing results about the existence and development of taboos in a given culture and in inter-cultural contact situations, one needs to be cautious. Is it *per se* possible to elicit direct evidence of deeply rooted taboos by asking those involved? As discussed before, taboos are by definition self-explicable, and they are acknowledged, but not defined exactly in a way that makes it almost impossible to formulate them (cf. Rammstedt 1964: 40). The function of taboos even pre-supposes their repression in the conscience of the person concerned since already the identifica-tion and naming of a taboo may mean a taboo breach. This implies the danger that we only become aware of those taboos that are not controlling us. As soon as the taboo can be reflected, it is no longer a taboo (Rammstedt 1964: 41).

Still, there is a vital difference between (only) talking about taboos and breaching them through actions. This becomes apparent by the verbal taboo violations in talk-shows which have become a mere gimmick. Taboo violations in talk-shows always have to be entertaining for the audience, so they do not reflect discourse practice of the relevant culture at all.[6]

Because of the reasons mentioned, questionnaires and interviews about taboos need to be enhanced by other methods. An important one is discourse analysis, since indications of the existence of taboos may be derived from the analysis of the way communication and speech take place. An intercultural dimension adds to the complexity of the concepts of *taboo* and *silence* and makes it even more difficult to interpret their occurrence in communication.

6. Conclusion

The word and the concept *tabu* has come to us from a distant language and cul-ture and the way it is used today has only little to do with its original meaning. It is useful and meaningful to use the concept in the analysis of modern soci-eties in general and in intercultural communication in particular. Taboos in the sense outlined in this article are characteristic for all forms of community,

---

[6] It could be very misleading and would result in disaster if subjects and discourse reflected in TV talk-shows were to be transferred to intercultural contact situations. Talk-shows misrepresent everyday discourse and pretend that everything, especially controversial topics, may be talked about without taboos.

because they are a prerequisite for organized coexistence, and prevent unnecessary dispute and conflict from occurring, without having to explicitly and directly regulate social interaction as a whole. The taboo complex is inseparably connected to taboo crossing and taboo violation, as well as breaking of taboos and de-tabooization.

We have provided an overview of the relevant theories and results achieved in research on taboo and silence in (intercultural) communication. Concrete examples have illustrated the benefits these results provide in practical terms and that there is a need for more studies, especially in intercultural contexts. Subjects of taboo research are:

- negative conventions of actions (taboos of action—"Don't do it")
- non-themes (zones of silence, i.e., communication taboos—"Don't speak about it!")
- etiquette themes (taboo discourse—"Don't speak about it that way!")
- linguistic expressions to be avoided (linguistic taboos—"Don't say that!")
- the possible relationships between verbal and non-verbal taboos.

A problem of modern societies and intercultural communication is that taboo rules cannot be stated explicitly. Taboos dealing with death, dying, and funerals are largely agreed upon; however, there are group-specific differences when it comes to taboos concerning sexuality. This is particularly true for homosexuality. The differences may vary with age, education, social background, as well as one's own sexual orientation.

Taboos ensure the stability of a society and are the basis for the identity of the individual and his/her group. Taboo breaches allow development and dynamics. No community can do without this taboo complex. Modern societies are also marked by taboos, though one can see an advancing de-tabooization in certain areas. This is balanced by the emergence of new taboos. Because of the progressive secularization and growing value pluralism, as well as an overall globalization of all areas of life, today's taboos are not always and in every case the same for all groups and individuals.

Taboos are rather context-sensitive; they have to be related to certain groups and situations. It is important to separate action and communication taboos. Communication taboos may be ambivalent because they include the concealment and repression of delicate subjects within a community and they can hinder development. Dealing with taboos and taboo violation in intercultural communication is difficult—as recently shown in the argument around the Mohammed caricature. In intercultural contact situations it is important to recognize and understand meaningful silence of the foreign and other. Taboo breach needs to be calculated and learned and, last but not least, this depends on the linguistic and communicative competence of the participants.

References

Allan, Keith and Kate Burridge. 1991. *Euphemism and Dysphemism. Language Used as Shield or Weapon*. New York/London: Oxford University Press.

Aman, Reinhold. 1982. Interlingual taboos in advertising: How not to name your product. In: Robert J. di Pretro (ed.), *Linguistics and the Professions*, 215–224. Norwood, NJ: Ablex.

Balle, Christel. 1990. *Tabus in der Sprache*. Frankfurt am Main: Peter Lang.

Betz, Werner. 1978. Tabu—Wörter und Wandel. In: *Meyers Enzyklopädisches Lexikon*. Band 23, 141–144. Mannheim: Bibliographisches Institut.

Bloomfield, Leonard. 1933. *Language*. New York/London: Holt.

Bubis, Naomi and Sharon Mehler. 1996. *Shtika: Versuch, das Tabu zu brechen*. Frankfurt am Main: Suhrkamp.

Collins. 1987. *Collins Cobuild English Language Dictionary*. London: Collins Publishers.

Danieli, Yael. 1980. Countertransference in the treatment and study of Nazi Holocaust survivors and their children. *Victimology* 5: 3–5.

Douglas, Mary. 1994. Taboo, Religious. In: *The Encyclopedia of Language and Linguistics*. Volume 9, 4511–4512. Oxford: Pergamon Press.

Encyclopaedia Britannica. 2007. Ultimate Reference Suite. DVD-ROM. United Soft Media.

Graupmann, Jürgen. 1998. *Das Lexikon der Tabus*. Bergisch Gladbach: Bastei Lübbe.

Günther, Ulla. 1992. "und aso das isch gar need es Tabu bi üs, nei, überhaupt need". Sprachliche Strategien bei Phone-in-Sendungen am Radio zu tabuisierten The-men. Bern: Peter Lang.

Havers, Wilhelm. 1946. *Neuere Literatur zum Sprachtabu*. (Abhandlung der philosophisch-historischen Klasse der Akademie der Wissenschaften in Wien 223,5.) Wien: Rohrer.

Holden, Lynn A. 2000. *Encyclopedia of Taboos*. Oxford: ABC-CLIO Ltd.

Jaworski, Adam (ed.). 1997. *Silence: Interdisciplinary Perspectives*. Berlin: Mouton de Gruyter.

Jaworski, Adam. 1997. Introduction: An overview. In: Adam Jaworski (ed.), *Silence: Interdisciplinary Perspectives*, 3–14. Berlin/New York: Mouton de Gruyter.

Jaworski, Adam. 1998. *The Power of Silence. Social and Pragmatic Perspectives*. London: Sage.

Jaworski, Adam. 1999. The power of silence in communication. In: Laura K. Guerrero, Joseph A. DeVito and Michael L. Hecht (eds.), *The Nonverbal Communication Reader. Classic and Contemporary Readings*, 156–162. Prospect Heights, IL: Waveland Press.

Jaworski, Adam, Anna Danielewicz, Wioleta Morszczyn and Monika Pawloska. 1990. Cross-cultural taboo and conflict: Politeness of topic selection in the native-foreign language situation. Unpublished paper given at the 25th Conference on Contrastive Linguistics.

Jenkins, Susan. 2000. Cultural and linguistic miscues: A case study of international teaching assistant and academic faculty miscommunication. *International Journal of Intercultural Relations* 24(4): 477–501.

Jensen, J. Vernon. 1973. Communicative functions of silence. *ETC. A Review of General Semantics* XXX: 249–257.

Knapp, Karlfried. 2000. Metaphorical and interactional uses of silence. *Erfurt Electronic Studies in English* 7/2000. http://www.uni-erfurt.de/eestudies/eese/journal-frame.html (last access: January 10, 2008).

Kraft, Hartmut. 2004. Tabu. Magie und soziale Wirklichkeit. Düsseldorf: Patmos.

Krajewski, Sabine. 2002. Life Goes on. And Sometimes it Doesn't. A Comparative Study of Medical Drama in the US, Great Britain and Germany. Frankfurt am Main: Peter Lang.

Kuhn, Fritz. 1987. Tabus. *Sprache und Literatur in Wissenschaft und Unterricht* 60: 9–35.

Kurzon, Dennis. 1997. *Discourse of Silence*. Amsterdam/Philadelphia: John Benjamins.

Luchtenberg, Sigrid. 1985. *Euphemismen im heutigen Deutsch. Mit einem Beitrag zu Deutsch als Fremdsprache*. Frankfurt am Main: Peter Lang.

Markkanen, Raija and Hartmut Schröder (eds.). 1997. *Hedging and Discourse. Approaches to the Analysis of a Pragmatic Phenomenon in Academic Texts*. Berlin/New York: de Gruyter.

Meillet, Antoine. 1921. *Linguistique Historique et Linguistique Générale*. Paris: Champion.

Müller, Sandra. 2004. *We, on Death Row—der Tod steht Ihnen gut*. Frankfurt am Main: Peter Lang.

Nakane, Ikuko. 2007. *Silence in Intercultural Communication: Perceptions and Performance*. Amsterdam: John Benjamins.

Niskanen, Tuija. 1999. More than sweaters and shocking pictures. On the corporate philosophy and communication stragegy of Benetton. In: Sam Inkinen (ed.), *Mediapolis. Aspects of Texts, Hypertexts and Multimedial Communication*, 358–381. Berlin/New York: Mouton de Gruyter.

Pelikan, Johanna. 1987. Die NS-Vergangenheit als Tabu-Thema in Österreich. Eine qualitative, textlinguistische Analyse des Hearings zum Präsidentschaftswahlkampf. *Wiener Linguistische Gazette* 38/39: 77–93.

Poyatos, Fernando. 2002. *Nonverbal Communication Across Disciplines: Paralanguage, Kinesics, Silence, Personal and Environmental Interaction*, Vol 2. Amsterdam/Philadelphia: John Benjamins.

Quirk, Randolph and Gabriele Stein. 1990. *English in Use*. London: Longman.

Rammstedt, Otthein. 1964. Tabus und Massenmedien. *Publizistik* 9: 40–45.

Redfern, Walter D. 1994. Euphemism. In: *The Encyclopedia of Language and Linguistics*. Volume 3, 1180–1181. Oxford: Pergamon Press.

Reimann, Horst. 1989. Tabu. In: *Staatslexikon. Recht Wirtschaft Gesellschaft in 5 Bänden*. Bd. 5, 420. Herausgegeben von der Görres-Gesellschaft. 7. Auflage. Freiburg: Herder.

Rothe, Matthias and Hartmut Schröder (eds.). 2002. *Ritualisierte Tabuverletzungen, Lachkultur und das Karnevaleske*. Frankfurt am Main: Peter Lang.

Rothe, Matthias and Hartmut Schröder (eds.). 2005. *Körpertabus und Umgehungsstrategien*. Berlin: Weidler Verlag.

Rudas, Stephan. 1994. Stichworte zur Sozialpsychologie der Tabus. In: Peter Bettelheim und Robert Streibel (ed.), *Tabu und Geschichte. Zur Kultur des kollektiven Erinnerns*, 17–20. Wien: Picus.

Sahlgren, Jöran. 1915. Blåkulla och blåkullafärderna. En språklig och mythistorisk undersökning. [The witches dance on the Blocksberg]. *Namn och Bygd. Tidskrift för nor-disk ortnamnsforskning* 3: 100–161.

Schank, Gerd. 1981. *Untersuchungen zum Ablauf natürlicher Dialoge*. München: Hueber.

Schorch, Stefan. 2000. *Euphemismen in der hebräischen Bibel*. Wiesbaden: Harrassowitz.

Schröder, Hartmut. 1995. Tabuforschung als Aufgabe interkultureller Germanistik. Ein Plädoyer. *Jahrbuch Deutsch als Fremdsprache* 21: 15–35.

Schröder, Hartmut. 1998. Tabus, interkulturelle Kommunikation und Fremdsprachenunterricht. Überlegungen zur Relevanz der Tabuforschung für die Fremdsprachendidaktik. In: Annelie Knapp-Potthoff and Martina Liedke (eds.), *Aspekte interkultureller Kommunikationsfähigkeit*, 93–106. München: iudicium.

Schröder, Hartmut. 2001. Sprachtabu und Euphemismen. Sprachwissenschaftliche Anmerkungen zu Stefan Schorchs "Euphemismen in der hebräischen Bibel". In: Annelies Häcki Buhofer, Harald Burger and Laurent Gautier (eds.), *Phraseologiae Amor. Aspekte europäischer Phraseologie*, 229–246. Baltmannsweiler: Schneider-Verlag Hohengehren.

Schröder, Hartmut. 2002. Semiotisch-rhetorische Aspekte von Sprachtabus. In: Eckhard Höfner, Hartmut Schröder and Roland Wittmann (eds.), *Valami más. Beiträge des Finnisch-Ungarischen Kultursemiotischen Symposiums "Zeichenhafte Aspekte der Veränderung"*, 169–187. Frankfurt am Main: Peter Lang.

Schröder, Hartmut. 2003. Tabu. In: Alois Wierlacher and Andrea Bogner (eds.), *Handbuch Interkulturelle Germanistik*, 307–315. Stuttgart/Weimar: Metzler.

Schröder, Hartmut. 2005. Phänomenologie und interkulturelle Aspekte des Tabus. Ein Essay. In: Tzveta Sofronieva (ed.), *Verbotene Wörter*, 287–314. München: Biblion Verlag.

Scott, Robert L. 1993. Dialectical tensions of speaking and silence. *Quarterly Journal of Speech* 79(1): 1–18.

Soanes, Catherine and Sara Hawker. 2005. *Compact Oxford English Dictionary of Current English*. 3rd edition. Oxford: Oxford University Press.

Struve, Ulrich. 1998. Erinnern=Leben. Jüdisches Leben in Deutschland. http://www.literaturcafe.de/erinnern/teil5.htm (last access: January 10, 2008).

Tannen, Deborah and Muriel Saville-Troike (eds.). 1985. *Perspectives on Silence*. Norwood, NJ: Ablex.

Treimer, Karl. 1954/1955. Tabu im Albanischen. *Lingua* 4: 42–62.

Trost, Pavel. 1936. Bemerkungen zum Sprachtabu. *Travaux du Cercle Linguistique de Prague* 6: 288–294.

Ullmann, Stephan. 1962. *Semantics. An Introduction to the Science of Meaning*. Oxford: Blackwell.

Walter, Joachim, Birgit Möller and Hubertus Adam. 2000/2001. Vom beredten Schweigen in der Kinder- und Familientherapie mit Flüchtlingsfamilien. *Zeitschrift für Politische Psychologie* 8/9: 549–560.

Watzlawick, Paul, Janet Beavin Bavelas and Don D. Jackson. 1980. Pragmatics of Human Communication: Study of Interactional Patterns, Pathologies and Paradoxes. New York: Norton.

Wrobel, Ursula. 2003. *Andere Länder—Andere Sites. Bewältigung von Tabudiskursen in Online-Produktwerbung mit Hilfe von Abschwächungsstrategien unter besonderer Berücksichtigung des Hedging. Ein Vergleich US-amerikanischer und deutscher Websites im Kontext interkultureller und werblicher Kommunikation.* Frankfurt am Main: Peter Lang.

Wundt, Wilhelm. 1926. *Völkerpsychologie. Eine Untersuchung der Entwicklungsgesetze von Sprache, Mythus und Stille.* 4. Band: Mythus und Religion. 1. Teil. Leipzig: Engelmann.

Zöllner, Nicole. 1997. *Der Euphemismus im alltäglichen und politischen Sprachgebrauch des Englischen.* Frankfurt am Main: Peter Lang.

Part II

Applied Intercultural Communication

11

Intercultural Communication in Healthcare Settings

Celia Roberts

1. Introduction

Most of the literature on cultural issues in healthcare settings stems from medical anthropology and does not focus on the details of interaction. The sociological and sociolinguistic studies take a more interactional perspective but are concerned with asymmetrical encounters generally rather than with intercultural communication. The applied linguistic literature on intercultural communication in healthcare would make up only a slim volume, although it is growing. It is important, therefore, to make connections with the wider literature, not least because of the contributions anthropology and sociology have made to an understanding of discourse, identity and equality in healthcare settings. The work on healthcare discourse has concentrated on the health professional–patient interaction. Following Goffman, this is the "front stage" work of professionals. However, hospitals and other healthcare institutions are held together as much by "backstage" work: the talk and text between health professionals, managers and other staff in healthcare organizations (Atkinson 1995). And the institution of medicine and the professions within it are largely maintained by the education, training and selection work that prepares and develops health professionals. Much of this is carried out in high stakes gate-keeping encounters. So, this "backstage" work is also included in this chapter.

Migration and the diaspora continue to produce a changing communicative ecology in public life. Stable ethnic minority populations co-exist alongside relatively new groups of migrants and asylum seekers. As with other caring and social services, both the research and policies in the health arena chart the changes in practices produced as a result of multilingual and culturally diverse client populations. These include changes in the medical and nursing undergraduate curriculum and postgraduate training, concerns about fairness and equal opportunities in assessment and selection processes, and research and policies around interpreter mediated consultations.

2. Professional–Patient Communication

It is estimated that over ten thousand articles have been written about health-care professional–patient communication. Most of these are written either by healthcare practitioners or psychologists (Ong, DeHaes, Hoos and Lammes 1995). In comparison, the output from linguistics has been small. Candlin and Candlin (2003: 135) with reference to the major applied and sociolinguistic journals remark that "one finds the occasional paper, but no real sense of ongoing commitment to the health care communication field". Only a very small fraction of these thousands of articles are focused on intercultural communication (Skelton, Kai and Loudon 2001).

3. Difference as "Cultural"

The research traditions of medical sociology and sociolinguistics, although not focused on ethnic notions of interculturality, conceptualize the health professional–patient encounter as one of difference in which the medical system is characterized as "a cultural system" (Kleinman 1988). The different perspectives and knowledge structures about, for example, AIDS or genetics, and managing social relations are broadly intercultural in that professionals and clients/patients are seen as voicing different world views (Mishler 1984). The sociolinguistic literature on healthcare settings has looked at inequalities in medical discourse (Freeman and Heller 1987), and healthcare generally (McKay and Pittam 2002) asymmetrical power relations (Ainsworth-Vaughn 1998, Wadak 1997) and how they are co-constructed in consultations (ten Have 1995) and, in particular, the gendered nature of such relations (Fisher 1995; West 1984), as well as social class (Todd 1984), the discursive representation of health and illness (Fisher and Todd 1983; Fleischman 2001; Hyden and Mishler 1999); and how different medical conditions shape the discourse of the consultation (Hamilton 2004).

The sociologically based studies of the consultation share with intercultural communication studies a concern with inferential processes and the potential for miscommunication which can feed into more structured social inequalities in healthcare. Cicourel (1983) examines the miscommunication when doctor and patient have different belief structures about the cause of an illness (see also Tannen and Wallet 1986). He argues that much of the misunderstanding that arises out of diagnostic reasoning stems from tacit clinical experience and from everyday understanding that is presumed to be shared knowledge. Similarly, Atkinson (1995) and Silverman (1987) drawing on seminal work on the ritual aspects of the consultation, analyse the powerful discourses that determine the patients' treatment.

As well as the cultural differences between health professional discourse and the lifeworld discourses of the patient, there are increasing tensions and instabilities between professional discourses and the wider institutional discourses of healthcare organization, as new types of communicative genres come into being (Iedema and Scheeres 2003; Cook-Gumperz and Messerman 1999).

Iedema (in press) describes the "interactive volatility" where there is increasing amount of talk in what might broadly be conceived of as intercultural encounters where professionals and others who inhabit different professional and organizational cultures now have to negotiate meanings together. This volatility is the result of new sites and practices where there are stuggles over how to interact, as professional roles and relationships have to be rethought. Research on the detailed interactional strategies of the consultation has been dominated by Conversation Analysis (CA). Although not addressed explicitly, Conversation Analysis looks at the differences in how professionals and patients communicate with each other. By looking at relatively large numbers of a particular phase of the consultation, CA has shown the patterns of turn design and their consequences for health professionals and their patients. CA studies in the USA, Finland and the UK, to name some of the main contributions to this tradition, have focused on particular phases such as openings, history taking and making a diagnosis (see Drew, Chatwin and Collins 2001 for an overview of CA in health-care settings). CA, in pursuing the quest for general patterns, has not focused on ethnic/linguistic diversity in communication and so the unpredictable and less determinate qualities of consultations when patient and doctor draw on different ethno-linguistic resources (see Gumperz and Cook-Gumperz 2007). However, CA methodology has influenced the interactional sociolinguistic research in healthcare settings described below.

It is not possible to look at all aspects of what Sarangi calls a developing "communicative mentality" (Sarangi 2004) in healthcare settings, nor to look at all the ways in which "diversity" affects interpretation in health encounters where diversity includes, as mentioned above, any difference in health professionals' and patients' perspectives.

The rest of the chapter will, therefore, focus on language and ethnicities in intercultural communication.

4. Cultural Differences and Medical Anthropology

Just as there are fuzzy boundaries between what is ethnically constituted as cultural difference and what is socially/institutionally constituted, as suggested, so the notion of "intercultural" is problematic. In other words "culture" can be conceived of too narrowly as *only* accounting for linguistic/ethnic differences or overused to explain *any* interaction where participants' ethnic/national origins differ. As Auer and Kern argue, an encounter is not intercultural just because people originate from different parts of the world and belong to different races and ethnicities. "Culture" can only be understood as part of action and interaction rather than standing outside it. Differences, difficulties and misunderstandings cannot be easily accounted for *because* people come from these different backgrounds. This may be the explanation but there are other reasons to do with "professional culture", individual differences, etc. which may account for differences (Auer and Kern 2000).

It is important to bear these arguments in mind when discussing the literature on health beliefs from medical anthropology. The significance of this approach in professional–patient consultations lies in the potential for misunderstandings when different explanatory models of illness, which patients bring to the encounter, clash with the diagnosis and explanation of the disease from the professional's perspective. Much of the early medical anthropology literature focused on non-western health beliefs and more recent studies have used this perspective to examine issues of cultural diversity in western healthcare settings (Kleinman 1988; Helman 1994), and in relation to mental illness (Rack 1991). These health beliefs may affect how the body is conceptualized, what is regarded as healthy and what causes disease and appropriate responses to it. Studies by medical anthropologists have also discussed different ways in which patients from different cultural backgrounds may present their symptoms, some highlighting objective signs and others the emotional or psychological aspects (Helman 1994). Another aspect of the cultural and linguistic relativity of health beliefs concerns pain and how it is responded to and expressed. Healthcare beliefs are also affected by different experiences of healthcare systems and this may affect practical issues such as adherence to treatment (Henley and Schott 1999). The culturally specific beliefs that patients bring to a consultation enter into the discourse of the encounter and cannot be ignored in a narrowly linguistic analysis. However, medical anthropology has not focused on the discursive and interactional aspects of the consultation (but see Manderson and Allotey 2003 for an exception). So, illuminating though this literature is, it tends to conceive of health beliefs as static sets of assumptions rather than active discourses which may be called up or not and which are mediated through different styles of self presentation. In contrast to much of the anthropological literature, recent studies in the UK suggest that patients from diverse backgrounds tend to use western medical models in their consultations with mainstream health professionals (Bhopal 1986).

Rather than fixed health beliefs, it is the discourse styles of relating to, and representing illness to the health professional that tend to make cultural issues relevant in the consultation (Anderson, Elfert and Lai 1989). As Pauwels (1991, 1994) indicates in her discussion of training health workers in Australia, broad differences in health beliefs were more readily available for comment than discourse and rhetorical features. So there is a tendency to focus on beliefs because they are easier to talk about than on ways of talking and interacting which are more hidden and require more technical understanding.

5. Health Professional–Patient Communication in Linguistically and Culturally Diverse Societies

In the clinical literature, cultural diversity tends to be treated in two different ways: either in terms of cultural awareness, drawing on the health beliefs literature described above or in terms of the "language barrier". Language and culture tend to be treated separately, rather than being "wired in together" (Agar 1994). While some research plays down language problems, most of the studies acknowledge them (Ahmad, Kernohan and Baker 1989; Ali 2003). And of these latter, nearly all are concerned with issues of interpreting; the majority with policy issues (Jacobs, Lauderdale, Meltzer, Shorey, Levinson and Thisted 2001) but others with the nature of mediated consultations and some of the drawbacks of them.

5.1. Interpreter-Mediated Consultations

The linguistic and sociolinguistic studies on interpreter mediated encounters in healthcare settings argue that the interpreter is not a neutral tool (Putsch 1985) or a "walking bilingual dictionary" (Ebden, Carey, Bhatt and Harrison 1988) but a linguistic and social intermediary, dealing with discourse and social interaction and not just a narrow definition of language:

> "Interpreters do not merely convey messages they shape, and in some very real sense, create those messages in the name of those for whom they speak." (Davidson 2000: 382).

Davidson's work also clearly shows that as well as managing the conversational flow of the consultation, interpreters also act as gatekeepers, often editing and even deleting utterances of the patients for whom they are interpreting. To this extent, they are certainly not acting as advocates or ambassadors. Nor are they neutral since they act as social agents within the jointly constructed discourse (Bührig 2001). It is not surprising, therefore, that interpreter-mediated consultations are often less patient-centred than non-mediated ones (Rivadeneyra, Elderkin-Thompson, Silver and Waitzkin 2000).

In most medical settings, more informal interpreters are used than professional ones, including staff in the hospital or clinic and family and friends of the patients (Meyer 2001; Bührig and Meyer 2005). Yet there is a dearth of literature in this area. One area where there are some studies is in the use of children as informal interpreters for their family. This research has focused on the views of healthcare professionals and has identified several problems including limited language skills and the difficulties of interpreting complicated and sensitive subjects (Cohen, Moran-Ellis and Smaje 1999). The term "language brokering" is used, derived from the notion of cultural brokering (Kaufert and Koolage 1984) which suggests that a "broker" is more independent than an interpreter in initiating action in an encounter. The term "brokering" focuses on the consultation as an intercultural event and not just on narrow issues of linguistic translation. Although the role of children in these intercultural encounters can lead to the kind of problems mentioned above, research on children as brokers showed a more mixed picture (Green, Free, Bhavnani and Newman 2005). The child brokers often felt ignored and, contrary to good practice for professional interpreters, wanted to be treated as full participants in the consultation. But they also felt there were benefits to child brokering in terms of the responsibility it gave them and the help they could offer their families.

The interpreter-mediated consultation can produce its own misunderstandings and this may be in part due to the health professionals' own competence in working with interpreters (Blackford 1997). Some patients prefer to communicate directly with their doctor and there is some evidence that patients are suspicious of cultural mediators who may talk *for* them. Uncertainty about how talk is interpreted may lead to mistrust that can slide into negative assumptions about the group that speaks that language (Collins and Slembrouck in press).

Collins and Slembrouck's study looks at alternatives to the face-to-face interpreter-mediated consultation: the use of translated medical terms and phrases and the use of telephone interpreters. In this ethnographic linguistic study of a local community clinic in Belgium, Collins and Slembrouck show that there is considerable unease with all these different strategies among the staff of the clinic. A manual that consisted of key phrases, symptoms and diseases was translated into those languages where there were few or no informal interpreters. However, this was found to be cumbersome and created its own linguistic and interactional problems. Doctors preferred direct and unmediated consultation where possible.

6. Intercultural Communication in the Majority Language

While many of the broader cultural issues of a diverse society have been treated in the sociological and sociolinguistic literature on health settings (see above), the interactional dimension has received less attention. Discourse analysis methodology has been used to focus on interactional differences and on misunderstandings in Australian settings (Pauwels 1991; Cass, Lowell, Christie, Snelling, Flack, Marrnganyin and Brown 2002; Manderson and Allotey 2003), in South Africa (Crawford 1994) and in comparing doctor–patient communication in the USA and Japan using quantitative discourse analysis (Ohtaki, Ohtakia and Fetters 2003).

The rest of this chapter will draw on interactional sociolinguistics (Gumperz 1982, 1996, 1999, Gumperz and Cook-Gumperz 2007) and on the detail of how conversational inferences are made and conversational involvement is sustained in ethnically and linguistically heterogeneous communities. Differences in communicative background enter into talk and affect how interpretations are made. Ways of talking are not separated from the socio-cultural knowledge that is brought along and brought about in the interaction or how social identity leaks out into the interaction through talk; for example, how to manage the moral self in consultations, what are allowable topics, how to structure an illness narrative; how direct to be in self-presentation or how to manage turns at talk with the professional. At a micro level, language and socio-cultural knowledge influence choice of words and idioms and a range of prosodic features, including intonation and rhythm. These are the "contextualization cues" (Gumperz 1982) which help to frame each phase of the consultation and channel the interpretive message of either professional or patient. Where these styles of speaking and conventions for interpreting the other's talk are not shared, misunderstandings frequently occur. Differences in communicative style can not only lead to overt misunderstandings but also to difficult or uncomfortable moments and to some of the small tragedies of everyday life (Levinson 1997); for example, if patients do not get access to scarce resources. Patients may be anywhere on a continuum of language ability in terms of lexico-grammatical accuracy, pragmatics and discursive strategies

(Ali 2003). Patterns of language difference are situated and contingent rather than absolute and systematic, so:

> "We need to be able to deal with degrees of differentiation and . . . learn to explore how such differentiation affects individuals' ability to sustain social interaction and have their goals and motives understood." (Gumperz 1982: 7).

7. Patients With Limited English and Doctors in General Practice

This final section is based on a series of studies drawn from a research project based at King's College London. The video data illustrated below form part of a corpus gathered for a programme of research on patient–family doctor interactions: Patients with Limited English and Doctors in General Practice: Education issues (the PLEDGE project), which used interactional sociolinguistic methods to explore how general practitioners (GPs) and patients negotiate meaning and collaborate to manage, repair or prevent understanding problems. 20% of the 232 video-recorded consultations were with patients from non-English speaking backgrounds or patients with a culturally specific style of communicating *and* featured frequent and profound misunderstandings.

Patients from these backgrounds ranged from those who had considerable difficulty conveying even their literal meaning, while others were more fluent, but have culturally different styles of communicating, influenced by their first languages.

The research looked at the potential for, and occasions of misunderstandings and awkward moments where the conditions for shared interpretation between patients and doctors cannot be created. The studies include: misunderstandings which occur when doctors fail to understand patients (Roberts et al. 2005), when the misunderstandings are caused by doctors and when both sides try to prevent and repair misunderstandings (Moss and Roberts 2005). We have also looked at phases in the consultation, for example, the opening phase (Roberts, Sarangi and Moss 2004) when differences in self-presentation can set the consultation off on the wrong footing.

Intercultural consultations challenge much of the received wisdom about good communication skills in the healthcare literature. The topsy-turvy, "looking glass" world of such consultations suggests that "patient-centred" models ("patients want their feelings elicited") and the idea that more talk is likely to mean less misunderstanding ("ask open questions") often do not work and even cause more confusion when talk itself is the problem. Communications research and textbooks argue that doctors should engage more with patients but in the PLEDGE data attempts to do so by the doctors through social chat and extended explanations were often closed down by the patients (Roberts, Moss, Wass, Sarangi and Jones 2005).

7.1. Problems With Patient-Centredness

Data example one: In the following example, a young mother from Somalia has brought her baby daughter to see the family doctor because she has been suffering from diarrhoea. At this stage in the consultation, the doctor has already taken a brief history from the patient's mother and, before examining the baby, has asked her some initial questions about breast feeding her:

Example 1.

```
 1  D   little bit (.) right so you're virtually stopped (.)
 2      so what sort of questions have you got in your mind for me today (.)
 3      what do you want me to do
 4      (1)
 5  P   mm no: =she say=
 6  D   =today=
 7  P   eh: the lady she say if you want to contacting doctor eh:
        you want eh: talk him
 8  D   yeah= =
 9  P   = =I say yes I am happy with e- with =you=
10  D   =right= right ok= =
11  P   = =because (.) definitely when I am coming with you
12      when I go back I will go back happy
13  D   ((laughs)) I hope so
14  P   because I will look to see you and your doctor K (.)
15      I like it
16  D   good= =
17  P   = =[cos] when when I come in will come in the you know ((tut))
18      when I go back my home I'm happy
19  D   right
20  P   ((laughs))
21  D   so you want me to- (.) check her over
```

At line one the doctor uses a number of contextualization cues to show that she is about to shift topic from discussing breast feeding. She pauses, uses the discourse marker "right" and sums up the patient's contribution. She then moves to a new frame, at line 2, to eliciting patient's concerns in classic patient-centred mode. The mother may well have missed the lexical and prosodic contextualization cues which mark the shift in topic and this exacerbates the difficulty in processing the questions in lines two and three. But the main difficulty seems to be that she cannot interpret the shift in frame marked by these open questions. She responds with a negative and then refers to the "lady" (probably the receptionist) and how she is happy to see this particular doctor. This is the beginning of a narrative account about coming in to see the doctor rather than an analytical account of her concerns. She then reformulates her perception of the doctor twice more. This repetition of how she likes this doctor and her colleague seems to shift the topic from the question she asked the receptionist (about seeing the doctor) to some general display of satisfaction. This may be because she is uncertain how to take the doctor's elicitation and/or because she sees it as culturally appropriate to praise her. This is not the footing which the doctor had anticipated in which the patient is offered a more equal social relationship with the doctor in indicating her concerns. The doctor's responses at lines 10, 16 and 19 are markers of possible change of frame rather than receipt tokens, particularly "right". However, the patient orients to them as the latter and on three occasions reiterates her positive evaluation of the doctor. When there is again a minimal response from the doctor at line 19 "right", the mother gives up on her praise and laughs, marking the closure of this unsuccessful attempt at patient-centredness. The doctor then speaks *for* the patient in line 21, thus undermining her original attempt to be patient-centred and shifting back to a more orthodox frame in which she pushes on with the next phase of the consultation (Roberts, Sarangi and Moss 2004).

Misunderstandings, as this example shows, are multi-causal and jointly accomplished: contextualization cues fail to be read; socio-cultural knowledge about patient roles is not shared and neither side has the appropriate linguistic resources to repair the misunderstanding. The origin of the problem may lie with the patient or with the doctor but together they either talk past each other or, in some cases, find other resources to repair and manage the interaction. Unsurprisingly, doctors had difficulties with patients' phonological differences, prosodic features, particularly contrastive stress and assessing speaker stance, and with grammatical and syntactical means of contextualizing. But the greatest difficulties were with patients' overall rhetorical style: with low self-display, with structuring their information and with two inter-related features of topic overload and overlapping/interrupting talk (Roberts, Moss, Wass, Sarangi and Jones 2005).

Topic management was also one of the elements of doctor talk which, on different occasions, either produced or prevented misunderstandings (see also Erickson and Rittenberg 1987). Rapid topic shift was a major cause of interactional difficulties. By contrast strategies for topic involvement and fostering chances of participation in which the patient could initiate the topic tended to prevent or help repair misunderstandings (Moss and Roberts 2005).

7.2. Presentation of Self and Symptoms

It is a commonplace in the intercultural literature to find evidence of the illusion of understanding and of awkward moments where there is no overt breakdown but the sense of orderliness and the underlying rhythm of a typical institutional encounter fails to be established or maintained. This is illustrated in the opening phases of symptom telling where local English styles of self and symptom presentation contrast with those used by patients whose dominant language is not English. These issues and the next two examples are discussed in more detail in Roberts, Sarangi and Moss (2004). There are three aspects to the initial self-reporting by patients: the description of symptoms, the context in which the symptoms occurred and the patient's stance. By stance here we include both "affective stance" and "epistemic stance" (Ochs 1996).

Example 2.
A young white woman who speaks a standard variety of English has brought her toddler to the surgery to have his infected eye checked out.
01 D   right so how can I help =you=
02 M   =o:h= =erm=

03 D =I'm sorry= you've had to come
04 M oh it's ok / (1) I think he's got conjuncti*vitis but =I'm not= sure (.) hes had
05 D =oh dear=
06 M it since la:st (0.5) he had a *gummy eye this side but {[ac]when he was born that was quite *gummy so I tolerated it}(.) then it *travelled to this one and got {[dc]progressively worse (0.5) over the weekend we were in Germany for a wedding so }= =
07 D = =oh right (nice time)
08 M yeah it was good
09 D ok
10 M erm it went *red underneath *there and *red just a*bove
11 D right
12 M {[dc]and it's been very *gunky}
13 D mm= =
14 M = = {[ac] [lo]as you can see I've sort of left it (.) erm }= =
15 D = =so this is for how many days now

Through her use of prosodic features, the mother focuses on the symptom and puts in the background the child's history of such infection. She does this by putting emphatic stress on key syllables "conjunctiVITis", "GUMmy", "RED" and so on and by speeding up her utterance at 6 when giving some of the background detail and then slowing down when she returns to the symptoms later in turn 6 and 12. The repetition "red" and the rhythmic stress in this turn and the next when she refers to the "gunky" eye reinforces the display of symptoms as the most important information. This enables the doctor to attend to the presentation of symptoms, and the rest can be put in the background.

By making the child's symptoms the focus of her opening turns, and the context and stance the background, this patient aligns herself with the GP and the medical model which she expects the GP to be working with. Since both doctor and patient share the same cultural resources for making meaning, in this case the same use of prosodic features to contextualise this phase of the consultation, the indirect messages conveyed in these contextualisation cues are readily interpretable by the GP.

The mother's epistemic stance is a subtle blend of the agentive–she "tolerated" the gummy eye but also somewhat deferential–"I've sort of left it". The patient's mother presents her "moral self" as a caring but not overly anxious mother who does not want to over treat her child and she interweaves this moral self with the medical model of symptom giving. As shown above, this is partly accomplished through her prosodic management of the opening report.

Patients whose expert language is not English face linguistic, pragmatic and rhetorical problems. Pragmatic and linguistic difficulties do not *necessarily* prevent such patients from managing the rhetoric of routine self-presentations. However, many patients talk about their problems with resources which are both linguistically and rhetorically different from those of the doctor.

In the next example, the patient focuses not on her symptoms but her inability to cope with them. She is an elderly woman of South Asian origin whose first language is Gujarati.

Example 3.

D   come in come in please come in [ ] good morning
P   good morning
D   have a seat
P   thank you
D   how are you today
P   oh: {[dc] [creaky voice]not very good}
D   not very good (.) what's happening
P   I *pain here (.) *too much (.) I can't cope you know
D   right
P   *yesterday (.) *whole day
D   right
P   and I eat (.) *three times (.) Paracetamol
D   right
P   two three hours it will be *all *right and then (.) *come *pain again (.) I *can't cope (.) Pain like
D   you can't cope with this pain
P   yeah very very bad (.) I don't know what's the wrong with me
D   sure how * long you have this

The patient slows down her speech with "not very good" and speaks in a creaky, tremulous voice. It as if she is as acting out the pain in her talk. The rest of her initial self report is delivered in short quite sharply contoured units with little distinction made prosodically between the description of the symptoms, the context, the self-treatment and her stance. The doctor does not immediately ask her about her symptoms but instead repeats what she has said, "you can't cope with this pain", which elicits more affective talk. And when he does ask about the symptoms, the question is, prosodically, more like a comment than a question and does not seem to function as directing back the patient to the facts of the condition. One reason why this example may be different from the previous one is that the doctor is also of South Asian origin, a Panjabi speaker, and is willing to stay with the affective stance as the focus of this self report, rather than moving immediately to the question about how long she has had these symptoms.

Both the English mother and the Gujarati patient were able to create the conditions for shared negotiation and appropriate presentation of self and symptoms because they shared linguistic and cultural resources with the doctor. When this is not the case, the orderliness of the opening stage of the consultation is challenged. Unexpected aspects of self-reporting are put in the foreground and the expected focus is lost. Sometimes, patients cannot combine symptom telling with a stance which tells the doctor what kind of patient they have sitting opposite them. As a result openings become protracted and harder work interactionally. Doctors may make judgements about patients based on a style of self-reporting that does not meet the doctor's expectations. Patients become labelled as "difficult" or "passive" and these labels become social facts. These facts constructed out of the discourse of patient–healthcare professionals, can also lead to generalisations and stereotypes in the backstage work of healthcare encounters (Roberts, Sarangi and Moss 2004).

8. Backstage Work

As with the health professional–patient communication, the relatively little work by socio- and applied linguistics on backstage work has not focused on intercultural communication. Meetings (Cook-Gumperz and Messerman 1999), doctors' rounds (Atkinson 1995), interaction in operating theatres (Pettinari 1988) as well as talk, for example, in medical laboratories are all backstage work where the teams reflect the diverse multilingual nature of western urban societies. However, linguistic and ethnic diversity is rarely the focus of attention except in educational and selection processes where issues of disadvantage, language and indirect racial discrimination are increasingly matters of concern. These issues can manifest themselves in subtle ways. For example, Erickson's case study of an African-American inexperienced doctor presenting a case to his white preceptor (experienced attending doctor) shows how "racial" tension is an implicit resource which the young doctor uses to distance himself from the black "street" patient. But in so doing he uses a more formal medical register than is expected between two medical colleagues and so may come across as insufficiently socialized (Erickson 1999).

The preparation, training and assessment of ethnic minority healthcare professionals, particularly those educated and/or trained overseas, raises questions about the adequacy and fairness of these high-stake intercultural encounters. A recurrent theme is the gap between medical knowledge and socio-cultural knowledge. Both aspiring healthcare professionals and their educators and assessors tend to overemphasize medical knowledge and down-play or remain unaware of the socio-cultural knowledge which constructs these encounters. This is the case with healthcare workers in Canada (Duff, Wong and Early 2000), with professionals subjected to language testing in Australia (McNamara 1997) and in the London-based research projects which end this paper.

9. Oral Assessment and Its Potential for Indirect Discrimination

The first of these studies concerns the oral examination for membership of the Royal College of General Practitioners and the possibility of discriminatory outcomes for certain groups of ethnic minority candidates (Roberts and Sarangi 1999). Video recordings of the examinations were analysed using interactional sociolinguistic methods. The study concluded that the "hybrid discourses" of the exam were particularly problematic for non-traditional candidates especially those trained overseas. The exam consisted of three different modes of question: institutional, professional and personal. However the exam criteria were institutionally driven. For those candidates not used to the institutional discourses of gate keeping oral assessments, however proficient they were as doctors, the examination remained an unfair hurdle.

A similar concern with equal opportunities for certain groups of ethnic minorities, led to research in a large London medical school on the final year undergraduate clinical examination which consists of role-played consultations with actor-patients (Roberts et al. 2003). Candidates who were rated highly were compared with those that failed and three components of their performance were identified as shedding light on the contrast in their marks: communicative style in which highly situated talk was contrasted with a schema driven agenda; thematic staging in which candidates either staged their arguments to persuade or closed off negotiating too early; and ideological assumptions about "slippery areas" to do with beliefs and values. Ethnic minority candidates from overseas who had performed well in medical knowledge tests tended to be marked lower in these three areas.

10. Conclusion

Discourse analysis and interactional sociolinguistics have started to look at the differences and misunderstandings which can occur in intercultural encounters in healthcare. Lack of shared assumptions about role-relations, differences in communicative style and a lack of resources on both sides to create conditions for negotiating understanding are fed by and feed into negative ethnic and linguistic ideologies. Inequalities in healthcare can result both for patients and for professionals working in healthcare settings. Studies of intercultural communication in such settings have made a contribution to the field of applied linguistics and shed new light on medical practices. Oral examinations are now looked at through the discourse analyst's lens. Judgements about candidates are no longer simply read off from their talk; and the interactional construction of the candidate by the examiner is now acknowledged (Roberts, Sarangi, Southgate, Wakeford and Wass 2000). Similarly, issues of language and ethnicity in doctor–patient communication are enriched by the applied discourse analyst's conceptual frameworks and analytic gaze. But there the contribution to medicine and health studies of interaction analysis is still only partially visible. The most important next step is for applied linguists to be widely published in mainstream medical and health journals.

Box 1. Transcription conventions

=word=	overlapping talk
word= =	latching (one speaker following another with no pause)
(.)	micro pause, less than one second
(2.0)	estimated length of pause of one second or more, to nearest 0.5 of a second
wor:d	segmental lengthening
wor-	truncation
[ ]	inaudible speech
[word]	unclear speech
((laughs))	non-lexical occurrence
{word}	talk overlaid by non-lexical occurrence
*	stressed syllable
[ac]	accelerated speech
[dc]	slown speech
[lo]	low pitch register
/\	rising–falling pitch movement

References

Agar, Michael. 1994. *Language Shock*. New York: William Morrow.

Ahmad, Waqar, E.E. Kernohan and M.R Baker. 1989. Patients' choice of general practitioner: Influence of patients' fluency in English and the ethnicity and sex of the doctor. *Journal of the Royal College of General Practitioners* 39: 153–155.

Ainsworth-Vaughn, Nancy. 1998. *Claiming Power in Doctor–Patient Talk*. Oxford: Oxford University Press.

Ali, Nasreen. 2003. Fluency in the consulting room. *British Journal of General Practitioners* 53: 514–515.

Anderson, Joan, Helen Elfert and Magdalene Lai. 1989. Ideology in the clinical context: chronic illness, ethnicity and the discourse on normalisation. *Sociology of Health and Illness* 11(3): 253–278.

Atkinson, Paul. 1995. *Medical Talk and Medical Work*. London: Sage.

Auer, Peter and Friederike Kern. 2000. Three ways of analysing communication between East and West Germans as intercultural communication. In: Aldo di Luzio, Susanne Günthner and Franca Orletti (eds.), *Culture in Communication: Analysis of Intercultural Situations*, 89–116. Amsterdam: John Benjamins.

Bhopal Raj. 1986. Asians' knowledge and behaviour on preventative health issues: smoking, alcohol, heart disease, pregnancy, rickets, malaria prophylaxis and surma. *Community Medicine* 8: 315–321.

Blackford, Jeanine. 1997. Breaking down barriers in clinical practice. *Contemporary Nurse* 6: 15–21.

Bührig, Kristin. 2001. Interpreting in hospitals. In: Sara Cagada, Silvia Gilardoni and Marinette Matthey (eds.), *Communicare in Ambiente Professionale Plurilingue*. Lugano: USI.

Bührig, Kristin and Bernd Meyer. 2005. Ad-hoc interpreting and the achievement of common purposes in doctorpatient communication. In: Juliana House and Jochen Rehbein (eds.), *Multilingual Communication*, 43–62. Amsterdam: John Benjamins.

Candlin, Christopher and Sally Candlin. 2003. Healthcare communication: A problematic site for applied linguistics research. *Annual Review of Applied Linguistics* 23, 134–154.

Cass, Alan, Anne Lowell, Michael Christie, Paul Snelling, Melinda Flack, Betty Marrnganyin and Isaac Brown. 2002. Sharing the true stories: Improving communication between aboriginal patients and health care workers. *Medical Journal of Australia* 176: 466–470.

Cicourel, Aaron. 1983. Hearing is not believing: Language and the structure of belief in medical communication. In: Sue Fisher and Alexandra D. Todd (eds.). 221–239.

Cohen, Suzanne, Jo Moran-Ellis and Chris Smaje. 1999. Children as informal interpreters in GP consultations: pragmatics and ideology. *Sociology of Health and Illness* 21(2): 163–186.

Collins, Jim and Stef Slembrouck. In press. 'You don't know what they translate': language, contact, institutional procedure, and literacy practice in neighbourhood health clinics in urban Flanders. *Journal of Linguistic Anthropology*.

Cook-Gumperz, Jenny and Lawrence Messerman. 1999. Local identities and institutional practices: Constructing the record of professional collaboration. In: Srikant Sarangi and Celia Roberts (eds.), 145–181.

Crawford, Anne. 1994. Black patients white doctors: Stories lost in translation. Cape Town: National Language Project, Cape Town.

Davidson, Brad. 2000. The interpreter as institutional gatekeeper: The sociolinguistic role of interpreters in Spanish–English medical discourse. *Journal of Sociolinguistics* 4/3: 379–405.

Drew, Paul, John Chatwin and Sarah Collins. 2001. Conversation analysis: a method for research into interactions between patients and healthcare professionals. *Health Expectations* 4/1: 58–70.

Duff, Patricia, Ping Wong and Margaret Early. 2000. Learning language for work and life: The linguistic socialisation of immigrant Canadians seeking careers in health care. *Canadian Modern Language Review* 57(1): 9–57.

Ebden, Phillip, Oliver Carey, Arvind Bhatt and Brian Harrison. 1988. The bi-lingual consultation. *Lancet* 1: 347.

Erickson, Frederick. 1999. Appropriation of voice and presentation of self as a fellow physician: aspects of a discourse of apprenticeship in medicine. In: Srikant Sarangi and Celia Roberts (eds.), 109–143.

Erickson, Frederick and William Rittenberg. 1987. Topic control and person control: A thorny problem for foreign physicians in interaction with American patients. *Discourse Processes* 10: 401–415.

Fisher, Sue. 1995. *Nursing Wounds: Nurse Practitioners/Doctors/Women Patients and the Negotiation of Meaning.* New Brunswick, NJ: Rutgers University Press.

Fisher, Sue and Alexandra D. Todd (eds.). 1983. *The Social Organisation of Doctor–Patient Communication.* Washington, DC: Centre for Applied Linguistics.

Fleischman, Suzanne. 2001. Language and medicine. In: Deborah Schiffrin, Deborah Tannen and Heidi Ehrenberger Hamilton (eds.), *Handbook of Discourse Analysis*: 470–502. Oxford: Blackwell.

Freeman, Sarah and Monica Heller (eds.). 1987. *Medical Discourse.* Special Issue of *Text* 7(1).

Goffman, Erving. 1974. *Frame Analysis.* New York: Harper and Row.

Green, Judith, Caroline Free, Vanita Bhavnani and Anthony Newman. 2005. Translators and mediators: bilingual young people's accounts of their interpreting work in health care. *Social Science and Medicine* 60: 2097–2110.

Gumperz, John. 1982. *Discourse Strategies.* Cambridge: Cambridge University Press.

Gumperz, John. 1996. The linguistic and cultural relativity of inference. In: John Gumperz and Stephen Levinson (eds.), 374–406.

Gumperz, John. 1999. On interactional sociolinguistic method. In: Srikant Sarangi and Celia Roberts (eds.), *Talk, Work and Institutional Order: Discourse in Medical, Mediation and Management Settings*, 453–471. Berlin: Mouton de Gruyter.

Gumperz, John and Stephen Levinson (eds.). 1996. *Rethinking Linguistic Relativity.* Cambridge: Cambridge University Press.

Gumperz, John and Jenny Cook-Gumperz. 2007. Discourse, cultural diversity and communication: a linguistic anthropological perspective. In: Helga Kotthoff and Helen Spencer-Oatey (eds.), *Handbook of Intercultural Communication*, 13–30. Berlin: Mouton de Gruyter.

Hamilton, Heidi. 2004. Symptoms and signs in particular: The influence of the medical concern on the shape of physician–patients talk. *Communication and Medicine* 1/1: 59–70.

ten Have, Paul. 1995. Medical ethnomethodology: an overview. *Human Studies* 18: 245–261.

Helman, Cecil. 1994. *Culture, Health and Illness*, third edition. Bristol: Wright.

Henley, Alix and Judith Schott. 1999. *Culture, Religion and Patient Care in a Multi-ethnic Society: A Handlbook for Professionals.* London: Age Concern.

Hyden, Lars-Christer and Elliot Mishler. 1999. Language and medicine. *Annual Review of Applied Linguistics* 19: 174–192.

Iedema, Rick and Hermine Scheeres. 2003. From doing to talking work: Renegotiating knowing, doing and identity. *Applied Linguistics* 24: 316–337.

Iedema, Rick, Carl Rhodes and Hermine Scheeres. In press. Surveillance, resistance, observance: exploring the teleo-affective intensity of identity (at) work. *Organization Studies.*

Jacobs, Elizabeth, Diane Lauderdale, David Meltzer, Jeanette Shorey, Wendy Levinson and Ronald Thisted. 2001. Impact of interpreter services on delivery of health care to limited Englishproficient patients. *Journal of General Internal Medicine* 16(7): 468–74.

Kaufert, Joseph and William Koolage. 1984. Role conflict among 'cultural brokers': the experience of native Canadian medical interpreters. *Social Science and Medicine* 18(3): 283–286.

Kleinman, Arthur. 1988. *The Illness Narratives: Suffering, Healing and the Human Condition.* New York: Basic Books.

Levinson, Stephen. 1997. Contextualising contextualisation cues. In: Susan Eerdmans, C. Previgagno and Paul Thibault (eds.), *Discussing Communication Analysis 1: John Gumperz*, 24–30. Lausanne: Beta Press.

Manderson, Lenora and Pascale Allotey. 2003. Cultural politics and clinical competence in the Australian Health Service. *Anthropology and Medicine* 10(1): 71–85.

McKay, Susan and Jeffery Pittam. 2002. *Language and Health Care.* Special Issue *Journal of Language and Social Psychology* 21(1).

McNamara, Tim. 1997. Problematising content validity: The Occupational English Test as a measure of medical communication. *Melbourne Papers in Language and Testing* 6(1).

Meyer, Bernd. 2001. How untrained interpreters handle medical terms. In: Ian Mason (ed.), *Triadic Exchanges. Studies in Dialogue Interpreting.* Manchester: St Jerome.

Mishler, Elliot. 1984. *The Discourse of Medicine: Dialectics of Medical Interviews.* Norwood, NJ: Ablex.

Moss, Becky and Celia Roberts. 2005. Explanations, explanations, explanations: How do patients with limited English construct narrative accounts? *Family Practice* 22(4) 412–418.

Ochs, Elinor. 1996. Linguistic resources for socialising humanity. In: John Gumperz and Stephen Levinson (eds.), Rethinking Linguistic Relativity 407–437.

Ohtaki, Sachiko, Toshio Ohtakia and Michael Fetters. 2003. Doctor–patient communication: a comparison of USA and Japan. *Family Practice* 20(3): 276–282.

Ong, L.M., J.C. DeHaes, A.M. Hoos and F.B. Lammes. 1995. Doctor–patient communication: a review of the literature. *Social Science and Medicine* 40/7: 903–918.

Pauwels, Anne (ed.). 1991. *Cross-cultural Communication in Medical Encounters*. Monash: Communicative Languages in the Profession Unit.

Pauwels, Anne. 1994. Applying linguistic insights in intercultural communication to professional training programmes. An Australian case study. *Multilingua* 13 1/2: 195–212.

Pettinari, Catherine. 1988. *Task, Talk and Text in the Operating Room: A Study in Medical Discourse*. Norwood, NJ: Ablex.

Putsch, R.W. 1985. Cross cultural communication: The special case of the interpreters in health care. *Journal of the American Medical Association* 254: 3344–334.

Rack, Philip. 1991. *Race, Culture and Mental Disorder*, Second edition. London: Routledge.

Rivedeneyra, R., V. Elderkin-Thompson, R. Silver and H. Waitzkin. 2000. Patient-centredness in medical encounters requiring an interpreter. *American Journal of Medicine* 108/6: 470–474.

Roberts, Celia and Srikant Sarangi. 1999. Hybridity in gatekeeping discourse: Issues of practical relevance for the researcher. In: Srikant Sarangi and Celia Roberts (eds.), 473–503.

Roberts, Celia, Srikant Sarangi, Lesley Southgate, Risheard Wakeford and Valerie Wass. 2000. Oral examinations, equal opportunities, ethnicity and fairness in the MRCGP. *British Medical Journal* 320: 370–374.

Roberts, Celia, Valerie Wass, Roger Jones, Srikant Sarangi and Annie Gillett. 2003. A discourse analysis study of 'good' and 'poor' communication in an OSCE: a proposed new framework for teaching students. *Medical Education* 37: 192–201.

Roberts, Celia, Srikant Sarangi and Becky Moss. 2004. Presentation of self and symptoms in primary care consultations involving patients from non-English speaking backgrounds. *Communication and Medicine* 1/2: 159–169.

Roberts, Celia, Becky Moss, Valerie Wass, Srikant Sarangi and Roger Jones. 2005. Misunderstandings: a qualitative study of primary care consultations in multilingual settings, and educational implications. *Medical Education* 39: 465–475.

Sarangi, Srikant. 2004. Towards a communicative mentality in medical and health care practice: Editorial. *Communication and Medicine* 1/2: 1–11.

Sarangi, Srikant and Celia Roberts (eds.). 1999. *Talk, Work and Institutional Order: Discourse in Medical, Mediation and Management Settings*. Berlin: Mouton de Gruyter.

Silverman, David. 1987. *Communication and Medical Practice*. London: Sage.

Skelton, John, Joe Kai, and Rhian Loudon. 2001. Cross-cultural communication in medicine: questions for educators. *Medical Education* 35/3, 257–261.

Tannen, Deborah and Cynthia Wallet. 1986. Medical professions and parents: A linguistic analysis of communication across contexts. *Language in Society* 15, 295–312.

Todd, Alexandra Dundas. 1984. The prescription of contraception. *Discourse Processes* 7: 171–200.

West, Candace. 1984. *Routine complications: Troubles in talk between doctors and patients*. Bloomington: Indiana University Press.

Wodak, Ruth. 1997. Discourse-sociolinguistics and the study of doctor–patient interaction. In: Britt-Louise Gunnarsson, Per Linell and Bengt Nordberg (eds.), *The Construction of Professional Discourse*, 173–2000. London: Longman.

12

Schools and Cultural Difference

Albert Scherr

As a rule, intercultural communication takes place between individuals who have been educated in schools, and these will, to some degree, have inculcated in them an understanding of their national statehood and culture. For indeed schools are politically mandated to transmit the basic elements of citizenship and national identity, in order to ensure the continuity and endurance of the political community. This is true not only in those states that actively promote national history, culture and identity; it is also true where prevailing political values explicitly reject nationalistic programs and ideologies. At the same time, schools are institutions that provoke some portion of their pupils to distance themselves from the identity the schools seek to promote. Youthful rebellion and the development of youth sub-cultures arise not the least from confrontation with the norms of the dominant culture represented in school curricula and practices (Willis 1977, Eckert 2000).

For the transmission of national collective identity, and more generally for the formation, transmission and acquisition of collective identifications of all sorts, language obviously plays a central role; and just as the acceptance of a tendered national identity usually goes hand in hand with the acquisition of a national standard language, independent linguistic varieties often arise in connection with collectively felt non-national, regional, ethnic or youth-culture identities (Eckert 2000; Harris and Rampton 2003). As Ben Rampton (2003: 403) argues, the use of dialects by minority pupils and codeswitching in schools can "constitute acts of resistance within a racist society".

Thus, with respect to school as the institution which is centrally important for language acquisition and the development of individuals' construction of their cultural membership, both aspects are systematically intertwined.

This contribution addresses, from an international, comparative perspective, the questions of how schools as national, state-managed institutions bring forth collective identities and distinctions, and of how they establish perspectives on important features of non-national cultural identity (e.g., regional, ethnic, religious). It will reveal that how social and cultural heterogeneity are treated in the context of school-based socialization and education is closely related to influential socio-political programs, and that these can only be understood against the background of the given interlocking structures of social inequality and cultural identification.

1. School, Nation, Culture, and Language

State-managed education of children and adolescents in schools is a fundamental characteristic of modern societies. Historically and socio-systematically, there is an intimate connection between industrial capitalism, nation-statehood, the establishment of state schools, and the enforcement of universal schooling, as has been pointed out by Talcott Parsons (Parsons 1971: 94.). On the one hand, the growth and enforcement of a state-managed educational system can be understood as a reaction to the social, spatial and temporal separations between family and wage-earning work that industrialization imposed, for industrial work meant that families were no longer in a position to give their children the knowledge needed to enter the work force. Thus, general education outside the family became the rule rather than the exception. On the other hand, however—and for the present purposes this is the decisive point— schools acquired essential significance in the effort to enforce the political idea of a unified national state with a homogeneous culture and language. Schools were to enable all future citizens to communicate in the standard national language, and they were meant to give them a historical and political understanding of themselves as citizens as well as a national identity (cf. Gellner 1983: Chapter 3).

The establishment and school-based transmission of a unified national linguistic standard, with a sharply drawn boundary to dialects and the linguistic standards of other nations, is by no means merely a response to functional demands of industrial capitalism or nation-state democracy. The "demand for the linguistically homogeneous nation and the clearly distinct national language" was, and for more than accidental reasons "remains a standard part of nationalist ideology" (Barbour 2000: 14). Calls to national patriotism and unity resonate most effectively with members of the national "imagined community" (Anderson 1991) when these, and no others, share the same common language. Seen in this light, the establishment of national languages is an essential part of the process that creates nation-states and national identities. Hence, it is hardly surprising that independence movements are often mingled with linguistic policies, and the development of new nations—as happened during the disintegration of Yugoslavia—is accompanied by efforts to emphasize and strengthen linguistic differences and boundaries (Barbour and Carmichael 2000).

Furthermore, to the extent that schools implement certain nationally oriented curricula (historical perspectives, national literary canons, geographic descriptions), they are made the means of instilling in children and adolescents a culture of the nation-state. From a socio-historical perspective the establishment of schools is part of the effort to establish a national culture and language and to marginalize traditional regional and class-specific cultures and languages, as well as to establish cultural boundaries to other nations (Hobsbawm 1990: 80). Out of a population excluded from political representation, living in local and regional frames of reference, schools are established to create citizens aware of their nation, who understand the language of their national government, feel themselves represented by it, are ready to serve in its armed forces, are willing to migrate within the national boundaries, and are prepared to accept the demands of working in its factories and living in its cities. Education is thus a key element in nation building, while schools and armies are an essential component of the state's communicative apparatus, meant "to spread the image and the heritage of the 'nation' and to inculcate attachment to it and to attach all to country and flag, often 'inventing traditions' or even nations for this purpose" (Hobsbawm 1990: 91).

Today, this patriotic amalgam of education with nation-state, national language and national culture still has its adherents, but world-wide it is by no means the only accepted model. To be sure, schools continue to be important socio-political institutions that must help to transmit a national language, as well as nationally significant knowledge, values and norms. Nevertheless, the experience of two world wars, the globalization of mass-media communications and trade, the social movements of the 1960s and 1970s and the large-scale, international migration of workers have led—especially in middle and northern Europe—to criticism of nationalist ideologies as well as to an influential reexamination of the idea that societies can only be conceived as nation-states, each with a uniform language and national culture. Processes of cultural pluralization, liberalization and differentiation, as well as the development of an increasingly trans-national culture, both popular and educated, have made the notion of autonomous national cultures less convincing. Additionally, the assertive political claims of migrants and minorities to an independent cultural status, the failure of the 'melting pot' in the USA and social developments in Canada have led to the political ideal of a 'multicultural society', that is, to the concept of a society still organized as a national state, distinguishing its citizens legally and politically from non-citizens and instituting a nationally defined legal system and standard language, but at the same time proclaiming linguistic, cultural and religious diversity as permitted or even welcome (Kymlicka 1995).

These developments have far-reaching consequences for the educational system and the schools of such states, as they change the socio-political norms to which pedagogical theory and practice are oriented. They tend to undermine the conception of the school as an institution meant to instill the values and norms of a national culture, and they lend more political and pedagogical weight to the goal of respecting cultural differences. This includes the discussion on the right of students to be instructed in their first language (Honeyford 2003). By no means, however, does this reduce the significance of national differences in educational practice, for the questions of what passes for 'culture and cultures', i.e., whether and in what sense education can claim to be founded on culture-neutral knowledge and universal values, and what place regional, religious and ethnic cultures can have in the educational program— these questions currently receive widely differing answers on political stages and in the resulting pedagogical discourses.

The following sections present some of the ways in which the schools and educational systems of three countries are approaching the treatment of culture and cultural differences. The interconnections of social policy, the reproduction of culture, and education will be discussed with reference to the educational systems of France, Britain and Canada, along with theories of intercultural pedagogy. The aim will be to show that the chosen socio-political frameworks not only have wide-reaching organizational and legal consequences, but that they also influence concrete behavioral features of the school environments.

2. Education, Reproduction of Culture and Multiculturalism

As social institutions, schools are charged with ensuring that all citizens acquire a common language as well as the knowledge, behavior patterns, value orientations and norms that are felt to be indispensable for life in their society. Universally mandatory schooling is an expression of this duty. Schooling thus is based, for one, on assumptions about the knowledge and skills necessary to meet the demands of industry and political life. Additionally, pedagogical theory and practice adopt assumptions about which skills, knowledge, moral and political convictions best fulfill current educational ideals. Now, pedagogically significant ideas about personality development and about worthwhile knowledge and skills are not autonomously derived from pedagogical theory, as has been repeatedly shown since the classic studies of Emile Durkheim (1922) and Siegfried Bernfeld (1973). Rather, they are expressions of socially dominant structures, models and norms, or of critical reactions to these in pedagogical theory and discourse. Accordingly, educational sociology regards the practice of schools as a constitutive element of societal reproduction, in the sense of its transmitting socially dominant values, norms and behavioral tendencies. Currently prominent theories and studies focus not only on the forms and content consciously known to their practitioners, but also on those structures and practices in which social demands reproduce themselves as self-evident and unquestioned background assumptions. This perspective displays educational practice as a component in the larger system that inculcates culture, in the sense of the restraining rules, norms, values, symbols, meanings and bodies of knowledge upon which the culture rests. Socio-historical, sociological and pedagogical studies have shown, furthermore, that school-induced socialization must be examined with respect to the question of how it contributes to enforcement of a particular social discipline and to the formation of personality structures typical of the culture (Apple 1982; Dreeben 1970; Foucault 1979; Holzkamp 1993).

Traditional pedagogical views have accordingly seen the task of schools as precisely that of upholding the basic postulates of the national culture, and they succeed to the extent that pupils acquire the conviction that these have no alternatives or are superior to those of other nations.

Seen this way, school-induced socialization has an enormous socio-political meaning, and as a result the forms and content of schooling are an enduring source of social conflict. School is thus not only the place where the hegemony of the dominant culture is played out and transmitted; it is also the scene of daily conflicts about legitimate vs. illegitimate behaviors and language, as well as about recognition of the social relevance of hegemonial values, norms and knowledge (Willis 1977). Here children from diverse cultural backgrounds come in contact and in conflict, and this alone demands an examination of the cultural norms of the schools' institutional frameworks as well as of their daily practice. Relevant questions concern the ways in which stereotypes of nation, race, ethnicity and religion affect communication in schools, how legitimate vs. illegitimate knowledge and language are distinguished, how normal and deviant behaviors are marked, and how national, religious, ethnic and sex-related identifications are established and represented. Discussions on the legitimate use of languages in schools in multilingual settings can so be linked to "struggles over the establishment of authority and legitimacy" (Heller and Martin-Jones 2003a: ix). One possibility of carrying out social conflicts is by means of the legitimate language and language uses (Heller and Martin Jones 2003b).

Hence theories and programs of multicultural education demand that pedagogical practice include sensitivity to cultural differences. They reject pedagogical models meant to enforce conformity to a nationally oriented culture and instead emphasize a perspective that accepts a multiplicity of differing and equally valuable nationally, religiously and ethnically formed cultures. In contrast to traditional social and pedagogical theories, they adopt a comparative view that sees the immediate social forms not as unquestionably given and natural, but rather as constitutive elements of various cultural frameworks. Adopting such a perspective imposes definite and pedagogically significant requirements for communication and understanding: individual knowledge and/or communicative activities must be interpreted within one of many possible cultural backgrounds. Accordingly, difficulties in mutual understanding among individuals and social groups are traced to differences among cultures. Problems and conflicts are likely when the participants in the intercultural dialogue—in contrast to scientific observers of the dialogue—remain naively caught in the perspective of their own culture, unable to adopt a larger view that would allow them to go beyond their own implicit assumptions and certainties. Thus, concepts for inter-and multicultural education attempt to instill awareness in all participants of the cultural embeddedness of individuals' experience and action. Further, multicultural education seeks to respond to the situation of socially disadvantaged migrants and minorities "so that students from diverse racial, ethnic, and social-class groups will experience educational equality" (Banks and Banks 2001: 3).

What is often overlooked in proposals for multicultural education is the difficulty of clearly and unambiguously identifying particular cultures and of assigning individuals or social groups to closed and clearly bounded cultural frameworks. Rather, it is necessary to look not just at cultures as a source of communicative problems, but also at the social conditions and practices by which cultures are created and differentiated from one another, not as closed communicative systems but as flexible interpretational frameworks; for every instance of 'intercultural' communication is in reality socially situated, that is, framed in a *single* encompassing system of social labellings and cultural differences, and the participants in intercultural communication operate with knowledge of their cultural membership, acquired in shared processes of socialization (Hall and du Gay 2002).

Educational socialization is relevant for the study of intercultural communication in four specific respects:

First, schools are institutions for the presentation and enforcement of national, ethnic and religious identifications—but also the locus of resistance against assimilation to the hegemonial culture. *Second,* schools are the central agents of socialization, so that much of the cultural background and cultural identification which individuals bring into intercultural dialogue have been acquired not in autonomously native cultures but in the schools themselves. *Third,* schools are social meeting points that are not isolated from the cultural differences, conflicts and adaptive dynamics found elsewhere; rather, they host a continuous background of 'doing culture', in which the interactions among pupils and teachers lead the participants to form ideas about various cultures and to differentiate themselves from others via cultural labels. Recognizing this, in pedagogical practice, 'culture' is often invoked as an explanatory scheme in reacting to difficult and irritating behavior, when it seems plausible to interpret the behavior as the expression of pupils' backgrounds and families. *Fourth,* in observations and analyses of interactions it has been shown that attributions to cultural and ethnic factors, 'enlightened' by cultural theory, are often simplistic and that they tend to go hand in hand with projective and grossly simplifying explanations of the observed behavior (cf. e.g. Schiffauer et al. 2002).

By contrast, numerous and various criticisms of an inadequately thought-through multiculturalism have pointed out that individuals in modern societies cannot be intelligibly understood solely as products of a culture, which alone determines their experiences, thoughts and actions. Instead, it is necessary to take the multiplicity of cultural and social influences in individuals' lives into account, as well as the individual and collective forms of critical distancing and creative transformations of cultural givens that are characteristic of modern societies.

3. Socio-Political Aspects and Educational Models for Dealing With Cultural Differences

Despite a widespread expectation to the contrary, supported by sociological theories of modernization, cultural differences and identifications have in fact lost importance neither in the world community nor within nation-states. Such identifications are not merely holdovers from hierarchical societies, religions, ethnic and regional traditions that have successfully resisted the pressure of national leveling. In fact, in modern social conflicts, elements of shared national, ethnic, racial or religious identification have been introduced again and again as part of the social dynamic of conflict (Castells 1995). This is true not only of so-called ethnic conflicts, carried out openly and even violently, but also of social relations between natives and migrants or majorities and minorities. Even in societies lacking visible signs of ethnic, national or religious conflict, migrants are often socially disadvantaged and suffer discriminatory labeling with specific characteristics. Under these conditions, cultural, ethnic and religious identifications serve as a kind of collective self-assertion against the situation imposed by the host society.

Socialization and education in schools are, of course, not insulated from these conflicts, and it is worthwhile to study how social and cultural identifications play out within them. To this end we can distinguish three problem areas:

- External social, political and legal conditions (including the economic, political, and legal status of migrants; dominant conceptions of national identity; linguistic and cultural policies; connections between cultural, ethnic and religious attributions and forms of social discrimination; prevalence of xenophobic or racial ideologies)
- Within the community, the roles schools assume in the area of conflict over cultural supremacy (in particular, administratively propagated ideas, norms and curricula; treatment of language and cultural symbols; policies concerning the composition of classes and of the faculty; relations to the local community)
- Within schools, how nationality, language, culture, race, ethnicity and religion are treated in the curricula and in the classroom, and how ethnic, cultural, linguistic, racial and religious attributions influence the evaluation and encouragement of pupils.

Comparative international studies (e.g., Schiffauer et al. 2002; Hormel and Scherr 2004) have shown factors in all of these areas to have important consequences.

Thus, teachers in Canadian schools are required to be sensitive to the ethnic and religious orientations of their pupils and to take these into account when choosing instructional materials and methods. In German schools, on the other hand, the dominant attitude requires teachers to give special attention to deficits in language and family background among immigrant children. French teachers, on the other hand, are deliberately not informed about the nationality and religion of their pupils, to promote equal treatment of all, unbiased by such factors. Further comparison of Canadian with German and French schools makes clear that assumptions about cultural 'stamps' are by no means independent of the social positions of immigrants and minorities, where the social and economic factors are frequently misunderstood as expressions of cultural difference—for example, when factors like social class and parents' formal education and occupation are ignored, and success or failure in school is attributed to cultural influences.

Studies of multicultural education have shown that in the interaction between teachers and pupils, popular ethnic, religious and cultural stereotypes shape teachers' expectations about the abilities of pupils who appear to come from corresponding backgrounds. In language education, for example, a recent German study shows that teachers tend to attribute linguistic deficits to children with immigrant backgrounds (Weber 2003). This phenomenon contributes to the judgment that immigrant children have low linguistic competence. Hugh Mehan et al. (2001) cite various studies demonstrating that in US schools, as well, deficiencies among minority pupils are attributed to cultural factors. With the introduction of multicultural approaches, with new forms of communication and new content, the effects of presumed cultural determinants disappeared, making evident the causal role of a particular combination of teaching approach with social and cultural backgrounds of the pupils.

Whether schools treat racism, xenophobia, and discrimination as challenges deserving a proactive effort, or as problems that can be neglected, is still a matter of great importance. Even where a commitment to facing the problems of multicultural education has been made, the various national approaches, which often derive from a nation-state's fundamental values and historical experience and support its claim to democratic legitimacy, lead to considerable differences in educational practice. Some of these will be sketched in the next section.

3.1. Education for Citizenship or Multicultural Education

In educational policy-making, cultural differences are seldom treated in the abstract but rather in reference to the situations of immigrants or in the framework of conflicts about adequate recognition of national, religious or ethnic minorities. This in itself establishes a problematic framework, insofar as imagined cultural differences among social groups can be projected onto the actual immigrants or minorities, while other potentially meaningful differences, like those between middle-class and working-class culture or between various political milieus, are neglected. Although a politically and pedagogically influential line of thought insists on recognizing the autonomy of national, ethnic and religious groupings, any discussion of cultural differences in an educational context cannot ignore the inevitable interdependency of cultural attributions and socioeconomic status. How educational practice recognizes and deals with these issues varies widely among states. Here we shall look at three representative approaches, in France, Britain and Canada.

One common feature of the policies in these countries is their goal of making schools places where pupils witness equality and fairness in the relationships between natives and immigrants, as well as between majorities and minorities. All, however, face one grave difficulty that repeatedly surfaces in sociological studies: unequal socio-economic backgrounds and resulting attitudes toward the educational system strongly affect pupils' relative chances for success, and the chances of the disadvantaged can be improved by compensatory schooling only to a limited degree (Bernstein 1977; Bourdieu and Passeron 1990; Dubet and Duru-Bellat 2000; McDonald 1999). The British and Canadian models differ from the French model, in that the former attempt to recognize cultural and social differences and implement compensatory measures, while the French system tries to insulate the educational system from differences in social status, nationality, religion and ethnicity. Simplified and idealized, France and Canada present a pair of maximally contrasting approaches—republican universalism vs. multiculturalism—in which the implications of the underlying assumptions can be seen with especial clarity. In France the ideal of a religiously, culturally and ethnically neutral state reigns, resting on consensually accepted ideals and values of the Enlightenment, of the Declaration of the Rights of Man and Citizen and of democracy, instituted in a republic of free and equal citizens. By contrast, Canada's population, long comprising two distinct national and linguistic groupings, has destined it to embrace most fully a multicultural conception of the national state, and with it, multicultural concepts of education.

3.2. Fundamental Differences Between Canadian Multiculturalism and French Republicanism

Following Kymlicka (1995, 1997), Canada can be characterized as a liberal state and a 'civic nation', in which neither ethnic membership nor cultural identity play a role in defining citizenship. What matters are continuous residence and a willingness to acquire one of the national languages as well as elementary knowledge of Canadian history. All residents are granted formally equal political and social rights, access to state services and to the labor market. Citizens and landed immigrants enjoy equal legal status with the exception that only citizens have the right to vote and stand for office. The socio-economic situation of immigrants and minorities is quite heterogeneous, resulting from a selective immigration policy that favors highly qualified workers, and many immigrants belong to a relatively privileged class. Problems associated with disadvantaged classes are found most often in the indigenous population (Adam 2002; Geißler 2003: 24). Thus, in contrast to many European countries, Canadian immigrants are not typically socio-economically disadvantaged, and they do not have lower than normal rates of success in the educational system.

As in England, Canadian educational policy and pedagogical practice are multicultural and anti-racist (McLeod 1992; Moodley 1992, 1995). Since 1971 a national policy of multiculturalism has been implemented that aims not only to understand the cultural backgrounds of immigrants but also to orient and differentiate the school curricula accordingly, to the point of adapting styles and methods of teaching to pupils' backgrounds. Cultural multiplicity is not reduced to folkloristic enrichment of the dominant culture nor to helping immigrants to assimilate successfully. In fact, the goal of having culturally neutral schooling is fundamentally relativized, and schools are opened to local communities so as to let all cultural groupings participate in their development.

The educational system of France presents a stark contrast to that of Canada, and to that of Great Britain, as well. Its guiding principle is not that of social and cultural diversity but rather the ideal of *égalité*, the political and legal equality of all citizens. The republican cast of French immigration and integration policy shows itself in the conviction that French culture (*civilisation*) realizes universal modern values. It postulates that recognition of these values is the foundation upon which social integration, and therefore the relevant educational concepts and programs, must build (Dubet and Duru-Bellat 2000: 62ff.; Wieviorka 2003: 21). The historical background can be found in the belief of French political and intellectual elites in their own historical superiority:

> At bottom the *école publique* of Jules Ferry [beginning of the nineteenth century—A.S.] wanted to open the way to the universal for both children of the mother country as well those from the colonies. It led the former out of the narrow bounds of their dialects, their villages and towns, and the latter out of their savagery.
>
> Wieviorka 2003: 23

It follows from the aim of transmitting universal culture that multicultural and community-oriented education must be strictly rejected. In 2003 this principle was again invoked in the debate over the wearing of scarves as religious dress in schools; the winning side argued for the assumed culturally neutral republican principles, and against allowing culture-specific symbols. These, in contrast to the modern, universal cultural framework of the schools, are thus implicitly suspected of being primitive and pre-democratic, and for them there can be no place in a society of free and equal citizens.

A further corollary of this basic orientation is that deliberate, compensatory support for minorities is not compatible with the principle of equality and equal treatment of all citizens. Racism and discrimination are to be overcome by an appropriate form of education, emphasizing republican values, rather than by recognizing cultural differences. Education for citizenship and political autonomy are thus central themes, and it is expected that a citizen brought up with these enlightened, universal principles will reject racism and ethnic discrimination. French educational policy and practice are thus guided not by the goal of instilling acceptance of, and willingness to communicate with other cultures, but rather the goal of superseding cultural particularism, so that cultural differences lose their significance.

The traditional republican concepts of *Citoyenneté* and *Civilité* are also invoked as elements of social measures meant to react to social conflicts in cities and suburban slums, regional segregation and ethnic stereotyping of social inequality (Bourdieu et al. 2002; Dubet and Lapeyronnie 1992). Nevertheless, immigrants in France suffer high rates of unemployment, and, statistically seen, their chances for social advancement are meager. A significant portion of the children and adolescents have difficult school careers, and even those who obtain higher levels of education must reckon with considerable discrimination in the labor market. Social marginalization is the fate of many second-generation immigrants.

It will not be surprising that the basic differences between Canadian and French education have important consequences on all levels of educational politics and practice, as some selected aspects of these will reveal.

3.3. Ethnic Labeling in Schools

In societies with sizable immigrant populations, the existence of and differences among various ethnic groups become topics of conversation, so that the society comes to postulate a number of distinct communities, each having a distinct history and culture, either claimed by the community or attributed to it by the others. The creation of ethnic differences and identifications is thus a social process, and schools are among the social participants. In Germany it can be shown that the social discrimination of pupils from immigrant backgrounds is a topic around which ethnically flavored group identities develop, finally being claimed as a positive point of reference in the groups' collective identities (Bommes and Scherr 1991; Tertilt 1996). Similar phenomena have been reported in France. In French schools, however, manifest symbolic references to religion or ethnicity are treated as illegitimate, so that ethnic symbols and labellings acquire an additional meaning they could not otherwise have: they signify rejection of the official program of ethnically neutral schooling.

In England and Canada, on the other hand, ethnic identification is seen in the political and educational spheres as a legitimate reference to distinctive cultural differences, and—differently from Germany and France—it can legitimately be invoked as an explanatory or justifying factor in official documents and proceedings. One reason for the acceptance of ethnicity in Britain is that immigrants from former colonies often possess British passports, and in Canada citizenship is attained with relative ease after immigration. Hence, immigrant groups cannot be excluded on the basis of legal status, and in Britain and Canada ethnicity tends to become a category that merely distinguishes groups within one and the same body politic.

In British schools ethnicity can be invoked in the context of proceedings that involve social inequality, social distance and racial discrimination. Pupils are categorized according to ethnically formulated criteria, which are also employed in gathering official statistics. The criteria are based on a heterogeneous set of attributes (race, nationality, religion, language, self-defined ethnicity) and are actually not strictly ethnic categories. A document from the Department for Education and Skills (DfES 2003: 8) prescribes the following set of categories: White, Mixed, Asian or Asian British, Black or Black British, Chinese. The category Asian is further sub-divided into Indian, Pakistani, etc. In schools such categories are used for collecting statistics on attendance, discrimination cases, and the treatment of racially motivated conflicts.

The guidelines established here for official and for self-classification are hardly suited for educational contexts, nor for characterizing actual cultural differences. They make evident a fundamental problem with proactive multicultural and anti-discriminatory programs: in order to observe and record specific difficulties that immigrants and minorities face, it is first necessary to obtain unambiguous categorizations or self-categorizations of all individuals who might be affected. This, however, indulges and confirms precisely the same categorizations that the programs are meant to overcome. No way out of this dilemma is visible, for all proactive measures must necessarily be directed to specific disadvantaged and discriminated groups.

3.4. Compensatory and Anti-Discriminatory Policies

In Canada and Britain schools participate in actively combating the disadvantaged status of immigrants and minorities. Special importance is given to measures directed at linguistic deficiencies. In the framework of an anti-discrimination program, the guidelines of the Ontario Ministry of Education for development of an 'inclusive curriculum' prescribe that pupils whose first language is neither English nor French shall receive adequate offerings to learn a school's language of instruction. Likewise, however, courses in the minority languages of the community are to be offered, and pupils are to be encouraged to develop their knowledge of their first language. Furthermore, the guidelines emphasize that dialects differing from Canadian Standard English are not to be stigmatized (Ministry of Education and Training Ontario 1993: 14). Thus,

Canadian educational policies differ radically from the French program of ethnically blind equality, whose efforts are concentrated on measures directed against intentional discrimination and racial insults.

3.5. Involvement and Exclusion of Communities

Opening schools to the communities they serve is a key measure in the school reforms that have been attempted in Canada and in Britain, one meant to draw the experience and concerns of immigrant and minority groups into the schools' development. The schools actively seek to improve communication with parents from immigrant populations, in order to compensate for these parents' under-representation in school activities, conferences and in the parent–teacher associations. Additional measures have been taken in Britain and Canada to overcome language barriers that hinder parents from participating in school affairs.

In France, on the other hand, schools are understood to be neutral institutions committed to republican universalism, and their task is therefore taken to be that of overcoming regional and ethnic identifications as well as cultural particularism. Pupils are to be perceived and treated above all as individuals and as citizens, not as members of groups, and this is meant to enable them to shake off traditional cultural and religious ties. This orientation brings with it the goal of insulating both pupils and educational practice from the parents' influence. Thus, in contrast to Britain and Canada, no special effort is made to involve parents in school affairs, as representatives of a community or of a culture of origin, and obtaining their participation is not a goal of French educational policy. Nevertheless, immigrants do join political initiatives that speak out on socially controversial issues, among them those that affect education. These attitudes toward schools' relationships to their immediate communities and their significant cultural symbols find expression in the architectural features of French schools, as a recent ethnographic study has shown (Schiffauer et al. 2002): they are typically isolated from their surroundings by walls, fences and closed gates, while British schools tend to lack such isolating elements.

3.6. Curricula

Adopting the goal of transmitting an adequate representation of the knowledge and history of its minorities, Canadian educational policy has committed itself to multiculturalism and the abandonment of a Europe-centric, dominant culture in its school curricula. An additional goal is to scrutinize all educational materials for cultural stereotypes and prejudices. Schools not only permit but encourage pupils to express their identities with cultural and religious symbols and clothing. In all school subjects an effort is made to make reference to the traditions and cultural accomplishments of various groups. So, for example, the mathematics curriculum includes both Chinese arithmetic and that of the 'first nations'. Such curricula are seen not only as necessary for improving the motivation of minorities and improving their chances of success, rather, on a more fundamental level it is assumed that how the elements of knowledge are presented and transmitted has a significant influence on attitudes that the majority groups develop with respect to the minorities. To this end, members of the majority culture are compelled to learn about cultural accomplishments and important items of knowledge that stem from the minority cultures.

Multiculturalism on this pattern is vehemently rejected in France and therefore plays no role in curricular development. In the framework of citizenship education, cultural differences and variety are primarily discussed in terms of defining the boundaries between legitimate claims to cultural particularity and the demands imposed by republican values and civil rights. In emphasizing the supreme claims of democratic values and norms, as well as of human rights, French curricula try to present an orientation having universal validity, superior to all traditional cultures (Centre nationale de documentation pédagogique 2000a, b).

Like the French *Education à la Citoyenneté*, the British *Citizenship Curriculum* takes a skeptical view of the labellings implicit in naive multiculturalism. This position has nevertheless led to quite different consequences. The *Citizenship Curriculum* recognizes the positive importance of social and individual alliances, as well as the ways in which cultural and ethnic labelling can lead to discrimination (Department of Education and Skills 2002).

4. Conclusions

The various ways of dealing with cultural differences in education can be understood adequately only against the background of each country's social and political situation and the goals underlying its national policies. These express socially influential assumptions about cultural differences and their significance which cannot be ignored in educational communication, and which are often felt by teachers, parents and pupils to be the correct view of their social reality.

Nationalistically oriented concepts of education have not lost favor and are still in force in many countries. However, programs like those of Canada and Britain, based on political and pedagogical multiculturalism and meant to encourage sensitive appreciation of cultural differences and to overcome social and economic disadvantages, have also become influential. These programs tend to distance themselves from the idea that cultural differences and problems in intercultural communication can be ignored in educational practice or overcome by assimilating all pupils to the same national culture. At the same time, multicultural education is by no means a panacea for social and cultural tensions, for the institutional recognition of ethnic differences goes hand in hand with tendencies to accept and fix ethnic labellings and prejudices (see Reisigl in this volume). This leads to the paradox of trying to overcome ethnicity as a mechanism of discrimination and repression by elevating ethnicity to the status of a legitimate category for steering social and educational practice. Thus, to reduce the importance of ethnic labelling, pupils are in fact ethnically labeled, in the end giving these labellings not a reduced, but a higher importance. Furthermore, by recognizing their ties to cultural groups, pupils are inhibited from achieving distance to these groups and individual autonomy, which can be of particular importance in conflicts with parents and 'members of one's own culture'. Growing up in modern, liberal societies, pupils are not compulsively bound to their ethnic-cultural backgrounds, and in accord with the values of these societies, they can legitimately free themselves from the claims of specific cultural traditions.

The contrary paradigm, represented in the policies of France, where they derive from a specific commitment to republican and democratic ideals, posits the essential unimportance of ethnicity and cultural difference. It, too, offers no complete answer to a situation in which social inequalities are merged with cultural differences and attributions, for the underlying premise of the school as an island that can be effectively insulated from disturbing social and parental influences is a fiction that cannot be upheld. Universalism and strict rejection of cultural particularity are not sufficient to overcome the drag of social disadvantage on individual aspirations, nor can a policy of equal treatment of all pupils, blind to ethnic and social groupings, react to the subtle forms of structural discriminated that are named and explicitly addressed in Canada and Great Britain. Against the background of the programmatic difficulties faced by both the multicultural and the republican orientations, intercultural research and pedagogical theory face the task of developing sensibility to forms of structural and institutional discrimination, and to the complex interaction of attributions, labellings and identifications with processes of distancing and achievement of personal autonomy.

References

Adam, Heribert. 2002. Wohlfahrtsstaat, Einwanderungspolitik und Minderheiten in Kanada: Modell für Deutschland und Europa? [Welfare state, immigration politics and minorities in Canada: A model for Germany and Europe]. In: Andreas Treichler (ed.), *Wohlfahrtsstaat, Einwanderung und ethnische Minderheiten* [Welfare state, immigration and ethnic minorities], 327–344. Wiesbaden: Westdeutscher Verlag.

Anderson, Benedict. 1991. *Imagined Communities. Reflections on the Origin and Spread of Nationalism*. London: Verso. Apple, Michael W. 1982. *Education and Power*. Boston: Routledge.

Banks, James A. and Cherry A. McGhee Banks (eds.). 2001. *Handbook of Research on Multicultural Education*. San Francisco: Jossey-Bass.

Barbour, Stephen. 2000. Nationalism, Language, Europe. In: Stephen Barbour and Cathie Carmichael (eds.), *Language and Nationalism in Europe*, 1–17. Oxford: Oxford University Press.

Barbour, Stephen and Cathie Carmichael (eds.). 2000. *Language and Nationalism in Europe*. Oxford: Oxford University Press.

Bernfeld, Siegfried. 1973. *Sisyphus, or The Limits of Education*. Berkeley: University of California Press.

Bernstein, Basil. 1977. *Class, Codes and Control: Towards a Theory of Educational Transmissions*, Vol. 3, 2nd edn. London: Routledge Kegan Paul.

Bommes, Michael and Albert Scherr. 1991. Der Gebrauchswert von Selbst- und Fremdethnisierung in Strukturen sozialer Ungleichheit [The usefulness of ethnicizing self and others in structures of social inequality]. *Prokla* 83(21): 291–316.

Bourdieu, Pierre et al. 2002. *Das Elend der Welt*. Konstanz: Universitätsverlag Bourdieu, Pierre and Claude Passeron. 1990. *Reproduction in Education, Society, and Culture*. London: Sage Publications.

Castells, Manuel. 1995. *The Power of Identity*. Malden: Blackwell.

Centre national de documentation pédagogique (CNDP). 2000a. *Education Civique, Juridique et Sociale. Classe de Seconde*. Document d'accompagnement. Paris: CNDP (http://www.cndp.fr/ textes_officiels/ lycee/ecjs/sec/pdf/eseec001.pdf).

Centre national de documentation pédagogique (CNDP). 2000b. *Education Civique, Juridique et Sociale. Classe de Première*. Document d'accompagnement. Paris: CNDP (http://www.cndp. fr/textes_officiels/ lycee/ecjs/pre/pdf/EPREC001.pdf).

Department of Education and Skills (DfES). 2002. *Citizenship. The National Curriculum for England*. London (http://www. dfes.gov.uk/citizenship).

Department of Education and Skills (DfES). 2003. *Minority Ethnic Attainment and Participation in Education and Training: The Evidence*. London: DfES (http://www.standards.dfes.gov.uk/ ethnicminorities/links_and_publications/763003/RTP01–03_Amended).

Dreeben, Robert S. 1970. *Nature of Teaching: Schools and the Work of Teachers*. San Francisco: Scott Foresman.

Dubet, Francois and Marie Duru-Bellat. 2000. *L'Hypocrisie Scolaire. Pour un Collège enfin Démocratique*. Paris: Editions du Seuil.

Dubet, Francois and Didier Lapeyronnie. 1992. *Les Quartiers d'Exil*. Paris: Editions du Seuil.

Durkheim, Emile. 1922. *Éducation et Sociologie*. Paris: Alain.

Eckert, Penelope. 2000. *Linguistic Variation as Social Practice*. Oxford: Blackwell.

Foucault, Michel. 1979. *Discipline and Punish: The Birth of the Prison*. London: Penguin.

Geißler, Rainer. 2003. Multikulturalismus. In: Kanada—Modell für Deutschland [Multicultural-ism in Canada—A model for Germany]. *Aus Politik und Zeitgeschichte* [From politics and current events] B26: 19–25.

Gellner, Ernest. 1983. *Nations and Nationalism*. Oxford: Blackwell.

Gumperz, John and Cook-Gumperz, Jenny. 2007. Discourse, cultural diversity and communica-tion: a linguistic anthropological perspective. In: Helga Kotthoff and Helen Spencer-Oatey (eds.), *Handbook of Intercultural Communication*, 13–30. Berlin: Mouton de Gruyter.

Hall, Stuart and Paul du Gay. 2002. *Questions of Cultural Identity*. London: Sage.

Harris, Roxy and Ben Rampton (eds.). 2003. *The Language, Ethnicity and Race Reader*. London: Routledge.

Heller, Monica and Marilyn Martin-Jones. 2003a. Introduction: symbolic domination, educa-tion and linguistic difference. In: Monica Heller and Marilyn Martin-Jones (eds.), *Voices of Authority*, ix–xi. Westport: Ablex Publishing.

Heller, Monica and Marilyn Martin-Jones. 2003b. Conclusion: education in multilingual settings. In: Monica Heller and Marilyn Martin-Jones (eds.), *Voices of Authority*, 419–424. Westport: Ablex Publishing.

Hobsbawm, Eric J. 1990. *Nations and Nationalism since 1780: Programme, Myth, Reality*. Cam-bridge: Cambridge University Press.

Holzkamp, Klaus. 1993. *Lernen. Eine subjektwissenschaftliche Grundlegung* [Learning. A sub-ject-founded study]. Frankfurt: Campus.

Honeyford, Ray. 2003. The language issue in multi-ethnic English schools. In: Roxy Harris and Ben Rampton (eds.), *The Language, Ethnicity and Race Reader*, 145–160. London: Routledge.

Hormel, Ulrike and Albert Scherr. 2004. *Bildung für die Einwanderungsgesellschaft* [Education for the immigrant society]. Wiesbaden: Westdeutscher Verlag.

Kymlicka, Will. 1995. *Multicultural Citizenship: a Liberal Theory of Minority Right*. Oxford: Oxford University Press.

Kymlicka, Will. 1997. *States, Nations and Cultures*. Assen: Van Gorum & Co.

McDonald, Kevin. 1999. *Struggles for Subjectivity*. Cambridge: Cambidge University Press.

McLeod, Keith A. 1992. Multiculturalism and multicultural education in Canada: human rights and human rights education. In: Kogila A. Moodley (ed.), *Beyond Multicultural Education*, 215–242. Calgary: Detselig Enterprises Ltd.

Mehan, Hugh et al. 2001. Ethnographic studies multicultural education in classrooms and schools. In: James A. Banks and Cherry A. McGhee Banks (eds.), *Handbook of Research on Multicultural Education*, 129–144. San Francisco: Jossey-Bass.

Ministry of Education and Training Ontario. 1993. *Antiracism and Ethnocultural Equity in School Boards*. Toronto: Ministry of Education and Training Ontario (www.edu.gov.on.ca/ eng/document/curricul/antiraci/antire.html).

Moodley, Kogila A. 1992. *Beyond Multicultural Education*. Calgary: Detselig Enterprises Ltd.

Moodley, Kogila A. 1995. Multicultural education in Canada: historical development and current status. In: James A. Banks and Cherry A. McGhee Banks (eds.), *Handbook of Research on Multicultural Education*, 801–820. San Francisco: Jossey-Bass.

Parsons, Talcott. 1971. *The System of Modern Societies*. Englewood Cliffs: Prentice-Hall.

Rampton, Ben. 2003. Youth, race and resistance: a sociolinguistic perspective in micropolitics in England. In: Monica Heller and Marilyn Martin-Jones (eds.), *Voices of Authority*, 403–417. Westport: Ablex Publishing.

Reisigl, Martin. This volume. Discrimination in discourses. Chapter 5.

Schiffauer, Werner, Gerd Baumann, Riva Kastoryano and Steven Vertovec (eds.). 2002. *Staat, Schule, Ethnizität* [State, school, ethnicity]. Münster: Waxmann.

Tertilt, Hermann. 1996. *Turkish Power Boys*. Frankfurt/M: Suhrkamp.

Weber, Martina. 2003. *Heterogenität im Schulalltag* [Heterogeneity in day-to-day school life]. Wiesbaden: Westdeutscher Verlag.

Wieviorka, Michel. 2003. *Kulturelle Differenzen und kollektive Identitäten* [Cultural differences and collective identities]. Hamburg: Hamburger Edition.

Willis, Paul. 1977. *Learning to Labour: How Working-class Kids get Working-class Jobs*. Farnborough: Saxon House.

13

The Cultural Context of
Media Interpretation

Perry Hinton

1. Introduction

In this chapter I will be examining the role of culture in the interpretation of the media. With the globalization of the media we now have a number of interesting academic questions that arise when media communications cross cultural boundaries. To what extent is the interpretation of these communications unique to the home culture in which they are produced? Are there universal aspects of media interpretation that cross cultural boundaries? How do people in one culture interpret the media output of another culture? We can explore these by examining two areas that at first glance show a strong aspect of universality. First, the concern over children and media portrayals of violence and secondly, the extraordinary popularity of soap operas (particularly the South American genre of 'telenovelas'), which have enjoyed world-wide success. One possible explanation for culture not being a major determinant in media interpretation is that there is enough commonality in the audience impact across cultures so that key aspects of the communication have similar effects regardless of the culture. Furthermore, it has been proposed that globalization has brought about this homogeneity. One argument is that, with the globalization of media, the dominance of Western producers—particularly from the United States of America—has resulted in a reduction of cultural difference in media interpretation (see Tomlinson 1999, 2004, although it is not Tomlinson's view).

In this chapter, however, I will be taking the opposing view and arguing that an examination of the cultural context of both the academic research and the audience reception is important to gain a full picture of what is happening in media interpretation. Indeed, from a range of disciplines, such as anthropology (e.g., from the ideas of Geertz 1973, 2000), social psychology (Moscovici 1981), cultural psychology (Stigler, Shweder and Herdt 1990), and cultural studies (e.g., Alasuutari 1999), there has been a shift towards analysing communication in terms of a cultural analysis. The research in 'audience reception', for example, examines a more complex relationship of the audience with the programme—as an integrated element within their everyday lives—encompassing their culture and what it means to them within the discourse of their everyday lives (Alasuutari 1999). Globalization may not therefore result in a promulgation of a dominant (Western) ideology but one contested and negotiated within the social practices of the different cultures (Tomlinson 2004).

2. Media Effects

Firstly, it is interesting to note that much of the work on the effect of the media within Communication Studies—especially the impact of television on its audience—has been undertaken apparently without particular reference to culture. For example, it is quite possible to examine major modern texts on 'media effects' and not find the word 'culture' in the index at all (see Bryant and Zillman 1994; Potter 1999). Hence, there is an apparent separation of the cultural context in which the debate arises and the outcomes of the research indicating a media effect—with the resultant implication that the effect could well be universal. With the globalization of media messages we also have the attendant globalization of the concerns about the effect of the media on the audience, particularly children. Indeed, Carlsson states "Many people suspect a correlation between the rising level of violence in daily life, particularly, that committed by children and youth, and the culture of violence our children encounter on television, in video films, in computer games and via Internet" (Carlsson 1999: 9). We could therefore argue that the fact that Bryant and Zillman and Potter are writing in the United States of America and Carlsson in Sweden is irrelevant to the research in this area and that we are dealing with an issue of equal concern across cultures. However, I wish to question the extent to which we can we divorce this concern from its cultural origin and create a discourse around 'the violence of youth' devoid of its cultural setting.

Much of the academic debate on the effect of media violence was stimulated by the work of Bandura and his colleagues in the early 1960s in the United States of America (e.g., Bandura, Ross and Ross 1963).[1] In their experiments, young children (3–6 years) were shown, in certain circumstances, to imitate an adult model whom they had observed punching and hitting a blow-up 'bobo' doll. This and subsequent studies refined the conditions under which modelling would or would not take place (Bandura 1977). As a result of these studies, television was seen as an exemplar role model in the shaping of children's imitative behaviour. Thus, the audience was viewed as susceptible under the right conditions (or wrong conditions depending on which way one looks at it) to the influence of the media. As a result, it was argued that watching violent televised behaviour could then lead to real-life violent behaviour. And we have evidence of an apparently universal effect.

Yet when we look for the context of the research on media effects, it often lies within a wider public discourse existing within the culture in which the research is based. There is no exception in this case. If we examine one of Bandura's early articles (Bandura, Ross and Ross 1963—the first specifically on film mediation), we find right at the beginning, within the introduction, the

---

[1] The research interest in media violence goes back to the 1920s with the public concerns about the effect of the cinema in the United States of America (Gunter 1994).

following quote: "A recent incident (San Francisco Chronicle 1961) in which a boy was seriously knifed during a re-enactment of a switchblade knife fight the boys had seen on a televised rerun of the James Dean movie *Rebel Without a Cause*, is a dramatic imitative influence of film stimulation" (Bandura, Ross and Ross 1963: 3). Notice that here at the beginning of the journal article, prior to the presentation of the research, the link between a media presentation and violence is stated. It clearly establishes the cultural context of the research that follows—youth violence in American society. Thus, the research is developing the discourse that had been stated publicly in the newspaper. Furthermore, the findings develop the concerns of a society seeking an explanation for the violent behaviour of its youth, and focus those concerns on the role of the media.

The public concern about the violence of youth in the United States of America has pervaded both the research and the government's interest in the media (see, for example, the U.S. Surgeon General's Scientific Advisory Committee on Television and Social Behavior 1972, and underlying a number of references within Youth Violence: A Report of the Surgeon General 2001). We can see the same underlying context in a comprehensive review of the media violence research (Potter 1999). The book states in the very first sentence on page 1: "Violence in America is a public health problem". Statistics on murders and other violent crime in the United Sates of America are described, along with a particular focus on teenagers. Thus, Potter is explicitly concerned about "the problem of violence in *our* culture" (1999: 2, my italics). So we should not be surprised at the lack of an index entry for 'culture' in this book, and that of Bryant and Zillman (1994), as the focus of the book is within the specific context of youth violence in the United States of America.

Potter (1999) is expressing concerns that are part of a public debate within American society that engages the US administration as well. The Surgeon General's Report on Youth Violence (2001) also focuses on the violence of youth in American society as a problem for examination and explanation. The first paragraph of the preface to this report notes the events in the Columbine high school in April 1999 when two students used guns to kill twelve fellow students and a teacher before turning the guns on themselves. Thus, it is the discourse within the culture of the United States of America that provides the impetus for the report. Whilst the report is not specifically about media portrayals of violence, exposure to television violence at an early age (6–11 years) is seen as one of the risk factors in youth violence (see Chapter 4, Box 4.1 of the report).

The issue for the modern global media environment is that the cultural context may often be lost when a text enters a different culture. An American author writing for an American audience does not need to spell out the concerns about the effects of the media within their common society—although clearly Potter helpfully does. The difficulty is that this society is not necessarily the same society for the reader as the author, when the book enters the global market. Whilst gun crime is an issue in Britain, its scale is minimal in comparison to Potter's figures from the United States with many British people never having had access to a gun and never actually having held one in their lives (including myself). As I mentioned elsewhere (Hinton 2000), the focus on the crime statistics presented in the preface of Potter's book may not have resonance in cities with little street crime such as Tokyo or countries where ordinary citizens do not have access to guns, such as the United Kingdom.

Indeed, when we examine a contemporary text for the British market, Gunter and McAleer (1997: viii), in their preface, make reference to the concerns about television violence "in the United States" (my emphasis) and their statistics from Britain simply provide demographic data on the availability of television, rather than setting up an image of British youth. The conclusion to their preface is that parents are responsible (along with broadcasters) for their children's viewing. So, the issue of media and children is set up in a very different manner in the British, compared to the American, text—and this may lead to a different view of the audience reception of the media.

If the research arising from the specific concerns about the possible causes of youth violence in the United States of America then enters the globalized academic debate on media violence (e.g., Carlsson 1999), the specific cultural context of the concerns is at risk of being ignored. Yet the research shows clear cultural differences, with the Surgeon General's Report on Youth Violence (2001) acknowledging lower levels of youth violence in a number of other countries in comparison to the USA. Furthermore, there is clear evidence of cultural differences in reaction to media portrayals of 'violence'. For example, Weigman, Kuttschreuter and Baarda (1992), in a study lasting three years and encompassing a number of different countries, found that there were significant correlations between aggressive behaviour and watching violent television for both boys and girls in the United States of America but not in the Netherlands or Australia. Indeed, it is not necessarily the case that we have the same context for the 'media violence' debate within the cultures of other countries.

There is also the question of what is meant by 'media violence'. Indeed, it is often the definition that is seen as the central problem for researchers (Gunter and McAleer 1997; Gauntlett 1998; Livingstone 1990). In fact, the focus and definition will reflect an ideology (Gauntlett 1998) that itself will provide a cultural context in the way that the particular audience is viewed within the research. Within the United States of America there is a public debate about youth violence, which provides a framework to the research within which the authors reside (e.g. Potter 1999). It is not surprising, in this context, that the research seeks to examine the media in order to determine its potential effects on the youth of America.

However, outside of the specific concerns of the United States of America, maybe it is more appropriate, in the global media environment to conclude, as Gunter and McAleer (1997: 116), writing in the United Kingdom, state, "The debate around television violence will continue both in the public and academic spheres. Whether or not there is too much violence in programmes is a subjective question as much as it is a scientific one: the answer lies, to a large extent, in the prevailing public taste and opinion." These public opinions, I would suggest, are the representations we are communicating and negotiating within a particular cultural context. Taking the example of the Hong Kong kung fu movie genre, one interpretation is that these movies contain a series of violent incidents. However, this is not the only interpretation. Bruce Lee, the superstar of the genre, preferred to class his work as 'action' rather than 'violence'

(Logan 1995). The performance of the other major star, Jackie Chan, is viewed by the audience as balletic and comedic (Clemetson 1996). Thus, we should not expect the same discourse of media violence for a community such as Hong Kong with its lower levels of youth violence and we would not expect the same connotation to be placed on children imitating their screen heroes.

If we look at the example of Japan, we can see that recently there have been public concerns about youth violence (e.g., Balasegaram 2001), particularly as a result of well-publicized murders by young people (despite Japan remaining a country with extremely low rates of crime, see Tamura 2004). Here, however, the debate about the causes of these crimes has focused on the nature of modern Japanese society, rather than specially on the media. It has been suggested that a social and economic system geared up for material success has led to a high degree of pressure on the young for academic success and many find it difficult to cope, becoming socially isolated (referred to as 'hikiko-mori'). Thus, the question of youth violence is contextualized within both the role of the education system and the nature of social relations within Japanese society in a period of change. Whilst there are discussions of how to deal with young people in the criminal justice system, much of the debate has focused on the social bonds and social control within the changing Japanese society and the spiritual and emotional well-being of the young within it (Japan Echo 2000a 2000b 2001 2005). Hence, in Japan, the recent publicity about youth violence has not led to an examination of the media per se, but rather to an examination of society itself.

3. Audience Interpretation

As well as the considerable amount of work on media effects, there has been a second strand of research that has examined the active role an audience plays in interpreting the meanings of media messages (Livingstone 1990). Much of this work, interestingly, has focused on audience involvement with television dramas, commonly referred to as soap operas. In the modern global marketplace, television programmes from the United States of America have been exported to many countries round the world and these programmes (many of them soap operas such as *Dallas* and series such as *Friends*) have frequently achieved very high audience figures in the host country. This has set the context for public debates in a number of countries where their own audiences are seen as being influenced by the 'cultural imperialism' of these programmes, undermining their indigenous cultural values and replacing them with those of the many imported programmes, particularly from the United States of America (Schiller 1976; see Thielmann in this volume on dominance in other aspects).

One of the most remarkable audience figures for a television programme was the 200 million people who watched the final episode of the soap opera *The Rich Also Cry* in Russia in 1992 (O'Donnell 1999). Its regular audience for the 249 episode run was in excess of 100 million people. These figures are quite extraordinary, with up to 70 % of the country watching the programme. However, one of the interesting features of this example is that the programme itself was not a Russian production at all, but a Mexican telenovela from 1979 with the original title of *Los Ricos También Lloran*, dubbed into Russian.

On the face of it we can see the phenomenal success of the programme as evidence for the wide appeal for certain television programmes, despite the transmission in a different country and many years after its original production. It could be that the Russians and the Mexicans share a common interest in the female-centred passionate, tragic love stories of the Mexican telenovelas (Arias-King 1998). Indeed, telenovelas, from Mexico, Brazil and a number of other South American countries, are watched in over one hundred countries world-wide, with estimates of a global audience of around two billion viewers (Schlefer 2004). Included in these are a range of countries from Eastern Europe, including the Czech Republic, Poland, Bulgaria and Russia (Sinclair 1999).

Yet the telenovelas are produced by different countries and are targeted to their home audience in their production. In Mexico, the two big producers are Televista and TV Azteca and in Brazil the major producer is TV Globo. The home audiences are large with 34 % regularly viewing telenovelas in Mexico and 73 % in Brazil, with the overall audience in Latin American countries of 54 % of the population between 12 and 64 years (Soong 1999). Interestingly, telenovelas are very much part of the home culture in both their choice of subject and their relationship to the audience. The telenovela *Nada Personal* from Mexico dealt with issues such as political corruption. The similarity of aspects of the storyline to real events would not have been lost on the Mexican audience. Also, TV Globo monitors audience reaction to its programmes and may modify a particular storyline development within a telenovela as a result (Soong 1999).

We could argue that this intimate relationship with the audience provides a local product (as opposed to programmes from other parts of the world) that audiences prefer (Sola Pool 1977). Furthermore the cultural attributes and the language (Spanish and Portuguese) of the telenovelas can be seen as engaging the common culture of the Latin American audiences and providing ways of engaging with cultural issues (such as the position of women in the culture) common to those audiences. Wilkinson (2003) refers to this cultural setting as the 'cultural linguistic market'. Within this market, researchers have examined the role of the telenovela in issues of national and cultural identity and the role they play in the everyday life of the culture; and, indeed, how they are contributing to the public debate of social issues within a culture (Acosta-Alzuru 2003)

Yet the qualities of both language and culture are altered when a production is exported across both language and time. So we do not have the same cultural context for a Mexican programme produced for the home market in the late 1970s when it is shown dubbed in Russian in the early 1990s. Hence the question arises: what does the programme mean to the Russians in contrast to the Mexicans or is there simply enough common power of the storyline to engage audiences across time and culture?

We can examine two aspects of the way an audience interprets a programme. First, we can examine the meanings that they give to the programme. How, for example, do the Russians interpret the storyline of a Mexican soap opera? What happens when a television programme from one country is shown in a different country? Are their differences in audience interpretation? Secondly, we can examine the aesthetic enjoyment of the programme. It is possible that an audience in one country may thoroughly enjoy a programme from another country for different reasons, such as the exotic 'otherness' of it, compared to those of the audience in the original country, which may be reflecting their everyday concerns.

Within the analysis of communication, early models presented the flow of communication as a process that would result in an effect upon the audience member (based on the communication model of Shannon and Weaver, 1949). Developments of this model have been more sophisticated: for example, watching a lot of television is seen to have a 'cultivation effect', in that it provides material for shaping the beliefs of the viewer (Shanahan and Morgan 1999). For example, if television programmes showed a higher rate of youth crime than existed in the actual criminal statistics, then a heavy television viewing audience might, through cultivation, develop a belief that the rate of youth crime was higher than it actually is. We could argue that through the watching of television programmes from another country its values may be cultivated within the host nation. This would also provide a theoretical explanation for the concerns that through the export of its media a country could be engaging in cultural imperialism (e.g., Schiller 1976; Dorfman and Mattelart 1975).

Within cultural studies, however, it was argued that an audience might produce a number of alternative meanings to a programme. Hall's (1980) model focused on the way in which programmes were encoded (by the producers) and decoded (by the audience). In this model audiences may decode the messages within the programme in terms of the preferred meanings (i.e., presented in the encoding of the programme) or in oppositional terms. In his work on the audience of the British early evening current affairs programme, *Nationwide*, Morley (1980) identified the different readings of different groups, such as trade unionists or students, of the programme. He showed the audience members were not necessarily accepting the dominant ideology of the programme in their reception of it (Morley 1993).

This led to the audience being seen as an 'active audience', making their own meaning from the programme (Livingstone 1990). In her own work on the British soap opera *Coronation Street*, Livingstone (1989) showed that the explanations for events, such as a potential adulterous affair, proposed in the programme through the script were not necessarily the ones chosen by audience members. Indeed, the audience offered explanations (such as 'being carried away with their feelings') that were not presented in the programme itself. Thus, if a programme is shown in a different culture we may have a different interpretation to that of the home audience.

This was supported by Liebes and Katz (1990) in their analysis of the hugely popular US soap opera *Dallas* (concerning a rich oil-owning family) with different cultural groups. The studies involved focus groups of three couples who watched an episode of the programme followed by a discussion with the researchers. Fifty-five groups were tested, with around ten groups from each of different cultures within Israel (Israeli kibbutz members, Israeli Arabs, Jewish immigrants from Morocco and recent Jewish immigrants from

Russia) as well as groups from Los Angeles in the United States. Katz and Liebes (1985) noted a range of differences and similarities in the interpretation
by the different groups. A common point throughout was that the rich were
unhappy. The researchers found that, in the discussions, the groups made
sense of the different issues raised through their own cultural backgrounds.
For example, the Russian viewers were more likely to cite the social roles (such
as 'businessman') in their discussions of motivation within the programme
whereas the Americans and kibbutz members tended to employ psychological
explanations (Katz and Liebes 1986). Also, the Arabs saw immorality in the
programme whereas the Russians focused on capitalism as the corrupting factor (Liebes and Katz 1989). The groups also differed in the way they discussed
the programme: 'critically', in terms of the structure and conventions of the
programme and 'referentially', in terms of their own experiences.

Interestingly, one country where *Dallas* was not popular was Japan, where
it was only shown for six months before being cancelled. Employing the same
methodology as earlier, Katz, Liebes and Iwao (1991) examined Japanese viewers' discussions of the programme. Here eleven focus groups were employed.
The authors argued that the Japanese groups were very critical of the programme due to its 'inconsistency' or 'incompatibility' both in the story and the
characters (Katz, Liebes and Iwao 1991: 102). They were the most critically
distant, as opposed to involved (or 'referential'), of the groups examined—it
was simply not a programme that they watched. Furthermore, it did not fit
with the conventions of Japanese own locally produced 'doramas'. The Japanese did appreciate the aesthetic form of the programme—yet it did not appeal
to them. Thus, in terms of an active audience approach, we should expect that
the Russian viewers of *The Rich Also Cry* would differ in their interpretation
of the programme in comparison to its original Mexican audience.

An active audience may have different interpretations of a programme
but do they also gain different enjoyment from it? The 'uses and gratifications
approach' (McQuaill 2001) proposes four reasons for a viewer choosing to watch
a television programme: a need to find out what is happening around us, as
a reference for our own sense of identity, as a form of relationship (with characters on the television), and as entertainment (diversion). Livingstone (1989)
in her analysis of viewers of the British soap opera *Coronation Street*, found
escapist entertainment was the major reason for watching and that four separate groups of viewers could be identified through the way they interpreted
the characters' actions and motivations. These were linked to the viewers'
relationships to the characters in the programme (through their experience of
watching the programme) as well as factors such as age and gender. Livingstone (1990) draws on the proposal by New-comb and Hirsh (1984) that television provides a 'cultural forum'—it is rich and complex and open to differences
in interpretation. Yet the enjoyment of the programme can be both from the
'reality' of it (we can make references to our own lives) and the 'unreality' of it
(it is exciting and glamorous).

In her work on the soap opera *Dallas*, Ang (1985) examined the written responses from Dutch viewers of the programme. The enjoyment these
women viewers found in the programme was not its representation of American life as such but the pleasure in the wealth of the characters, the style of

the programme, the luxury in the clothes, the cars and houses—all as features of melodrama. It was not the capitalist values that were presented within the programme (which personally the viewers may have opposed) but the dramatic playing out of the problems of the rich family at the centre that appealed to the viewers. The programme had an appeal as fantasy and as melodrama that led to an emotional enjoyment of it. Interestingly, her research led her to argue that television programmes should not be seen as presenting a dominant meaning (as would be argued from a 'cultural imperialism' stand-point) with a possible oppositional reading by the viewer. For Ang (1985) the 'effect' of the programme was much more 'local' and cultural (see also Ang 1990a) and hence more complex.

There has been some debate concerning the nature of the 'active audience' in its freedom of choice in constructing meanings (Morley 1993). The power of the media organizations which produce and distribute the programmes (producing their dominant meanings) is greater than that of the audience in interpreting and reinterpreting those messages (Morley 1993; Ang 1990b). Whilst the 'active audience' model undermines the view that audiences are pawns of powerful media effects in their making of meaning, they have little choice in the media production and delivery and therefore their enjoyment and interpretation of television programmes exists within the framework of the media industries. For example, the telenovela *The Rich Also Cry* was the first opportunity for a Russian audience to view this type of show after a diet of dull broadcasts (Baldwin 1995). Also Miller and Philo (2001) argue against the view that the audience can interpret a programme in any way: audiences usually can understand the intended message but they may accept or reject it. Their only exception is where language and culture are very different between the producers of the message and the audience.[2] As we shall consider below, the dubbing and the cultural differences between the Mexicans and the Russians could have led to differences in the interpretation of *The Rich Also Cry*. However, its focus on the life of its central female character could have the same appeal to Russian women as it had to the Mexican women thirteen years earlier.

One explanation for the global success of the telenovela is that, like Ang's analysis of *Dallas*, it provides the enjoyment of melodrama for a majority female audience (see Gledhill 1992). Telenovelas have a finite number of episodes (around 200) so, unlike some soap operas, they do have a conclusion. Traditionally, there is a romantic couple at the centre of the drama, with many difficulties providing obstacles to their love. Many telenovelas, such as the Mexican *Simplemente Maria*—a Cinderella story that was also successful in Russia—have a strong female lead at the heart of the story. Thus, the success of telenovelas across the world, both in their own countries of origin and in Russia or the Czech Republic lies in their emotional expression through melodrama. Their success in Bulgaria can be attributed to women's pleasure, in that they construct a feminine aesthetic that provides a validation of female emotional power and romantic relationships (Kotzeva 2001). However,

---

[2] Stone (1993) cites an example of a Chinese film comedy that was viewed by Western critics and audiences as a melodrama.

we should be cautious in proposing an explanation that ignores the cultural context of the television experience. Baldwin (1995) argues that the success of *The Rich Also Cry* in Russia can be linked to the particular cultural context of Russia at the time of screening. Furthermore, there may be subtle culturally-specific features of the content within the programme that are only available to the knowing audience of the indigenous 'cultural-linguistic market' (Wilkinson 2003) and not to an audience from a different culture.

Acosta-Alzuru (2003) interviewed Venezuelan viewers of *El País de las Mujeres* (*The Country of Women*), a non-traditional Venezuelan telenovela drawing on social issues current within the culture, including sexual harassment, domestic abuse, abortion and homosexuality. She found that issues such as domestic violence, which had been part of the public debate for some while, were accepted by the audience but other issues, such as abortion and homosexuality, which were problematic issues within Venezuelan culture, were much less acceptable, so the character choosing not to have an abortion was approved of by the viewers. Acosta-Alzuru (2003) argued that this showed the relationship between Venezuelan culture and the programme—and controversial issues, that were not part of the public debate, produced a concern in the audience. The stories and characters in the telenovelas are features of public discourse with friends and fellow workers, and hence the viewers felt discomfort when unspoken issues (such as sexual harassment) entered the public domain through the telenovela.

We can see a second example of the cultural links for the home culture in the Japanese drama, *Oshin* (the name of the central female character). This was highly successful in Japan in the 1980s and also in over forty other countries (Harvey 1995). The story spans the life of *Oshin* from her birth in 1901 to the 1980s, and charts her trials and tribulations through life. Thus, it can be enjoyed as the triumph of the female character over adversity during the most turbulent periods of the 20th century. However, as Harvey (1995) points out, there are covert meanings within the programme provided for a Japanese audience. The central character's strength, contrary to the Western stereotype of the Japanese woman, but clearly identifiable to the Japanese viewer, embodies the iconic quality of 'endurance', a quality that is seen as a key feature of the Japanese themselves in their progress though the 20th century. As Harvey (1995) shows, the central character *is* Japan and her life is a mirror of Japanese history. Within the programme the audience is provided with explanations for aspects of their own history through the experiences of *Oshin*.

Returning to the success of *The Rich Also Cry* in Russia, Baldwin (1995) links this to the contemporary culture of the host nation. "What the show's popularity can tell us about Russian culture in and on the post-communist stage is that the switch of a good/evil paradigm from that of communist/capitalist to capitalist/communist marks a radical change in the way knowledge about gender in contemporary Russia is socially constructed" (Baldwin 1995: 287). The programme was cheap to buy and came at a time when the Russian audience had little experience of this form of television. Yet the viewers took on the story of the female central character 'as their own'. As Kotzeva (2001: 78) acknowledges for the Bulgarian women viewers of telenovelas: "A post-communist reading of gender through construction of melodramatic identifications of female viewers could be further linked to the opening up of the nation to a consumerist global TV world".

In both Russia and Bulgaria the telenovela phenomenon extended beyond the personal in that the arrival of actors from the programmes led to huge numbers of fans turning out to see them and politicians meeting them (Kotzeva 2001; Baldwin 1995). Even the Russian President Boris Yeltsin met Veronica Castro, star of *The Rich Also Cry* when she visited the country in 1992 (Baldwin 1995). This, in itself, becomes an interesting cultural phenomenon in its own right. Hence, the success of the telenovelas outside their countries of origin can be seen as the host nation taking them into their own culture. They become part of the communication within the culture, the subject of everyday discussion and a vehicle for engaging in issues such as gender and relationships in a changing society.

4. Concluding Comments

In conclusion, we should not view globalization as a mechanism that necessarily leads to a homogeneity of media interpretation, but rather as "a process of complex connectivity" (Tomlinson 2004: 26). It is a dynamic process by which media products interact with their home culture to structure the discourse around such societal concerns as youth violence or gender roles. When media messages, such as television programmes are exported to other cultures, we should not expect this audience to interpret the programmes in the same way but to actively make sense of them in terms of their own cultural expectations.

Traditionally, the academic analysis of the media has focused on individuals and the effect that the media message can have upon them, leading to a tendency to ignore cultural differences or to see them as a 'backdrop' to experience. However, the development of a more cultural focus in analysis, such as in cultural psychology within the field of psychology (e.g., Stigler, Shweder and Herdt 1990), has placed culture at the heart of understanding audience interpretation. Rather than examining cultural difference, as cross-cultural psychology does, cultural psychology examines the interrelationship between the mind and culture (Shweder 1991) and the set of cultural practices that develop within a culture. Thus, the focus of study is the involvement of culture in interpretation and understanding. We can examine this through an examination of cultural products such as beliefs, traditions and the interpretation of the media.

One way of viewing this process is through Moscovici's theory of social representations (Moscovici 1981, 1998). He argues that people within a culture share common representations, such as the English view of the French. This idea of representation bears similarity with the idea of schema in cognitive psychology (Augostinos and Innes 1990); however, Moscovici (1998) emphasizes that representations are not static features in the individual mind but are dynamic and that representations are being constantly developed through communication within a culture. So newspapers, television and everyday conversations within a culture provide the forum for the negotiation of the cultural representations. Moscovici (1998) uses the analogy with money to explain this. I have 'my' money in 'my' pocket but I can give it to you. I will happily exchange two £5 notes for one £10 note. So the specific notes are not the important feature. Just like the exchange of money, ideas flow within a culture, developing these cultural models. Thus, both home-produced and foreign media products provide communications that can enter the discourse of the audience and interpretation becomes a complex process of structuring and developing that discourse within their culture.

Whilst concepts such as 'media violence' or 'women's consumption of melodrama' can be examined without reference to the cultural setting, a focus on the cultural context reveals a richer understanding of an audience's engagement with the media. With respect to both media violence and television soap operas, they are more than simply different media communications. Rather they are cultural products. A key feature of soap operas or telenovelas is that they become part of the communication within the culture, both through magazines and television reporting on them, and through the everyday conversations of the audience. Within the original culture the specific cultural references, as in *Oshin* or *The Country of Women*, can offer representations that are linked to ideas that develop the viewer's sense of national and cultural identity (Acosta-Alzuru 2003). To the host culture, some programmes may be rejected (such as *Dallas* in Japan) but others may be used within the culture to develop their own representations of themselves, within the frameworks of their own lives (Kotzeva 2001). Across cultures there may be shared concerns about, and pleasures in, the media products but media interpretation takes place within a cultural context.

References

Acosta-Alzuru, Carolina. 2003. Tackling the issues: meaning making in a *telenovela*. *Popular Communication* 1(4): 193–215.

Alasuutari, Pertti. 1999. Introduction: three phases of reception studies. In: Pertti Alasuutari (ed.), *Rethinking the Media Audience*, 1–21. London: Sage.

Ang, Ien. 1985. *Watching Dallas: Soap Opera and the Melodramatic Imagination*. New York: Methuen.

Ang, Ien. 1990a. Melodramatic identifications: television fiction and women's fantasy. In: Mary E. Brown (ed.), *Television and Women's Culture*, 75–88. London: Sage.

Ang, Ien. 1990b. The nature of the audience. In: John D.H. Downing, Ali Mohammadi and Annabelle Sregerny-Mohammadi (eds.), *Questioning the Media: A Critical Introduction*, 155–165. Newbury Park: Sage Publications.

Arias-King, Fredo. 1998. Is it power or principle? A footnote on Clinton's Russia policy. *Johnson's Russia List*. http://www.cdi.org/russia/johnson/2475.html [Accessed 31 January 2007].

Augoustinos, Martha and John M. Innes. 1990. Towards an integration of social representations and social schema theory. *British Journal of Social Psychology* 29: 213–231.

Balasegaram, Mangai. 2001. Violent crime stalks Japan's youth. *BBC News Online*. http://news.bbc.co.uk/1/hi/asia-pacific/1377781.stm [Accessed 31 January 2007].

Baldwin, Kate. 1995. Montezuma's revenge: Reading Los Ricos También Lloran in Russia. In: Robert C. Allen (ed.), *To be Continued . . . Soap Operas Around the World*, 285–300. London: Routledge.

Bandura, Albert. 1977. *Social Learning Theory*. Englewood Cliffs, NJ: Prentice Hall.

Bandura, Albert, Dorothea Ross and Sheila A. Ross. 1963. Imitation of film-mediated aggressive models. *Journal of Abnormal and Social Psychology* 66(1): 3–11.

Bryant, Jennings and Dolf Zillman (eds.). 1994. *Media Effects: Advances in Theory and Research.* Hillsdale, NJ: Lawrence Erlbaum Associates.

Carlsson, Ulla. 1999. Foreword. In: Cecilia von Feilitzen and Ulla Carlsson (eds.), *Children and Media: Image, Education, Participation*, 9–11. Göteborg: The UNESCO International Clearinghouse on Children and Violence on the Screen at Nordicom.

Clemetson, Lynette. 1996. Return of the dragon. *Far Eastern Economic Review* March: 46–47.

Dorfman, Ariel and Armand Mattelart. 1975. *How to Read Donald Duck: Imperialist Ideology in the Disney Comic.* New York: International General Editions (originally published 1971).

Gauntlett, David. 1998. Ten things wrong with the effects model. In: Roger Dickinson, Ramaswami Harindrath and Olga Linné (eds.), *Approaches to Audiences—A Reader*, 120–130. London: Arnold.

Geertz, Clifford. 1973. *The Interpretation of Cultures.* New York: Basic Books.

Geertz, Clifford. 2000. *Available Light: Anthropological Reflections on Philosophical Topics.* Princeton, NJ: Princeton University Press.

Gledhill, Christine. 1992. Speculations on the relationship between soap opera and melodrama. *Quarterly Review of Film and Video* 1–2(14): 103–124.

Gunter, Barrie. 1994. The question of media violence. In: Jennings Bryant and Dolf Zillman (eds.), *Media Effects: Advances in Theory and Research*, 163–211. Hillsdale, NJ: Lawrence Erlbaum Associates.

Gunter, Barrie and Jill McAleer. 1997. *Children and Television*, 2nd edn. London: Routledge.

Hall, Stuart. 1980. Encoding/decoding. In: Stuart Hall, Dorothy Hobson, Andrew Lowe and Paul Willis (eds.), *Culture, Media, Language*, 128–138. London: Hutchinson.

Harvey, Paul A.S. 1995. Interpreting *Oshin*—war, history and women in modern Japan. In: Lise Skov and Brian Moeran (eds.), *Women, Media and Consumption in Japan*, 75–110. Richmond: Curzon Press.

Hinton, Perry R. 2000. Review of 'W.J.Potter, On Media Violence'. Thousand Oaks, CA: Sage, 1999. 304pp. *European Journal of Communication* 15(3): 434–436.

Japan Echo. 2000a. Juvenile crime. *Japan Echo*, 27 5. http://www.japanecho.co.jp/sum/2000/270510.html [Accessed 31 January 2007].

Japan Echo. 2000b. Educational reform. *Japan Echo* 27, 6. http://www.japanecho.co.jp/sum/2000/270603.html [Accessed 31 January 2007].

Japan Echo. 2001. A new class of drifters. *Japan Echo* 28, 5. http://www.japanecho.co.jp/sum/2001/280515.html [Accessed 31 January 2007].

Japan Echo. 2005. Japan's new misfits. *Japan Echo* 32, 1. http://www.japanecho.co.jp/sum/2005/320103.html [Accessed 31 January 2007].

Katz, Elihu and Tamar Liebes. 1985. Mutual aid in the decoding of Dallas: preliminary notes from a cross-cultural study. In: Phillip Drummond and Richard Patterson (eds.), *Television in Transition*, 187–198. London: British Film Institute.

Katz, Elihu and Tamar Liebes. 1986. Patterns of involvement in television fiction: A comparative analysis. *European Journal of Communication* 1(2): 151–171.

Katz, Elihu, Tamar Liebes and Sumiko Iwao. 1991. Neither here nor there: Why 'Dallas' failed in Japan. *Communication* 12: 99–110.

Kotzeva, Tatyana. 2001. Private fantasies, public policies: Watching Latin American telenovelas in Bulgaria. *Journal of Mundane Behavior* 2(1): 68–83.

Liebes, Tamar and Elihu Katz. 1989. On the critical abilities of television viewers. In: Ellen Seiter, Hans Borchers, Gabrille Kreutzner and Eva-Maria Warth (eds.), *Remote Control: Television, Audiences and Cultural Power*, 204–222. London: Routledge.

Liebes, Tamar and Elihu Katz. 1990. *The Export of Meaning: Cross-Cultural Readings of Dallas.* Oxford: Oxford University Press.

Livingstone, Sonia M. 1989. Interpreting a television narrative: how different viewers see a story. *Journal of Communication* 40(1): 72–85.

Livingstone, Sonia M. 1990. *Making Sense of Television: The Psychology of Audience Interpretation* Oxford: Butterworth-Heinemann.

Logan, Bey. 1995. *Hong Kong Action Cinema.* New York: Overlook.

McQuaill, Dennis. 2001. With more hindsight: conceptual problems and some ways forward for media use research. *Communications* 26(4): 337–350.

Miller, David and Greg Philo. 2001. The active audience and wrong turns in media studies. *Soundscapes—Journal on Media Culture*. http://www.icce.rug.nl/~soundscapes/VOLUME04/ Active _audience.html [Accessed 1 February 2007].

Morley, David. 1980. *The Nationwide Audience:Structure and Decoding*. British Film Institute Television Monograph no. 11. London: British Film Institute.

Morley, David. 1993. Active audience theory: Pendulums and pitfalls. *Journal of Communication* 43(1): 13–19.

Moscovici, Serge. 1981. On social representations. In: Joseph P. Forgas (ed.), *Social Cognition: Perspective on Everyday Understanding*, 181–209. London: Academic Press.

Moscovici, Serge. 1998. The history and actuality of social representations. In: Uwe Flick (ed.), *The Psychology of the Social*, 209–247. Cambridge: Cambridge University Press.

Newcomb, Horace and Paul J. Hirsch. 1984. Television as a cultural forum: Implications for research. In: William D. Rowland and Bruce Watkins (eds.), *Interpreting Television: Current Research Perspectives*, 58–73. Beverly Hills,CA: Sage.

O'Donnell, Hugh. 1999. *Good Times, Bad Times: Soap Operas and Society in Western Europe*. London: Leicester University Press.

Potter, W. James. 1999. *On Media Violence*. Thousand Oaks, CA: Sage.

Schiller, Herbert I. 1976. *Communication and Cultural Domination*. New York: International Arts and Sciences Press.

Schlefer, Jonathan. 2004. Global must-see TV. *Boston Globe* 04. 01. 2004. http://www.boston. com/ news/globe/magazine/articles/2004/01/04/global_must_see_tv/ [Accessed 31 January 2007].

Shanahan, James and Michael Morgan. 1999. *Television and its Viewers: Cultivation Theory and Research*. Cambridge: Cambridge University Press.

Shannon, Claude E. and Warren Weaver. 1949. *The Mathematical Theory of Communication*. Urbana, IL: University of Illinois Press.

Sinclair, John. 1999. *Latin American Television: A Global View*. New York: Oxford.

Sola Pool, Ithiel de. 1977. The changing flow of television. *Journal of Communication* 27(2): 139–179.

Soong Roland. 1999. Telenovelas in Latin America. http://www.zonalatina.com/Zldata70.htm [Accessed 31 January 2007].

Stigler, James W., Richard A. Shweder and Gilbert S. Herdt (eds.). 1990. *Cultural Psychology: Essays in Comparative Human Development*. New York: Cambridge University Press.

Stone, Alan A. 1993. Comedy and culture. *Boston Review* September/October. http://www. boston review.net/BR18.5/alanstone.html [Accessed 31 January 2007].

Shweder, Richard A. (ed.). 1991. *Thinking Through Cultures: Expeditions in Cultural Psychology*. Cambridge: Harvard University Press.

Surgeon General's Report on Youth Violence. 2001. *Youth Violence: A Report of the Surgeon General*. U.S. Department of Health and Human Services. http://www.surgeongeneral.gov/ library/ youthviolence/report.html [Accessed 31 January 2007].

Tamura, Masahiro. 2004. Changing Japanese attitudes towards crime and safety. *Japan Echo* 31, 4. http://www.japanecho.co.jp/sum/2004/310406.html [Accessed 31 January 2007].

Thielmann, Winfried. This volume. Power and dominance in intercultural communication, Chaper 6.

Tomlinson, John. 1999. *Globalisation and Culture*. Cambridge: Polity Press.

Tomlinson, John. 2004. Globalisation and national identity. In: John Sinclair and Graeme Turner (eds.), *Contemporary World Television*, 24–28. London: British Film Institute.

U.S. Surgeon General's Scientific Advisory Committee on Television and Social Behavior. 1972. *Television and Growing Up: The Impact of Televised Violence*, DHEW Publication No. HSM 72–9086. Washington, DC: U.S. Department of Health and Human Services.

Weigman, Oene, Margot Kuttschreuter and Ben Baarda. 1992. A longitudinal study of the effects of television viewing on aggressive and prosocial behaviours. *British Journal of Social Psychology* 31: 147–164.

Wilkinson, Kenton T. 2003. Language differences in the telenovela trade. *Global Media Journal* 2(2). http://lass.calumet.purdue.edu/cca/gmj/sp03/gmj-sp03-wilkinson.htm [Accessed 31 January 2007].

14

Cross-Cultural Communication in Intimate Relationships

Ingrid Piller

1. Introduction

In this article I will attempt to provide an overview of recent research in cross-cultural intimate relationships. Of course, such an undertaking immediately poses the question: what is a cross-cultural intimate relationship? I will focus on only one type of intimate relationship, namely romantic and sexual couple relationships with various degrees of duration, commitment and exclusivity, ranging from life-long monogamous marriage on the one hand to short-lived prostitution encounters on the other. It could be argued that couple communication can never be cross-cultural as each couple forms their own personal 'mini-culture' no matter where the partners come from. Alternatively, it has also been suggested that men and women each have their gender-specific cultures (Maltz and Borker 1982; Tannen 1986, 1990), and in this view each and every heterosexual couple would engage in a cross-cultural relationship. For the purposes of this paper, I will engage with neither of these two extremes on the definitional cline [see the Intoduction by Spencer-Oatey and Kotthoff]. Rather, I will consider an endogamous relationship one in which the partners share the same national and linguistic background, and, conversely, a cross-cultural couple one in which the partners come from different national and/ or linguistic backgrounds. I will thus ignore couple relationships where the partners come from different class, racial, regional or religious backgrounds although many studies of intermarriage focus on these (e.g., Stoltzfus 1996; Breger and Hill 1998; Ata 2000; Sollors 2000).

The paper is organized as follows: in the next section I will explore beliefs about exogamy and endogamy, as these provide the context in which cross-cultural communication in intimate relationships occurs. I will then provide demographic evidence for a sharp increase in international intimate relationships over the past 30 years and will discuss some of the reasons for this trend. I will argue that globalization in its various forms has facilitated meetings for partners from diverse backgrounds. Three aspects of globalization in particular are relevant, and I will discuss each in turn: increased international mobility, increased international data flow, and increased international cultural exchange. Throughout, I will concentrate on cross-cultural communication during the "early days" of an intimate relationship, i.e. when the relationship is considered or is just being established. I do so for two reasons: first, I have explored communication issues once a cross-cultural relationship has been established elsewhere (Piller 2001a, 2001b, 2002, in press), particularly language choice, the assumption that communication in cross-cultural intimate relationships is a "problem" per se, arguments, and the bilingual education of children in such relationships. Second, and more importantly, it would be wrong to assume that an intimate relationship is characterized by cross-cultural communication for an extended period just because the partners come from different national and/or linguistic backgrounds. As elsewhere, cross-cultural communication cannot be defined on the basis of the identities of the interactants, but rather on the basis of what it is that interactants orient to: only if they orient to cultural difference and culture as a category is actively constructed, can a communicative event be considered cross-cultural (Piller 2000; Scollon and Scollon 2001, Spreckels and Kotthoff in this volume). The more established a cross-cultural intimate relationship becomes, the rarer cross-cultural communication will be.

2. Endogamy and Exogamy

Many societies around the world see endogamous relationships—marriage within one's own group—as the norm, and intermarriage as the exception from the norm that is in need of explanation. By contrast, a relatively small number of societies routinely practice exogamy, and consider intra-cultural marriage a deviation from what is typically done. Examples of traditional societies that consider intermarriage the norm include the Banoni on the Solomon Islands (Lincoln 1979) and the Tucanoan in the Vaupés region in the North West Amazon Basin of Brazil and Colombia (Jackson 1983). The Tucanoan have a strong taboo against endogamy, and group membership is defined on the basis of one's "native" language. Residence is patri-local and language usage is dual-lingual, i.e. each partner speaks their "native" language and receives the partner's "native" language back. A child grows up hearing the father's language spoken widely, but also the language of the mother, and those of other female relatives, all of whom would be in-married. Thus, children grow up multilingual but consider their father's language their "native" language. Intermarriage is also fast becoming the predominant practice in some non-traditional societies such as Australia, where a 2004 newspaper article reported that "love is changing the face of Australia" (Gibbs and Delaney 2004). According to Gibbs and Delaney (2004), 22 % of the Australian population claimed more than one ancestry in the 2001 national census—a figure that reflects the intermarriage rate of previous generations, and is presumably significantly higher today.

It is against this background of different ideologies about intermarriage that intimate cross-cultural communication occurs. Ideology may be clearly stated as societal rules or taboos as in the Tucanoan case, or it may be implicit in practice as in the Australian case. Clearly, ideologies that consider intermarriage the norm are the exception globally. Even if ideology is implicit in practice, assumptions about intermarriage as exceptional may continue to exist simultaneously. Gibbs and Delaney (2004) provide an example: after having reported on the demographic findings regarding increased intermarriage in Australia, the authors go on to note with a certain air of surprise that "it appears that intermarriage is well-received". The interview excerpts with partners in cross-cultural relationships that follow clearly indicate that the interview question was regarding any negative experiences, and are summed up as follows: "The *Herald* talked to a dozen couples who said they experienced negligible racism in Sydney. They searched in vain to find examples of a hostile look or whispered taunt".

Therefore, in the following I will concentrate on cross-cultural intimate communication in contexts where intermarriage is exceptional and/or regarded as exceptional (usually both).

3. Cross-Cultural Intimate Relationships and Globalization

In 1960, 19,458 German citizens married a non-citizen in a state-registered ceremony in Germany. By 1995, that number had risen to 50,686 (Statistisches Bundesamt 1997: 22). An even steeper increase can be observed in Japan: in 1965, 3,500 marriages between a Japanese citizen and a non-citizen were registered. By 1997, that number had risen to 27,000 (Radford and Tsutsumi 2004). The figures for the USA provide the same picture of an increase in international marriages: in 1992, 128,396 immigrants were admitted as spouses of US citizens. Ten years later, in 2002, 294,798 spouses of US citizens were admitted.[1] These three examples must suffice to prove the point that international marriages have, on a world-wide scale, increased enormously over the past decades. Furthermore, it must be borne in mind that marriage is only one form of an intimate cross-cultural relationship: it is difficult, if not impossible, to provide statistics on intimate relationships other than those sanctioned by the state. Intimate cross-cultural relationships not included in the marriage statistics take many different forms, and would, *inter alia*, include gay and lesbian couples, cohabitation and de facto relationships, and short-term relationships. Statistics that can be considered indicators of these types of relationships further confirm the finding of a tremendous increase in intimate cross-cultural relationships in recent decades. For instance, an indicator would be the figures of women who enter a country on an "entertainer visa" in countries where such a visa class exists, as it does in Japan. In the 1990s around 60,000 "entertainers" annually entered Japan from the Philippines (Radford and Tsutsumi 2004) to work in bars, cabarets and nightclubs, in other words to provide some form of "intimate labor", be it sexual or non-sexual companionship.

This increase in cross-cultural intimate relationships is directly linked to globalization. Globalization can be defined as "a social change, an increased connectivity among societies and their elements [. . .]; the explosive evolution of transport and communication technologies to facilitate international cultural

---

[1] http://uscis.gov/graphics/shared/aboutus/statistics/; last accessed on 29/09/2004.

and economic exchange".[2] Three aspects of globalization in particular can be isolated that have facilitated cross-cultural intimate relationships: increased international mobility; increased international data flow; and increased international cultural exchange. I will discuss each in turn.

4. Increased International Mobility

Globalization is characterized by unprecedented numbers of people moving around the world, be it for the purposes of study, employment, pleasure, or to flee from persecution, to name but a few. Obviously each instance of international mobility increases the chances for people to meet and find a partner from elsewhere. For instance, in my research with English-and-German-speaking couples (Piller 2002), I found that the majority of participating couples had met while one partner was abroad as an exchange student. Others met while one or both partners were working abroad, where "work" includes military service. Indeed, statistical evidence that the mere fact of overseas residence increases cross-cultural relationships comes from marriages between male US citizens and female German citizens registered in Germany (Statistisches Bundesamt 1997: 23). This is the only group of international marriages registered in Germany that saw a significant decrease in the period from 1960 to 1994. In 1960, 6,062 German women married a US national (which was then by far the largest group of foreign men to enter marriage with a German woman in Germany; the second largest group were Italian men with 1,215 registered marriages). However, in 1994, only 1,728 German women married a US national. As it happens this decrease—during a period where international marriages overall increased around 2.5 times (see above)—runs parallel to the stationing and eventual draw-down of US troops (Herget, Kremp and Rödel 1995). In another example, Walters (1996) points out that a number of the Anglophone wives of Tunisian men in his study first met their partner while they served as Peace Corps volunteers in Tunisia. Waldis' (1998: 196) research with Swiss–Tunisian couples where the female partner is Swiss and the male partner is Tunisian found that there were three circumstances in which the partners had met: while the Tunisian men studied overseas in Switzerland, while the Tunisian men worked overseas in Switzerland, while both partners studied or worked abroad in France, or while the Swiss women holidayed in Tunisia as overseas tourists.

In addition to the fact that increased international mobility for a range of purposes creates chances for cross-cultural intimate relationships to emerge, people may actually engage in international travel with the express aim of entering an intimate relationship as is the case in travel for sex and romance. Travel for sex and romance is not in itself a new phenomenon: the scarcity of women in the American West in the 19th century, for instance, saw many Chinese women migrate to the US for relationship reasons (White-Parks 1993). They either came as "picture brides" of Chinese men, where the marriage had been arranged by their families back in China, or they came

---

[2] http://en.wikipedia.org/wiki/Globalisation; last accessed 29/09/2004.

as prostitutes, often having been sold or forced into the sex trade. Old as the practice may be, travel for sex and romance has exploded in recent decades. It is useful to make a distinction between travel for sex, or, less euphemistically, "prostitution travel", which is illegal in many contexts and oftentimes involves slavery and human trafficking, and romance travel, which centers around the mail-order bride industry and where both partners choose to enter a cross-cultural intimate relationship under legitimate circumstances. At the same time, there is a fine line between the two, as has become apparent, for instance, in cases of internet relationship scams. Given that the demand and supply countries for both sex and romance travel tend to be the same, it could also be argued that sex and romance travel are two sides of the same coin.

The extent of international prostitution travel can be gleaned from websites devoted to the fight against the sexual exploitation of women and children.[3] These show that throughout the 1990s the international mobility of both prostitutes and their clients increased tremendously. For instance, approximately 500,000 women annually are trafficked as prostitutes into Western Europe (Hughes et al. 1999). In many Western European countries, migrant prostitutes significantly outnumber local prostitutes, as for instance in Germany, where 75 % of prostitutes are foreigners (Hughes et al. 1999). At the same time, an estimated 200,000–400,000 German men annually travel abroad as prostitution tourists, with the Philippines, Thailand, South Korea, Sri Lanka and Hong Kong as their main destinations (Hughes et al. 1999). Figures for other industrialized countries show a similar picture of high demand for international prostitution, both as regards in-bound prostitutes and out-bound clients: Japan, for instance, has about 150,000 foreign women in prostitution, and Japanese men constitute the largest group of prostitution tourists in Asia (Hughes et al. 1999). The suppliers in this global division of sexual labor come from impoverished nations in Asia and Latin America, and, since the end of the Cold War, Russia and Eastern Europe.

Global economic inequality similarly underlies the legitimate side of the business od romance travel, which centers around the mail-order bride industry. Kojima (2001) analyses the mail-order bride industry as a system for the global division of reproductive labor. Women in industrialized countries have on an individual level been successful in freeing themselves from the imperative to marry and have children, but they have not succeeded in changing the underlying system of capitalism and patriarchy which depends upon gendered unpaid work for social and human reproduction. Consequently, the gap is being filled by migrant wives and mothers. Like prostitution travel, romance travel is immensely gendered: men from industrialized nations go on "romance tours" to choose an overseas bride, while women from underdeveloped nations migrate to join their overseas husbands and take up residency with them. A "romance tour" is a form of package tourism where a mail-order bride agency organizes for a client to meet a number of available women in a

---

[3] E.g. *End Child Prostitution, Child Pornography and Trafficking of Children for Sexual Purposes* at http://www.ecpat.com/eng/index.asp; *Coalition Against Trafficking in Women* at http://www.catwinternational.org/.

given destination with the aim of marriage. The package typically includes airfare and hotel, arranged meetings with individual women or parties with a number of women, marriage contracts and legal assistance, and wedding arrangements. "Cherry Blossoms", a US-based international marriage agency, for instance, offers romance tours to Shenzhen (China), Lima (Peru), Cebu City (Philippines), Bangkok (Thailand), and Ho Chi Min City (Vietnam), where the agency introduces the client to five women per day for a period of up to seven days "or as needed if you do not need so many. Most of our men go for at least two weeks so once they have time to get to know some of the women they have met better before returning home". "Cherry Blossoms" claims on their website that over 90 % of the men who use their tour services get engaged and then marry within a year of their tour.[4] Instead of or along with individual introductions, agencies also organize "socials" for the men to attend along with a number of local women seeking marriage. The male–female ratio in some such socials is 12:2,000 (O'Rourke 2002). Indeed, many of the clients who provide testimonies about their experience with the US-based agency "Russian Brides" gush about the wide selection, as this correspondent: "I picked four that I liked the best, Sveta, Maria, Natasha, and Nadia. I had a wonderful time with all four. It was hard to choose between them. In the week I spent in Moscow, I had more dates and fun than I've had in the past ten years with American women".[5] Romance tours, as well as the mail-order bride industry more generally, have been enormously facilitated, if not enabled, by the internet, and it is to this medium that I will now turn.

5. Increased International Data Flow

It is not only increased international travel that has resulted in the tremendous increase in cross-cultural intimate relationships, but also increased international data flow, using such technologies as the Internet. Today, virtual meetings are as common as physical meetings. My students, who are in their 20s often tell me stories of how they met their partners online, or that they are conducting virtual relationships, with only very limited actual physical encounters—something I, in my late 30s, still find remarkable. The internet has removed some, even if not all, of the constraints of space on love. It is in this space that dating and matchmaking agencies of all kinds are booming, including mail-order bride services. The modern mail-order bride industry began in the early 1970s with personal ads and print mail-order catalogues (O'Rourke 2002). However, it was only with the spread of internet access that the industry started to boom. In 2002, O'Rourke (2002) estimated that, at the time, there were around 2,700 agencies worldwide, with around 500 based in the US. From the mid-1980s onwards an estimated 5,000 mail-order brides from the Philippines alone entered the US each year, a total

---

[4] http://www.blossoms.com/cgi-bin/htmlos.cgi/28173.1.418454620598222596; last accessed on 30/09/2004 All quotes from mailorder bride websites are verbatim.
[5] http://www.russianbrides.com/client_comments8.html; last accessed on 30/09/2004.

of 55,000 as of 1997 (Hughes et al. 1999). The advantages of the web-based agency over newspaper ads or print catalogues are obvious: To begin with, the database can be kept up-to-date at all times, so that customers do not need to worry that the prospective partners they are interested in might already have been taken. Most sites emphasize this fact in their advertising, for instance:

> If you watch our site closely, you will notice that 50 beautiful women are added to it every week. But what you might not notice, unless you book-marked many ladies' profiles, is that we also de-activate many profiles every week. Approximately 5–25 such deactivations each week result from daily client requests and contacts from ladies asking to be removed from our site as they have entered a serious relationship. We honor these requests without hesitation.[6]

Furthermore, the genre of the personal ads has changed with the new medium. Personal ads are no longer a minimalist genre where the advertiser has to be concise because they are paying per word or even per letter (Bruthiaux 1996). Web-ads typically include a closed list of attributes (age, physical measurements, ethnicity, religion, smoking status, etc.), plus a photo, and two open-ended sections where the advertiser can describe themselves and their desired other.

Finally, prospective partners do not have to rely on the personal ad in isolation, rather the membership system of many sites offers an opportunity for instantaneous communication. If a client is interested in an advertiser they can initiate a chat session with them. Cristina, whose "real-life success story" is featured on "Filipina Heart" describes the process as follows:

> I dont know where to start my fairytail like story. I was in filipinaheart only to chat with my friends but i did not expect that i will meet the man that will give me happiness, love, and everything to me. one day, i go to the internet cafe to close my profile in filipinaheart because i am so busy studying but there is this man named garry that popped up in my computer screen only a few minutes before i can close my profile. i am not really interested to talk that day but i felt something for him and that talk last for hours and we promised to talk everyday either in filipinaheart or phone. we communicate everyday [. . .][7]

If a site does not offer a membership system (where the men pay for access to the data of all the women advertising on a site), the client can purchase the contact details of the women they are interested in on a case-by-case basis ("add to shopping cart"), usually with discounts for bulk buyers. The liberalization of the telephone market has also meant that even frequent and long international telephone calls to conduct a romantic relationship have become affordable from many industrialized countries. Indeed, some mail-order bride

---

[6] http://www.russianbrides.com/faq1.htm; last accessed on 30/09/2004.
[7] http://www.filipinaheart.com/success.cfm; last accessed on 30/09/2004.

websites also offer telephone deals: "[W]e have found a pre-paid phone card company that offers incredibly low rates for all of your domestic and foreign calling needs. Calling the Philippines used to be very expensive to say the least. Now, it can be done at a very attractive price. Do your wallet a favor, and take a moment to check out these cards through our link."[8]

Thus, websites offer far greater choice to their customers, both quantitatively (number of potential partners) and qualitatively (extended basis on which a choice is being made). While the internet offers many advantages for cross-cultural intimate communication, it also has well-known dangers. Mail-order bride sites often function as "shop-fronts" for organized crime and lure women into prostitution, and even if they do not, the danger of entering an abusive relationship is high. The mail-order bride industry is poorly regulated, and most of the regulations aim to prevent immigration fraud rather than protecting the women who enter a country as mail-order brides, and who are oftentimes dependent on their new husband in many ways, not least for their residency status. Unsurprisingly, the incidence of domestic violence in such marriages is higher than in marriages resulting from other encounters (O'Rourke 2002). Intimate cross-cultural encounters on the internet can thus easily become a vehicle of exploitation as in this case of a Russian mail-order bride in the US:

> My internet meeting with Ed led to my being victimized in three ways. I was a victim of domestic violence, of sexual assault, and trafficking . . . There were no pimps or organized crime rings. In my case, the internet was the vehicle for my sexual exploitation. It enabled Ed, a sexual predator, to lure me across the world into a situation in which I had no choice but to submit to his sexual demands. I was not his first victim, and I will not be his last. I have heard that he has a new Russian bride, and my heart bleeds for her.[9]

6. Increased International Cultural Exchange

Globalization is also characterized by an increase in international cultural exchange, in particular through cultural exports emanating from "cultural centers" such as the movie industry in Hollywood and Bollywood, or the music industry in London, New York, and Hong Kong. Increased international mobility and increased international data flow explain the increase in cross-cultural intimate relationships as a function of increased chances for cross-cultural encounters. However, at the same time, the fact remains that some people actively seek out a partner from a different cultural background as the mail-order bride phenomenon makes abundantly clear. Therefore, in this section, I will argue that it is globalization as increased international cultural exchange that is instrumental in encouraging an increasing number of people to actively seek out a cross-cultural intimate relationship. Cross-cultural desires in this view are not some kind of inner state, but rather a discursive construction (see

[8] http://www.manilabeauty.com; last accessed on 01/10/2004.
[9] http://action.web.ca/home/catw/attach/catw2003report.pdf; last accessed on 30/09/ 2004.

Cameron and Kulick 2003a, 2003b for a full discussion of desire as a discursive construction). In this understanding public discourses—be they a Hollywood movie or a pop song—provide structures that individuals can draw on. In previous work (Piller 2002, in press), I have described that a number of the partners in long-standing cross-cultural intimate relationships I interviewed explained that, at the beginning of their relationship, the fact that their partner came from another culture was part of the attraction. One German woman, for instance, said of her US-American husband, "I always wanted to marry a cowboy". Another German woman has the following exchange with her British partner:

> Erika[10] @and if you weren't an Englishman, you wouldn't stand no chance. not like a snowball in hell, so.@ @@@ das hat fuer mich ne grosse Bedeutung, dass du Englaender bist. ((*that is very important for me that you are an Englishman.*))
> Michael immer noch? ich glaube am Anfang war das mal. *is that still the case? I think that used to be so in the beginning.*

My data show that partners in a cross-cultural intimate relationship may initially see each other as a representative of their culture. The more established the relationship is the less partners see each other as cultural representatives, and the more they see each other as individuals. In her study of Russian–American marriages, Visson (1998: 102) similarly observes that partners tended to see themselves as individuals, but their spouses in cultural terms, "as products of a 'foreign' culture".

Takahashi's PhD research provides a further important contribution to our understanding of cross-cultural desire as a discursive construction within a specific context: this researcher shows that some Japanese women actively seek out an English-speaking partner because they take them to be good-looking and considerate ladies' men, similar to the media images of celebrities such as David Beckham, Tom Cruise or Brad Pitt (Piller and Takahashi 2006; Takahashi 2006). There are numerous sources from which these images of Western men as attractive, caring, loving, and giving emanate: there are of course Hollywood movies and numerous other US cultural products, but, more crucially for our discussion, international cultural interconnectedness has reached such levels that these images also emanate from Japanese cultural products, such as *manga* and *anime*, Japanese pop songs (as opposed to American ones, which are available simultaneously), women's magazines, and the advertising for the English-language-teaching industry. As Takahashi's (2006) ethnographic research shows it is particularly in situations where Japanese women experience serious dissatisfaction with Japanese society, and particularly Japanese

---

[10] All the names are pseudonyms. The transcription conventions are as follows:
Intonation and tone units
,   clause final intonation ("more to come")
.   clause final falling intonation
Paralanguage
@   laughter (one @ per syllable, i.e. @@@ = "hahaha")
Translation
italics translations of speech that was originally in German are in italics.

men, as for instance the experience of severe bullying or divorce from a cheating husband, that they decide to actively pursue the possibility of meeting a Western partner.

Dissatisfaction with Western women also emerges as the main reason that mail-order bride websites give for American men to pursue a partner from outside their own culture. I will now shift away from the focus on women that has previously dominated research in cross-cultural desires (as in most languageand-gender-related enquiry; see, e.g. Piller and Pavlenko 2004), and explore the cross-cultural desires expressed by Western men on these sites in greater detail. There are four aspects to these discursive constructions: representations of what Western men are like and what they desire in a relationship; representations of what Western women are like and why these "default partners" are not being considered; representations of foreign women—I will concentrate on Filipinas—and what makes them desirable; representations of Filipino men, their "default partners", and what makes them undesirable or unsuitable partners for Filipinas. I will briefly discuss each. To begin with, it is important to bear in mind that categories such as "Western man" and "Filipina" are member categorizations (Sacks 1992; Antaki and Widdicombe 1998, Spreckels and Kotthoff in this volume) on the websites. One site, for instance, has the following slogan: "Western Man + Filipina = Happiness. You do not have to be good with Algebra to know that is a winning equation!!"[11] In this example, as in numerous others, the categorization is a member categorization as it is used on the site, and it also provides evidence for the fact that advertisers on this website (be they Western men or Filipinas) approach each other (initially) in cultural categories, i.e. as representatives of their respective cultures.

Western Men

According to O'Rourke (2002: 477), surveys have repeatedly shown the following characteristics of US-American men who seek the services of a mail-order bride agency:

> [A] median age of 37, where ninety-four percent were white; fifty percent had two or more years of college, while less than one percent lacked high school diplomas; fifty-seven percent had been married at least once before; and seventy-five percent hoped to father children through the mailorder marriage. Additionally, the men surveyed were, for the most part, politically and ideologically conservative and financially successful.

In her analysis of 60 personal ads placed by men on the "Filipinaheart" site in early 2004, Mooring (2004a) also found—on the basis of their demographic details which form part of a check-list on this site, as they do on most—that the majority of these advertisers (75 %) were 36 years or older (up to 65). Most were Christians (only 22 % identified as "Other", "No Religion", "Buddhist"

---

[11] http://www.everlastinglove.com/match.htm; last accessed on 30/09/2004.

or "Jewish", in this order). In their open-ended self-descriptions the most frequently occurring attributes, in descending order, were: "attractive/good looking", "honest", "financially secure/successful", "great sense of humor", "loving", "caring", "romantic", "family-oriented", "religious/god-fearing", "fun-loving", "understanding", "simple", "faithful", and "open-minded". The composite picture produced from those 60 ads is one of a traditional head-of-the-family, breadwinner husband-and-father. This is also the image espoused in the marketing statements of the websites themselves. The following is an example:

> This site caters to the classical American gentlemen. Men who understand that man and women are different, and someone a lot smarter than us made us different for very good reasons. What you are looking for is someone 100% loyal and who fulfills all the other roles a traditional wife fills. What I found is that women from the Philippines meet that criteria and are more compatible with American gentlemen than American women. [. . .] I've seen an understanding of the social order from Philippine people I've not seen in any American younger than 60 to 70 years old. What this means is **the Philippine people teach social and family skills that Americans have abandoned**. But not all Americans. There are still plenty of American men who appreciate and desire those skills and understanding.[12]

Western Women

The above quotation also mentions that American women lack compatibility with American men. Negative representations of Western women are pervasive on these websites and their frequency testifies to the fact that the writers see endogamy as the norm, and feel they need to justify their search for a foreign partner (see above). Western women are represented as "liberated" (which is always used in quotation marks), selfish, aggressive, and materialistic. Statements such as this one abound:

> I know many of you are tired of the US or Canadian singles scene like I was. You know . . . insincere girls who like to play games or expect constant material gifts. But these Asian ladies are honest, faithful, rarely lose their figures as they age, are extremely supportive, and care more about your heart than your wallet. For them, nice guys finish first! I know that is a new concept to many who are reading this . . . I know it was for me. Don't settle for a demanding and unappreciative woman. The age of the internet has opened up a whole new world of opportunity. It's time you meet the woman you truly deserve! Life is too short to settle for a "6" when you can have a "10"![13]

Much of what is said about Western women is said by implication, through contrasting them, implicitly or explicitly, with Filipinas, as in "they rarely lose their figures when they age", which implies that Western women do.

---

[12] http://www.filipinalove.com/offer.shtml; last accessed on 01/10/2004; emphasis in the original.
[13] http://www.manilabeauty.com; last accessed on 01/10/2004; my emphasis.

Filipinas

Foreign women are everything that Western women are not, or are no longer. They are the ideal of conventional femininity: beautiful, petite, devoted, religious, obedient, submissive, and sexy. Previous research has shown that Orientalist images (Said 1978, 1993; Spurr 1993) predominate in the images of Asian women in the West, and particularly in the US (Marchetti 1993; Uchida 1998). The image of Asian women is dominated by the "Madame Butterfly", or, more recently, "Miss Saigon" stereotype, which portrays Asian women as exotic, sexually available, submissive, obedient, domestic, sweet and passive. For her honours thesis, Mooring (2004b) collected generalizations about Filipinas from six different mail-order bride sites,[14] and found that they largely coincide with the image described by Uchida (1998). The following is typical:

> Filipina women are renowned for their beauty, femininity and traditional family values. They are sincere, devoted and they believe in a lasting marriage. The majority of our members are in the Philippines. Our personal opinion reflects the fact that Filipina women stand out among Asian women in terms of charm, openness, intelligence, education and trustworthiness. In addition, Filipina women make excellent wives, and they excel and value their husbands as their priority. They are very affectionate and romantic, and their focus and goals is giving their man tender loving care, surpasses all the women in South East Asia. They are well educated in their different respective professions and you'll find them very mature in their thinking. They are mature for their age and view older men as more stable and responsible partner. These ladies are very feminine and gentle, cultured and passionate. They enjoy the outdoors as much as indoor activities. Their outer physical beauties coupled with their wonderful personality, high level of intelligence, sense of humor and sincere devotion to their man creates one of the strongest relationships you could ever hope to find.[15]

On many sites, as on this one, there is also evidence of defending the "Filipina brand" against competitors, namely other Asian women. The strongest "selling points" in this respect are their English ability and their Christianity, but other differences that make Filipinas more attractive to Western men than other Asian women are mentioned as well:

> We are different from most Asian cultures. We are loyal to family unit more than country. We are comfortable loving and marrying men of other race, while most Asians "lose face" if marry outside their on culture. [. . .] Marry a Filipina, and you not have to eat with chopsticks or bow all time.[16]

The same competition can be observed on Russian mail-order bride websites, where Russian women, who are relative newcomers to the scene, with the indus-

---

[14] http://www.filipina-ladies-personals.com; http://www.filipinaconnection.net/; http:// www. filipinacupid.com; http://www.filipinalove.com; http://www.manilabeauty.com/; http://www.everlastinglove.com.

[15] http://www.filipina-ladies-personals.com/new/meetfilipina.htm; last accessed on 30/ 09/2004.

[16] http://www.everlastinglove.com/match.htm; last accessed on 01/10/2004.

try only dating from the end of the Cold War, are positioned vis-à-vis Asian women: "Western men see Russian women as more mature and usually more educated than their Asian counterparts".[17] However, their main competitive edge seems to be their race: Russian women are similarly exoticized as Asian women, but they have the added bonus of being White: they "have a European face but the patience of an Asian".[18] Similarly, a feature in the *Sydney Morning Herald Magazine* entitled "Reds in the beds" (Phelan 2000) described Russian mail-order brides as "sexy, willing [. . .] Olgas, Svetlanas, and Natashas." The "earthy, exotic soul of Russian women [is said to be] very attractive, partly because the Russians have a much more traditional approach to relationships and forming a comfortable home life". In sum, "here are exotic white women who know their place".

Filipinos

The emasculation of Asian men is a frequent trope in Orientalist discourse (Marchetti 1993; Spurr 1993; Pennycook 1998), and mail-order bride websites are no exception. In the same way that Filipinas are everything that Western women are not, Western men are everything that Filipinos are not, as in this example:

> We, being Filipinas in general, think of Western gentlemen, particularly Western European and North American men as God-fearing, hardworking, and deserving of much love, respect, and admiration. Please understand this the right way, but frankly we take pleasure in being submissive to the reasonable demands of our husband. Western men make us feel comfortable, and even protected, as we naturally look to Western men for high moral and spiritual integrity. Ok, so we like taller guys and Western features, maybe because of movie heroes. <u>Too many boys here playboy, drinker, gambler, and abuser</u>. American (USA & Canada) man have reputation of treating wife in good manner.[19]

Indeed, the fear of (sexual) abuse and violence which the anonymity of the internet engenders, and which is well-founded given the high incidence of international sexual exploitation (see above), is always present on these websites. However, it is banished in two ways: either it is projected on scamming competitor websites or, more frequently, on foreign men. In addition to projecting fears, negative representations of non-Western men also allow the Western suitor to take up another traditional male subject position, namely that of the knight-in-shining-armor who comes to the rescue of the damsel-in-distress. Numerous male advertisers mention their abhorrence of women being mistreated, for example: "I am searching for a Life Partner. I can and will offer her my understanding and love. I am very responsible and loving and <u>I don't like it</u>

---

[17] http://www.american.edu/TED/bride.htm; last accessed on 01/10/2004.
[18] http://www.american.edu/TED/bride.htm; last accessed on 28/09/2004.
[19] http://www.everlastinglove.com/match.htm; last accessed on 01/10/2004; my emphasis.

<u>when a man mistreats a woman</u>. I am looking for a woman that I can give all of my love to [. . .]".[20]

Summary: Increased International Cultural Representations

Orientalist discourses that emerged with the colonial expansion of European nations and, later the USA, continue to persist. However, while Said's (1978) original analysis focused on representations of "high culture" such as novels and academic scholarship, they are now well and truly engrained and almost universally disseminated through pop culture. The "Madame Butterfly" stereotype is a good example: while the Puccini opera (first performed in 1904) is a typical product of high-culture with the limited distribution that entails, the "Miss Saigon" musical ran for over 10 years each in both London and on Broadway and toured internationally, ensuring a much wider distribution. It has always been one feature of Orientalist discourse to represent the relationship between the colonizer and the colonized as a sexual one where the colonizer is associated with masculinity and the colonized with femininity (Hyam 1990; Spurr 1993). The expanded dissemination of Orientalist discourses has also led to an expansion of sexual relationships between men from industrialized countries, and women from underdeveloped ones. In the era of globalization, a Western man no longer has to be a colonialist to enjoy "exotic" romance.

While I have focused on the desires expressed by Western men, my discussion would be incomplete without a short mention of the desires expressed by the women, even if only to avoid the impression that the women are passive victims of neo-colonial relations. They are not. Like the men they are part of a similar international cultural realm, and many of the women actually mention movie stars in describing some desired traits of their prospective partners. Many of the women advertisers are college-educated and, technologically speaking, they have internet access. It is apparent that it is precisely those Filipinas who have access to international cultural exchange who choose to seek a partner from elsewhere.

7. Conclusion

Intimate communication is often perceived as an immensely private space that is not accessible to observation and research. Like others (e.g. Dryden 1999; Gubrium and Holstein 1987, 1990; McElhinny 1997), my analysis here, as well as my previous work with cross-cultural couples (particularly Piller 2002, in press; Piller and Takahashi 2006) demonstrates that the private–public distinction cannot hold. The positioning of a cross-cultural intimate relationships occurs within a societal space in which intermarriage is either seen as the norm, or—usually—as an exception that needs to be justified and accounted for. Furthermore, large societal-level processes such as globalization provide the

---

[20] http://www.blossoms.com/cgi-bin/htmlos.cgi/30505.19.936980826016707861; last accessed on 28/09/04; my emphasis.

structure within which individuals can agentively develop and pursue cross-cultural desires. I have here focused on the ways in which globalization as a macro-process is interlinked with cross-cultural intimate relationships (see also Reisigl in this volume). I have singled out three aspects of globalization that mediate cross-cultural intimate relationships and have exemplified those with data from previous research and, particularly, mail-order bride websites. These aspects of globalization are increases in three domains: international mobility, international data flow, and international cultural exchange. These provide increased chances for partners from different cultural backgrounds to meet but they also turn on the desires of individuals to meet a cross-cultural partner. Internationally disseminated ideologies of gender, race, and family pitch (in the present case study) American men against American women, and Filipinas against Filipinos, and other Asian women. These positionings find their parallel in international economic relationships: in the same way that other forms of labor have been outsourced from industrialized countries, sexual, reproductive and emotional labor is being outsourced. In the same way that other international outsourcing has removed employment regulations from the control of the state and the unions and has weakened workers' rights internationally, "intimate outsourcing" is weakening the cause of gender equality internationally. It is within this larger framework that individuals pursue their personal happiness.

References

Antaki, Charles and Sue Widdicombe S. (eds.). 1998. *Identities in Talk*. London: Sage.

Ata, Abe W. 2000. *Intermarriage between Christians and Muslims: A West Bank Study*. Ringwood, Victoria: David Lovell Publishing.

Breger, Rosemary and Rosanna Hill (eds.). 1998. *Cross-cultural Marriage: Identity and Choice*. Oxford and New York:

Berg. Bruthiaux, Paul. 1996. *The Discourse of Classified Advertising: Exploring the Nature of Linguistic Simplicity*. New York and Oxford: Oxford University Press.

Cameron, Deborah and Don Kulick. 2003a. Introduction: Language and desire in theory and practice. *Language and Communication* 23: 93–105.

Cameron, Deborah and Don Kulick. 2003b. *Language and Sexuality*. Cambridge: Cambridge University Press.

Dryden, Caroline. 1999. *Being Married, Doing Gender: A Critical Analysis of Gender Relationships in Marriage*. London: Routledge.

Gibbs, Stephen and Brigid Delaney. 2004. Mix and match. *Sydney Morning Herald*, 14 June 2004.

Gubrium, Jaber F. and James A. Holstein. 1987. The private image: experiential and method in family studies. *Journal of Marriage and the Family* 49: 773–786.

Gubrium, Jaber F. and James A. Holstein. 1990. *What is Family?* Mountain View, CA: Mayfield.

Herget, Wilfried, Werner Kremp and Walter G. Rödel (eds.). 1995. *Nachbar Amerika: 50 Jahre Amerikaner in Rheinland-Pfalz [Neighbor America: Americans in Rhineland-Palatinate, 1945–1995]*. Trier: WVT Wissenschaftlicher Verlag Trier.

Hughes, Donna M., Laura Joy Sporcic, Nadine Z. Mendelsohn and Vanessa Chirgwin. 1999. *The Factbook on Global Sexual Exploitation*. Coalition Against Trafficking in Women. Retrieved 29/09/2004 from the World Wide Web: http://www. uri.edu/artsci/wms/hughes/factbook. htm

Hyam, Ronald. 1990. *Empire and Sexuality: The British Experience*. Manchester: Manchester University Press.

Jackson, Jean E. 1983. *The Fish People: Linguistic Exogamy and Tukanoan Identity in Northwest Amazonia.* Cambridge: Cambridge University Press.

Kojima, Yu. 2001. In the business of cultural reproduction: theoretical implications of the mail-order bride phenomenon. *Women's Studies International Forum* 24(2): 199–210.

Lincoln, Peter C. 1979. Dual-lingualism: passive bilingualism in action. *Te Reo* 22, 65–72.

Maltz, Daniel and Ruth Borker. 1982. A cultural approach to male-female miscommunication. In: John J. Gumperz (ed.), *Language and Social Identity,* 196–206. Cambridge: Cambridge University Press.

Marchetti, Gina. 1993. *Romance and the "Yellow Peril": Race, Sex, and Discursive Strategies in Hollywood Fiction.* Berkeley: University of California Press.

McElhinny, Bonnie. 1997. Ideologies of public and private language in sociolinguistics. In: Ruth Wodak (ed.), *Gender and Discourse,*106–139. London: Sage.

Mooring, Ylana. 2004a. Attractive Western man seeks honest Filipina mail order bride: ideology of gender relationships in advertisements seeking Filipina mail order brides. Unpublished Honours Essay, University of Sydney, Sydney.

Mooring, Ylana. 2004b. The discourse of Filipina mail-order bride websites. Unpublished Honours Thesis, University of Sydney, Sydney.

O'Rourke, Kate. 2002. To have and to hold: A postmodern feminist response to the mailorder bride industry. *Denver Journal of International Law and Policy* 30(4): 476–498.

Pennycook, Alastair. 1998. *English and the Discourses of Colonialism.* London: Routledge.

Phelan, A. 2000. Reds in the beds. *Sydney Morning Herald Magazine,* 1 April 2000, 49–52.

Piller, Ingrid. 2000. Language choice in bilingual, cross-cultural interpersonal communication. *Linguistik Online* 5(1) http://www.linguistik-online.com/1_00/index.html.

Piller, Ingrid. 2001a. Linguistic intermarriage: language choice and negotiation of identity. In: Aneta Pavlenko, Adrian Blackledge, Ingrid Piller and Marya Teutsch-Dwyer (eds.), *Multilingualism, Second Language Learning and Gender,* 199–230. Berlin and New York: Mouton de Gruyter.

Piller, Ingrid. 2001b. Private language planning: the best of both worlds? *Estudios de Sociolingüística* 2(1): 61–80.

Piller, Ingrid. 2002. *Bilingual Couples Talk: The Discursive Construction of Hybridity.* Amsterdam: Benjamins.

Piller, Ingrid. In press. "I always wanted to marry a cowboy": bilingual couples, language and desire. In: Terry A. Karris and Kyle Killian (eds.), *Cross Cultural Couple Relationships.* Binghampton, NY: Haworth.

Piller, Ingrid and Aneta Pavlenko. 2004. Bilingualism and gender. In: Tej K. Bhatia and William C. Ritchie (eds.), *The Handbook of Bilingualism,* 489–511. Oxford: Blackwell.

Piller, Ingrid and Kimie Takahashi. 2006. A passion for English: desire and the language market. In: Aneta Pavlenko (ed.), *Languages and Emotions of Multilingual Speakers,* 59–83. Clevedon: Multilingual Matters.

Radford, Lorraine and Kaname Tsutsumi. 2004. Globalization and violence against women—inequalities in risks, responsibilities and blame in the UK and Japan. *Women's Studies International Forum* 27: 1–12.

Sacks, Harvey. 1992. *Lectures on Conversation.* Oxford: Blackwell.

Said, Edward W. 1978. *Orientalism.* London: Routledge & Kegan Paul.

Said, Edward W. 1993. *Culture and imperialism.* London: Vintage.

Scollon, Ronald and Suzanne W. Scollon. 2001. Discourse and intercultural communication. In: Deborah Schiffrin, Deborah Tannen and Heidi Ehrenberger Hamilton (eds.), *The Handbook of Discourse Analysis,* 538–547. Malden, MA, and Oxford: Blackwell.

Sollors, Werner (ed.). 2000. *Interracialism: Black–White Intermarriage in American History, Literature, and Law.* New York: Oxford University Press.

Spreckels, Janet and Kotthoff, Helga. This volume. Identity in intercultural communication. Chapter 7.

Spurr, Davis. 1993. *The Rhetoric of Empire: Colonial Discourse in Journalism, Travel Writing, and Imperial Administration.* Durham: Duke University Press.

Statistisches Bundesamt. 1997. *Strukturdaten über die ausländische Bevölkerung.* Wiesbaden: Metzler & Poeschel.

Stoltzfus, Nathan. 1996. *Resistance of the Heart: Intermarriage and the Rosenstrasse Protest in Nazi Germany.* New York: W.W. Norton.

Takahashi, Kimie. 2006. Akogare and English language learning: Japanese women in Australia. Unpublished PhD, University of Sydney, Sydney.

Tannen, Deborah. 1986. *That's not what I Meant! How Conversational Style Makes or Breaks Relationships.* New York: Ballantine Books.

Tannen, Deborah. 1990. *You Just don't Understand: Women and Men in Conversation.* New York: Ballantine Books.

Uchida, Aki. 1998. The orientalization of Asian women in America. *Women's Studies International Forum* 21(2): 161–174.

Visson, Lynn. 1998. *Wedded Strangers: The Challenges of Russian–American Marriages.* New York: Hippocrene.

Waldis, Barbara. 1998. Trotz der Differenz: Interkulturelle Kommunikation bei maghrebinisch–europäischen Paarbeziehungen in der Schweiz und in Tunesien. [Despite the difference: Intercultural communication in Maghrebine-European relationships in Switzerland and Tunisia] Münster: Waxmann.

Walters, Keith. 1996. Gender, identity, and the political economy of language: Anglophone wives in Tunisia. *Language in Society* 25: 515–555.

White-Parks, Annette. 1993. Journey to the golden mountain: Chinese immigrant women. In: Bonnie Frederick and Susan H. McLeod (eds.), *Women and the Journey: The Female Travel Experience,* 101–117. Pullman, WA: Washington State University Press.

15

Adapting Authentic Workplace Talk for Workplace Intercultural Communication Training

Jonathan Newton

1. Introduction

This paper describes the challenge of selecting and adapting recordings of authentic workplace interactions for use in a workplace language programme. The programme is designed to assist migrants to acculturate to the communicative practices of the New Zealand workplace. Authentic interactions were taken from a large corpus of recordings made in a wide range of blue and white collar workplaces. While the interactions are largely intracultural, using this authentic language allows us to identify important sociopragmatic features of workplace language that are rarely highlighted in artificial materials used in intercultural communication training and provides participants with resources that are directly relevant to their needs.

2. Using Transcripts of Authentic Workplace Talk to Develop Intercultural Communication Skills[1]

The use of authentic language in second language instruction has attracted lively discussion and debate. The relevant issues are captured in a recent article by Richard Day (2003), *Authentic materials, a wolf in sheep's clothing.* Debate on the topic is wide-ranging, encompassing areas such as: the nature of authenticity (Widdowson 1978; Breen 1985); distinctions between text and task authenticity (Guariento and Morley 2001); the role of corpora of authentic

[1] I am a member of the Wellington Language in the Workplace Project (LWP). All references to 'we' and 'us' refer to fellow team members. I would like to thank in particular, Janet Holmes and Meredith Marra for assistance with preparing this paper for publication. Nicky Riddiford assisted with valuable comments and insights on the teaching programme which forms the basis for the analysis in this paper. LWP transcribers made the material available for analysis. Finally, I thank those who allowed their workplace interactions to be recorded. This research was supported by a Victoria University Research Fund Grant.

language in materials design and curricula (Carter 1998; Cook 1998; Kennedy 2003)—as exemplified in the COBUILD project (Sinclair 1987); the value of simplification and simplified materials for reading instruction (Widdowson 1978; Lynch 1996, Nation and Wang 1999); and classroom uses of authentic material (Burns, Gollin and Joyce 1997; and detractors Cook 1997; Day 2003).

Among those who argue the case for authentic materials, Burns, Gollin and Joyce (1997) claim that authentic spoken texts provide an important link to interaction outside the classroom, and prepare students for the unpredictability of everyday communication. Carter (1998) uses corpus data to demonstrate how frequently occurring features of authentic conversation such as three-part exchanges, vague language, ellipsis, hedging, widespread use of discourse markers and interruptions, are absent from scripted dialogues in published ELT materials.

On the other hand, Day (2003) argues that authentic materials are too difficult for many typical language students and can have a damaging effect on motivation and attitude. Day suggests that instead of a concern with authenticity, teachers should focus on *appropriateness,* that is, materials that match the needs and level of the learners. Cook (1997: 230) also warns against overvaluing authentic language, arguing that the language classroom is a "play world in which people can practice and prepare" and not "a real world where behaviour has serious consequences".

While Day and Cook are right to caution against authenticity for its own sake (what has been referred to as 'the cult of authenticity'), I believe that their concerns are largely unfounded within the context of workplace communication training (and the general field of language for specific purposes). Here, the goal of preparing participants for the workplace calls for a closer alignment rather than a disjuncture between language training programmes and worksites (the play world and the real world in Cook's terms).

One obvious way to accentuate this alignment is through using authentic language from the workplace in the training context, the topic that I explore in this chapter. And yet authentic spoken interaction is rarely used in commercially published materials for workplace training (Holmes 2005). Instead, recourse to invented interactions and scenarios is widespread. From a practical point of view this is hardly surprising since recordings of authentic conversational workplace language are not easy to obtain. Not least among the challenges is identifying and gaining permission from workers in appropriate and willing work-sites, and carefully managing ethical matters and confidentiality. Even when recordings are obtained, transcribing interactional data and extracting useful and useable material for instruction is a time-consuming process.

Workplace interactions are embedded in localized contexts reflecting the discourse history of particular communities of practice and referring to contextual artifacts or shared procedures not accessible to a listener or the reader of a transcription. Further, a single interaction, even when framed with opening and closing moves, is typically shaped by its role as a small part of a much larger and ongoing conversation involving past and future interactions between interlocutors (Vine 2004). The relevance of the larger conversation is frequently signaled in comments that pick up on previous conversations. When a conversation is transcribed, these and other features of the conversation can make for complex, idiosyncratic, unruly conversational artifacts that belie the perceived ease with which we all carry out conversations in our native language.

In sum, while authentic spoken interaction offers unique opportunities to look 'inside' workplace talk and to bring the workplace and training programmes together, the task of making such material useable is logistically challenging. As Dumitrescu (2000: 22) argues, "while authentic materials hold great promise for trainees who are focused on practical language use, the use of authentic language contexts does not relieve the instructor's burden of materials development".

3. The Data Source and Workplace Training Context

This challenge provides the impetus for the current chapter. The corpus of workplace interactions which provides the raw data for the chapter was collected by the Language in the Workplace Project (LWP)[2] at Victoria University of Wellington which, since 1996, has been developing a large corpus of transcribed recordings of workplace talk from a range of blue and white collar workplaces. More than 2500 interactions have been recorded from twenty one worksites, and involving around 5000 participants. This material has been used extensively for research purposes (see Holmes and Stubbe 2003; see also Marra and Holmes 2007), but until recently it has been relatively underused as a resource for workplace language training (although see Stubbe and Brown 2002; Holmes and Fillary 2000; Malthus, Holmes and Major 2005).

We saw an opportunity to address this gap when, in 2005, the university was contracted to provide language-focused training courses for skilled migrants who had been unable to find work in their chosen professions in New Zealand for at least two years. Applicants for the courses are required to be proficient in English at a level comparable to at least an IELTS score of 6.0 (roughly equating to intermediate proficiency) and to be trained and experienced in a profession. Professions represented by participants in the programme include law, stock broking, finance and economics, teaching, academia, design, economics, accountancy, and IT and telecommunications consultants. Applicants reported a number of barriers to employment prior to joining the course. Primary among these are limited language proficiency (especially in relation to job interviews) and the need for professional work experience in the New Zealand context before many employers will consider employing them.

The twelve-week course is divided into a five-week in-class component followed by a six-week workplace placement (with each Friday spent back in class) and concludes with a final week in class. The initial five week block focuses on job interview technique and other aspects of finding employment as well as on developing awareness of critical aspects of communication in the NZ workplace

---

[2] For more details, see the Language in the Workplace website, http://www.vuw.ac.nz/ lals/lwp [Accessed 31 January 2007]

in preparation for the six week work placement and it is to this end that we harnessed the LWP corpus. Using such a large quantity of workplace talk for intercultural communication training requires careful planning around three critical issues:[3]

1. Identifying pragmatic targets for instruction;
2. Selecting suitable samples of workplace talk;
3. Choosing appropriate instructional methods to exploit authentic work-place talk.

The remainder of this chapter addresses each of these issues in turn, and in so doing provides guidelines for approaching intercultural communication training through the use of authentic materials.

4. Identifying Pragmatic Targets for Instruction

Workplace interaction contains a wealth of sociopragmatic features suitable for intercultural communication training as examples (1) and (2) in following sections illustrate. But as Montgomery (2003: ix) notes, " . . . cultures are boundless and it is difficult to anticipate what features of context will be significant for communication." To resolve this difficulty and approach the data in a coherent way, we identified the following general sociopragmatic principles that not only provided instructional targets but also guided the search for suitable interactions:

a. talk is functionally complex; an utterance performs more than one function at the same time and one form often has many layers of meaning (e.g., informative, relational, attitudinal);
b. expressing degrees of politeness involves selecting contextually appropriate discourse strategies;
c. interpreting polite and impolite behaviour involves taking account of appropriateness in context;
d. language provides a range of strategies and devices for boosting and softening the strength of an utterance;
e. language provides direct and indirect ways of expressing meaning.

The generality of the principles is useful in programmes involving participants from a range of nationalities who are preparing for a range of types of work. The intercultural dimension of these principles is not explicit here, but is an essential part of the application of the principles to targeted interactions. Participants are always encouraged to be mindful of their culture of origin, aware of "the possibility of difference" (Corbett 2003: 24) and prepared for the "decentring from one's own taken-for-granted world" (Byram and Flemming

---

[3] A fourth critical issue is, of course, monitoring and assessment of the effectiveness of instruction. This however, lies beyond the scope of this chapter.

1998: 7, cited in Corbett 2003: 24). We see this in Task 4 discussed later in the chapter where participants are asked to imagine an interaction that they have just studied taking place in their culture of origin and to identify ways in which the communication might differ in the two contexts.

Principles (b) and (c) stress the importance of context for judging appropriateness. Context involves not only the broad cultural context as represented in the work of social psychologists and management scientists such as Hofstede (2001) but also features of micro-context such as the physical environment and shared histories of participants (Lo Bianco 2003: 29; cf. Gumperz and Cook-Gumperz 2007). It is essential that study of the sociopragmatic features of an authentic interaction takes these factors into account, although such exploration may be somewhat speculative given the limited availability of this kind of information. Let me use example (1) to illustrate this point.

Example 1.   Context: Tom enters Greg's office to request a day's leave

Tom: can I just have a quick word
Greg: yeah sure, have a seat
Tom: [sitting down] great weather, eh?
Greg: mm
Tom: yeah, been a good week did you get away skiing at the weekend Greg: yeah, we did now how can I help you
Tom: I was just wondering if I could take Friday off and make it a long weekend
Greg: mm I don't see any problem with that + you will have finished that report by then won't you

In this example Tom uses small talk and an informal communicative style in his approach to a superior to request a day's leave. Without more information about the worksite and the interlocutors in this conversation it is a question of speculation whether the level of informality we see here reflects a particularly friendly relationship between Tom and Greg that overrides status differences, a workplace in which informality is encouraged, or a more general feature of the New Zealand culture within which this interaction takes place.

5. Selecting Suitable Samples of Workplace Talk

In order to define our data search and to address the most obvious needs of intercultural communication training we narrowed the materials to a focus on face-threatening speech acts (often referred to as 'difficult talk' in ESOL teaching materials). Face threatening speech acts are particularly problematic in intercultural communication because of the role culture plays in constructing face and in shaping the strategic and linguistic realizations of politeness and face work (Brown and Levinson 1987; Blum-Kulka, House and Kaspar 1989; Kasper and Blum-Kulka 1993; Trosberg 1995; Gass and Neu 1996; Spencer Oatey 2000; Kasper and Rose 2003). Furthermore, for the purposes of instruction in sociopragmatic competence, face threatening speech acts are likely to furnish plenty of examples of the sociopragmatic principles identified in the

previous section and of indirectness, hedging, boosting and softening strategies which often cause difficulty in intercultural communication.

Face threatening speech acts encompass a broad but finite set of speech acts,
and in order to manage the scope of the materials for instruction we restricted
our attention to the following four broad categories of such speech acts:

1. Making requests, giving and receiving instructions, and refusing;
2. Making and receiving complaints, and giving and receiving feedback;
3. Expressing opinions, making suggestions and disagreeing;
4. Giving and receiving apologies.

The decision to organize the programme around particular groupings of face-threatening speech acts made first stage data sorting relatively
straightforward since the corpus was also coded by speech act. We were thus
able to extract from the data base of 2500 interactions a smaller sample of the
targeted speech acts and their surrounding conversational moves. In order to
select a finite set of useable interactions from these large data sets our two
primary criteria were first, that an interaction contain salient examples of the
sociopragmatic principles identified in the previous section, and second, that
the speech act occurred within a coherent bounded speech event that would be
comprehensible as a stand-alone episode. Example (1) discussed above clearly
meets these criteria. It is not particularly difficult or complex but nevertheless
displays some revealing pragmatic choices around the use of small talk and
downsizers in a request made by a subordinate to a superior.

Clear cut interactions such as this were the exception rather than the
rule however. As the data search continued, it quickly became clear that relatively few episodes would meet the second criterion of being stand-alone episodes that made sense to an external reader without needing to supply an
extensive description of the background and context. The highly situated and
contextualized nature of spoken discourse produces meanings that emerge
from shared physical context, shared histories and previous conversations,
all of which are difficult for a third party reading a transcript to access. It
was immediately apparent just how different this authentic material was
from artificial interactions constructed for instructional purposes. While it
could be claimed that selective sampling of 'ideal' authentic interactions leads
to similar distortions, I would argue that the features of interaction that can
be lost in the selection process (e.g., widespread exophoric reference, lack of
boundedness) are not those that deserve attention in intercultural communication training. We finally selected material which resembled as closely
as possible the workplace contexts of the students on our language-focused
training courses for skilled migrants.

6. Choosing Appropriate Instructional Methods to Exploit Authentic Workplace Talk

There is considerable support for an approach to second language instruction
which emphasizes awareness rather than performance as the critical factor in

successful second language acquisition (Schmidt 1990; Gass 1997; Ellis 1999). 'Awareness' in this case refers both to "forming some kind of explicit representation of a target form" (Ellis 1999: 15) and to *noticing* formal qualities of the input (Gass 1997). While Ellis is referring here to grammar instruction, Kasper and Rose (2003) propose that such an approach is a valid starting point for instruction in interlanguage pragmatics. As they note,

> [t]eachers can explicitly model and guide students in their use of target practices, engage students in awareness-raising activities of L2 pragmatics, and provide feedback on students' productions. Peer activities enable students to collaboratively work on tasks and support each other's development of pragmatic ability through using the target language and metapragmatic discussion
>
> Kasper and Rose (2003: 233)

Their extensive review of empirical research on acquiring pragmatic competence in a second language shows convincingly that learners provided with metapragmatic information ('explicit representation of a target form' in Ellis's formulation) outperform those without this information (Kasper and Rose 2003: 268).

'Awareness' is approached somewhat differently, though compatibly, in Tomlinson and Masuhara (2004). The authors distinguish *cultural awareness* from *cultural knowledge*, the former defined as "a gradually developing inner sense of the equality of cultures, an increased understanding of your own and other people's cultures, and a positive interest in how cultures both connect and differ" (Tomlinson 2001: 5, cited in Tomlinson and Masuhara 2004: 7). Instruction focused on cultural awareness makes use of probing, exploring, reflecting and comparing, with the ultimate goal of raising sensitivity to cultural differences and producing learners more able to navigate intercultural encounters. Typically, this awareness is internal, dynamic, variable, multidimensional and interactive (Tomlinson and Masuhara 2004: 6).

In contrast, they define *cultural knowledge* as static and stereotypical generalizations about the cultural norms that distinguish different cultures (e.g. Germans are direct, the English are reserved). This is the conventional view of cultural knowledge as external, static, articulated, stereotypical, and reduced (Tomlinson and Masuhara 2004: 6), a view which *essentializes* culture. While cultural knowledge is quick and efficient to dispense in intercultural communication training, the authors note that such an approach to culture all too easily overlooks the heterogeneity and dynamic nature of culture (Tomlinson and Masuhara 2004: 6).

In choosing an instructional method that best utilizes authentic spoken interactions we sought to give primacy to the goal of awareness-raising both in the sense of awareness used in the SLA literature and in Tomlinson and Masuhara's formulation discussed above. Communicative practice also plays an integral role, both emerging from and priming opportunities to reflect on principles of intercultural communication and to apply these principles to the interpretation of authentic workplace interactions. The integral connections between performance, awareness-raising and text interpretation can be seen in the materials discussed below. The materials refer to the following scenario:

The Scenario

The workplace: A ministry of the New Zealand Government

The people:

- Sara (53) is the manager of a team within this ministry.
- Ripeka (48) is communications manager for the ministry.
- Ella (42), Simon (37), and Marisse (34) are all report writers who work in the team.
- The team have worked together for about one year.

The situation:

Sara is holding a weekly meeting with her team. She has noticed an increasing number of writing errors in documents produced by the team. These documents include letters sent to the public, and reports posted on the ministry website and sent to government officials.

6.1. Communicative Practice

Performative practice (i.e. role play) plays an essential role in awareness raising (Swain 1995) and fulfils this role particularly well when it precedes awareness-raising and interpretation activities. Positioned thus, practice primes participants to *notice the gap* between their performance of a difficult workplace communicative event and the performance of the original interaction. Task 1 provides an example of this approach based on the scenario presented above. In this task the participants are asked to analyse a short, constructed segment of talk (deliberately designed to portray ineffective and inappropriate communication strategies) and then to work with others to produce improved versions of the talk (they will later listen to and analyse the original interaction).

Task 1.   Here is one way that Sara could raise the problem:

"Look, I'm very unhappy with the quality of your writing. It's full of mistakes and I'm really embarrassed by it. It gives us all a bad name. You need to do something about it or else there might be consequences."

a. What could be wrong with this approach? Find at least three possible problems with the way Sara communicates here.
b. Now work together with another participant and role-play ways Sara could address this problem more effectively.

Communicative practice can also be facilitated by providing trainees with a scenario along with a partial transcript of the original interaction containing either the initial turn(s) or with critical turns omitted and with the requirement that they work in pairs or groups to complete the interaction. Various versions can then be presented by the trainees and discussed and compared with the original interaction. Mak et al. (1999: 84–85) discuss the advantages of such role-based approaches to developing sociopragmatic competence. These include opportunities for diagnosis by a facilitator, opportunities for observing a range of ways of managing a speech event, opportunities for obtaining feedback from other group members, and opportunities for supported experimentation with different ways of managing communication.

6.2. Awareness-Raising and Interpretation Tasks

Awareness-raising and interpretation tasks are concerned with awareness both as attention to *explicit knowledge* and as *noticing*. These two dimensions of awareness are discussed below.

6.2.1. AWARENESS AS ATTENTION TO EXPLICIT KNOWLEDGE. We can distinguish two forms of explicit knowledge for attention in intercultural communication training: knowledge of broad principles of culture and language (sociopragmatic knowledge), and knowledge of appropriate and polite linguistic forms and strategies (pragmalinguistic knowledge). Both are addressed in the principles outlined in section 4 above. At a sociopragmatic level, trainees reflect on their interpretation and performance of linguistic action with reference to first language values. At a pragmalinguistic level, they instantiate their sociolinguistic knowledge in the form of particular communication strategies and linguistic devices.

Analysis of Sara's talk from the interaction provided in the appendix illustrates a number of these principles. Sara's two main turns in the interaction are also presented below in example (2) as a single stretch of discourse.

Example 2.

Sara: and that's the um issue of writing [deep breath]. Um when, um whenever you—er—we're drafting, well, I've noticed a couple of mistakes creeping into our work. That's stuff that, that even that *I've* looked at. I notice it because the letters go through—all the letters that go out of the ministry go through what's called the day file. They also go through, er, each manager as well as our own staff. Sometimes suddenly as I'm re-reading I spot a spelling mistake which I didn't see the first time or a grammatical mistake. I really ask for all of you to make sure that you take it to one other person at least to, um, to look at before you, before you post it. Even when you send it to me to look at it must also be checked by others. Of course when you're doing a big chunk of work then that's normal for us t--we always do that checking. Even with just simple letters make sure that they're looked at. It's so easy to overlook just a simple mistake and the less mistakes we send out the better

Sara is a team leader (i.e. manager) in a Government department, and her gentle way of giving the team a directive as well as negative feedback about their writing reflects a 'team' culture in this particular workplace. Sara manages by consensus and collaboration rather than coercion and directive. At a pragmalinguistic level we see this in features of her talk such as the use of inclusive third person pronouns ('we're drafting'), downsizers ('a *couple* of mistakes'), indirect speech acts ('I really ask for all of you to . . . '), expressions of understanding ('It's so easy to overlook just a simple mistake'), and extended explanation leading up to the negative feedback and directive. These are all potentially valuable targets for awareness-raising that highlight culturally specific ways of doing workplace talk.

6.2.2. AWARENESS AS NOTICING. Analysis of Sara's talk leads us to the second formulation of awareness: awareness as noticing. Tasks which require learners to analyse and interpret authentic workplace talk encourage awareness as *noticing* of salient sociopragmatic features of talk. As noted above, noticing of features in input is facilitated by practice opportunities that make learners aware of a gap between their performance and the performance that they are exposed to in an authentic interaction. It is also aided by the provision of explicit knowledge which makes non-obvious or ambiguous features of input more salient.

Prompt questions are a simple yet effective way of encouraging noticing since the questions themselves require learners to take a critical look at communication and to become more aware of the processes involved in identifying and interpreting the multiple meanings bound up in everyday interactions. The following prompt questions lend themselves to interpretation of a range of sociopragmatic features of workplace talk:

- What is the basic proposition?
- What other social meanings are being communicated? (e.g., disapproval, surprise)
- How are these meanings being communicated (wording, tone, non-verbal language)?
- What does the way people are talking to each other tell you about their relationship with each other?
- How would you interpret the [speech act/episode]?
- How does the addressee interpret the [speech act/episode]?
- How would you rate the politeness of the [speech act/episode]?
- How would you rate the appropriateness of the [speech act/episode]?

The following tasks (Tasks 2 to 4) require participants to interpret the interaction provided in the Appendix. (Note that the numbering of the tasks reflects the sequence in the original materials.) In Task 2, participants assess the sociopragmatic qualities of the interaction which they have listened to, and then in Task 3 look for evidence of pragmalinguistic strategies and forms that realize politeness and directness in the interaction and that support the interpretations they made in the previous task. The question *'How would you rate the effectiveness of Sara's communication style?'* in Task 2 is particularly interesting in that it encourages participants to consider the qualities that make communication effective or ineffective, thus drawing attention to the face-work being done by Sara as she seeks to address the sensitive issue of the poor quality writing produced by her team.

Task 2.

Listen to the interaction and rate how Sara communicates with her team on the scales below (circle a number in each scale).

How polite was Sara?

Polite			Impolite
1	2	3	4

How direct was Sara?

Direct			Indirect
1	2	3	4

How would you rate the effectiveness of Sara's communication style?

Very Effective			Not at all Effective
1	2	3	4

To answer this third item you need to define *effectiveness* You can do this by identfying the outcomes that would you expect from "effective" communication. What might these be?

Task 3.

Now read the interaction as you listen again. Underline words or phrases that Sara uses to convey her message *constructively* and *effectively*. Note also any other ways that she communicates effectively (e.g., pausing, use of voice quality, the structure of the message).

Task 3 provides a series of prompt questions that mirror the generic questions provided above, but with encouragement for participants to consider the interaction in the light of their cultural background.

Task 4.

a. What does Sara ask her team to do to reduce the number of mistakes that they make in their writing? What words does Sara use to soften this instruction?
b. Compare Sara's complaint with the complaint you created [see sample tasks 4 below]. What differences do you notice?
c. Imagine the same situation in your culture of origin. Would you expect a manager to communicate in the way that Sara has communicated here? In what ways might the situation and the communication be different?
d. Work with a partner to identify five ways to communicate effectively based on your analysis of Sara's communication.

The various options for awareness-raising and text interpretation described above combined with communicative practice offer a varied but integrated approach to using authentic talk in intercultural communication training for the workplace.

7. Conclusions

Our research in a wide range of workplaces indicates that the sociolinguistic and sociopragmatic demands of integrating into a new workplace are often very daunting. Learning ways of interacting which are appropriate and normal in a workplace is an important aspect of fitting in and becoming an integrated member of the workplace as a community of practice. Sociopragmatic competence is an often underestimated aspect of workplace success.

Even those born and brought up in an English-speaking speech community may find the process of learning how to do things appropriately with words at work very challenging. Fitting into the workplace involves learning the sociolinguistic and sociopragmatic rules of expression which are particular to the specific community of practice one is joining. Managing workplace discourse, knowing how to make a complaint appropriately, how to make a joke, how to disagree without causing offence, and how to refuse effectively—these are examples of areas which can present pitfalls to people from cultures with different norms from those of their co-workers.

Our use of authentic workplace talk in an intercultural communication training course strongly supports an approach to teaching and training which is rooted in real workplace language. Our analyses of the complexities of authentic workplace interaction suggest that teaching materials need to move beyond formulaic phrases and artificially constructed text book dialogues, which bear little relation to genuine workplace talk. The evidence surveyed in this paper indicates that distinctive ways of doing things develop in particular communities of practice. Our experience suggests that teachers therefore need to make use of multi-media resources for work-oriented communications skills courses, based, preferably, on authentic interaction in the organizations and worksites in which their students will be working.

In conclusion, authentic materials are a valuable resource for assisting migrants to become more informed, sensitive, flexible, and strategically equipped communicators in their second language (Tomlinson and Masuhara 2004: 7). Such materials can be instrumental in encouraging critical awareness of the assumptions and values that lie beneath utterances and behaviour, and in developing the ability to assess situations and recognize multiple interpretations. Most importantly for intercultural communication training purposes, such materials can help alert trainees to likely areas of cultural difference thus enabling them to better negotiate the distance between their own and the new culture. In sum, our work on authentic materials provides evidence that the expensive and complex business of collecting and analysing authentic workplace interaction has worthwhile practical outcomes for those engaged in preparing people for the communicative demands of the workplace.

Appendix

'Mistakes creeping into our work'

<u>The workplace</u>: A ministry of the New Zealand Government

<u>The people</u>:
- Sara (53) is the manager of a team within this ministry.
- Ripeka (48) is communications manager for the ministry.
- Ella (42), Simon (37), and Marisse (34) are all report writers who work in the team.
- The team have worked together for about one year.

<u>The situation</u>: Sara is holding a weekly meeting with her team. She has noticed an increasing number of writing errors in documents produced by the team. These documents include letters sent to the public, and reports posted on the ministry website and sent to government officials.

Sara	. . . which leads me onto one other item which I haven't got on the um agenda ah is it alright if I . . . ?
Ripeka	yep, sure
Sara	and that's the um issue of writing [deep breath]. Um when, um whenever you—er—we're drafting, well, I've noticed a couple of mistakes creeping into our work. That's stuff that, that even that *I've* looked at. I notice it because the letters go through—all the letters that go out of the ministry go through what's called the day file. They also go through, er, each manager as well as our own staff. Sometimes suddenly as I'm rereading I spot a spelling mistake which I didn't see the first time or a grammatical mistake
Simon/Ella/Ripeka	mm, yeah
Sara	I really ask for all of you to make sure that you take it to one other person at least to, um, to look at before you, before you post it. Even when you send it to me to look at it must also be checked by others. Of course when you're doing a big chunk of work then that's normal for us t-—we always do that checking. Even with just simple letters make sure that they're looked at. It's so easy to overlook just a simple mistake and the less mistakes we send out the better
Ella	I'm doing that eh [laughs]
Simon	yeah, kia ora
Ripeka	I'd like to take that a bit further too cos if we're going to use other languages in the letters, make sure they are also checked as well okay
Sara	Kia ora

References

Blum-Kulka, Shoshana, Juliane House and Gabriele Kasper (eds.). 1989. *Cross-cultural Pragmatics: Requests and Apologies*. Norwood, NJ: Ablex.

Breen, Micheal P. 1985. Authenticity in the language classroom. *Applied Linguistics* 6(1): 60–70.

Brown, Penelope and Stephen C. Levinson. 1987. *Politeness. Some Universals in Language Usage*. Cambridge: Cambridge University Press.

Burns, Ann, Sandra Gollin and Helen Joyce. 1997. Authentic spoken texts in the language class-room. *Prospect* 12(2): 72–86.

Byram, M and M. Flemming (eds.). 1998. *Language Learning in Intercultural Perspective: Approaches through Drama and Ethnography.* Cambridge: Cambridge University Press.

Carter, Ronald. 1998. Orders of reality: CANCODE, communication, and culture. *ELT Journal* 52(1): 43–56.

Cook, Guy. 1997. Language play, language learning. *ELT Journal* 51(3): 224–231.

Cook, Guy. 1998. The uses of reality: a reply to Ronald Carter. *ELT Journal* 52: 57–63.

Corbett, John. 2003. *An Intercultural Approach to English Language Teaching.* Clevedon: Multilingual Matters.

Day, Richard. 2003. Authentic materials: A wolf in sheep's clothing. *Guidelines* 25(2): 21–24.

Dumitrescu, Valeriu. 2000. Authentic materials: Selection and implementation in exercise language training. *English Teaching Forum* 38(2): 20–23.

Ellis, Rod. 1999. The place of grammar instruction in the second/foreign language curriculum. *New Zealand Studies in Applied Linguistics* 5: 1–21.

Gass, S.. 1997. *Input, Interaction and the Second Language Learner.* Mahway, NJ: Lawrence Erlbaum.

Gass, Susan and Joyce Neu (eds.). 1996. *Speech Acts across Cultures: Challenges to Communication in a Second Language.* Berlin/New York: Mouton de Gruyter.

Guariento, William and John Morley. 2001. Text and task authenticity in the EFL classroom. *ELT Journal* 55(4): 347–52.

Gumperz, John and Jenny Cook-Gumperz. 2007. Discourse, cultural diversity and communication: a linguistic anthropological perspective. In: Helga Kotthoff and Helen Spencer-Oatey (eds.), *Handbook of Intercultural Communication,* 13–30. Berlin: Mouton de Gruyter.

Hofstede, Geert. 2001. *Culture's Consequences. Comparing Values, Behaviors, Institutions, and Organizations Across Nations,* 2nd edn. Beverly Hills, CA: Sage.

Holmes, Janet. 2005. Socio-pragmatic aspects of workplace talk. In: Yuji Kawaguchi, Susumu Zaima, Toshihiro Takagaki, Kohji Shibano and Mayumi Usami (eds.), *Linguistic Informatics—State of the Art and the Future: The First International Conference on Linguistic Informatics,* 196–220. Amsterdam: John Benjamins.

Holmes, Janet and Rose Fillary. 2000. Handling small talk at work: Challenges for workers with intellectual disabilities. *International Journal of Disability, Development and Education* 47(3): 273–291.

Holmes, Janet and Maria Stubbe. 2003. *Power and Politeness in the Workplace. A Sociolinguistic Analysis of Talk at Work.* London: Pearson Education.

Kasper, Gabriele and Shoshana Blum-Kulka (eds.). 1993. *Interlanguage Pragmatics.* Oxford: Oxford University Press.

Kasper, Gabriele and Kenneth R. Rose. 2003. Pragmatic development in a second language. *Language Learning* 52: Suppl. 1.

Kennedy, Graeme. 2003. Amplifier collocations in the British National Corpus: Implications for English language teaching. *TESOL Quarterly* 37(3): 467–489.

Lo Bianco, Joseph. 2003. Culture, visible, invisible and multiple. In: Joseph Lo Bianco and Chantal Crozet (eds.), *Teaching Invisible Culture: Classroom Practice and Theory,* 11–38. Melbourne: Language Australia.

Lynch, Tony. 1996. *Communication in the Language Classroom.* Oxford: Oxford University Press.

Mak, Anita, Marvin Westwood, F. Ishu Ishiyama and Michelle Barker. 1999. Optimising conditions for learning sociocultural competencies for success. *International Journal of Intercultural Relations* 23(1): 77–90.

Malthus, Caroline, Janet Holmes and George Major. 2005. Completing the circle: Research-based classroom practice with EAL nursing students. *New Zealand Studies in Applied Linguistics* 11(1): 65–91.

Marra, Meredith and Janet Holmes. 2007. Humour across cultures: joking in the multicultural workplace. In: Helga Kotthoff and Helen Spencer-Oatey (eds.), *Handbook of Intercultural Communication,* 153–172. Berlin: Mouton de Gruyter.

Montgomery, Martin. 2003. Forward: In: John Corbett (ed.), *An Intercultural Approach to English Language Teaching,* ix–x. Clevedon: Multilingual Matters.

Nation, I.S. Paul and Karen Ming-Tsu Wang. 1999. Graded readers and vocabulary. *Reading in a Foreign Language* 12(2): 355–380.

Schmidt, Richard. 1990. The role of consciousness in second language learning. *Applied Linguistics* 11(2): 17–46.

Sinclair, John M. 1987. *Looking Up: An Account of the Cobuild Project in Lexical Computing.* London and Glasgow: Collins.

Spencer Oatey, Helen (ed.). 2000. *Culturally Speaking: Managing Rapport in Talk Across Cultures.* London: Continuum.

Stubbe, Maria and Pascal Brown. 2002. *Talk That Works. Communication in Successful Factory Teams: A Training Resource Kit.* Wellington: School of Linguistics and Applied Language Studies, Victoria University of Wellington.

Swain, Merill. 1995. Three functions of output in second language learning In: Guy Cook and Barbara Seidlhofer (eds.), *Principles and Practice in Applied Linguistics*, 125–144. Oxford: Oxford University Press.

Tomlinson, Brian and Hitomi Masuhara. 2004. Developing cultural awareness. *Modern English Teacher* 13(1): 5–11.

Trosberg, Anna. 1995. *Interlanguage Pragmatics.* Berlin: Mouton de Gruyter.

Vine, Bernadette. 2004. *Getting Things Done at Work.* Amsterdam: John Benjamins.

Widdowson, Henry G. 1978. *Teaching Language as Communication.* Oxford: Oxford University Press.

16

Intercultural Training[1]

Martina Rost-Roth

Intercultural training is of increasing importance and has already tradition. The *Handbook of Intercultural Communication,* edited by Asante, Newmark and Blake, was published in 1979 and contains many useful contributions on training methods. A few years later, Landis and Brislin's (1983) *Handbook of Intercultural Training* was published, and the papers and overviews in this three-volume work show how extensive and versatile the training programs on offer at this point were.

Another sign of the increasing importance of the training area is the setting up of professional organizations. SIETAR, the 'Society for Intercultural Education, Training and Research', was founded in the USA in 1974, and unites the activities of those working in the area of training. 'SIETAR Europa' was founded in 1991 and 'SIETAR Deutschland' in 1994. The SIETAR homepages offer various services, providing information on the organization, journals and other publications, and training programs on offer.[2]

1. Need for Training

The literature on internationalization in the business world frequently refers to the necessity of preparing employees for intercultural contact (Scherm 1995: 249–250), yet companies have long been aware that many expatriate assignments are unsuccessful. Vance and Ensher (2002: 447) point out that 16 to 40% of managers posted abroad return home prematurely, either because their performance is inadequate, or because they or their families have problems adjusting to the new culture.[3] Additionally, intercultural training is becoming more important not only with regard to postings abroad, but also for business travellers and multicultural teams. The costs of insufficient preparation can have a negative effect not only in the case of premature returners, but also in the form of poor negotiation outcomes. For example, Lanier (1979: 178) makes the point that an estimated 50 % of employees sent abroad do not work

---

[1] I am greatly indebted to Helen Spencer-Oatey for her editorial advice and Peter Franklin for helpful comments and hints.

[2] http://www.sietar-europa.org/, 12. 02. 2006

[3] See also Black and Gregersen (1999) and Black and Mendenhall (1992: 178), who refer to various studies.

efficiently, due to inadequate cultural adjustment. Trimpop and Meynhardt make an even stronger claim:

> The companies assess the success of their foreign postings at less than 30%. That means they admit that over 70 % of all postings abroad are failures! The number of assignments which thus worked well or very well is likely to be around the 10% mark. (Trimpop and Meynhardt 2003: 188, translation by the author)

According to Black and Mendenhall (1992: 178), the annual costs of insufficient preparation are estimated to be from 50,000 to 150,000 US dollars in individual cases and several tens of millions of dollars for a company with several hundred expatriate employees.

Black and Gregersen (1999: 53) see an increasing need for training, in view of the fact that 80 % of medium-sized and large companies send employees abroad, and 45 % of these companies plan to increase this figure. Yet the need for intercultural training is rarely adequately recognized. According to Black and Mendenhall (1992: 178), 70 % of US employees who are sent abroad, and 90 % of their families, go overseas without any prior intercultural training; similarly, according to a Price Waterhouse study (1997), only 13 % of companies offer cultural awareness training for all their staff on a regular basis. Black and Mendenhall (1992) complain that in some cases, companies still maintain the basic assumption that managers who work well at home will also deliver good performance abroad. Nevertheless, the number of shorter intercultural preparation courses (briefings for culturally 'challenging' postings) did increase to 47 %, compared to 21 % in 1995 (Dowling et al. 1999: 156).

International mergers are also frequently unsuccessful (Niedermeyer 2001: 65). An increasing need for training is thus seen in cross-border mergers and joint ventures. In recent years, there has been a rise in the number of mergers with companies from Eastern Europe. In such cases, difficulties arise because these companies, on the one hand, want 'new' Western know-how, but on the other hand are returning to their own traditions more strongly. Companies can be more successful in this context if they "sensitize their managers to intercultural issues", because conflicts arising from the "implementation of Western management methods" are anticipated and better dealt with (Thomas and Hagemann 1992: 197; Bolten and Dahte 1995).

According to Bolten and Schröter, the wave of mergers and acquisitions since the late 1990s "has led to changes in the international corporate landscape". In their experience, these corporate mergers are "very sensitive and susceptible to disturbance" (Bolten and Schröter 2001: 9). With this in mind, Kammhuber (2001: 78) describes merger consulting as a new working area, and also refers to experiences from the Daimler/Chrysler merger in this context.

Finally, to plan effective intercultural training, it is useful to examine how successful postings are handled. Black and Gregersen (1999) take this approach, and study what characterizes companies with successful outcomes of foreign postings and employees working abroad. They identify three key factors: 1. "knowledge creation and global leadership development", 2.

intercultural competence, and 3. well-designed reintegration programs (Black and Gregersen 1999: 54).

2. Target Groups

Gudykunst and Hammer (1983: 143) discuss the question of who should be trained. In the business world, the following areas of application can be distinguished:

- intercultural training for management,
- intercultural training for integration of foreign employees and the building of multinational teams,
- intercultural training for staff in marketing, product management and PR divisions,
- intercultural training for international negotiation,
- intercultural training for family members.

Marketing, product management and public relations are becoming increasingly important areas. Problems of intercultural contact arise in these fields in particular, due to the fact that many symbols are dependent on culture, and thus cannot be 'exported' directly. For example, whereas a stork is a symbol of the (happy) birth of a child in Germany, in Singapore it symbolizes death in childbirth. Colour symbolism is also highly dependent on culture (see Kotthoff 2007). For instance, the colour white is connected with cleanliness and hygiene in western countries, but with mourning and death in Asian cultures. Taking account of such differences is not only absolutely crucial for the success of advertising, but is also important for corporate image representation. In the case of creating a uniform corporate identity, it is essential that the elements chosen do not have a counterproductive effect due to cultural differences.

Intercultural training for multinational teams is also essential for other areas, such as international administration, or for teams of doctors or nursing staff in the medical field (see Roberts in this volume). Thomas and Hagemann (1992) maintain that more problems and conflicts arise in groups comprising three or more cultures than in less culturally diverse groups, and that more time is needed to carry out tasks.

Yet multicultural teams can also provide the potential for creative problem-solving. Adler (2002), for example, demonstrates how intercultural teams can be used to develop valuable synergies. So one task of culture-oriented training programs is to promote appreciation of other cultural approaches.

Another area which is subject to increasing attention is negotiations in international and multicultural contexts (Thomas and Hagemann 1992: 196; Bolten 1992; Ehlich and Wagner 1995).

Family members of staff posted abroad are also receiving increasing attention, as experience shows that the success of the actual employee's work depends crucially on the well-being and support of his or her family. As family members are usually less well integrated, they can experience particular problems. Children over 13 years tend to have particular difficulties. Another frequently occurring problem is that partners have no possibility of being able to work. Referring to the findings of Tung and Andersen (1997) and the Price Waterhouse study (1997–1998), Dowling et al. (1999: 163–164) establish that increasing awareness of the need to involve families is evolving. Thus, for example, training material for children has also been developed (Kalten-häuser and Swol-Ulbrich 2002).

3. Types of Training

There have been a number of attempts to systematize the range of approaches to intercultural training that now exist in the literature. Brislin, Landis and Brandt (1983: 181) distinguish six different approaches, according to type of learning or training:

- Information or fact-oriented training
- Attribution training (culture assimilator or intercultural sensitizer, learning about values)
- Cultural awareness
- Cognitive behavior modification
- Experiential learning (emphasis on learning through actual experience)
- Interaction training

Another way in which training programs can be categorized is in relation to their timing, with the following threefold classification:

- (Pre-departure) Orientation training
- Training abroad
- Reintegration training (Thomas 1996).

Gudykunst and Hammer (1983: 126) distinguish training programmes in two ways, firstly, according to whether they are based primarily on the presentation of information ("didactic") or on an experiential approach ("experiential"), and secondly, on whether they prepare participants for encountering other cultures in general or for dealing with specific individual cultures. Using this system, Gudykunst, Guzley and Hammer (1996) differentiate between four types of training:

I. Experiential culture-general training
II. Experiential culture-specific training
III. Didactic culture-general training
IV. Didactic culture-specific training

The authors provide numerous examples of training techniques for these different types, and also discuss studies evaluating them.

References to this classification can be found frequently throughout the more recent literature. For instance, Bolten (2001) discusses the advantages and disadvantages of various training concepts with reference to this categorization:

Table 1. Trading concepts (Bolten 2001:9–10, translation by the author)

Culture-general informative training concepts	Culture-specific informative training concepts
– Culture-general assimilator – Seminars on intercultural communication theory, cultural anthropology and comparative cultural psychology – Training videos – Discourse-analysis-based training – Case study analysis Positive: High cognitive learning effect in relation to the understanding of intercultural communication processes. Negative: Mainly rather academic approach, which is regarded as too abstract by management staff.	– Culture-specific assimilator – Language classes – Culture-specific seminars on history, everyday history and changing values of a cultural area – Case study analysis Positive: Thorough understanding in relation to the development of a specific cultural system is possible, as long as the approach is not only descriptive but also explanatory. Negative: With a descriptive or factbased historical approach, reduction to Do's and Taboos; thus a risk of intensifying stereotypes.

Culture-general interaction-oriented training concepts	Culture-specific interaction-oriented training concepts
– Intercultural workshops (multicultural groups) – Simulations, role plays for intercultural sensitization – Self-assessment questionnaires Positive: Mixed groups can experience interculturality directly. Negative: Simulations etc. are often fictitious and are not taken seriously by the participants.	– Bicultural communication workshops – Culture-specific simulations – Negotiation role plays – Sensitivity training Positive: Semi-authentic experience of business-related intercultural actions, as long as the training group is bi-cultural. Negative: Culture-specific knowledge is not passed on as a rule.

There is not enough scope in this context to describe all the forms of training in detail (for an overview of further types of training, see also Fowler and Mumford 1999, Cushner and Brislin 1997, and Newton in this volume). However, examples of different conceptions will be provided below.

4. Simulations and Role Plays

Simulations and role plays with various guidelines are among the 'classics' in the field of intercultural training. Gudykunst and Hammer (1983) and Gudykunst, Guzley and Hammer (1996) provide an overview of various approaches, concepts and estimations of their effectiveness.

One of the most well-known is certainly 'Bafa Bafa'. This is an experience-oriented method used as general preparation for other cultures. Participants are divided into two groups, which stand for different cultures. Each group initially has to learn certain rules which are crucial for their own culture. Observers are then sent into 'the other culture' to find out its rules. Finally, 'visitors' are exchanged.

> In Bafa Bafa participants simulate two hypothetical cultures: Alpha culture, a male dominated, collectivist culture, and Beta culture, a female dominated, individualistic culture. Trainees typically spend 30 minutes learning the rules to their respective cultures before engaging in brief exchanges between the two. After every one has had a chance to interact with the other culture, trainees attempt to describe and explain what it is that they experienced. Debriefing can explore such issues as attribution formation, anxiety, verbal and nonverbal communication, culture shock, a feeling of 'home' on return to one's 'own group', and so forth. A minimum of three hours is typically required to carry out the simulation with a debriefing. Two trainers are required.
>
> (Cushner and Brislin 1997: 5)

As with many other training programs, Bafa Bafa was first developed as an instrument for the military (Gudykunst and Hammer 1983: 133). Another well-known simulation is the 'Albatros'. The Albatros aims at bringing the participants into a situation in which they are confronted with behaviour and experiences new to them. It serves to show that many things are interpreted wrongly at first sight.

There are also approaches that make use of language learning experience in intercultural training programmes: 'Piglish: A Language Learning Simulation' is regarded as useful, not only for sensitizing individuals without previous language learning experience, but also for experienced language teachers (Hartley and Lapinsky 1999).

Gudykunst et al. (1996) and Fowler and Mumford (1995: 17–126) describe a large number of role plays and simulation games which are used repeatedly in modified forms in various training concepts. For an overview of the possibilities of using simulation games, see also Sisk (1995).

Finally, experimental games and video conferences are also of interest as simulations, and are described below along with other recent developments (see section 9).

5. Critical Incidents and Culture Assimilator

The 'culture assimilator'—also known as the 'intercultural sensitizer'—was developed in the 1960s. The first assimilator was based on a study of Arab students in the USA, who were questioned on cultural conflict situations. Dealing with such conflict-relevant situations, referred to as 'critical incidents', forms the central content of the training programs.[4]

---

[4] On the original idea of 'culture assimilators', see Fiedler and Triandis (1971). The technique of centering discussion on critical incidents originates from Flanagan (1954). Ideal critical incidents

The training program is provided as written material, which can be either used as it is or integrated as an element of a course program. The objective is to prepare participants for encountering their own and other cultural orientation systems by means of cognitive insights.

Albert (1983: 196) provides an overview of early 'culture assimilators'. Firstly, there are culture assimilators for preparing participants for specific target cultures. Target groups and cultures in this area include, for example, Iran, Honduras and Thailand. Secondly, there are also programs for individual target groups and for dealing with minorities.[5] There are also cultural assimilators that aim to sensitize participants in general (Brislin et al. 1983).

The material is divided into sections, each focusing on specific 'critical incidents' as case studies. There are alternative explanations for every case study. Both adequate explanations from the perspective of the host country are offered as well as false interpretations typical of the participants' own culture or ignorance of cultural influences. Participants select which explanations apply. The programs then set out why certain alternatives can be regarded as correct and others not. Thomas (1996) gives the following example:

> *"1. Critical interaction situation 'computer training'*
> Due to my working focus on the computer sector, I also hold computer training courses in China. I always ask the participants repeatedly during the courses whether they have understood everything, so that I can carry on with the material. They all answer 'yes'. However, when I then ask a specific question, no one can answer it. I now assume that many participants have not understood the material, although they nod in reply to my question as to whether they have understood. This behaviour on the part of the Chinese always surprises me.
>
> Why don't the Chinese students admit that they haven't understood something? Read through all the possible answers below. Then tick one of the four scale points given for every alternative.
>
> *2. Alternative explanations*
>
> a) The Chinese students don't want to admit to not understanding because they are afraid of punishment
> most applicable—quite applicable—not very applicable—least applicable.
>
> b) In this learning situation, the pupils don't tell the truth because they want to conceal their weakness and don't want to criticize the teacher.
> most applicable—quite applicable—not very applicable—least applicable
>
> c) [. . .]
>
> d) [. . .]

---

for culture assimilators are seen as fulfilling the following criteria (in this case formulated for Americans as the addressees of the training): a) a common occurrence in which an American and a host national interact, b) a situation which the American finds conflictful, puzzling, or which he is likely to misinterpret and c) a situation which can be interpreted in a fairly unequivocal manner, given sufficient knowledge about the culture. (Fiedler, Mitchell, Triandis 1971: 97)

[5] See for example Slobodin et al. (1992) *The Culture Assimilator: For Interaction with the Economically Disadvantaged* or Landis and Miller (1973) *The Army Culture Assimilator: Interacting with Black Soldiers* or Müller and Thomas (1991) *Interkulturelles Orientierungstraining für die USA,* or Brüch and Thomas 1995 *Beruflich in Südkorea. Interkulturelles Orientierungstraining für Manager, Fach- und Führungskräfte.*

3. Justification of the explanations

Explanation a) This answer is not quite correct. A German teacher is unlikely to want or be able to make Chinese students so scared of punishment that they therefore don't admit to not understanding. [. . .]

Explanation b) This answer is correct. For us, too, it is difficult to admit that we haven't really understood something that we ought to. In China teachers are very well respected. Especially if they teach such important subjects as computing it is particularly difficult for students to admit that they do not understand. [. . .]

(Thomas 1996: 122–123, translation by the author)

At the end of each individual unit, information is given on basic 'cultural standards', at a higher level of abstraction. Thomas understands cultural standards as norms and benchmarks for producing and evaluating behavior, whereby the aim is to differentiate various orientation systems. The basic assumption is that cultural standards can be reconstructed via the analysis of critical incidents (Thomas 1996 and 1999: 115; see also Franklin 2007). In the training material, the description of cultural standards is included. For example, the following standards are seen as significant for dealing with the Chinese culture:

- social harmony (HE*)*
- hierarchy
- relationships ('GUANXI' and 'RENQING', 'RENJI GUANXI')
- 'work unit', 'unit where you live' ('DANWEI')
- face (MIANZI)
- respect, Politeness ('QIANGONG XING')
- 'relativism of rules'(Liang/Kammhuber 2003: 171–182, translation by the author)

In most cases, around 10 standards are listed per target culture. The descriptions in the materials are frequently found useful as an initial orientation. However, critics also see a risk that the descriptions of cultural standards in the training material become absolute. The authors Müller and Thomas (1991: 12) themselves refer to the critical aspect that differences are emphasized, whereas common factors tend to remain in the background.

6. Linguistic Awareness of Cultures

Training programs that prepare participants not only for specific target cultures, but also for more general problems in contact situations with other cultures, centre on differences in behaviour. Programs such as 'Linguistic Awareness of Cultures' make reference to discourse and more subtle linguistic areas. This training program was essentially initiated by Müller-Jacquier, and was developed as part of the research project 'Intercultural Behavioral Training' (Helmolt and Müller 1991: 518), whereby the program also makes reference to Gumperz (Müller-Jacquier 2000: 33).[6]

---

[6] See also Knapp/Knapp-Potthoff (1990) for general strategies for enhancing mutual understanding.

The term 'Linguistic Awareness of Cultures' (abbreviated hereafter as LAC) refers back to the term 'Cultural Awareness Training'. One key aspect of this training concept is that it attempts to make participants aware of differences in communicative behavior. Another crucial point is that it is not only concerned with passing on knowledge of individual differences in communication habits, but also aims to teach strategies for deriving cultural differences. Here, Müller-Jacquier opposes normative problem-solving strategies, such as those that principally form the basis of the culture assimilators, and the explanatory patterns these offer, which primarily emphasize psychological insights and differing value orientations (Müller-Jacquier 2000: 20–22). In contrast, he attempts to make participants aware that there are often (only) differences in conventions. This approach is based on teaching linguistic categories to describe typical intercultural interaction problems, which arise from differing communication rules. The program illustrates how individual linguistic and communicative areas can be influenced by culture and determined by different conventions and behavioral expectations.

Different linguistic areas are illustrated with the help of examples, which are also presented to a certain extent as 'critical incidents'. However, the objective is not to carry out 'isomorphic attributions' and ascriptions, but to make cross-culturally functioning mechanisms visible (Müller-Jacquier 2000: 8). The overriding learning target is a more general sensitization to everyday communication and problems of intercultural communication, and the following linguistic areas are addressed (Müller-Jacquier 2000: 27–39):

1) The program illustrates that *lexical items and social meanings* often cannot be transferred directly from one language or culture to another, as they reflect cross-sections of social reality in each case, and these can be very different in different cultural contexts. Examples of terms which show such differing culturally influenced conceptions include *Sunday, friend, friendliness, coziness, order, school, church, going for a walk*. It also points out that sometimes there is no equivalent in other languages for certain words, or that different terms 'coincide'. The Japanese word *'kyaku'* is used as one example of differing conceptualizations; the term covers the German or English/American words *'Kunde'*/ *'customer'* and *'Gast'*/ *'guest'*.

2) *Speech acts* may be realized in different forms, and speech acts that appear identical may be based on differing interpretations. Different conventions are illustrated, for example, by means of responses to compliments, and conventions for giving invitations in which different formulations imply different levels of commitment (Müller-Jacquier 2000: 28–29).

3) *Conversational organization and conventions of discourse sequence:* In this context, the program thematizes differences in the organization of speaker exchanges (rather long silent phases in Japanese; different realizations of overlapping and interruption in French and German), or different realizations of conversational conditions (see Günthner 2007). Differences are also displayed in overriding structures and expectations of the course of conversations. For example, Spanish people may not be used to German expectations that points

on an agenda should be discussed in a fixed order and should not be taken up
or questioned later on (Müller-Jacquier 2000: 29–31).

4) The program shows that there are also differing taboo *subjects*, and that
tabooization may differ depending on situations or points in time.

5) Training approaches that do not simply contrast two cultures, but refer
to several cultures in comparison, have a decisive advantage in sensitizing
participants to differing *levels of directness*:

> If one establishes comparatively that, for example, Germans are direct
> with regard to communicative disclosure of speech intentions, and Swedes
> are indirect [. . .], it is easy to forget to point out—as in many comparative
> approaches—that these statements are to be regarded as relational, and
> that, for example, a number of Asian speakers would describe Swedes as
> very direct. (Müller-Jacquier 2000: 31)

This makes it clear that contrasts and qualifications do not exist as absolute
quantities, but that qualifications and assessments arise from different starting points and perspectives.

6) Participants are made aware of *register differences* and that speakers select
language variants and speech styles depending on the situation, status of conversational partners, etc. Differing formality grades play a particular role in
this register selection. This is shown, for example, in differing forms of greetings and address and their evaluation for defining the situation and relationship (see Kotthoff 2007).

7) *Paraverbal communication* is an extremely interesting area, which is
neglected in most other training programs. The objective is to clarify the differing effects of intonation and prosodic phenomena. For instance, Japanese
intonation often sounds monotonous to German listeners. Germans often find
that a certain high tone of voice frequently heard among French native speakers sounds affected. Differing assessments are also displayed with regard to
speech volume.

   Speaking quietly is seen as an expression of control over one's emotions in
Japan, and positively evaluated. Pauses in speech are also valued positively,
as they are seen as a sign of reflection. However, in other cultures, speaking
quietly with long pauses may be interpreted as an expression of insecurity, and
judged negatively.

8) The field of *nonverbal communication*, which is particularly prone to false
interpretation in cultural comparisons as it is rarely perceived consciously, is
also integrated into the training program. There are considerable differences,
for example, in the area of eye contact. In Japan, speakers tend to make eye
contact less frequently and for shorter periods than in Germany. Gestures also
show differences in cultural conventions.

   There are differing expectations and interpretations in relation to posture and body language, too: in Japan, a calm position is assessed as an

expression of good manners, and women who fold their arms are often seen as arrogant. With regard to aspects of facial expressions such as smiling, there are also considerable differences. Thus, smiling is also used in Japan, for example—unlike in Western societies—to conceal anger. Differences in the area of proximity are also critical, as bodily closeness or distance is often interpreted psychologically.

9) The program shows that *value orientation and attitudes* are manifested in the form of interaction. It quotes, e.g., the dimensions introduced by Hofstede—i.e. individualism/collectivism, high/low power distance, high/low uncertainty avoidance, masculinity/femininity, long-term/short-term life planning. The aim is to illustrate that differences only appear via contrasts, and that such orientations affect all the other areas of speech behavior described here.

10) As a further area, *rituals* in the various life domains are also thematized (Kotthoff 2007). Thus, for example, representatives of other cultures find it strange that guests knock on the table of a public house or bar in Germany, or that adults shake children's hands to congratulate them on their birthdays.

By means of cross-linguistic and cross-cultural comparison for these communication areas, 'Linguistic Awareness of Cultures' attempts to make participants aware that linguistic behavior may be based on diverse conventions.

The training is delivered through interactively designed presentations, group work and self-learning phases. Recently, video material has also been made available. The objectives include practicing 'proposing alternative explanatory hypotheses' and promoting meta-communicative skills.

"The following case illustrates our points:

Dr. Greiner has just been appointed department head in a German company's branch office in Seoul, Korea. After he arrives, he calls his first team meeting. He prepared questions in advance to help him get oriented to the work at that branch, to gather important information, and, at the same time, to begin to "socialize" with his future colleagues. However, not very long into the meeting, he realizes that his Korean colleagues' answers are very vague. Indeed, they seem to become increasingly vague and even evasive the more precisely he phrases his questions. To ensure that they understand his English, he repeats his questions whenever the answers are provided reluctantly. He smiles and attempts to make eye contact. Finally, he states that if his colleagues have any questions, he would be very happy to answer them. But there are none. After the meeting he does not know much more than he did before and is quite irritated. He assumes they have hidden agendas and want something from him. He resolves to gather some of the needed information in formal and informal face-toface conversations (in his office and also at the lunch table) and to phrase his questions even more precisely at the next meeting.

Many leaders would, like Dr. Greiner, attempt to find culturally oriented explanations and solutions to their experience; however, the results would be limited. We propose that a truly effective leader will also generate hypotheses about the different linguistic conventions that might explain the situation. A linguistic analysis would yield a number of additional hypotheses. For example, relying on a linguistic explanation of directness and indirectness, leaders might consider that the Korean colleagues are giving contextualized answers to the questions. However, they would note that Dr. Greiner seems to be misinterpreting these context-sensitive statements as vague even though, according to Korean conventions, they are quite clear. Therefore, he cannot understand why he was not provided with concrete information. Linguistically sensitive leaders might also propose that speech acts explain the situation. They might hypothesize that Dr. Greiner posed questions in a way that seemed to be calling for a decision or yes/no response without realizing that in a high-context culture (. . .) like Korea, such questions may be seen as requiring a face-threatening commitment that the Koreans want to avoid.

Third, they could propose that Dr. Greiner was not introduced according to Korean discourse conventions. Because proper introductions may be an important prerequisite for communication in first-contact situations, the Koreans may have been hesitant to respond to his questions.

Relying on the linguistic perspective of nonverbal communication, leaders might contemplate that Dr. Greiner wrongly interpreted his colleagues' lowered eyes as a sign of embarrassment or ignorance. He may not have recognized it as a gesture of politeness towards their superior.

Global leaders would also benefit from analyzing Dr. Greiner's reactions to the Koreans' responses using a linguistic-interactionist point of view. Considering the effects of foreign behavior on the situation and relying on the linguistic notion of speech acts, they might propose that Dr. Greiner's reaction to his interpretation of the Korean answers of asking even more concrete decision questions was unsuitable for the situation. Thereby, he provoked his colleagues to give even vaguer answers and avoid eye contact more strongly, interactively causing even more misunderstanding. In addition, they may analyze the nonverbal communication, noting that Dr. Greiner reacted to the Korean's convention of avoidance of eye contact by trying even harder to obtain it. Thereby, he might have provoked an even more intense avoidance of eye contact.

Finally, linguistically savvy leaders would analyze the conventions of discourse and observe that Dr. Greiner caused further insecurity in the response behavior of his coparticipants by repeating questions that had been understood and even answered already. This analysis illustrates how important it is to come up with multiple explanations for reconstructed critical incidents (regardless of whether they are personal experiences or documented in the literature). All the explanatory hypotheses have the potential of being accurate, for the given case study as well as for other German-Korean or U.S.-Korean interactions." (Müller-Jacquier and Whitener 2001: 236–238)

The program is further characterized by an interactionist perspective, which takes the interculturality of conflict situations into account. The authors work on the assumption that participants in intercultural encounters not only act on the basis of the principles of their own cultural socialization, but also display new forms as they react and adjust to their interlocutors.

One factor worth remarking on is that the ability to form alternative and multiple explanatory hypotheses is seen as the basis for fostering intercultural competence (see also Wiseman 2002); it is a skill that is more helpful overall for intercultural contact situations than the need for knowing correct solutions.

7. Discourse Analysis-Based Training

Training programs based on discourse analysis explicitly target communication problems in everyday working life. The aim is to promote behavioral changes through participants reflecting on their own practical work. This approach requires relatively intensive advance preparation, as participants deal with case studies from their own work. The basic principles are presented in Liedke, Redder and Scheiter (1999). The first aim is to reveal fundamental communicative problems, not to pass on "magic recipes" (Liedke, Redder and Scheiter 1999: 158). The second aim is to attempt to generate behavioural changes principally by analyzing situations occurring in sound transcripts or video recordings, and by extending these in role plays. This training concept has been put into practice mainly in the field of governmental communication and training for public administration staff who deal with foreign clients.

Ten Thije (2001) also presents a discourse analysis-based training program. It is worth noting in this context that the selection of case studies and discussions is not limited to dealing with misunderstandings,[7] but also seeks to focus on other aspects of intercultural situations, such as creating common ground (see also Koole and ten Thije 1994 on the theoretical foundation of this aspect). Reflecting on the scope for action is regarded as particularly important. For a program adapting authentic workplace talk for training purposes, see Newton in this volume.

8. Coaching, Consulting, Training on the Job—Recent Tendencies in Intercultural Competence Training

The terms 'coaching' and 'consulting' are gaining increasing significance (see particularly Bolten 2001). Bolten attributes the demand for such new forms of training to the fact that preparation time prior to foreign assignments, and thus the time available for preparatory 'off-the-job' measures and training is being reduced.

Furthermore, findings such as those of Stahl (1998: 157 and 171) indicate that many problems that occur during periods abroad do not decrease with longer lengths of stay. This can also be seen as one reason why 'on-the-job' training—in contrast to outsourced 'off-the-job' courses—is gaining in importance. Correspondingly, Dowling et al. (1999: 157) and Oechsler (2002: 876–878) cite support in everyday work as an important component for supporting foreign assignments and a prerequisite for success.

Bolten (2001) compares 'on-the-job' and 'off-the-job' training schemes:

---

[7] For literature on miscommunication and misunderstanding see Coupland, Wiemann and Giles [sic!] (1991) and Rost-Roth (2006).

Table 2.   Training schemes (Bolten 2001: 3, translation by the author)

Off-the-job	On-the-job
Intercultural training as conventional cognitive and awareness training;	*Intercultural mediation* Mediating activity in open and concealed conflicts in multicultural teams
Intercultural experimental games Professionally oriented experimental games, in which intercultural on-the-job situations are simulated	
Intercultural consulting Providing intercultural advice to management personnel on issues of staffing international teams and in assignment and reintegration processes	*Intercultural coaching* Coaching and supervising multicultural teams with the aim of making them aware of their own culture-specific actions, and formulating synergy potentials as targets

One prime advantage of on-the-job programs, in comparison to traditional off-the-job training, is that they enable more direct reactions to dysfunctional situations. Bolten (2001) sees two main roles for coaches: firstly, the coach as a metacommunicator, supervisor and moderator who has high-level analytic skills for understanding communication and interaction processes, and secondly, the coach as a moderator and expert, who also helps to implement the suggestions of consultants. The job of consultants, in turn, consists mainly of providing advice for making decisions over staffing teams, foreign assignments or re-integration programs.

The use of mediators is a further 'on-the-job' measure. Mediators, as independent persons, can be used to facilitate communication and to work with parties involved in conflicts. The mediator attempts to take all the different interests into account, in order to come up with mutually agreed solutions (Bolten 2001 and Mayer and Boness 2005).

A further tendency that can be observed is an increase in efforts to integrate experience in the location itself (Vance and Ensher 2002). Thus, companies attempt to use the 'Host Country Workforce (HCW)' as an additional source of information and potential. This opens up possibilities for passing on critical incidents and information on workplace standards directly, as a resource for mentoring and on-the-job coaching.

A further recent tendency is experimental games training for staff (usually managers) involved in foreign assignments, or in bi-national or multinational groups, along with representatives of the target country. Training can also take place via video conference. Participants are set tasks which they have to solve jointly with representatives of the other culture or other company. The trainers intervene to point out cultural differences and initiate behavioral modification. 'Interact' (Bolten 1999) is an experimental game specifically related to the participants' everyday work. The participants form groups which differ according to the cultural origin and native languages of the members. The groups are placed in different places or rooms with one trainer each.

One task of the game is to enter into cooperative negotiations. This training method uses work-related tasks and highly specialized demands to create a 'semi-authentic scenario', enabling participants and trainers to recognize typical behavior patterns in intercultural interactions, which are supposed to be reflected in the context of the training.

9. Video Material, CD ROMs, and Websites

There are an increasing number of training programs in the form of video material. One well known and relatively widespread example is Copeland und Griggs' (1985) *Going International*. This program covers the following elements:

- Bridging the culture gap
- Managing the overseas assignment
- Beyond culture shock
- Welcome home, stranger
- Working in the USA
- Living in the USA
- Going international—safely
- Cross-cultural relationships and workshops

Each tape includes critical incidents, interviews with experts, and advice. Gudykunst, Guzley and Hammer (1996) comment that particularly *Bridging the Cultural Gap*, *Beyond Culture Shock* and *Welcome Home Stranger* can be put to good use to illustrate intercultural communication processes. Information on these programs can be found at http://www.griggs.com/videos/giser. shtml/ (accessed 12. 02. 2006). This site promotes video products by stating an increasing need for training due to increasing globalization, and estimating the cost to the economy ("each year billions of dollars are lost"). The video material is supplemented by a users' guide. The site also recommends using the series *Global Contrasts* as an additional resource.

The series *Valuing Diversity*[8] is also well known. These films primarily aim to make viewers aware of the dynamics underlying encounters between individuals with different backgrounds. The series also aims to promote self-reflection.

Another set of training material is *Diversophy*, developed by George Simons International, which is available as a card game set or in an online version and as *Tele-diversophy* for mobile phones. It is aimed at varied occupational groups, and is developed for different cultural contexts. Its objective is to create "a low-risk environment where participants feel free to confront their prejudices and increase awareness".[9]

Summerfield (1993) provides references to numerous film and video material. More recent examples are the video materials produced under the direction of Trickey and Ewington, which aim "to illustrate cultural diversity

---

[8] http://www.griggs.com/videos/vdser.shtml, 12. 02. 2006
[9] http://www.diversophy.com, 12. 02. 2006

in multicultural teams"[10] and to specify "competencies required for managing in an international context"[11] or Jonamay, Myers and Simons (2000) as a CDROM assisted handbook of training exercises for professionals.

There is also increasing interest in instruments that assess competences and provide profiles of people who work in intercultural and international settings. For example, *The International Profiler* questionnaire, developed by interculturalists and psychometricians at WorldWork Ltd., London, and available in various languages, supplies licensed consultants with a respondent's profile across 'a set of of ten competencies (with 22 associated skills, attitudes and areas of knowledge) that define the special capabilities required to transfer leadership, managerial and professional skills to an international context'.[12] The *INCA project* assessment tools, which are also designed to be used by different cultural groups, are available online in English, German and Czech.[13] For more information on assessment and self-assessment of intercultural competence, see also Prechtl and Davidson Lund 2007.

For further up-to-date information on this steadily growing field, readers should consult the relevant journals,[14] which are also represented on the internet, and the homepage and links of SIETAR.[15] Instructions for the development and use of video programmes in different contexts can be found in Fowler and Mumford (1999). For opportunities to develop CD-Roms and online materials, see especially Simons and Quappe (2000).

10. Selection Criteria for Training Programs

Since intercultural training courses are based on very different training approaches, the question of what criteria to use in practice for selecting a training program is complicated. Scherm (1995), with reference to other studies, regards three criteria as important:

- Length of the foreign assignment;
- Extent of the interaction in the foreign culture, i.e. frequency and intensity of contacts to the cultural surroundings;
- Divergence between the host and the home culture (degree of unfamiliarity). (Scherm 1995: 248, translation by the author).

Black and Mendenhall (1992) also address the question of what criteria should be used for selecting training programs. They initially establish that up to now, there is no systematic way of comparing different intercultural training

---

[10] http://www.tco-international.com/team.asp, 12. 02. 2006

[11] http://www.tco-international.com/competencies.asp, 12. 02. 2006

[12] http://www.worldwork.biz/legacy/www/downloads/Introduction.pdf, 12. 02. 2006

[13] http://www.incaproject.org, 12. 02. 2006

[14] See for instance the *European Journal of Intercultural Studies* (http://www.intercultural.at/, 12. 02. 2006), *Interculture-Online* (http://www.interculture-online.info/ index.php?bereich=bac kissues&ausg=1&inhalt=1&lang=deu, 12. 02. 06, or *'International Journal of Human Resource Management'* (http://www.tandf.co.uk/journals/titles/09585192.asp, 12. 02. 2006).

[15] http://www.sietar.de/SIETARproject/3.0Interculturale-learning.html, 23. 11. 2005

courses and their characteristics. So they regard the question of how to determine different forms of training intensity (i.e. 'rigour') as central. The intensity is partly determined by the way in which the training concepts integrate learners. The learning theory assumption that the level of difficulty of grasping something is partly dependent on how new or unfamiliar the behavior to be learned is, is translated into contact with other cultures. Linguistic contrasts and the previous experience of the parties are also taken into account. Further factors are the length of the assignment and 'job novelty'.

11. Effectiveness of Intercultural Training

The evaluation of training is a broad-based area of research, to which this article can only make a marginal reference. Problems of evaluating training programs are described in the first volume of Landis and Brislin's *Handbook of Intercultural Training* (1983). There has also been a great deal of literature dealing with the problem of evaluation since then (see particularly Blake and Heslin 1983; Kinast 1998: 20–54 for methodological problems; see also Trimpop and Meynhardt 2003; Morris and Robie 2001). Blake and Heslin discuss the following research methods and data sources:

1. self reports;
2. judgments of significant others [. . .];
3. archival/objective measures;
4. evaluator observations; and
5. measures of one's overt behavior.

Assessing training effectiveness often entails using the model developed by Kirkpatrick. According to Kirkpatrick (1994) evaluation of training should explore reactions of trainees, learning, transfer/behaviour and results at successive levels, each level providing information important for the next level:

1. reactions (measures how participants react to the training program),
2. learning (attempts to assess the amount of learning, e.g. skills, knowledge, attitude),
3. transfer (how the newly acquired skills, knowledge, or attitude are being used),
4. results (improved quality, decreased costs?).

Brislin et al. (1983) maintain that the possible positive effects of training fall into three areas:

- Changes in thinking,
- Changes in feelings,
- Changes in behavior. (Brislin et al. 1983: 7–8)

Black and Mendenhall (1992) summarize findings on the effect of intercultural training programs from various studies as follows:

9 out of 10 studies that examined the relationship between training and self-confidence in the ability to behave effectively in intercultural situations, established a positive connection; 16 out of 16 found positive correlations with more suitable perceptions in intercultural contact; 9 out of 9 found a positive correlation with adjustment processes (for a summary of the findings, see Black and Mendenhall 1992: 179).

Hammer (1999) also provides an overview of the effects of intercultural training, and lists the following factors as being significant for success:

There are three fundamental outcomes that indicate the success or failure of expatriate adaptation and that guide the development of cross-cultural training efforts: personal/family adjustment and satisfaction, intercultural interaction, and professional effectiveness (Hammer 1999: 9).

Drawing on the findings from Black and Mendenhall's studies, Hammer summarizes them as follows:

In short, cross-cultural training has been shown to develop cross-cultural skills that affect subsequent success in an overseas assignment, improve expatriates' psychological comfort and satisfaction with living and working in a foreign culture, and improve task accomplishment in the cross-cultural environment. (Hammer 1999: 8)

Of course, the effectiveness of training programs is highly dependent on the trainer's abilities.[16]

To conclude, 'intercultural competence' is an extremely complex phenomenon, and a combination of different training methods seems desirable, because combining different training approaches makes optimal use of their advantages while compensating for their shortcomings.

References

Adler, Nancy J. 2002. *International Dimensions of Organizational Behavior.* 4th edition. Cincinnati Ohio: South-Western.

Albert, Rosita D. 1983. The intercultural sensitizer or culture assimilator. In: Dan Landis and Richard Brislin (eds.), *Handbook of Intercultural Training Volume I: Issues in Theory and Design,* 186–217. New York: Pergamon.

Asante, Molefi Kete, Eileen Newmark and Cecil A. Blake (eds.). 1979. *Handbook of Intercultural Communication.* London: Sage.

Bennett, Milton and Jane Bennett. 1992. *Audio-Visual Resources: Selected Reference Materialis for Using Films and Videos.* [http://www.iaccp.org/teaching/films/bennett.pdf, 12. 02. 2006].

Black, J. Stewart and Mark Mendenhall. 1992. A practical but theory-based framework for selecting cross-cultural training methods. In: Mark Mendenhall and Gary Oddou (eds.): *International human resource management,* 177–204. Boston: PWS-Kent.

Black, J. Stewart and Hal B. Gregersen. 1999. The Right Way to Manage Expats. *Harvard Buisness Review,* 52–63.

---

[16] Paige (1996) goes into more detail on the required skills for trainers.

Blake, Brian F. and Richard Heslin. 1983. Evaluating Cross-Cultural Training. In: Dan Landis and Richard Brislin (eds.): *Handbook of Intercultural Training Volume I: Issues in Theory and Design*, 203–223. New York: Pergamon.

Bolten, Jürgen. 1992. Interkulturelles Verhandlungstraining [Intercultural Negotiation Training]. *Jahrbuch Deutsch als Fremdsprache*, 18, 269–287. München: iudicium.

Bolten, Jürgen. 1999. InterAct: Zur Konzeption eines interkulturellen Unternehmensplanspiels [Interact: The Conception of an Intercultural Business Simulation]. In: *InterAct: Ein wirtschaftsbezogenes interkulturelles Planspiel für die Zielkulturen Australien, Deutschland, Frankreich, Italien, Großbritannien, Niederlande, Ostasien, Rußland, Spanien und USA*, [*InterAct: The Conception of an Intercultural Business Simulation Game for the Target Cultures Australia, Germany, France, Italy, Great Britain, The Netherlands, East Asia, Russia, Spain and the USA*], 94–99. Sternenfels: Wissenschaft und Praxis.

Bolten, Jürgen. 2001. Interkulturelles Coaching, Mediation, Training und Consulting als Aufgaben des Personalmanagements internationaler Unternehmen [Intercultural Coaching, Mediation, Training and Consulting as Tasks for Human Resources Managers in International Corporations]. In: Alois Clermont, Wilhelm Schmeisser and Dieter Krimphove (eds.), *Strategisches Personal-management in Globalen Unternehmen* [*Strategic Human Resource Management in Global Corporations*], 1–16. München: Vahlen. [http://www2. uni-jena.de/ philosophie/iwk/forschung/Publikationen/Coaching.pdf, 30. 1. 2005].

Bolten, Jürgen and Marion Dahte (eds.). 1995. Transformation und Integration: Aktuelle Probleme und Perspektiven west-/ost-europäischer Wirtschaftsbeziehungen [Transformation and Integration: Western/Eastern European Business Relations: Current Problems and Perspectives], Sternenfels: Verlag Wissenschaft und Praxis.

Bolten, Jürgen and Daniela Schröter (eds.). 2001. *Im Netzwerk interkulturellen Handelns*. [*In the Network of Intercultural Action*] Sternenfels: Verlag Wissenschaft und Praxis.

Brislin, Richard, Dan Landis and Mary E. Brandt. 1983. Conceptualizations of Intercultural Behavior and Training. In: Dan Landis and Richard Brislin (eds.), *Handbook of Intercultural Training. Volume I: Issues in Theory and Design*, 1–35. New York: Pergamon.

Brown, Penelope and Stephen Levinson. 1978. Universals in Language Usage: Politeness Phenomena. In: Esther N. Goody (ed.), *Questions and Politeness: Strategies in Social interaction*, 56–289. Cambridge: Cambridge University Press.

Brüch, Andreas and Alexander Thomas. 1995. Beruflich in Südkorea: Interkulturelles Orientierungstraining für Manager, Fach- und Führungskräfte [On business in South Korea: Intercultural Orientation Training for Managers, Professionals, and Executives]. Heidelberg: Roland Asanger.

Copeland, Lennie and Lewis Griggs. 1985. *Going International*. New York: Random House.

Coupland, Nikolas, Howard Giles and John M. Wiemann (eds.). 1991. *Miscommunication and Problematic Talk*. Newbury Park/ London/ New Delhi: Sage.

Coupland, Nikolas, John M. Wiemann and Howard Giles. 1991. Talk as 'Problem' and Communication as 'Miscommunication': An Integrative Analysis. In: Nikolas Coupland, Howard Giles, and John M. Wiemann (eds.): *Miscommunication and Problematic Talk*, 1–49. Newbury Park/ London/ New Delhi: Sage.

Cushner, Kenneth and Richard W. Brislin. 1996. *Intercultural interactions: A practical guide*, Thousand Oaks: Sage.

Cushner, Kenneth and Richard W. Brislin. 1997. *Improving Intercultural Interactions: Modules for Cross-Cultural Training Programs*. Volume 2. Thousand Oaks: Sage.

Dowling, Peter J., Denice E. Welch and Randall S. Schuler. 1999. *International Human Resource Management: Managing People in a Multinational Context*. Cincinnati: South Western College Publishing.

Ehlich, Konrad and Johannes Wagner (eds.). 1995. *The Discourse of Business Negotiation*. Berlin/ New York: Mouton de Gruyter.

Fiedler, Fred E., Terence Mitchell and Harry C. Triandis. 1971. The Culture Assimilator: An Approach to Cross-cultural Training. *Journal of Applied Psychology*, 55, 95–102.

Flanagan, John C. 1954. The Critical Incident Technique, 327–358. In: *Psychological Bulletin*, 51.

Fowler, Sandra M. and Monica G. Mumford. 1995. *Intercultural Sourcebook: Cross-Cultural Training Methods*, Volume 1, Yarmouth: Intercultural.

Fowler, Sandra M. and Monica G. Mumford. 1999. *Intercultural Sourcebook: Cross-Cultural Training Methods*, Volume 2, Yarmouth: Intercultural.

Franklin, Peter. 2007. Differences & difficulties in intercultural management interaction. In: Helga Kotthoff and Helen Spencer-Oatey (eds.), *Handbook of Intercultural Communication*, 263–289. Berlin: Mouton de Gruyter.

Gudykunst, William B. and Mitchell Hammer. 1983. Basic Training Design: Approaches to Intercultural Training. In: Dan Landis and Richard Brislin (eds.): *Handbook of Intercultural Training, Volume I: Issues in Theory and Design*, 118–154. New York: Pergamon.

Gudykunst, William B., Ruth Guzley and Mitchell Hammer. 1996. Designing Intercultural Training. In: Dan Landis and Rubi Bhagat (eds.), *Handbook of Intercultural Training*. 2nd edition, 61–80. Thousand Oaks: Sage.

Gudykunst, William B. and Bella Mody (eds.). 2002. *International and Intercultural Communication*. Thousand Oaks: Sage.

Günthner, Susanne. 2007. Intercultural communication and the relevance of cultural specific reper*toires of communicative genres*. In: Helga Kotthoff and Helen Spencer-Oatey (eds.), *Handbook of Intercultural Communication*, 127–152. Berlin: Mouton de Gruyter.

Gumperz, John J. 1982. *Discourse Strategies*. Cambridge: Cambridge University Press.

Gumperz, John J., Tom Jupp and Celia Roberts. 1979. *Crosstalk: A Study of Crosscultural Communication*. Southall: NCILT National Centre for Industrial Language Training.

Hammer, Mitchell R. 1999. Cross-Cultural Training: The Research Connection. In: Sandra M. Fowler and Monica G. Mumford (eds.), *Intercultural Sourcebook: Cross-Cultural Training Methods*. Volume 2, 1–18. Yarmouth: Intercultural.

Hartley, Cay and Terri Lapinsky. 1999. Piglish: A Language Learning Simulation. In: Sandra M. Fowler and Monica G. Mumford (eds.), *Intercultural Sourcebook: Cross-Cultural Training Methods*. Volume 2, 131–141. Yarmouth: Intercultural.

Helmolt, Katharina v. and Bernd-Dietrich Müller. 1991. Zur Vermittlung interkultureller Kompetenzen [Teaching Intercultural Skills]. In: Bernd-Dietrich Müller (ed.), *Interkulturelle Wirtschaftskommunikation* [*Intercultural Business Communication*], 509–548. München: iudicium.

Inman, Marianne. 1985. Language and Cross-Cultural Training in American Multinational Corporations. *The Modern Language Journal*, 69, 3, 247–255.

Jonamay, Lambert, Selma Myers and George Simons. 2000. *Global Competence: 50 Training Activities for Succeeding in International Business*. Amherst MA: Human Resource Development.

Kaltenhäuser, Bettina and Hilly v. Swol-Ulbrich. 2006. *Andere Länder, andere Kinder* [*Other Countries. Other*]. Frankfurt a. M.: VAS Verlag.

Kammhuber, Stefan. 2001. Interkulturelle Trainingsforschung: Bestandsaufnahme und Perspektiven [Intercultural Training Research: Overview and Perspectives]. In: Jürgen Bolten and Daniela Schröter (eds.), *Im Netzwerk interkulturellen Handelns* [*In the Network of Intercultural Action*], 78–93. Sternenfels: Verlag Wissenschaft und Praxis.

Kinast, Eva-Ulrike. 1998. *Evaluation interkultureller Trainings* [*Evaluation of intercultural training*], Berlin: Papst Science.

Kirkpatrick, Donald L. 1994. *Evaluating Training Programs: The Four Levels*. San Francisco CA: Berrett-Koehler.

Knapp, Karlfried and Knapp-Potthoff, Annelie. 1990. Interkulturelle Kommunikation, *Zeitschrift für Fremdsprachenforschung* [Journal of Foreign Language Research], 1: 62–93

Koole, Tom and Jan D. ten Thije. 1994. *The Construction of Intercultural Discourse*. Amsterdam/Atlanta: Editions Rodopi.

Kotthoff, Helga. 2007. Ritual and Style in Intercultural Communication. In: Helga Kotthoff and Helen Spencer-Oatey (eds.), *Handbook of Intercultural Communication*, 173–198. Berlin: Mouton de Gruyter.

Landis, Dan and Richard W. Brislin (eds.). 1983. *Handbook of Intercultural Training Volume I: Issues in Theory and Design*. Volume 2. *Issues in Teaching Methodology. Volume 3. Area Studies in Intercultural Training*. New York: Pergamon.

Landis, Dan and Radhika Baghat (eds.). 1996. *Handbook of Intercultural Training*. 2nd edition. Thousand Oaks CA: Sage.

Landis, Dan and Miller, A. (sic). 1973. The Army Culture assimilator. Lukeacting with black soldiers. Philadelphia: Center for Social Development.

Lanier, Alison R. 1979. Selection and Preparation for Overseas Transfers. *Personnel Journal*, 58, 160–163.

Liang, Yong and Stefan Kammhuber. 2003. Ostasien: China [East Asia: China]. In: Alexander Thomas, Stefan Kammhuber and Sylvia Schroll-Machl (eds.), *Handbuch Interkulturelle Kommunikation und Kooperation. Vol. 2: Länder, Kulturen und Interkulturelle Berufstätigkeit [Handbook of intercultural communication and Cooperation. Vol. 2. Countries, Cultures, and Intercultural Employment]*, 171–185, Göttingen: Vandenhoeck & Ruprecht.

Lieberman, Simma, George Simons and Kate Berardo. 2003. *Putting Diversity to Work: What to know and do to get the best out of a diverse workforce*. Canada: Crisp.

Liedke, Martina, Angelika Redder and Susanne Scheiter. 1999. Interkulturelles Handeln lehren—ein diskursanalytischer Trainingsansatz [Teaching Intercultural Action—A Discourse Analytic Approach]. In: Gisela Brünner, Reinhard Fiehler and Walther Kindt (eds.), *Angewandte Diskursforschung, Bd. 2. Methoden und Anwendungsbereiche [Applied Discourse Research. Vol. 2. Methods and Areas of Practice]*, 148–179. Opladen: Westdeutscher Verlag.

Macharzina, Klaus and Michael-Jörg Oesterle (eds.). 2002. *Handbuch Internationales Management: Grundlagen—Instrumente—Perspektiven [Handbook of International Management: Basics—Instruments—Perspectives]*. 2nd edition. Wiesbaden: Gabler.

Mayer, Claude-Hélène and Christian M. Boness. 2005. *Intercultural Mediation & Conflict Resolution*, Stuttgart: ibidem.

Morris, Mark A. and Chet Robie. 2001. A meta-analysis of the effects of cross-cultural training on expatriate performance and adjustment. *International Journal of Training and Development*, 5, 112–125.

Müller, Andrea and Alexander Thomas. 1991. *Interkulturelles Orientierungstraining für die USA [Intercultural Orientation Training for the USA]*. Saarbrücken: Breitenbach (new edition: Asanger).

Müller, Bernd-Dietrich. 1991. Die Bedeutung der interkulturellen Kommunikation für die Wirtschaft [The importance of intercultural communication for Business]. In: Bernd-Dietrich Müller (ed.), *Interkulturelle Wirtschaftskommunikation [Intercultural Business Communication]*, 27–42. München: iudicium.

Müller-Jacquier, Bernd. 2000. Linguistic Awareness of Cultures: Grundlagen eines Trainingsmoduls [Linguistic Awareness of Cultures: Basics of a Training Modul]. In: Jürgen Bolten (ed.), *Studien zur internationalen Unternehmenskommunikation [Studies in International Business Communication]*, 27–51. Leipzig: H. Popp.

Müller-Jacquier, Bernd and Ellen M. Whitener. 2001. Effective Global Leadership: The Role of Linguistic Analysis of Intercultural Communications. In: Torsten Kuhlmann, Mark Mendenhall and Gunter L. Stahl (eds.), *Developing Global Business Leaders: Policies, Processes, and Innovations*, 225–241. Westport CT: Quorum Books.

Newton, Jonathan. This volume. Adapting authentic workplace talk for workplace communication training. Chapter 15.

Niedermeyer, Manfred. 2001. Interkulturelle Trainings in der deutschen Wirtschaft: eine Bestandsaufnahme [Intercultural Training in the German Business Sector: An Overview]. In: Jürgen Bolten and Daniela Schröter (eds.), *Im Netzwerk interkulturellen Handelns [In the Network of Intercultural Action]*, 62–77. Sternenfels: Verlag Wissenschaft und Praxis.

Oechsler, Walter A. 1997. Verfahren zur Auswahl, Vorbereitung und Entsendung von Stammhausdelegierten ins Ausland [Procedures for the Selection, Preparation, and Assignment of Company Delegates Abroad]. In: Klaus Macharzina and Michael-Jörg Oesterle (eds.), *Handbuch Internationales Management: Grundlagen-Instrumente-Perspektiven [Handbook of international management: Principles, Instruments, Perspectives]*, 771–784. Wiesbaden: Gabler.

Oechsler, Walter A. 2002. Verfahren zur Auswahl, Vorbereitung und Entsendung von Stammhausdelegierten [Procedures for the Selection, Preparation, and Assignment of Company Delegates Abroad]. In: Klaus Macharzina and Michael-Jörg Oesterle (eds.), *Handbuch Internationales Management: Grundlagen—Instrumente—Perspektiven [Handbook of international management. Principles, Instruments, Perspectives]*. 2nd edition, 865–880. Wiesbaden: Gabler.

Paige, Michael R. 1996. Intercultural Trainer Competencies. In: Dan Landis and Rubi Bhagat (eds.), *Handbook of Intercultural Training*. 2nd edition, 149–161. Thousand Oaks: Sage.

Prechtl, Elisabeth and Anne Davidson Lund. 2007. Intercultural competence and assessment: perspectives from the INCA Project. In: Helga Kotthoff and Helen Spencer-Oatey (eds.), *Handbook of Intercultural Communication*, 467–490. Berlin: Mouton de Gruyter.

Price Waterhouse. 1997–1998. *International Assignments: European Policy and Practice*, Europe. Berlin: Price Waterhouse.

Roberts, Celia. This volume. Intercultural Communication in Healthcare Settings. Chapter 11.

Rost-Roth, Martina. 2006. Intercultural Communication in Institutional Settings: Counseling Sessions. In: Kristin Bührig and Jan D. ten Thije (eds.), *Beyond misunderstanding. The linguistic analysis of intercultural communication*, 189–215. Amsterdam/ Philadelphia: Benjamins.

Scherm, Ewald. 1995. *Internationales Personalmanagement [International Human Resources Management]*. München, Wien: Oldenbourg Verlag.

Simons, George F., Carmen Vázquez and Philip R. Harris. 1993. *Transcultural Leadership: Empowering the diverse workforce*. Houston Texas: Gulf Publishing Company.

Simons, George F. and Stephanie Quappe. 2000. *Four books, four websites & four games later . . . What we have learned about working across cultures in a virtual world.* A paper presented at the SIETAR Europa Congress, Bruxelles, March 17, 2000, [http://www.diversophy.com/gsi/ Articles/4bks.pdf, 12. 02. 2006].

Sisk, Dorothy. 1995. Simulation Games as Training Tools. In: Sandra Fowler and Monica Mumford (eds.), *Intercultural Sourcebook: Cross-Cultural Training Methods*. Volume 1, 81–92. Yarmouth: Intercultural.

Slobodin, L. et al. 1972. Culture Assimilator. For Interaction with the economically disadvantaged. Washington D.C.: Department of Health, Education and Welfare.

Stahl, Günter. 1998. Internationaler Einsatz von Führungskräften [International Assignment of Executives]. München/ Wien: Oldenbourg.

Stahl, Günter. 1999. Geschäftlich in den USA: ein interkulturelles Trainingshandbuch [On Business in the USA: An Intercultural Training Handbook]. Wien: Wirtschaftsverlag Ueberreuter.

Stüdlein, Yvonne. 1997. *Management von Kulturunterschieden: Phasenkonzept für internationale strategische Allianzen [Managing Cultural Differences: A Phase Concept for International Strategic Alliances]*. Wiesbaden: Gabler.

Summerfield, Ellen. 1993. *Crossing Cultures Through Film*. Yamouth Maine: Intercultural.

ten Thije, Jan D. 2001. Ein diskursanalytisches Konzept zum interkulturellen Kommunikationstraining [A Discourse Analytic Concept of Intercultural Communication Training]. In: Jürgen Bolten and Klaus Schröter (eds.), *Im Netzwerk interkulturellen Handelns: Theoretische und praktische Perspektiven der interkulturellen Kommunikationsforschung [In the Network of Intercultural Action: Theoretical and practical perspectives on Intercultural Communication Research]*, 176–204. Sternenfels: Wissenschaft und Praxis.

Thomas, Alexander. 1996. Analyse der Handlungswirksamkeit von Kulturstandards [Analysis of the Effectiveness of Cultural Standards]. In: Alexander Thomas (ed.), *Psychologie interkulturellen Handelns [Psychology of Intercultural Action]*, 107–135. Göttingen: Hogrefe.

Thomas, Alexander. 1999. Kultur als Orientierungssystem und Kulturstandards als Bauteile [Culture as an Orientation System and Cultural Standards as Components]. *IMIS-Beiträge*, 10, 91–130.

Thomas, Alexander and Katja Hagemann. 1992. Training interkultureller Kompetenz [Training of Intercultural Competence] In: Niels Bergemann and Andreas L. J. Sourisseaux (eds.), *Interkulturelles Management [Intercultural Management]*, 173–199. Heidelberg: Physica.

Thomas, Alexander, Eva-Ulrike Kinast and Sylvia Schroll-Machl (eds.). 2003. *Handbuch Interkulturelle Kommunikation und Kooperation. Vol. 1: Grundlagen und Praxisfelder [Handbook of Intercultural Communication and Cooperation. Vol.: Principles and Areas of Practice]*. Göttingen: Vandenhock & Ruprecht.

Thomas, Alexander, Stefan Kammhuber and Sylvia Schroll-Machl (eds.). 2003. Handbuch Interkulturelle Kommunikation und Kooperation. Vol. 2: Länder, Kulturen und Interkulturelle Berufstätigkeit [Handbook of intercultural communication and Cooperation. Vol. 2. Countries, Cultures, and Intercultural Employment]. Göttingen: Vandenhoeck & Ruprecht.

Trimpop, Rüdiger M. and Timo Meynhardt. 2003. Interkulturelle Trainings und Einsätze: Psychische Kompetenzen und Wirkungsmessungen [Intercultural Training and Assignments: Psychological Skills and Measurements of Efficacy]. In: Klaus Götz (ed.), Interkulturelles

Lernen/ Interkulturelles Training [Intercultural Learning/ Intercultural Training]. 5th edition, 187–220. München: Rainer Hampp.

Tung, Rosalie L. and Arthur Andersen. 1997. *Exploring International Assignees' Viewpoints: A Study of the Expatriation/ Repatriation Process*. Chicago: Arthur Andersen Worldwide.

Vance, Charles and Ellen A. Ensher. 2002. The Voice of the host country workforce: A key source for improving the effectiveness of expatriate training and performance. *International Journal of Intercultural Relations*, 448–461.

Wiseman, Richard L. 2002. Intercultural Communication Competence. In: Gudykunst, William B. and Bella Mody (eds.), *International and Intercultural Communication*, 207–224. Thousand Oaks: Sage.

Wottawa, Heinrich and Heike Thierau. 2003. *Lehrbuch Evaluation [Textbook of Evaluation]*. third edition. Bern et al.: Hans Huber.

Index